Software Engineering:

A Project Oriented Approach

D1397068

Charles D. Sigwart
Northern Illinois University

Gretchen L. Van Meer
Northern Illinois University

John C. Hansen
Central Michigan University

Franklin, Beedle, & Associates, Inc.
4521 Campus Drive, 327
Irvine, CA 92715-9877

Dedication

To Julia - daughter of two of the three authors. . .

Publisher	Jim Leisy, Jr.
Production Coordinator	Lisa Cannon
Manuscript Editor	Sheryl Rose
Interior Design and Composition	Associated Printers
Cover Design and Production	Neo Nova
Illustrations	Rob Nesler

Rights and Permissions

Franklin, Beedle & Associates, Inc.

4521 Campus Drive, #327

Irvine, California 92715-9877

Library of Congress Cataloging-in-Publication Data
Sigwart, Charles D.,
   Software engineering : a project oriented approach / by Charles D. Sigwart, Gretchen L. Van Meer, John C. Hansen.
    p. cm.
  Includes bibliographical references (p.) and index.
  ISBN 0-938661-27-2 :
   1. Software engineering.   I: Van Meer, Cretchen L.,
II. Hansen, John C.,   . III. Title.
QA76.758.S49 1990
005. 1--dc20

              90-13935
              CIP

PREFACE

Those of us in the practice [in the 1950's] were a little uncomfortable with computer science. It put a neat and tidy framework around some things that to us weren't that neat and tidy, no matter how much we wanted them to be.

But when software engineering came along, it was like a trip home after a long absence. Software engineering seemed to care about what the good programmers had been doing for a decade and a half; it was based on the reality of the practice. ...

Software engineering involves understanding] both the theories of computer science and the realities of software practice.

> *- Robert L. Glass, "Software Engineering and Computer Science: How Do They Differ?" in Software Engineering Education,*
> *Springer-Verlag, New York, 1987*

Intended for Junior/Senior Level Software Engineering Courses

This book is intended for an undergraduate level introductory software engineering course that has a project as a major component. The emphasis is on the specification, organization, implementation, testing and documentation of software. It describes in some detail the foundation for carrying out a project. It is organized in a way that will lend itself to various types of projects. Documents that students are expected to write are described clearly and in detail. These documents all adhere to ANSI/IEEE Software Engineering Standards. The book could be used for a one or two term course.

We assume a knowledge of programming, including flow- charting and possibly object oriented design. Background in data structures and file handling is helpful. An understanding of machine architecture is useful. Structured programming and object oriented design are reviewed briefly.

There is a brief introduction to systems analysis in Part I, with a detailed chapter, Systems Analysis, in Part III. We assume that some projects will focus on immediate needs of project implementation by starting with an existing specification so that some of the topics must be deferred. Any of the chapters in Part III may be considered earlier in the course depending on the emphasis or needs of a particular project.

An area in which we depart from the sequence of other textbooks is in test planning and testing. We expect students to write a Test Planning Document as part of the specification. Chapter 5, Planning for Testing, introduces the concepts needed for producing a test plan, and Chapter 8, Testing, describes the actual testing process, emphasizing the need for good documentation. Ideally on the job, implementation and testing tasks will be done by separate teams, but this may not be feasible in the classroom.

A Project Oriented Approach

The impetus to write this text came from our experience in teaching a course with an intensive group software project. A major problem with many texts was that they were either too heavily weighted toward one specific aspect, or they were so broad that students with no work experience could not see how the material could be applied.

It may be audacious to write a textbook of any kind in a changing discipline such as computer science. Software engineering in particular is undergoing rapid changes. However, we believe that there are several very basic aspects of software engineering that are important now, and will continue to be important for the foreseeable future. These include:

- how to work as part of a team,
- how to specify a system unambiguously and correctly, and
- how to create documentation that is clear, correct, consistent, and will help in making software maintainable.

One objective of a project course in software engineering is to create a group situation that simulates on-the-job conditions and problems as nearly as is realistically possible. However, in so doing, we must come to grips with the inherent clash of values between the academic world and the world of industry. This clash was eloquently described by Robert L. Glass in Software Soliloquies:

> In the academic world, the student functions as a competing individual among competing individuals, and group activity is often thought of as cheating.

> In the industrial world, the employee functions as a team member, and group activity is the primary way things happen.

> In the academic world the individual is given credit for what he or she does.

> In the industrial world, the individual's role often dissolves into anonymity.

> ...The transition from competition to cooperation is unexpected.

> The transition from individual importance to anonymity may be painful.

We can attempt to simulate an industrial environment within limits. We can assign group projects, giving students the opportunity to learn about teamwork. But unlike the products of their industrial counterparts, the primary outcome should be a judgment of individual achievement rather than a judgment of the success of the project. It is possible to grade the project in terms of individual learning experiences. Our approach to this is described in an article in the ACM SIGCSE Bulletin, June 1985, "Evaluation of Group Projects in a Software Engineering Course," by Charles D. Sigwart and Gretchen L. Van Meer. An expanded version is included in the Instructor's Guide.

The choice of a chapter sequence has not been easy, either for teaching the subject or for writing this book. We are continually reminded of the adage: "In order to most effectively study a subject, be sure you understand it thoroughly before you begin." The idea is to present the topics in the order in which they are likely to be needed.

This book is designed as a textbook (although we hope it may be also useful as a reference pointing to further study of selected topics). As such it has several features designed specifically for the academic environment:

- Many examples throughout the text come from course projects. These include two continuing examples: a Computer Dating Service, and an interactive game, "Spies on a Grid." Aspects of these are used to illustrate several concepts. These examples are explored further in the chapter exercises.
- Appendix A is a suggested documentation standard.
- Appendix B is an interactive trace system useful for testing and debugging. While source level debugging tools are commercially available, many academic institutions do not have adequate support to buy all the software tools that might be desired. This system is simple, and works well.
- We have incorporated several topics we feel are important in the classroom but are not covered in other texts. We have added them because we feel that they are not self-evident. These include group formation, user interface, error trapping, software security and protection, and ethics.
- Many ideas are illustrated with source code, though the text is intended to be language independent. The specifics of programming are only very minimally addressed. The source code examples are in a variety of languages, and documented so that they should be understood by someone who is an experienced programmer.
- The subject of group dynamics is addressed, with descriptions of normal phases of group interactions, suggestions for running effective group meetings and enhancing communication skills (including a brief description of brainstorming), comments on selection of a group leader, and some types of problems for which to be alert.
- The Instructor's Guide discusses several aspects of group project

work. There are suggestions for: grading individuals in a group project; group selection and group size; group leader, responsibilities and rewards; what to do when a group impeaches its leader; and project demonstrations.

- The bibliography at the end of each chapter has annotations to help locate material to support particular topics. We have included some classic references in software engineering and in other disciplines that are relevant to further explore the material.

- One aspect that has caused our students a great deal of confusion is the terminology. In the past, terminology has evolved in inconsistent, and sometimes contradictory ways. We define a consistent set of terms based on IEEE Std 729-1983, Glossary of Software Engineering Terminology, and have included a glossary based on these definitions.

This book does not pretend to cover all areas of software engineering. Of course, we would like to cover everything, and in complete detail. On the other hand, we would like to get this book finished, and of a size that can be carried by one person.

ACKNOWLEDGEMENTS

No textbook can be produced without the efforts of many people. The authors wish to express their appreciation to the many people who offered helpful suggestions and comments on this text while it was in preparation. These include our publisher, James F. Leisy, Jr.; Frances L. Van Scoy, West Virginia University; Robert L. Glass, Computing Trends; Rodney Angotti, Northern Illinois University; Jerald a. Kabell, Central Michigan University; James P. Kelsh, Central Michigan University; David Ballew, Western Illinois University; Philip D. Beffrey, Digital Arts; Lili Shashaani, Duquesne University; Kathy Kerr, Harrison, Michigan; Karin Sergel, Kutztown University; Edward Yourdon, Yourdon Press; Laurie Werth, University of Texas, Austin; Thomas Hicks, Trinity University; Bradley J. Brown, The Boeing Company, Wichita, KS; and James E. Burns, Georgia Institute of Technology. We also wish to thank the companies that supplied us with software, including Mark Williams Company for "C Development System," and Rational Systems, Inc. for "Instant C." In addition, we wish to thank the following people who reviewed the manuscript and made comments: Ali Behforooz, Towson State University; William S. Curran, Southeastern Louisiana University; John J. Cupak, Jr.; George Davida, University of Wisconsin - Milwaukee; Peggy Forbes, TRG Consulting; Philip Gilbert, California State University, Northridge; David A. Gustafson, Kansas State University; Robert W. Hon, Columbia University; Greg Jones, Utah State University; Clifford D. Layton, Rogers State College; K. L. Modesitt, California State University; Kourosh Mortezapour,

Southwest State University; John F. Passefiume, Georgia Institute of Technology; C. L. Pelletier, Central Connecticut State University; Michael Petricig, Chapman College; P. A. Rhodes, San Diego; David D. Riley, University of Wisconsin - La Crosse; Walter Scacchi, University of Southern California; Wing C. Tam, Harvey Mudd College; Theodore C. Tenny, University of Oklahoma; Richard H. Thayer, Carmichael, California; Lee Tichnor, Western Illinois University; William Verbugge, Aurora University; Thomas Winfield, Cerritos, California; and Stuart H. Zweben, Ohio State University.

Special thanks to Dr. Robert S. Feder of Northwestern University Medical School, the ophthalmologist whose skill restored Charles Sigwart's eyesight after his disastrous accident in June 1989. Without him, this book would not have been finished.

Table of Contents

PART I

SYSTEM SPECIFICATION AND PLANNING

The Blind Men, The Elephant, and Software
with apologies to John Godfrey Saxe (1816 - 1887)

It was six men of Indostan, to learning much inclined,
Who went to see the elephant (though all of them were blind),
That each by observation might satisfy his mind.

The first approached the elephant, and, happening to fall
Against his broad and sturdy side, at once began to call:
"I see," said he, "the elephant is very like a wall!"

The second, feeling of the tusk, cried, "Ho! What have we here
So very round and smooth and sharp? To me 'tis mighty clear
This wonder of an elephant is very like a spear!"

The third approached the animal, and, happening to take
The squirming trunk within his hands, thus boldly up and spake,
"I see," said he, "the elephant is very like a snake!"

The fourth reached out his eager hand and felt about the knee:
"What most this wondrous beast is like is mighty plain," said he,
"Tis clear enough the elephant is very like a tree!"

The fifth, who chanced to touch the ear, said, "E'en the blindest man
Can tell what this resembles most. Deny the fact who can,
This marvel of an elephant is very like a fan!"

The sixth no sooner had begun about the beast to grope,
Than, seizing on the swinging tail that fell within his scope,
"I see," said he, "the elephant is very like a rope!"

And so those men of Indostan disputed loud and long,
Each in his own opinion exceeding stiff and strong,
Though each was partly in the right, and all were in the wrong!

So oft in software projects, the members of the team
Rail on in utter ignorance of what each other mean,
As if it were an elephant not one of them has seen.

Modification by G. L. Van Meer

The creation of a successful software system begins with good planning. This includes documenting system specifications for evaluation by the user and writing system and test plans for evaluation by management and for use by the software development team. Much careful effort and documentation is needed before development begins. All these activities are usually done by teams. Part I describes how to produce these documents. Part II describes the actual development of the software, which begins with writing code.

Chapter 1 gives a short history of software engineering and a definition of the software life cycle. This includes a discussion of terminology used by software engineers, and a description of the way this terminology has changed over the years until it was recently standardized (ANSI/IEEE Standard 729-1983). Then, since team activity is often different from the way things are done in classrooms, some aspects of group interactions are addressed.

For a classroom software engineering project, the first thing that needs to be done, after forming a group, is to define the problem that is to be solved by software. The instructor probably will have done a feasibility study, so we defer a discussion of this, along with an in-depth look at systems analysis, until Part III. This section emphasizes the production of preliminary documents that will completely describe the system to be created.

The specific documents may have a variety of names and formats, depending on the project, your background, and your instructor's preference. We use the terms Software Requirements Specification, System Plan, and Test Plan, which are consistent with the Documentation Standard given in Appendix A. These are based on ANSI/IEEE Standard 830-1984, Guide to Software Requirements Specification.

The Software Requirements Specification is described in Chapter 2. This should also include a high-level system design, which is described in Chapter 3.

Chapter 4 describes scheduling procedures for the project and how to create a schedule for the System Plan. Chapter 5 addresses the matter of testing. Although testing is actually done after the code is written, it must be planned.

After these documents have been written and accepted, the actual development of the system begins. Development is the subject of Part II. Absolutely no code should be written during the specification and planning part of the software life cycle. That is work that is only done if and when the system specification is accepted by the user and the system and test plans are accepted by the manager of the software development group. In the classroom, the instructor usually plays both roles.

CHAPTER 1

INTRODUCTION TO SOFTWARE ENGINEERING

The anomaly is not that software progress is so slow, but that computer hardware progress is so fast. No other technology since civilization began has seen six orders of magnitude in performance-price gains in 30 years. In no other technology can one choose to take the gain in either *improved performance* or *in reduced costs.*

-Frederick P. Brooks, Jr., "No Silver Bullet"

Software is hard!

-Donald E. Knuth

Software Life Cycle

Entire life cycle

> I. Software need
> II. Preliminary feasibility judgment
> III. Requirements analysis and feasibility study
> IV. Requirements specification
> V. Preliminary software design and planning
> VI. Software development
>   Detailed design
>   Coding and unit testing
>   Integration
>   System testing
> VII. Software maintenance

Project: Team formation and group interactions

1.A. Software Engineering and the Software Life Cycle

What is software engineering?

Software engineering is the systematic approach to the specification, development, operation, maintenance, and retirement of software. It is far more than just writing code. In fact, for a project in a software engineering course, writing the actual code generally will take at most 10% to 20% of the effort needed.

Although software engineering can be defined in a single sentence as above, software engineering has many aspects.

- Software engineering includes system specification. Someone has to decide what a program is supposed to do. This is perhaps the most difficult aspect of software engineering-and you are going to be doing it first! Worse yet, every aspect of your project depends on how well you do the specification. Well, no one said it was going to be easy.

- Software engineering includes writing large programs. What is a large program? The Department of Defense (DOD) considers a large program to be one with more than a million lines of code. (No, you won't be writing a program that size for this course). Then what is a small program? By DOD standards, a small program is one with less than 100,000 lines of code. That is the size that a course project will normally be.

- Software engineering includes documentation. You know how to put comments in your code, and if you are doing it right, you do that first. But documentation is more than just source code comments. It includes the software requirements specification; some overall diagrams of the system, such as the data flow diagram and hierarchy diagram that you use to specify the system in the first place; a user's manual; and a set of test documents.

- Software engineering includes testing and integrating code. All modules should be individually (unit) tested and integrated in a top-down, depth-first manner. And don't expect the integrated code to work just because the individual modules did.

- Software engineering includes creating maintainable code. This means keeping records, preferably in readable, organized form, of every step in the software development process. Were the specifications changed? Don't throw away the old specifications-keep a record of everything you've done, including reasons for the change. Did you change the design because something didn't work? Keep a record of it to help prevent someone from repeating your error. Keep version numbers **(configuration management)** on all modules - and everything else.

- Software engineering includes using tools. The tools you have used up to now most likely include a text editor and a compiler (or at least an interpreter). Probably you've used at least one operating system, and if you're lucky, some kind of debugger. Your next acquisitions may be a data dictionary generator and a pretty printer. You may even join the ranks of those who say, "I'd rather write programs to write programs, than write programs."

- Software engineering includes **quality assurance**. What is quality? That depends on the particular project requirements. It may include effectiveness in supporting the intended application, a high level of reliability, speed, the ability to perform within memory limitations, or some combination of these.

The **software life cycle** is the period of time that starts when a software product is conceived and ends when the product is no longer available for use. The software life cycle typically includes a **feasibility study, requirements analysis, specification, design, testing, installation and checkout, operation and maintenance,** and eventually **retirement.** The phases covered in this book are shown in Table 1.1, along with the chapter in which each topic is addressed.

Table 1.1   Software Life Cycle

		I. Software need	Chapter 10
S Y S T E M S	**A N A L Y S I S**	II. Preliminary feasibility judgment	Chapters 2, 10
		III. Requirements analysis and feasibility study	Chapter 2
		IV. Specification	Chapters 2, 3
		V. Preliminary software design and planning	Chapters 3, 4, 5
S Y S T E M S	**D E V E L O P M E N T**	VI. Software development:	
		Detailed design	Chapters 6, 7
		Coding and unit testing	Chapter 7
		Integration	Chapter 8
		System testing	Chapter 8
		VII. Software maintenance	Chapter 9

Other Issues:
Software tools	Chapter 11
Quality assurance	Chapter 12
Software security and protection	Chapter 13

The phases that are covered in a course project will not cover the entire life cycle. In general, a typical project will include some requirements analysis, specification, preliminary design and planning, detailed design, coding, testing, and integration. However, a project may be limited to specification, design and development, or it might be a maintenance project.

Figure 1.1 shows the percentages of time spent in each activity for a typical student project. This will vary according to factors such as how completely the project is specified and whether it is a new system or a modification to an existing system.

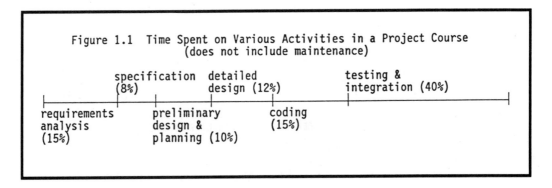

Figure 1.1   Time Spent on Various Activities in a Project Course (does not include maintenance)

Although the topics are addressed approximately in the order in which they are needed, it is important to keep in mind that the software life cycle is not linear, but iterative. That is, the cycle does not necessarily progress nicely from one step to the next, but often requires going back to an earlier phase to rethink and perhaps redesign some aspect of the system. This iterative aspect is shown in Figure 1.2.

1.B. The Inevitability of Change

Although the history of computer science is relatively short, it has been characterized by virtually constant change. This is likely to continue, with rapid changes taking place in both hardware and software. However, it will be some time before software can catch up with the current state of hardware.

1.B.1. Historical Perspective

Once upon a time, computer hardware represented the dominant cost in all aspects of computer use. Computer memory was limited. Since these beginnings the price of computers in general and memory in particular has dropped so dramatically that the typical desktop computer now has more power than the mainframes of only a few decades ago. If the automobile industry had done what the computer industry has done in the past thirty years, a BMW might cost $2.50 and get 20,000,000 miles per gallon.

Computer software, however has not kept pace with the advances in hardware. For example, in 1986, the Intel 80386 microprocessor, capable of addressing 4 gigabytes of memory, came into use with the Compaq Deskpro 386 microcomputer. The operating system available for it, however, was the Microsoft MS-DOS 3.1, which was designed for 640 kilobytes of memory. Enormous development tasks remain to be done to bring software up to the potential of the microprocessor.

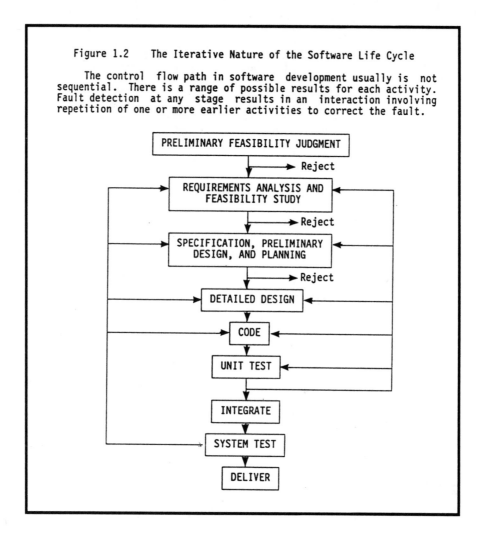

Figure 1.2   The Iterative Nature of the Software Life Cycle

The control flow path in software development usually is not sequential. There is a range of possible results for each activity. Fault detection at any stage results in an interaction involving repetition of one or more earlier activities to correct the fault.

1.B.2. Impact on Software

Today we have a large number of tools for use in software development. On the other hand, the size and complexity of programs often make their development more difficult.

In this text, we address both of these aspects of software. We will introduce a number of techniques that help in managing software development and in creating software that can be modified and updated.

One of the reasons for applying software engineering principles to large software projects is to increase productivity. Such increased software productivity is likely to be a slow accumulation of improvements from applying good practices. No major breakthrough is visible on the horizon. As Frederick P. Brooks, Jr., has said (April 1987,):

> *Software entities are more complex for their size than perhaps any other human construct because no two parts are alike (at least above the statement level). If they are, we make the two similar parts into a subroutine- open or closed. In this respect software systems differ profoundly from computers, buildings, or automobiles, where repeated elements abound.*

1.C. Standards

Several organizations set and certify software engineereing standards. These organizations include the **American National Standards Institute (ANSI)**, the **Institute of Electrical and Electronics Engineers (IEEE)**, and the **International Standards Organization (ISO)**. The standards are reviewed approximately every five years by committees of professionals from a broad spectrum of organizations in the United States and from other countries.

The practices described in this book are consistent with ANSI/IEEE software engineering standards. There are several reasons for this. One is that the ANSI/IEEE software engineering standards are internally consistent and often refer to each other. Another is that the ANSI/IEEE standards are readily available. A list of ANSI/IEEE software engineering standards used in this book is shown in Table 1.2.

[handwritten: standards are consistent and readily available]

Most companies have standards; many have their own internal standards. Not all correspond to ANSI/IEEE standards. This is partly because software engineering practice has been around much longer than these standards, and companies have created internal standards to meet the needs they perceive. On the job, you will need to find out what your company's standards are and adhere to them.

1.D. Terminology

One of the more confusing aspects of software engineering is the terminology. In the past, not only have multiple terms been in use for various aspects of the software life cycle, but also different sources use the same terms in different ways. As a simple example, for a long time there was no universal agreement on what is meant by the term software. Does software consist of source code or object code? Does it include documentation?

[handwritten: one term has diff. meanings]

The answer to the question is "all of the above." Software consists of programs in source and object form, documentation of the specifications and design, and any associated documentation of procedures or rules for the operation of the computerized system.

Table 1.2   Software Engineering Standards from the American National
            Standards Institute (ANSI) and the Institute of Electrical
            and Electronics Engineers (IEEE).

Each standard defines the scope and terminology for a particular life
activity and describes a set of practices required for compliance with
the standard. Other practices are recommended as optional practices.

ANSI/IEEE Std 729-1983, Glossary of Software Engineering Terminology
ANSI/IEEE Std 730-1984, Software Quality Assurance Plans
ANSI/IEEE Std 828-1983, Software Configuration Management Plans
ANSI/IEEE Std 829-1983, Software Test Documentation
ANSI/IEEE Std 830-1984, Software Requirements Specifications
ANSI/IEEE Std 983-1986, Software Quality Assurance Planning
ANSI/IEEE Std 1008-1987, Software Unit Testing
ANSI/IEEE Std 1012-1986, Software Verification and Validation Plans
ANSI Std X 3.5-1970, American National Standard Flowchart Symbols
                         and their Usage in Information Processing
IEEE Std 1016-1987, Software Design Descriptions

In this book we follow a standard set of terminology adopted by the American National Standards Institute (ANSI) and the Institute of Electrical and Electronics Engineers (IEEE), **ANSI/IEEE Standard 729-1983**, on which the glossary in this book is based. Standards for specific practices relating to various aspects of the software life cycle also have definitions of terms. We have added some terms that are not in ANSI/IEEE's *Standard Glossary* (1984). Furthermore, terms in the Glossary are cross-referenced for similar or related terms.

The problem you will find on the job is the contradiction in terminology in documents that were created before the standards were published. Software engineering is a relatively young field. People have used a variety of terms to refer to more or less the same parts of the software life cycle. The collection of terminology from six sources, shown in Table 1.3, illustrates the wide differences. The terms from each source are listed from top to bottom. They are arranged so that comparisons can be made horizontally.

You will encounter many programs, documentation, and publications that were written before the standards came into existence. It is important that you have some idea of how definitions have evolved so that you can interpret your sources.

In addition, keep in mind that just because a term is clearly defined in one source, it is not necessarily used that way uniformly. Many people continue to use older terminology, either because they are unaware of the current standard usage or because they are unwilling to change.

Table 1.3 Software engineering terminology that has been in use based on the references below. The terms describe phases of the software life cycle in chronological order from top to bottom for each source.

Authors of the Phases					
Brandon & Gray	Daly	Benjamin	Freeman	Metzger	Boehm
Application Identification and Project Selection	Planning	Feasibility Study	Needs Analysis	Definition	no term
System Survey					System Requirements
Data Gathering	Specify	System Specification	Specification		Software Requirements
System Analysis			Architectural Design	Design	Preliminary Design
System Design	Design	System Engineering	Detail Design		Detailed Design
Programming	Code	Programming and Procedure Development	Implementation	Programming	Code & Debug
Program Testing	Test				Test and Preoperations
System Testing		Implementation		System Test	
				Acceptance	
Conversion and Installation	no term		no term	Installation & Operations	
System Maintenance	no term	Maintenance	Maintenance		Operations and Maintenance
System Evaluation	Evaluation				

Benjamin, R. I. *Control of the Information System Development Cycle.* New York: Wiley Interscience, 1971.

Boehm, B. W. "Software Engineering." *IEEE Transactions on Computers* C-25, no. 12 (1976): 1226-1241.

Brandon, D. H., Gray, M. *Project Control Standards.* Princeton, NJ: Brandon Systems Press, 1970.

Daly, E. B. "Management of Software Development." *IEEE Transactions on Software Engineering* SE-3, no. 3 (1977): 229-242.

Freeman, P. "Tutorial on Software Design Techniques." IEEE Computer Society, 1976

Metzger, P.W. *Managing a Programming Project.* Englewood Cliffs, NJ: Prentice-Hall, 1973.

For example, one of the most abused terms in software engineering in recent years is *systems analyst*. Presumably, a systems analyst is someone who does **systems analysis**, defined as "the art of investigating the need for a system, determining the requirements, costs, benefits and feasibility of proposed systems and the preliminary design and planning of system development." This is an extremely difficult job, requiring a great deal of experience and background not only in software but in the details of the application at hand. It is aptly described as an art because it requires insight into human nature as well as knowledge of a host of technical problems.

On the other hand, a number of jobs have the title of systems analyst when the job itself may require many other talents. It has been used as something of a catch-all term, and is likely to continue that way. Therefore, you need to remember two things about this term. One is what systems analysis really is, and the other is that when the job title is systems analyst, you should find out what is really involved.

In addition to terminology, there are other areas of software engineering in which standards are useful. Software engineering involves a large number of different activities and a correspondingly large number of related documents. To help promote understanding and communication, practices are standardized. Therefore, as you become interested in more specialized areas of software practices, you should read the standards documents to understand what you are dealing with.

1.E. Prototyping

A **prototype** of a system is an initial or trial version under development. Generally it will not be completely functional within the system specifications. It may be used to test system concepts and as a basis for developing the eventual system.

In most engineering activity, developing a prototype is common. The prototype acts as a sort of test vehicle. It does not have to satisfy every requirement of the final system. This is especially important in developing complex mechanical products where the production facilities for manufacture require a major capital commitment. In software products the cost of manufacture is negligible; however, the complexity is so great that prototyping can be essential in investigating details of specification before committing resources to development of the entire system.

In software engineering the most common requirements to be relaxed for a prototype are performance requirements, followed by error actions, reliability requirements, and quality requirements. Since the prototype is intended to demonstrate only some of the functional aspects of a system it can be developed at a cost significantly lower than that of the final system. Some systems, of course, are critically dependent on performance. In such cases a prototype to demonstrate a kernel of a critical processing activity may be required to prove the feasibility of the system.

To create a quick prototype oriented to user interface specification, the performance characteristics of the system such as speed, size of data handled, accuracy, security, or completeness of error handling are most often compromised. This is a deviation from the traditional life cycle model, but it is frequently very useful in data processing and database applications. Very often those aspects of the system that pose the greatest risk are prototyped first. Getting early feedback from the client is usually desirable, because it is often difficult to get adequate communication of user needs during requirements analysis of software systems.

Another consideration that should be delayed is optimization. It is appropriate to apply anything you have already learned about efficiency (for example, if you need to sort anything, use an appropriate, system-supplied sort utility rather than the bubble sort you learned in your introductory programming course). However, a full discussion of optimization is beyond the scope of this course. In general, a small amount of code accounts for a large amount of run time, and often these "hot spots" can be found later, using a tool such as a profiler. For now, the guiding principle to keep in mind is, "First make it work, then make it work fast."

[handwritten margin note: Use system utilities to make the work fast.]

1.E.1. Rapid Prototyping

For a prospective computer application program, a prototype may be primarily an empty shell with a user interface to display user data entry screens and prompts and to generate report formats using simulated data, without performing any significant data processing. In other cases a working but preliminary system is produced without any attempt at optimization and without meeting many performance requirements of the eventual system. The production of such simulations is referred to as **rapid prototyping**.

The goal of rapid prototyping is to quickly get a working model that the user community can try out to evaluate the input and output formats for functionality and content. If a prototype can be produced on a time scale of a few days to several weeks, then it can be used as a serious tool in refining the requirements analysis and the detailed specifications before a major part of the development starts.

Rapid prototyping allows early visualization of the finished product. This is a great advantage in developing the type of system in which the user interface is a dominant aspect of the design. In many information management systems rapid prototyping is a valuable tool in completing and verifying system specifications by getting user evaluations of the prototype.

[handwritten margin note: useful when]

Prototypes are invaluable for interactive systems. They allow a user to play with a version of the system much like the final one. After using the prototype the user should have a better understanding of what is really needed and a modified requirements specification can be designed, if necessary. Revising a prototype is usually much less expensive than revising a finished system.

Rapid prototyping depends on the ability to put together, quickly and inexpensively, a system that will look to the customer something like the expected system. This raises an interesting question. Will it take almost as much work to make a prototype as to make the final system? Fortunately the answer to this question usually is no. This is true if a prototype is allowed to show the look and feel of the product, without actually performing all the required tasks. In general, a prototype will usually fake most of the internal data processing. In most cases a relatively small amount of effort will produce most of what is wanted.

Rapid prototyping blurs distinctions between requirements analysis and design as separate life cycle stages. However, it is very effective in getting users involved in the specification and design processes in a meaningful way.

1.E.2. Prototype - Use or Throw Away?

One of the major questions about the concept of prototyping is, "What do we do with the prototype after it has served its initial purpose?" Should the prototype be extended to become the final product or should it only be used to write requirements for the final program and then be thrown away? There are advantages to both approaches.

Extending a rough prototype to become the final program may lead to a sloppily written program that is hard to maintain. Some techniques that produce a running program quickly can be difficult to extend to a fully implemented system. If this is the case, the best procedure is to throw away the prototype and write a new program to the specifications using the insights gained during prototyping.

The strategy for producing the final version should be decided at the beginning. Some tools are specialized for quickly producing an empty shell with a user interface but are not extendable. Another approach might be to use a database management system such as dBASE III, which is implemented as an interpreter and which has good support for quickly building a user interface. Such a prototype system can be developed in a final version with higher performance by using a compiler for the database language. Alternatively, there are also dBASE to C translators to move the application to a programming language-based environment for further development.

On the other hand, a well-executed top-down approach often leads to a prototype developed in a conventional programming language, which can be extended into the final system. If the prototype proves adequate in terms of performance, it becomes the system. Otherwise more efficient modules are written where needed and exchanged for the prototype modules in building the final system.

1.E.3. Application to Group Project

For a group project in a software engineering course, it is often useful to think of creating a prototype rather than a finished product, largely because of the time constraints involved. For several types of applications a reasonable prototype can be developed in two to three months. That time frame fits into the usual course term.

Another reason for thinking in terms of developing a prototype is that it may help to maintain priorities. Although it is important to write a user interface that is readable, meaningful, and crash-proof, it is not reasonable to spend a lot of time revising the format of the user interface to make it as pretty as possible. Nor is it appropriate to focus a major part of your work on efficiency and optimization tasks in a course that covers a broad introduction to software creation. These areas are very important to the creation of real products, but they are secondary to demonstrating that the system works as it is supposed to.

1.F. Course Project: Group Formation

Your project will most likely be done on a group basis. The size and structure of the group will be determined by a number of factors, including the background of the students, the size of the class, and the nature of the project. There are several different group organization techniques; your instructor will decide which is most appropriate for the project.

One important aspect of group communication at the initial meeting for a class project is to exchange schedules, phone numbers, and electronic mail (E-mail) addresses. A software development team that works for one company has a common schedule and common office space. Students, unless they have class time devoted exclusively to group work, have no similar advantages and may have to establish their own meeting times and places.

Throughout the project you may want to refer to the section on group interactions at the end of this chapter. The comments there or in the references listed at the end of the chapter provide some helpful insights on group problems.

1.G. Beyond a Course Project: Industry Example

On the job, as in the classroom, there are a variety of ways of establishing teams. We discuss one of these, the chief programmer team. This is a description of a common and very effective type of team for large software projects, but it is normally unsuitable for use in the classroom without major modification. This is because of the number of people involved and the extensive resources used on the job, which may not be available to students. Please keep in mind the difference between a course project, which will probably be no more than a prototype, and a software system that takes many person-years to develop and includes hundreds of thousands or perhaps millions of lines of code.

The classical description of a programming team is that of the **chief programmer team** by Baker (1972). This team consists of a chief programmer, a backup programmer, a librarian, a technical staff consisting of programmers and possibly a specialist such as a database expert, and support staff for activities such as word processing, accounting, and clerical duties. Variants of that structure have been widely used in forming software development teams. This structure is illustrated in Figure 1.3.

One of the original virtues of having a separate librarian was to force centralization of control of and access to code and documents. That was a means of enforcing the concept that the code belongs to the group, not to individual programmers. In combination with programming standards and systematic reviews, this is a major contribution to assuring the quality of software.

In the era of batch computing and punched cards, clerks had the heavy duty of keypunching. Now it is usual for programmers to enter their own code with interactive editing terminals and to do documentation with various word processing tools.

The ideal of having a librarian and support staff is certainly not attainable for student project teams. This can be mitigated by intelligent use of word processors and other tools now widely available on microcomputers. Thus explicit policies must be in force to ensure that the entire team has access to project code and documentation. Although some of the librarian and clerical duties may be handled by each member of a student team, all the source code and working documents must be shared. That is, the information is to be available to all team members, regardless of the author of any specific module.

The idea of the software development team has been expanded in recent years. Large projects employ many types of teams working on specialized parts of the life cycle or subcomponents of a life cycle stage. A list of different team types that might work on a large software project is shown in Table 1.4. A major reason for splitting duties into different team domains is that it can avoid conflict of interest. Designers or coders want to believe that "their" code is correct. The quality assurance team needs to ensure that products conform to requirements. The job of test designers and testing teams is to find as many faults as possible. Overall system success is enhanced by having checks and balances between the roles of different teams.

Figure 1.3   Structure of a Chief Programmer Team

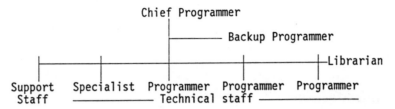

Chief programmer: The arbiter of design decisions. Coordinates and
    directs the team. Generally the most senior and experienced
    programmer.

Backup programmer: Assistant to the chief. Stand-in for chief
    when needed. Consults with chief on design decisions. An
    experienced programmer

Librarian: Manager of documents. Manages all code, maintains records,
    configuration management. May participate in unit testing.

Technical staff: Includes 2 to 5 personnel, primarily programmers,
    but might include a specialist.

Specialist: Such as systems analyst, data base expert, etc.

Programmer: Less experienced. Duties include coding, unit testing,
    debugging.

Support staff: Accounting, word processing, clerical.

Table 1.4 Team Types That Might Work on a Large Software
           Project

- Project management - coordination, planning and cost control
- Requirements - analysis, management and change control
- Configuration - review and management
- Quality assurance - planning, analysis, and review
- System architecture and design
- Coding and unit testing
- Tools development
- Integration testing
- System testing
- Training users and operators
- Maintenance

Team Organization and Group Management

This section is based in part on "Effective Group Interactions: Some Aspects of Group Projects in Computer Science Courses," by Gretchen L. Van Meer and Charles D. Sigwart, ACM SIGCSE Bulletin, Volume 21, Number 4, December 1989.

Introduction

Team formation is usually a response to a problem that cannot be solved by one person. Most software systems are large enough that it is not reasonable for one person to do it all. Team selection involves finding team members who can contribute to the solution of the problem.

The usual way to organize large software projects is to split the project into functional subsystems, each of which is assigned to a small team. The number of teams and the amount of management hierarchy required to manage and coordinate teams depends on the project size. A major part of software engineering deals with how software can be constructed with such teams.

A team is more than just several people working on a common project, but the level of teamwork will vary from one team to another. At one extreme, there may be a group of individuals carrying out related but individual assignments. At the other, there may be a team that works as a group at a fairly detailed level throughout the entire project.

There are major differences between individual work and teamwork. For example, to be an **effective team member**, a person should desire to be part of something that exceeds the limits of individual capabilities; should have an interest in doing a job with a higher degree of social interaction than is required by individual work; and should be interested in obtaining external criticism. (Criticism does not necessarily mean fault-finding; it means evaluating someone else's work for both its positive and negative attributes.) Effective team members also want to learn by association with others who are perceived as being knowledgeable. And they have a genuine interest in sharing their own knowledge with others. This is sometimes difficult for programmers who may have a hard time asking someone else to evaluate their work or suggest any changes.

Furthermore, a team approach to a project usually generates a greater degree of conflict than many people are accustomed to. Effective teamwork requires additional job skills. Working in a team environment on a class project can help to develop those skills. Teams, more than individuals, have a greater need for structured approaches such as top-down development and stepwise refinement. And remember that teamwork is the primary way that things are done on the job.

On the job, team selection is often made after the project is selected, and team members are acquired who have the necessary skills. In the classroom, skills are developing. The learning process happens at different rates for different individuals, which complicates the group interaction process. There is no way of knowing, when a group is formed, how the rates of learning of its members will vary. This can have a major impact on the effectiveness of a team.

In addition to all these limitations, the number of choices for team-mates is usually limited to those registered in the same class. This number may be relatively small. Therefore, the composition of any given team may be largely a matter of luck.

On the other hand, in the classroom everyone's background is likely to be similar. Furthermore, with the current shortage of skilled software engineers, there is no assurance that one will find better qualified team-mates anywhere else, either in another class or on the job.

Group Formation

The ideal size for a software project group depends on the project and the duties of the group. Work done in the 1950's by Robert F. Bales (1954) indicates that in general, the optimum team size is five. Based on an IEEE recommendation, the optimum team size for a software engineering project course is five. Of course, for large software projects, group sizes will vary and there will be many types of group other than programming teams. If the duties of a team require communication-intensive interaction among all members, then an upper bound on team size may be five or six. However, if the duties can be organized based on a hierarchy of com-munication paths between group members, then group size can be larger. Realistically, most projects require more than four to six people and will be subdivided into several smaller working units.

Bigger is not necessarily better, especially in a software engineering team. The first reaction of students tends to be that if there are more people, each will have less work to do. However, in coordinating a project, com-munication is vital at all levels. A greater number of people in a team results in more necessary lines of communication. This can quickly offset any advantage of having fewer subtasks per person.

Another drawback of larger group size is that members find it more difficult to get to know one another. Also, in a larger group, there may be a problem if one member feels that his or her contribution doesn't matter, since there are so many others. This may be less true of software develop-ment than other group activities, but in software development it is more serious if someone does feel this way.

In order to work most effectively in a team effort, it is important that the atmosphere encourage cooperation rather than competition. Team members must understand that their action (or inaction) affects the team effort, and this must supersede individual concerns.

Although classroom projects may or may not be graded on an individual basis, for most group efforts on the job, the group succeeds or fails as a group. Either all group members succeed, or all fail. Understanding this aspect of teamwork can make a substantial difference in becoming an effective team member.

Team Formation Phases

For this topic, we look at information from a field of study known as group dynamics. Courses in this subject are found in the areas of speech communication and psychology.

There are basically four phases of team formation and interaction. They can be referred to as *forming, storming, norming,* and *performing.* The *forming* phase is very short, usually limited to the initial meeting. The *storming* phase is slightly longer, including selection of a leader and developing a strategy. The *norming* phase is the longest, comprising as much as 90% of the group interaction and group effort. The *performing* phase includes the documentation of work done, and in a software project will be an ongoing process.

Forming

The first thing that must be done as a group is to establish the reason for being a group. This involves an orientation process. Each group member tries to figure out where each person fits into the group, what skills the various group members have, and how much and what kind of influence each person is likely to have on the group.

The purpose of the first meeting of any group involves getting acquainted and assessing each other's group participation skills and knowledge. In addition, the group must consider the general aspects of the group project and the requirements of the task at hand, and establish a method of interpersonal behavior.

The most important aspects of the project to address are a determination of what the task includes and what it does not include. Personal interaction aspects are more complicated. Often the people in the group do not know each other's backgrounds, schedules, areas of expertise, or personalities, and need to spend time finding out these things.

The initial meeting may seem disorganized as group members jump from one topic to another, from one point of view to another. While the focus may change in seemingly unrelated ways, this is an attempt on the part of the participants to assess the resources of the group. This is a normal component of group interaction.

One very important aspect of group communication at the initial meeting for a class project is to exchange schedules, phone numbers, and

E-mail addresses. Students, unlike their industrial counterparts, usually need to establish their own meeting times and places.

Storming

In the storming phase, the group must agree on the procedures it will follow. The name refers to two things: one, this phase is characterized by conflict; two, in this phase brainstorming (described below) is an excellent technique for developing a strategy. Conflict in this phase is normal. It means that various approaches are being considered. This type of conflict is preferable to a group whose members all wait for someone else to suggest a strategy.

To start ideas flowing, the technique of brainstorming may be used to help develop creative thinking. Group members, in turn, present concepts, with no judgments attached to the presentation or the reception of the concepts. The idea is to keep an open mind with regard to possibilities and consider many concepts.

As an introduction to brainstorming, the group might try this exercise. Take an ordinary word and have each group member, in turn, give an example of a use or context of the word, with no judgment attached. For example, take the ordinary word "bit." Computer science people are likely to give examples such as "high bit," "parity bit," "byte," and "nibble." But equally likely in a brainstorming session are responses such as "the dog bit me," "piece," or "bitter." The idea is to avoid self-imposed limitations that can unnecessarily constrict creativity. The same technique can be used to develop ideas on how to create an appropriate software system.

When different ideas about the course software project are presented, they should be considered and discussed by the group. When done in a spirit of cooperation, rather than engaging in a power struggle, this can result in higher quality software.

In this phase, the group agrees on a strategy and chooses a leader. Group leaders tend to emerge, whether formally elected or not. This decision will have been made, in part, in the forming phase. One of the aspects of that phase includes figuring out who is not a suitable group leader. This process usually excludes those who are either too quiet or too outspoken. Selection is likely to be based on the individual's approach to the project.

Norming

In this phase, norms are established. That is, group members agree on patterns of behavior and an approach to the project. Group cohesion begins to develop and considerable time is spent discussing project-related ideas. This is the longest phase; in a software development effort it may be

[handwritten margin note: selection of a leader, & developing strategy.]

[handwritten margin note: collects info, processes it, creates something coherent]

90% of the group interaction. It is in this phase that the team collects information, processes it, and creates something coherent.

Performing

In this phase, the documentation is put together in its final form. In a software engineering project, this is an ongoing phase. Documentation standards are likely to be clearly defined before you begin, possibly based on the standard given in Appendix A. The effort in this phase will be in producing, reviewing and editing the documentation, rather than in deciding the form it is to take.

[margin note: Producing - reviewing - editing the documentation.]

An Effective Team Environment

Team effectiveness depends on a number of factors. These include the level of work effort on each person's part, the amount of expertise in the group, and the appropriateness and effectiveness of the strategies that the group uses. In a class project, the level of expertise should be determined by the prerequisites for the course. The level of work effort depends to some extent on the makeup of the group and the partitioning of the project work, but also on individual motivation. The effectiveness of the strategies used will, we hope, be enhanced by the descriptions in this section.

Some specific problems are likely to arise. Some of these apply to groups in general, others to software engineering groups. We look at the most common of both kinds, which have to do with individual performance by group members. We address some means of resolving conflicts and enhancing interpersonal communication, injecting a caution about group cohesion.

Individual Performance

A problem that can be self-perpetuating in a group situation occurs when one member seems to be doing less than his or her share. Any perception of dissatisfaction on the part of the other group members can cause the guilty party to withdraw, causing the group to effectively lose a member. This is a common problem in a student project group when a member who is not performing up to standard is criticized. The problem is likely to be that the person does not understand some aspect of the project. The important thing to do is to make an effort to bring the person back into the group.

[margin note: ① not doing assigned work of his/her share & then withdraw because the class is criticized & he/she is criticizing results in losing one member. Try to bring the person back into group.]

Another type of problem can arise when an individual is reluctant to express his or her opinion about a concern because no one else has mentioned it. The rationale is something like, "Everyone else agrees to the proposed strategy so I guess it must be all right." Sometimes each group member, sharing the same reservation, will refrain from commenting. This has been referred to as "groupthink" and has led to some major disasters, not just in computer projects.

Another common problem is with group members who become competitive rather than cooperative. The result is endless arguments about technical details, turning minor problems into power struggles.

Conflict Resolution

Conflict among group members is indicative of the introduction of a variety of ideas. This is a positive attribute of a group. Conflict, therefore, should not be seen as inherently a problem. However, there needs to be an established mechanism for conflict resolution and decision making.

Conflict management is essentially a selection between alternative actions. In software projects, there is generally no one right way of doing things. Making a decision and getting on with the project is much more critical than arguing over whose ideas should be used.

Conflict resolution can occur by compromise, forcing, avoidance, or confrontation. While compromise has great appeal in some situations, in software projects it indicates a tendency to avoid the real issue. The converse of this is forcing, where one person insists that it be done a particular way. Neither of these methods is particularly effective.

Avoidance consists of ignoring the conflict, hoping it will go away. A moment's thought should indicate that there is no real solution in this, and worse, the avoidance process is a drain on the group energy, which can detract from the project.

As it turns out, confrontation is the most effective method of conflict resolution. By insisting that the group examine the areas of disagreement, discussion of differences is brought into the open. This is likely to result in an attempt to find the solution that is most likely to succeed, and will therefore be acceptable to all parties. Once the alternatives are clearly defined, decisions can be made by voting if necessary.

Interpersonal Communication

There are many purposes of interpersonal communication within a team. One is to define the internal organization of the team and each member's position in it. A second is to define the team's strategies. Third, the group members need to share information and to educate each other on various details of the project. In addition, the team must be able not only to identify the resources available to it, but also to communicate this information among themselves. Finally, the project activities must be coordinated.

Clearly, it is to the advantage of the entire team for each team member to develop interpersonal communication skills. Group members, to create an effective team, need to get acquainted with each other. They need to share their feelings about the project as well as their levels of expertise.

While willingness to express ideas is crucial, the success of group interaction also rests heavily on understanding other group members' feelings and methods of communication. Sometimes communication can be enhanced by each group member asking for feedback from others in the group. However, those who talk the most don't necessarily say the most.

Other methods of improving communication are for group members to listen carefully for feeling as well as content (e.g., how strongly does this team member feel about this idea?), and to watch for nonverbal clues (e.g., withdrawing from discussion). The group leader can start a discussion, and thereby improve communication, by asking open-ended questions (e.g., who can we get to try our system to see if it's really crash-proof?)

Group Cohesion

Group cohesiveness is a step toward cooperation. Satisfied members in cohesive groups communicate more. Unfortunately, a very cohesive group will not necessarily get the most done on a project. Group effectiveness is not necessarily related to the amount of time spent on group interaction. The team that spends a large amount of time together may indeed be spending a great deal of productive effort on project development. On the other hand, they might be just spending that time socializing together.

Meeting Techniques

People who have worked successfully on teams have used a number of different techniques and developed some basic principles for group meetings and interactions which seem to work well. The following is some advice for scheduling, preparation and procedures for meetings; and group interactions.

Note that there are suggestions on when to schedule meetings. Whether these are applicable to your project depends on the circumstances of your institution and whether you have class time allocated specifically for group meetings. The system of having an agenda and publishing minutes is very effective for any group, as they force the group members to evaluate in specific terms exactly what they are supposed to be doing and how well they are doing it.

Scheduling

- Team meetings should be scheduled as early as possible (early in the day, as well as early in the term).
- Meetings should only be scheduled at times that everyone can make.
- A meeting should be scheduled for a time and place with suitable size, setting, and time allowed for each member to be able to communicate directly with each other member.
- The meeting should be started only when everyone has arrived.
- The meeting should be canceled if 20 minutes have passed and someone is missing.

Preparation

- A detailed agenda should be prepared for each meeting, with copies for each team member.
- Before a meeting, copies of a list of items that have been agreed to for the next meeting should be circulated among all team members with a request for additions.

Procedures

- Each agenda item should be completed before going on to the next.
- Discussion should start with facts. Even when the facts are thought to be well known to all the members, a short review is a good idea. Three questions should be addressed for each major agenda item, in this order:

  What are the facts pertaining to the problem?
  How do we feel about them?
  What shall we do about the problem?

- Criticism and comment should be actively solicited from all team members. (Invite some controversy if there is none.)
- Doing (however tentative) should be encouraged, as opposed to discussing what must be done.
- The opinions and experiences of others should be solicited, especially when there are disagreements. (People may think they disagree when they are actually not talking about the same experiences. They must draw each other out far enough to realize what their differences are.)
- Each person must leave the meeting with something specific to do before the next meeting, whether individually or with others.

Group Interactions

- When somebody is talking, the other group members should not only listen, but also actively indicate their reactions. The speaker probably cannot read minds, and he or she needs the honest reactions of the other group members.

- The speaker should keep his or her eyes on the group, talking to the group as a whole (rather than to a crony or a special opponent.) The speaker should constantly watch for reactions. A lot of nonverbal communication goes on. A good undercurrent of direct eye contact can improve the harmony of the group.

- When problems arise, one tactic to break off an argument is to backtrack, to further work on the facts and direct experience. Sometimes it is a good idea to go out and get more information before proceeding on a specific topic.

General advice for successful group interaction from Robert F. Bales (1954) is:

> *Keep your ear to the ground. No recipe or set of rules can substitute for constant, sensitive, and sympathetic attention to what is going on in the relations between members. Do not get so engrossed in getting the job done that you lose track of what is the first prerequisite of success- keeping the committee in good operating condition.*

Summary

Software engineering and the software life cycle are defined and examined briefly from a historical perspective. Because software engineering is concerned not only with the creation of new software systems but also with the maintenance of existing software, it is sometimes very important to become acquainted with past practices. Chapter 1 discusses terminology. The current ANSI/IEEE Std 729-1983 is the basis for this book and its Glossary; however, the reader is cautioned about past usages of various terms.

A brief history of software engineering is given, with emphasis on the need to plan for change in software systems. Prototyping is described, since not only is this an important concept on the job, but also because a one-term classroom project effectively constitutes a prototype.

Because software development is generally a team activity and because the class project is likely to be done on a team basis, some aspects of team formation and group management are addressed. The four classic phases of team formation are described and suggestions for improving team productivity and group communication are discussed. Baker's classic chief programmer team is described as an industry example.

Keywords

American National Standards Institute (ANSI)
ANSI/IEEE Standard 729-1983
chief programmer team
configuration management
development
effective team member
feasibility study
Institute of Electrical and Electronics Engineers (IEEE)
maintenance
prototype
quality assurance
rapid prototyping
requirements analysis
software engineering
software life cycle
system specification
systems analysis

Review Questions

1.1   What is software engineering?

1.2   Name the phases of the software life cycle.

1.3   How consistent is software engineering terminology? How consistent has it been in the past?

1.4   Has software engineering become easier or more difficult?

1.5   How does the history of hardware development compare with software development?

1.6   What is a prototype and what is its purpose?

1.7   Why is software engineering usually done by teams?

1.8   What are the characteristics of an effective team member?

1.9   What is the ideal team size for a software development project?

1.10 Why is resource allocation needed in software engineering?

1.11 Describe the four phases of team formation and interaction.

1.12 Describe some problems that are likely to arise in programming groups.

1.13 Describe some methods of conflict resolution and the likelihood of the effectiveness of each.

1.14 What is the relationship between group cohesion and group effectiveness?

1.15 List several techniques for successful teamwork, and ways to apply them in a classroom project.

Exercises

1.1 What is the difference between prototyping a mechanical system such as an aircraft and prototyping a software system?

1.2 Your team has designed an information processing system and written the code. In trying out the system you find it is incompatible with the file formats of eight out of twelve other existing systems with which it must interact. What do you do next? To which previous stage of the software life cycle do you go?

1.3 Describe a committee or group in which you have participated that worked effectively. How did the group organization contribute to that effectiveness?

1.4 From your previous experience, describe an ineffective group activity and indicate what caused the group to be ineffective.

1.5 Compare your organization's standard for a particular set of software practices against the comparable ANSI/IEEE standard from Table 1.2. What topics are treated differently? What topics are not included? In what way do practices covered by the standards differ?

References

Baker, F. T. "Chief Programmer Team Management of Production Programming." *IBM Systems J.* 11,1 (1972): 56-73.

> Classic description of chief programmer team organization.

Bales, Robert F. "In Conference." *Harvard Business Rev.* 32 (1954): 44-50.

> Analysis of group interactions; classical study that determined that the ideal group size is five.

Bartol, K. M. "Building Synergistic EDP Teams." Proceedings of the Fifteenth Annual Computer Personnel Research Conference, ed. T. C. Willoughby. Arlington, VA: Aug. 18-19, 1977, pp.18-30.

> Reviews factors in team productivity, team structure (membership, size, reward system, resource allocation), and process factors (communication skill, leadership, conflict resolution).

Basili, V. R., and Zelkowitz, M. V. "The Software Engineering Laboratory Objectives." Proceedings of the Fifteenth Annual Computer Personnel Research Conference, ed. T. C. Willoughby. Arlington, VA: Aug. 18-19, 1977, pp.254-269.

Description of research program to investigate software engineering methods and practices.

Boar, Bernard H. Application Prototyping. New York: Wiley, 1984.

A systematic discussion of software prototypes, their relation to systems specification, and the management of development.

Brilhart, John K. Effective Group Discussion, 5th ed. Dubuque, IA: Wm. C. Brown, 1986.

Includes description of group phases: "forming, norming, storming, performing."

Brooks, Frederick P., Jr., The Mythical Man-Month, Essays on Software Engineering. Massachusetts: Addison-Wesley, 1975, reprinted 1982.

Considered a classic of software engineering. Brooks presents the results of his experience as the project manager for the IBM OS 360. A clear exposition of the non-linearity of manpower and project duration effects on software project management.

Brooks, Frederick P., Jr., "No Silver Bullet." IEEE Computer 20, no. 4 (April 1987): 10-19.

Fashioning complex conceptual constructs is the essence; accidental tasks arise in representing the constructs in language. Past progress has so reduced the accidental tasks that future progress now depends on addressing the essence.

Budde, Reinhard, et al., eds., "Approaches to Prototyping." *Proceedings of the Working Conference on Prototyping*. Nemur, Belgium: October 1983; Springer Verlag, 1984.

A collection of 35 papers on prototyping concepts, methodology, environments, and tools.

Cathcart, Robert S., and Samover, Larry A. Small Group Communication. Dubuque, IA: W. C. Brown, 1970.

Excellent collection of articles dealing with many aspects of small group interaction.

Delbecq, A. L. Van de Ven, A. H., and Gustafson, D. H. Group Techniques for Program Planning, A Guide to Nominal Group and Delphi Processes. San Francisco: Scott, Foresman, 1973.

Guide to group interaction processes, explaining two specific techniques for getting things done.

Fairley, Richard. Software Engineering Concepts. New York: McGraw-Hill, 1985.

Good coverage on concepts of design and development.

Forsyth, Donelson R. An Introduction to Group Dynamics. Monterey, CA: Brooks-Cole, 1983.

Includes a description of brainstorming, its origin and technique.

Gibbs, Norman E. and Fairley, Richard E. eds., Software Engineering Education: The Educational Needs of the Software Community, Springer-Verlag, 1987.

Papers presented at the Software Engineering Education Workshop, held at the Carnegie-Mellon University Software Engineering Institute Feb. 27-28, 1986. Includes "Software Engineering and Computer Science: How Do They Differ?" by Robert L. Glass.

The Institute of Electrical and Electronics Engineers, Inc., Software Engineering Standards, Distributed in cooperation with Wiley-Interscience, a division of John Wiley & Sons, Inc., October 1987.

> A collection of 13 standards documents published as one volume. Standards are revised at least once every 5 years and additional standards are under development. Individual standards are also published by the IEEE Computer Society Press.

> Includes "ANSI/IEEE Std 729-1983, Glossary of Software Engineering Terminology," which defines more than 500 terms in general use in the software engineering field.

Janis, Irving L. Victims of Groupthink: A Psychological Study of Foreign-Policy Decisions and Fiascos. Boston: Houghton Mifflin, 1982.

> This classic analysis of defective decision making at high levels of government is applicable to any group.

Kidder, Tracy. The Soul of a New Machine. New York: Bantam Books, 1982.

> Pulitzer Prize-winning account of the effects on the people involved in a bottom-up design and implementation of a computer and its systems software.

Peters, Lawrence J. and Tripp, Leonard L. "A Model of Software Engineering." Proceedings, Third International Conference on Software Engineering, IEEE, pp. May 1978.

> Has table indicating various uses of software engineering terminology in different organizations and at different times.

Pressman, Roger S. Software Engineering, A Beginner's Guide. New York: McGraw-Hill, 1987.

> Introductory book intended for freshman or sophomore level. Good descriptions of need for and application of software engineering.

Semprevivo, Philip. "A Critical Assessment of Team Approaches to Systems Development." Proceedings of the Fifteenth Annual Computer Personnel Research Conference, ed. T. C. Willoughby. Arlington, VA: Aug. 18-19, 1977, pp. 94-103.

> Description of team vs. individual effort; includes discussion of team member selection, dealing with conflict, and descriptions of techniques used by successful teams.

Shaw, Marvin E. Group Dynamics: The Psychology of Small Group Behavior. New York: McGraw-Hill, 1981.

> General description of group decision making and behavior; not applied to software engineering.

Sheil, B.A. "The Psychological Study of Programming." Computing Surveys 13, 1 (March 1981): pp. 101-120.

> Reviews the psychological research on programming and argues that the research's ineffectiveness is the result of unsophisticated experimental technique and a shallow view of the nature of programming skill.

Tubbs, Stewart L. A Systems Approach to Small Group Interaction, 2d ed., New york: Random House, 1984.

> Textbook on group dynamics; of particular interest is a chapter entitled "Defensive Communication" by Jack R. Gibb.

Unger, Brian, and Walker, Sheldon. "Improving Productivity in System Software Development." Proceedings of the Fifteenth Annual Computer Personnel Research Conference, ed. T. C. Willoughby. Arlington, VA: Aug. 18-19, 1977, pp. 104-115.

Based on experiences with groups in operating systems project courses; claim improved productivity by using a facilitator to lead student team group meetings.

Weinberg, Gerald M. The Psychology of Computer Programming. New York: Van Nostrand-Reinhold, 1971.

The first attempt to systematically describe programming. Its anecdotal style makes it highly readable; includes exposition of "egoless programming."

Woodfield, S. N., and Collofello, J. S. "Some Insights and Experiences in Teaching Team Project Courses." *SIGCSE Bull.* 14 (1983): 62-65.

Description of experiences teaching team project courses at Arizona State University, Tempe.

Yourdon, Edward, ed. Classics in Software Engineering. New York: Yourdon Press, 1979.

Reprints of 24 classic papers, including Baker's paper on Chief Programmer Teams cited above, and "Chief Programmer Teams" by Baker and H.D. Mills.

CHAPTER 2

THE SOFTWARE REQUIREMENTS SPECIFICATION

From the Minutes of a Borough Council Meeting:

Councillor Trafford took exception to the proposed notice at the entrance of South Park: "No dogs must be brought to this Park except on a lead." He pointed out that this order would not prevent an owner from releasing his pets, or pet, from a lead when once safely inside the Park.

The Chairman (Colonel Vine): What alternative wording would you propose, Councillor?

Councillor Trafford: "Dogs are not allowed in this Park without leads."

Councillor Hogg: Mr. Chairman, I object. The order should be addressed to the owners, not to the dogs.

Councillor Trafford: That is a nice point. Very well then: "Owners of dogs are not allowed in this Park unless they keep them on leads."

Councillor Hogg: Mr. Chairman, I object. Strictly speaking, this would prevent me as a dog-owner from leaving my dog in the back-garden at home and walking with Mrs. Hogg across the Park.

Councillor Trafford: Mr. Chairman, I suggest that our legalistic friend be asked to redraft the notice himself.

Councillor Hogg: Mr. Chairman, since Councillor Trafford finds it so difficult to improve on my original wording, I accept. "Nobody without his dog on a lead is allowed in this Park."

Councillor Trafford: Mr. Chairman, I object. Strictly speaking, this notice would prevent me, as a citizen, who owns no dog, from walking in the Park without first acquiring one.

Councillor Hogg (with some warmth): Very simply, then: "Dogs must be led in this Park."

Councillor Trafford: Mr. Chairman, I object: this reads as if it were a general injunction to the Borough to lead their dogs into the Park.

Councillor Hogg interposed a remark for which he was called to order; upon his withdrawing it, it was directed to be expunged from the Minutes.

The Chairman: Councillor Trafford, Councillor Hogg has had three tries; you have had only two . . .

Councillor Trafford: "All dogs must be kept on leads in this Park."

The Chairman: I see Councillor Hogg rising quite rightly to raise another objection. May I anticipate him with another amendment: "All dogs in this Park must be kept on the lead."

This draft was put to the vote and carried unanimously, with two abstentions.

> *- Robert Graves and Alan Hodge*
>
> *The Reader Over Your Shoulder, A Handbook for Writers of English Prose*

The manual, or written specification, is a necessary tool, though not a sufficient one. The manual is the external specification of the product. It describes and prescribes every detail of what the user sees. . . . For the sake of implementers it is important that the changes be quantized - and that there be dated versions appearing on a schedule.

The manual must not only describe everything the user does see, including all interfaces; it must also refrain from describing what the user does not see. That is the implementer's business, and there his design freedom must be unconstrained.

> *- Frederick P. Brooks, Jr., The Mythical Man-Month*

Software Life Cycle

Requirements analysis and specification

I. Software need
II. Preliminary feasibility judgment
III. Requirements analysis and feasibility study
IV. Requirements specification
V. Preliminary software design and planning
VI. Software development
    Detailed design
    Coding and unit testing
    Integration
    System testing
VII. Software maintenance

Project: Software Requirements Specification

2.A. Introduction

The beginning of a software project may be something as vague as the statement "Write a computer dating service." You know that you need to design the system, write the code, and get it to work. There are several other steps in the process, such as writing the Software Requirements Specification, including a Preliminary User's Manual; writing a System Plan; scheduling the entire project; writing a Test Specification Document; and getting the user's approval. All this must be done before you start writing any code for the system.

In Chapter 2 we will address the first step, writing the Software Requirements Specification.

2.B. Software Need and Feasibility Judgment

The **Software Requirements Specification (SRS)** is not the first thing that goes into the creation of a software system, but for a course project some things have already been done, such as a statement of need and a preliminary feasibility study. We will briefly explain what goes into these, although we defer a detailed description until Chapter 10.

The software life cycle begins with a statement of a **need**, followed by a preliminary decision as to whether the fulfillment of that need by software is feasible. That means deciding whether the available hardware, software, personnel, and time are sufficient and the need great enough to justify doing the system development.

If the decision is to go ahead, the next step is the requirements analysis and feasibility study. Requirements analysis is perhaps the most difficult aspect of software engineering. For the purposes of this chapter, we assume that the statement of need has been made and that a preliminary feasibility study has already determined that the course project can be done with the resources available. We proceed on the assumption that you are doing a limited amount of requirements analysis and address that topic briefly. We then turn to the subject of how to specify these requirements unambiguously. The format used is based on the ANSI/IEEE Standard 830-1984, Guide to Software Requirements Specification.

2.C. Requirements Analysis

2.C.1. An Introduction

Requirements analysis is probably the most difficult part of software engineering. Basically, it means figuring out exactly what the users want (not limited to what they say they want) and creating a system that will satisfy them. A moment's reflection on the specification "write a computer dating service" should tell you that this information is inadequate to start writing code.

The requirements analysis phase produces a documented set of requirements, features, and performance measures that the system and software must have in order to satisfy the recognized software need.

A **requirement**, in the context of systems analysis, is a condition or capability needed by a user to solve a problem or achieve an objective; or a condition that must be met by a system to satisfy a user need. For example, a statement of a requirement may be a fast system response time in an interactive system.

A **specification** is a concise statement of requirements to be satisfied and a procedure for determining if they are satisfied. For the fast interactive response time needed, the specification may be that the system must respond to the user within 1 second. As another example, a specification may state that a report must be printed within a certain page format, such as 8.5" by 11". These specifications can be verified by running the program and observing the result. Specification may also mean a document that prescribes the requirements. The document must be written in a complete, precise, verifiable manner.

Requirements analysis is a preliminary step in producing a specification of requirements. Information must be collected, analyzed, and organized. Management needs this information to make a decision about whether proceeding with software development will be worth the money. The steps in this process are summarized in Table 2.1 (and are addressed in detail in Chapter 10).

```
Table 2.1   Steps Leading to Management Approval for
            System Development

1. Developing an understanding of user needs and requirements
2. Determining the software requirements of the application
3. Achieving user community concurrence on requirements
4. Documenting software requirements specifications
5. Preparing preliminary designs for systems
6. Identifying resources needed for development
7. Creating development and implementation plans
8. Reviewing and verifying the designs and plans against the
   user community's needs and requirements.

For a  small group  project the first major  milestone may be
the decision  to carry out development.  At the  time of this
decision, no  more  than 33%  of the  effort to  deliver  the
system should have been expended, as indicated in Figure 1.1.
```

The formalization of system requirements is normally done before any development work is undertaken. The importance of this becomes obvious if we consider the possibility that management's decision will be to abandon the proposal. The formalization of a proposal is usually in the form of a Software Requirements Specification. In fact, several proposals may be prepared, supported by a cost/benefit analysis of each.

The Software Requirements Specification should answer the question, "Exactly what is it that the user(s) want the system to do, and how?" The Software Requirements Specification should specify a list of characteristics sufficient to ensure that a system has been designed to satisfy the identified needs and constraints. It should *not* detail the actual structure of the software system or the implementation. A separate document, the System Plan (see Chapter 4), should specify the outline of the actual development with schedules, cost estimates, resources, and staffing requirements.

2.C.2. Resource Requirements

By resources we mean time, effort, money, computer time, and equipment. Another incredibly difficult task is that of initially estimating the resources that will be used during the life of a software development project.

If the initial estimate is not done well the project can be doomed from the start. If the initial estimate does not provide for adequate resources, the project is bound to fail, because no matter what is said or done the project will have an overrun. It is extremely easy to underestimate the resources needed for a project. Software developers have been notorious for their optimism. To make matters worse, customers and supervisors tend to believe that resource requirements have been overestimated. Typical responses to resource estimates are:

"Why can't you do it for less?"

"The company can't possibly spend that much money."

"How can such a simple task take so much time and money?"

Because of these attitudes a software developer has some difficulty defending cautious estimates. Remember that the estimated resources must be roughly adequate so that the project can be completed within an acceptable margin of allocated resources.

At this point we should make sure that we know the difference between **requirements** and **needs.** An organization may decide that it needs an inventory control system. It would be very dangerous to present this need to its data processing department and expect to get an acceptable working software system. Based only on a statement of need, there is absolutely no basis for assuming that a system produced would be what the users want. We couldn't even be sure that it would inventory the right products.

As another example, a company may decide that it needs a computer dating service. Consider for a moment how you would write software that would satisfy this need. Without a specification of requirements we couldn't be sure that the system would conform to the user's expectations. What is needed is a detailed and complete specification of the requirements. An example of a requirement for a computer dating service might be, "The system must produce at least one match for each applicant."

2.C.3. Partitioning a System: Software, Hardware, Manual Procedures

The Software Requirements Specification should specify exactly which activities of the proposed system are to be allocated to hardware, which to software, and which to manual procedures.

Those processes to be performed by software that is specified for development must be clearly delineated. Only then can a specification of software development be established by the Software Requirements Specification.

To do this effectively, procedures that are to be handled manually or by hardware must be clearly defined. Manual procedures are those that are relevant to the system and done entirely by people. There is no need to get overly enthusiastic about automating every detail of a system. Some things are more trouble to do by machine than by hand. For example, most home computerized checkbook systems require more work than using a checkbook and a pocket calculator, and they are less portable.

2.C.4. Target Machine vs. Development Machine

The hardware used in software development is not necessarily the same hardware on which the software will ultimately run. The computer system for which the software is being developed is the **target machine**, and the system that is being used in development is the **development machine**. Resource requirements need to be stated for the target machine; however, it is important to determine that adequate resources are available for the development machine. We look first at **resource requirements** for the target machine.

The resources required for the target machine environment include memory size, mass storage type and size, choice of CPU, system architecture, choice of operating system, number and types of I/O channels, and choice of supporting software. Each of these factors may affect the system performance.

In specifying the **resource limits** required of the target machine, it is wise not to underestimate space requirements. If the memory or storage available is not saturated, it is often possible to trade memory space for speed improvement when the time for optimizing the code arrives. The labor required to squeeze more performance or more features into a system can be enormous if the space limit is already reached.

Resource requirements for the development machine may be considerably greater for the target machine. For example, the development machine may have to support a compiler and other tools in addition to all the features of the target machine. Presumably the system will not be compiled while it is in use.

For a course project, it is likely that the target machine and the development machine will be the same. However, it is important to understand that this is often not the case.

2.D. Presenting the Results of Analysis

In order to make sure that the analysts and users agree on the specifications for a system, there must be a written document. This document is often called the Software Requirements Specification.

The Software Requirements Specification should follow a standard form. A documentation standard is often explicitly adopted by an organization for all projects. The standard outline form given in Table 2.2 is from the ANSI/IEEE Standard 830-1984. This standard is referred to, along with some practical details of coverage, in Appendix A.

```
            Table 2.2  Software Requirement Specification Document
                            Sample  Outline

  Title Page

  Table of Contents

  1.0. Introduction
          1.1. Purpose and Origin of the Need for This System
          1.2. Scope of the System Specified
          1.3. Definitions, Acronyms, and Abbreviations
          1.4. References to Related and Supporting Documents
          1.5. Overview of the System

  2.0. General Description
          2.1. Product Perspective
          2.2. Product Functions
          2.3. User Characteristics
          2.4. General Constraints
          2.5. Assumptions and Dependencies

  3.0. Specific Requirements
          3.1. Functional Requirements
          3.2. External Interface Requirements
          3.3. Performance Requirements
          3.4. Design Constraints
          3.5. Attributes
          3.6. Other Requirements

  Appendixes (optional)

  Glossary

  Index
```

A standard form for the contents of a document permits a more efficient review process. An experienced reviewer who knows the format will know where a particular aspect of a system should be described in the document structure and will be able to check quickly for content or omissions.

The version of the ANSI/IEEE Software Requirements Specification standard in Table 2.2 includes an Introduction, a General Description, and Specific Requirements. In the next section we look at these, with some examples.

It is important to keep in mind that the Software Requirements Specification should not detail the actual structure of the software system or the implementation details. The algorithmic detail and implementation strategy should be left to the development phase, which might be the work of some other group of people than those doing the requirements analysis. The task here is to specify a list of requirements sufficient and only sufficient to unambiguously specify (and later verify) that a system has been designed to satisfy the identified needs and constraints. For example, the Software Requirements Specification would *not* include a specification of variable names, data structures, or detailed algorithms.

The Software Requirements Specification does need to be flexible enough to accommodate modifications that may be incorporated. Changes and additions are much easier to insert in the earlier stages of the software life cycle. Furthermore, because the Software Requirements Specification will be used during the entire software life cycle, it should be written in a way that can incorporate changes at any stage. This includes maintenance, which will be done after the system is delivered.

Keep in mind that this information should be clear even when it is read several years from now by someone who may be completely unfamiliar with the system. It is important to be complete and accurate. The characteristics of a good Software Requirements Specification are summarized in Table 2.3. These characteristics are described further in this chapter and in later chapters.

Table 2.3 Characteristics of a Good Software Requirements
          Specification

- It is unambiguous.
- It is complete.
- It is modifiable.
- It is internally consistent.
- It is verifiable.
- It is traceable.
- It is usable during development, operation, and maintenance.

All this is an overview of what the managers and users of the new system should expect. It also provides the background for the developers to understand the priorities of various detailed requirements to use when making design and implementation decisions.

Although these and other constraints may result in documents you would find dry or stuffy because of their formalism, keep in mind that the purpose is to make all details absolutely clear even if ponderous. This is the opposite of marketing or advertising literature, which has the goal of extolling the product, with as appealing a description as possible without making any outright lies about it.

2.E. Contents of the Software Requirements Specification

The goal of the Introduction and General Description sections is to provide a detailed perspective on what the system is proposed to do: why it is needed, what it will do in functional terms, how it will interact with existing systems, and what the benefits of the system will be. In many cases an important part is a description of what the system will not do. As an example of something that a computer dating service system does not do, there may be a statement that matches are not guaranteed if no suitable candidates are available.

The Introduction should state the software need and its background. It should address the question of where the system came from and why it is needed. This includes information as to whether the system is a new one or a modification of an existing one.

The General Description should include an overview of the product. This section does not state specific requirements; it only makes those requirements easier to understand. For example, for Fig Leaf Enterprises Computer Dating Service, this would include a list of the information to be collected from each client, the nature of the matching criteria, and a description of the level of security that is needed.

The third section of the Software Requirements Specification, the Specific Requirements, is the most detailed. This section should include all details that are necessary and sufficient for the developers to design, code and implement the system. Hence this section must be absolutely unambiguous. Every statement must be reviewed to be sure that there are no interpretations that are inconsistent with the intent of the analysts. Some ways of doing this are described in detail in Section 2.G below.

It is in the Specific Requirements Section that the characteristics listed in the General Description are specified in detail. For example, if a needed level of security was mentioned in the General Description, it should be specified in this part.

We will now briefly look at the specific sections of the Software Requirements Specification as listed in Table 2.2. Not all sections need to be used for every project. This is generally true for whatever document standard you are using. If any section of the standard document outline is not applicable, however, the corresponding section must still be present but should merely contain a comment such as: "This section is not applicable."

2.E.1. INTRODUCTION

Section 1.1, Purpose and Origin of the Need for This System indicates where the project originated, why you are doing it, and who the intended audience for the Software Requirements Specification is. For a course project, this may be something like: "This project was assigned to be done for course credit in Computer Science 475, Software Engineering...."

Section 1.2, Scope of the System Specified, should identify the system by name, for example, "Computer Dating Service." It should explain what the software will and, if necessary, will not do, in terms of a general overview.

Section 1.3, Definitions, Acronyms, and Abbreviations, includes any terminology that is either specific to the system to be developed or needed by the user. Every discipline has its own jargon, and those in the business get so used to using it that they forget how strange the terms may sound to an outsider. Because software systems are usually created for use by people outside the software business, it is important for the analysts to refrain from imposing their terminology on the user. It is also important for the analysts to learn the user's terminology. This problem is discussed further in Chapter 10.

This section is for the benefit of the development team as well as for review by the user. Any acronyms or abbreviations should be defined here so that when someone is reading the specification and comes across an abbreviation (such as SRS), he or she won't have to rely on memory for the definition. This section may be extremely important in ensuring good communication between the users and the analysts. This information can be put into an appendix and referred to in this section if it gets to be too long.

Section 1.4, References to Related and Supporting Documents, should provide a complete list of all documents referenced anywhere in the Software Requirements Specification and tell how to get a copy. This section is especially important when the system under development is a modification of an existing system. The need for finding existing documents is discussed in more detail in Chapters 9 and 10.

Section 1.5, Overview of the System, should describe what the rest of the Software Requirements Specification contains and how it is organized.

2.E.2. GENERAL DESCRIPTION

Section 2.1, Product Perspective, gives a brief description of the application of the product. It also indicates the relationship of the described

Figure 2.1　Partial Example of Software Requirements Specifications, Fig
　　　　　　Leaf Enterprises Computer Dating Service

2.2.　Product Functions

Each applicant will be expected to answer a set of questions on a variety of subjects. This information will be used to find matches with the best possible candidates from a file of available candidates. The applicant may also become an available candidate for other applicants.

The candidate that matches the highest number of applicant responses will be considered the best possible prospective date. The applicant will be provided with up to three possible candidates for a date; however, there is no guarantee that there will be a minimum number of matches. If there are no available prospective dates, an appropriate message will be sent.

.
.

2.3.　User (Applicant) Characteristics

The dating service will be a user-friendly, interactive system for selecting the most compatible dates for the applicant from a file of candidates.

The system may be used directly by the applicant at a terminal, or the applicant may fill out a form and have a Fig Leaf Enterprises employee process the information.

The applicant will be prompted with forty (40) questions to be answered in order to get a match. These questions are listed in the Preliminary User's Manual. All responses entered will be checked for validity, and in the case of an invalid response the user will be given an appropriate error message and be reprompted for correct data. The results will be used to select candidates. The applicant will have the option of changing the responses to these questions at any time during the session.

An applicant using the system will have the choice of four options from a menu:

(1) adding personal information to the system,
(2) being matched with a date,
(3) updating information previously entered,
(4) terminating the session.

.
.

system to existing systems, if any. For a course project you may be doing a completely new and independent project. If so, make a statement to that effect here. On the other hand, you may be doing something that builds on work that others have done, especially if you are doing projects on software tools. In that case, describe all related systems and their interfaces with the new system. Block diagrams showing the relations to other systems are appropriate.

Section 2.2, Product Functions, should summarize the functions that the product will perform. Section 2.3, User Characteristics, should describe the characteristics of the users of the product that will affect the specific requirements. A partial example of a General Description for a computer dating service is given in Figure 2.1 for Sections 2.2 and 2.3.

Under Section 2.4, General Constraints, there should be a general description of anything that will limit the developer's freedom, such as existing hardware, interfaces to other equipment or applications, company policies, government regulations, or safety and legal considerations.

Section 2.5, Assumptions and Dependencies, lists factors whose change would affect other requirements. For example, if it is assumed that your project will be done on a particular computer or using a particular language and/or operating system, any change in that assumption could alter the requirements for the system.

2.E.3. SPECIFIC REQUIREMENTS

Section 3.1, Functional Requirements, should specify how inputs to the software system are transformed into outputs, describing the fundamental actions that are to take place in the software. This description may include a data flow diagram or other high level model of the system. These models are described in Chapter 3.

Section 3.2, External Interface Requirements, includes the user interface, hardware interface, software interfaces, and communications interfaces. The user interface is normally in the form of a Preliminary User's Manual. Depending on its size, this may be referred to and added as an appendix to the SRS.

A partial example of a Preliminary User's Manual for Fig Leaf Enterprises Computer Dating Service is given in Figure 2.2. This example includes a relatively simple user interface that can be implemented on any system without any previous experience other than interactive programming. Somewhat more sophisticated user interfaces are described in Chapter 6.

Section 3.3, Performance Requirements, should specify the numerical requirements, both static and dynamic. Static numerical requirements include such things as the number of files and records to be used, the sizes of files and tables, and the number of terminals and users to be supported. Dynamic numerical requirements include such things as time constraints on the system. These must be stated in numeric, verifiable terms, for example, "95% of the time the system response to the user will take place in less than 1/2 second." If applicable, this section may distinguish between normal work conditions and peak workload conditions, with separate criteria for the two.

Section 3.4, Design Constraints, are those things imposed by other regulations, format standards, and hardware limitations. They include such things as format specification, audit tracing, and size of available memory.

Section 3.5, Attributes, includes such things as availability and security. In the case of the computer dating service, this might include a description of who would have access to the system. It would indicate

Figure 2.2 Sample Partial Contents of a Preliminary User's Manual

Fig Leaf Enterprises Computer Dating Service
Software Requirements Specifications

3.2.   External Interface Requirements - User's Manual
3.2.1. Introduction and Overview
.
.
3.2.2. Available Services, Fees, and Limits of Legal Liability
.
.
3.2.3. Procedure for Logging On to the System
.
.
3.2.4. Initial Interaction with the Dating Service

Once you have started the program, the initial menu will appear on the screen, like this:

```
Welcome to Fig Leaf Enterprises Computer Dating Service

Would you like to:

    A-add your personal information to the service
    D-be matched with a date
    U-update your personal information
    Q-terminate the session (quit)
Enter your selection and press Return
?
```

The question mark is the computer's way of telling you it is ready for a response from you. When you see the question mark, you must enter one of the above listed options and then press the carriage return. Either upper- or lowercase letters A, D, U, and Q are valid. (Don't worry about accidentally typing Q, as you will be asked for verification and given another chance to stay in the system.) However, typing anything other than the above choices will give you an error message.

For example, if you enter an incorrect response, such as M or 2, the screen will look like this (user replies are in boldface, everything else is generated by the computer):

```
Enter your selection and press Return
?M
ERROR - you must enter A, D, U, or Q
Enter your selection and press Return
?2
ERROR - you must enter A, D, U, or Q
Enter your selection and press Return
?
```

After you make an appropriate selection, you will be prompted for further information. When you see the question mark, the computer is waiting for an answer from you. Don't worry about making a mistake; you will always be given another chance, and an error message will try to help you figure out what was expected.

whether the clients use the system directly or whether a Fig Leaf
Enterprises employee will interview clients and then enter and retrieve
data. For example, if Fig Leaf Enterprises wants customers to use its system, security concerns might be addressed, as shown in Figure 2.3.

```
Figure 2.3   Fig Leaf Enterprises Computer Dating Service Software
             Requirements Specifications Security Concerns

2.0. General Description
   :

2.4. General Constraints
    Users may not have access to information contained in
anyone's file but their own.
   :

3.0. Specific Requirements
   :

3.5. Attributes
    File access shall be obtainable only with a password.
This password may be changed only by the master user.
   :
```

Section 3.6, Other Requirements, is for requirements that don't fit
into any other category. This may include the need for access to some
resource outside the development company. An example is given in Figure
2.4.

2.F. Contractual Aspects of Specification

Before beginning the Software Requirements Specification, you
must understand the magnitude of its importance. Keep in mind that you
are actually writing a contract, and in so doing you are making a commitment on behalf of yourself and your organization. This commitment is
legally binding, and the implications must be thought through carefully.

2.F.1. Definition of a Contract

The Software Requirements Specification is a contract to produce
the specified system. A **contract** is a legally binding agreement between
the parties involved to produce and deliver some specified goods or services of value under the conditions and terms of compensation specified.

Figure 2.4   Fig Leaf Enterprises Computer Dating Service
             Software Requirements Specification

   .
   .

3.6. Other Requirements
    Fig Leaf Enterprises wants to run an automated credit check on each
client for its proposed computer dating service. The system will need
access to the computer at the Dewey, Cheetum, and Howe Credit Company.
   .
   .

When the development is to produce a product to be sold (or licensed to) some set of users it is crucial to understand that there is a risk that the development will fail to meet one or more of the terms that are specified. Therefore the contractual terms should include not only the specified terms for acceptance and the schedule, but also what the penalties will be if the acceptance criteria are not adhered to. It is in the developer's interest to place a limit on its liability in the event that the development does not succeed.

2.F.2. Significance of the Contract

The organizational relation of the developers to the users is critical in defining the legal status of a Software Requirements Specification. If the developers and users are different divisions of the same company there may be much less concern about the consequences of deviations from a specification. However, in the long run all concerned are likely to have better working relationships if specifications are treated as a legally binding contract even in an in-house project.

The degree of formality may depend on the relation of the parties. It may be very informal if it is for the in-house development of an application to be used only within the same organizational subdivision. This is likely to be the case with your course project. However, it needs to be very formal and reviewed with extreme care if the development is to be produced as a product for an external user, especially if there is a diverse group of potential users spread across a large organization.

If developers and users represent legally distinct organizations, then the specification is a contract or a part of a contract binding the parties. A properly drawn contract must define the responsibilities of all parties to it and the compensation to be paid. In addition to being a definition for the developers of what they must produce, a Software Requirements Specification also defines what the users are entitled to get, for the agreed price.

Some aspects of development contracts for software projects are summarized in Figure 2.5.

Figure 2.5   Some Typical Contractual Pitfalls of a Development Contract

- How will changes in the specifications and any resulting costs be negotiated?
- What will the penalties be if the schedule is not maintained?
- What will the penalties and limits of liability be if the system does not conform to specific performance or functional specifications?
- Who is responsible for providing training for users?
- Who is responsible for maintenance?
- Who provides any special resources?

The importance of the contract cannot be overstated. It is something that is difficult to appreciate when one has done only classroom projects. The difference you have to look forward to on the job is enormous. We cannot improve on the following description by Robert L. Glass and Sue DeNim (1980).

> One of the things that separates the academic computer science world from the industrial software engineering world is the contract. Contracts may be bad, or contracts may be good . . . but there is one thing that contracts almost always are, and that is firm. If the contract says to do it, then short of an act of God, it will probably happen.
>
> Because of its importance, the contract is the focal point of jockeying for position. If you want to do it, get it in. If you can't do it keep it out. If it's hard to do and it's in, and you'd rally rather not, then weaken it. The art of contracting is much more of an art than the art of computing. . . .
>
> And the message here? Pay attention to the contract. The job you save may be your own.

2.G. Documenting Specifications

There are many ways to write specifications. This section is an introduction to some methods that we feel are appropriate for the types of projects you are likely to be doing now. This is neither a comprehensive survey of all possible methods, nor broad coverage of any one method. Further information on these and other methods can be found in the references at the end of the chapter.

The method selected for the project for this course as well as on the job will depend on a number of factors. These include the nature of the project, the tools that may be available, and the boss's preference.

2.G.1. Functional vs. Structural Descriptions

Writing specifications is not easy. The problem of finding an unambiguous exposition of what we wish to specify is well illustrated by our opening quotation about a dog walking ordinance.

A specification should communicate between users, managers, and developers. At present we do not have a body of research results to show us the best way to present specifications that bridge the communication gap between users and developers. The search for a common language between analyst, user, manager, and developer is a difficult one. Developers and analysts might be happy with a formal specification language. But while such a construct may permit automated checks on internal consistency and validity, it generally will not be useful to communicate with users and managers to check against their understanding of the requirements specified.

In the previous section we saw an outline of the requirements specification documentation for a system. Next we need to consider some practical techniques for presenting details of the requirements in a working Software Requirement Specification. The language used must be carefully structured and restricted to avoid ambiguity. The structure of the document must be organized to permit cross-referencing each point of the specification for later verification. In addition, what the system promises to do must be clearly stated because the documents will be interpreted as a contract.

Our introductory quotation is intended in a humorous vein to point out that it is by no means trivial to find a correct phrasing for a requirement in ordinary English. The difficult task is to specify exactly the subset of conditions that is intended. Therefore, it should not be surprising that we need to discuss some alternative ways to define specifications.

The Software Requirement Specification is to give a rationale, an explanation of the environment, and a functional description of a system to be designed and implemented. The functional description must be independent of implementation details. Hence it is inappropriate to link functional properties to any details of software structure.

It may well be that the design of the software structure may be decomposed into a hierarchy that is related to some obvious way to structure the data required by the system as inputs or outputs. However, the designers should be left free to choose the software structure to satisfy performance and other constraints. What may appear obvious to the analyst may not be obvious to the developers.

Figure 2.6 illustrates the difference between a **functional description** and a **structural description**. Two examples of a specification for a screwdriver are given. The first is functional; the second, structural. Notice that the structural description constrains the physical implementation by specifying details that are not required for someone to use the tool for its intended purpose. Your goal in writing specifications is to make them of the functional form.

We now look at several methods for specifying requirements.

```
Figure 2.6   Two Examples of a Specification for a Screwdriver

A.  Functional:
1.0  Aircraft maintenance screwdriver  #000-0001-1987, common description:
     Slotted head  screwdriver,  with  1/4-inch blade,  4-inch shaft,  and
     overall length not to exceed 8 inches.

B.  Structural:
2.0  Screwdriver blade tip to fit into slotted  head fasteners
     2.1  The blade tip width is required
          2.1.1  to be greater than 0.22 inch and
          2.1.2  not greater than 0.25 inch.
     2.2  The blade tip thickness shall be between
          2.2.1  0.005 inch minimum and
          2.2.2  0.008 inch maximum and
          ...
```

2.G.2. Specification Methods

Some means of specifying requirements are English (a natural language), structured English, formal specification language, decision tables, finite state machines, data structure models, and data flow diagrams. Table 2.4 gives a summary description of each of these methods. We will look at examples in the rest of this chapter and the next chapter.

One of the primary dangers in using natural language for describing anything of a technical nature is that our language is too rich in ambiguity. Such ambiguity may be wonderful for creating literary work by supporting multiple levels of interpretation. We, however, have the task of producing documentation of systems which can be unambiguously understood. One way to do this is to use a special, constrained subset of natural language structures and a restricted vocabulary. Such a subset language is called structured English.

2.G.2.a. Structured English

In one sense, writing **structured English** is equivalent to writing good pseudocode. We are concerned with expressing the algorithmic description of some set of user organization policies or procedures. Ultimately this is a constraint on the system (and software) that will carry them out. The intent of specification is to define the constraints, not to set the specific algorithmic detail of any particular software module(s).

Table 2.4 Alternative Systems for Expressing Specifications

Natural language - A description in ordinary English, for example, as a narrative description.

Structured English - A description in English with sentences that have severe restrictions on structural complexity and that contain only a restricted vocabulary of nouns, verbs, and qualifiers.

Formal specification language - A special language, or mathematical notation, employing defined operators and syntactic rules for expressing relations and constraints.

Decision tables (or decision trees) - A formal method of specifying a set of alternative conditions as cases and the actions that are to result in each possible case in the form of a table (or as a graphical tree with each of the leaves being the possible actions).

Finite state machine - A 5-tuple consisting of a set of states including initial and final states, and functions that map pairs to states and pairs to actions.

Data structure model - Graphical notation used to represent relationships between all the data entities of a system.

Data flow diagram - Graphical notation used to represent flow of information through the system.

The chance for ambiguity is limited by systematically minimizing the vocabulary used for actions, operators, and objects. Structured English is written using only names of items from the data dictionary (described in Chapter 3) as the subject or object of a sentence. The description of a procedure as a set of simple sentences is limited to the structured constructs: sequence, repetition and decisions. Some guidelines for writing structured English are given in Figure 2.7.

Figure 2.7 Guidelines for Structured English

- Use only simple declarative sentences.
- Use only imperative forms of verbs.
- Make the subject and object of every sentence a name of an object in the data dictionary.
- Do not use synonyms.
- Limit the structure of procedures to sequences, decisions, or repetitions.
- Do not use ambiguous verbs such as **process** or **handle**.
- Base decisions on a closed set.

The only allowed decision structure constructs are:

IF condition THEN procedure1 OTHERWISE procedure2
    OR
IF condition1 THEN procedure1
ELSE IF condition2 THEN procedure2

.

.

OTHERWISE procedureN

In a simple alternative decision, this requires that all cases must fall within 'condition' and result in 'procedure1' or fail to meet 'condition' and result in 'procedure2'. In a multiway decision, any case that does not fall within 'condition1' . . . 'conditionN' must be subject to an 'OTHERWISE procedure'. This satisfies the requirement that decisions be made on a closed set.

Repetitions must correspond to either a 'test at top' construct or a 'test at bottom' construct:

WHILE condition THEN procedure
    OR
REPEAT procedure UNTIL condition

A description in structured English should use indentation to indicate the scope of nested procedures. If it is necessary to satisfy users, a structured English description can be expanded and converted to narrative by adding some phrasing. The documentation produced using it should be unambiguous. Probably most people will find it very dull to read. However, keeping in mind the implications of a contract, structured English may be effectively used to produce a specification that is readable by both users and developers.

Since the representation in structured English is not rigorous, it is *not* subject to automatic translation. The potential for translation and automatic verification procedures make other specification strategies appealing to computer scientists. Unfortunately the pursuit of rigor takes us away from the possibility of having users verify that a specification meets their needs.

2.G.2.b. Formal Specification

Formal specification means producing a mathematically rigorous expression of a set of requirements. There are many ways to do this. We offer here one example based on the definitions given in Table 2.5. The first four definitions in Table 2.5 provide a theoretical foundation needed to deal with program specification and verification.

Table 2.5 Definitions to Support a Formalized Specification

Def 1: A state variable is a variable together with an associated domain. The variable may take on values from the domain.

Def 2: A state variable set is a set of state variables.

Def 3: A state is an assignment of values to all the variables of a state variable set.

Def 4: A state space is all possible states that a state variable set may assume.

Def 5: A boundary condition of an input class Z is a condition that must be satisfied by every state in Z.

Def 6: An error condition is the negation of a boundary condition.

Def 7: A boundary condition of an output class Z is a condition that must be satisfied by output state in Z.

Def 8: A finite state machine (FSM) is a 5-tuple:

(Q, q, f, NEXT, ACTION) where

1. Q is a finite set of states.
2. q in Q is a special state called the initial state.
3. NEXT is a function that maps (state, input symbol) pairs to states.
4. ACTION is a function that maps (state, input symbol) pairs to actions.
5. f in Q is a special state called the final state.

For a given problem, it is a relatively simple matter to describe it in these terms. Choose a **state space** that is rich enough to fully describe the problem. The system can then be described in terms of a mapping from a set of initial states, which we call the input class, to a new set of states, the output class. Look at Example 2.1.

Example 2.1 - States

Let a state variable set contain two state variables X and Y. Let the domain of X be { 1,2,3 } and the domain of Y be { a,b }. An example of a state is [X=1,Y=a]. In this case the state space is finite and contains six states. These states are [X=1,Y=a], [X=1,Y=b], [X=2,Y=a], [X=2,Y=b], [X=3,Y=a], and [X=3,Y=b].

Each time a program executes, it starts at one state and produces another state. We call the state in which a program starts the input state and the state the program produces the output state. Many times there are restrictions on what can be a valid input state other than being a member of the state space. These restrictions, which define the planned input class of the problem, are called boundary conditions of an input class (Definition 5 in Table 2.5) and error conditions (Definition 6 in Table 2.5). Examples are given below.

Example 2.2 - Boundary Condition of an Input Class

Consider a state variable set with one variable M whose domain is the set of all matrices. Suppose we were writing a program to invert matrices. One boundary condition that we would have to include would be: Each input matrix must be square.

Example 2.3 - Error Condition

The error condition associated with the boundary condition of Example 2.2 would be: There exists an input matrix that is not square.

The restrictions imposed by boundary conditions strongly influence the specification of a system. The systems analyst must take great care to see that these restrictions are chosen to conform to the problem, rather than for the programmer's convenience.

Every condition divides a set into two or more disjoint subsets, as shown in Example 2.4.

Example 2.4 - Condition That Divides a Set into Two Disjoint Subsets

Consider a payroll program. The way the processing is carried out will most likely vary according to whether or not the following condition is true or false: Hours worked are greater than 40.

2.G.2.c. Decision Tables

The processing of each input state depends on conditions met by that state. These conditions define different subclasses where each subclass meets a different combination of conditions and has its own processing function. If we calculate the subclasses and list the processing functions for each in tabular form we have a **decision table**. The steps shown in Table 2.6 can be considered as an algorithm for deriving a decision table.

```
Table 2.6  Algorithm for Deriving a Decision Table

1. Choose a planned input class.  The input class may be finite or
   infinite and may include erroneous inputs.
2. Choose a planned output class.
3. Determine which conditions cause the processing rules to vary.
4. For each condition in step 3 do the following:
   a. Determine the subclasses created by the condition and the range of
      values the condition has in each subclass.
   b. Determine the processing rule that yields the desired output class
      for each subclass.
```

Example 2.5 - Creation of a Decision Table

Suppose an automobile insurance agency has the following decision rules for deciding whom to insure and how much those people will pay:

1. A person pays the basic rate if he or she has had fewer than two accidents in the past five years and is either married or older than 30 years of age.

2. A person is uninsurable if he or she has had two or more accidents in the last five years and is 30 or younger.

3. A person pays an additional surcharge if he or she has had two or more accidents in the last five years and is older than 30, or if he or she is single and 30 or younger but has not had two or more accidents in the last five years.

The planned input class is yes or no answers to the following three questions:

    1. Married?

    2. Age is 30 or less?

    3. Two or more accidents in the last five years?

The planned output class consists of three actions:

    A. Deny the application.

    B. Accept the application at the basic rate.

    C. Accept the application at the basic rate plus surcharge.

The stated algorithm yields the decision table in Figure 2.8 for the given input classes, output classes, and conditions.

The decision table is divided into four quadrants by the horizontal and vertical double lines. The questions in the upper left quadrant are called the condition stubs. The statements in the lower left quadrant are called the action stubs. The entries in the upper right quadrant are called the condition entries and may take on the values Y (yes), N (no), and - (don't care). The entries in the lower right-hand quadrant are called action entries, and are either blank or X. The action entries represent the intersection of the condition entries and the action stubs. The columns are called rules. The action entries indicate what action is to be taken for each rule. In this example only one action is taken for each rule. This does not necessarily have to be the case.

Figure 2.8   Decision Table for Example 2.5

	1	2	3	4	5
1. Married?	-	N	-	N	Y
2. Age is 30 or less?	Y	Y	N	N	-
3. Two or more accidents in last five years?	Y	N	Y	N	N
A. Deny the application.	X				
B. Accept at basic rate.				X	X
C. Accept at basic rate plus surcharge.		X	X		

2.G.2.d. Finite State Machines

A technique similar to decision tables for problem specification is the use of **finite state machines** (FSM). We will use a general definition of a finite state machine, given as Definition 8 in Table 2.5.

We can represent a finite state machine as a digraph. The circles are the states. There is an arrow from state 1 to state 2 if NEXT (state 1, input) is followed by state 2. The arrow has the label input/ACTION (state 1, input). This is shown in Figure 2.9.

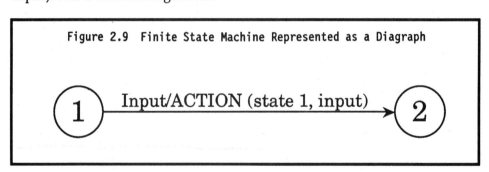

Figure 2.9 Finite State Machine Represented as a Diagraph

1 Input/ACTION (state 1, input) 2

The finite state machine can also be represented by two matrices, the next state matrix and the action matrix. The rows of the matrices correspond to the states of the finite state machine and the columns correspond to input classes.

For example, suppose we want to know the value of the parity of a bit string. We need to know whether the number of 1's in an input string is even or odd. We can do this by initializing a parity bit to zero. Then we use the finite state machine diagrammed in Figure 2.10. There are three states in this diagram. The start state is *begin*. If an input bit is zero, we want to go to state *even*, and the action is to do nothing with the parity bit. If the input bit is 1, we want to complement the parity bit and go to state *odd*.

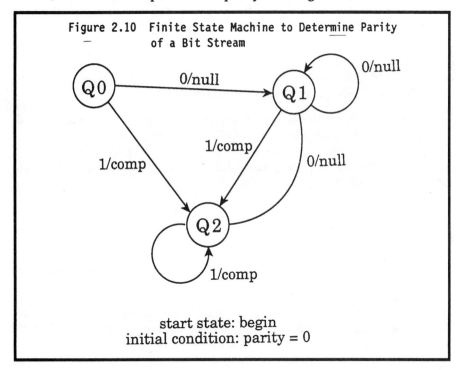

Figure 2.10   Finite State Machine to Determine Parity
of a Bit Stream

start state: begin
initial condition: parity = 0

We can represent the next state matrix and the action matrix as shown in Figure 2.11. The inputs, 0 or 1, are specified as the columns. The states, begin, even, and odd, are specified as the rows. The next state matrix shows which state is next for each input. The action matrix indicates the action to be taken with each change of state, complement parity or do nothing.

If the problem can be specified as a finite state machine, it is a simple matter to turn it into a program. In essence all that is needed is a next state table, an action table, a driver program, and procedures to carry out the actions.

```
          Figure 2.11 Matrices to Represent the Finite State Machine
                  in Figure 2.10 to Determine Parity of a Bit String

              Next State Matrix                        Action Matrix

                    1       0                              1          0

        begin │  odd  │  even │              begin │ complement │ null │

        even  │  odd  │  even │              even  │ complement │ null │

         odd  │  even │  odd  │               odd  │ complement │ null │
```

2.H. Course Project:
The Software Requirements Specification

In order to write the specifications, you must have obtained and organized all the details about the requirements for the project. If you have been given an informal specification of the project, this may be primarily an effort at organizing the information and producing a formal document. If, however, the information about the project is incomplete or inconsistent, you may have to put a great deal of effort into building a model of the system, along with analysis to determine the unanswered questions. Techniques for constructing system models are described in Chapter 3.

The system must be specified to the user's satisfaction. As a practical matter, for a course project the person you have to satisfy is your instructor. You may be able to impose many of your own ideas onto the system.

Your instructor may accept any feasible system specification. If so, remember that this may never happen again- most users have very definite ideas of what they want in a system! (However, they often have problems expressing their wishes. This is discussed further in Chapter 10.)

You may be given the opportunity to interview a user. If so, we recommend reading Section A.3. in Chapter 10, "Interviews and Their Pitfalls."

Although we have described a standard documentation format, you may be given another document standard to follow. This is especially likely if you are doing a modification of an existing system rather than a completely new system.

2.I. Beyond a Course Project: Choice of Specification Form

There is a wide range of options for specifying requirements. Some specifications can easily be turned into programs by direct translation.

There is a great deal of variety in standards used by various industries, and later, on the job, you will need to determine the appropriate standard for your company.

The technique chosen depends on such factors as the nature of the system being specified, whether the proposed system is new or a modification of an existing system, and the requirements and standards of a particular software organization. In other words, if your company has a preference for a particular specification procedure, then that is the one you use.

If your company does any defense contract work, the documentation standard will be one mandated by the Department of Defense, such as DOD-Std-2167A.

Summary

Chapter 2 should be used in conjunction with the next chapter on system models, because such a model is an important component of the Software Requirements Specification.

The first document to be produced for a course project will be the specification document. A Software Requirements Specification, based on ANSI/IEEE Standard 830-1984, is described in this chapter as an example. This description is consistent with the documentation standard in Appendix A.

Requirements analysis involves first doing a feasibility study. In a classroom project this usually will have been done, and the project will be feasible. On the job you will have no such assurances, and you will need to carefully evaluate costs and benefits, resource requirements, any constraints on the system in terms of both performance and resources, and plans for change.

Some aspects of a system can be handled by either hardware or software, and it is important to determine which is which in advance. Manual procedures should also be specified. Not every aspect of a system has to be automated; those things best done by humans should be left to humans.

The Software Requirements Specification must be unambiguous. It must be a standard form so that anything can be cross-referenced. Each part must be verifiable. Descriptions should be functional, that is, specify what is to be done, rather than structural, or how it is to be done.

The standard form of the Software Requirements Specification, based on ANSI/IEEE Std 830-1984, includes an Introduction, a General Description, and a Specific Requirements Section. The Introduction states the specific need and any relevant background. The General Description gives an overview. The Specific Requirements section includes the details. One part of the Specific Requirements, the External Interface Requirements, is normally in the form of a Preliminary User's Manual. The section on Assumptions and Dependencies should be in the form of a system model such as a data flow diagram, which is described in Chapter 3.

The Software Requirements Specification constitutes a contract. On the job it is extremely important that the contract be carefully written and thoroughly understood.

Several means of specifying requirements include natural language, structured English, formal specification languages, and decision tables. Natural language and even structured English have problems with ambiguity. Formal specification languages and decision tables have the advantage of being able to specify unambiguously. Data flow diagrams and data structure models are graphical means of representing the relationships between entities. The final specification document may include combinations of these.

Keywords

ANSI/IEEE Standard 830-1984
contract
decision tables
development machine
DOD Std 2167A
external interface
finite state machine (FSM)
formal specification languages
functional description
natural language
need
Preliminary User's Manual
requirement
requirements analysis
resource limits
resource requirements
Software Requirements Specification (SRS)
specification
state
state space
state variable
structured description
structured English
target machine
unambiguous specification

Review Questions

2.1.   What is meant by requirements analysis?

2.2.   What happens to a software system if the proposal is rejected?

2.3.   What are the necessary resources to be listed in the Software Requirements Specification? Which are important to a classroom project?

2.4.   What is the difference between specification and requirement? Between needs and requirements?

2.5.   Why is it important to leave algorithmic details and implementation strategy out of the Software Requirements Specification?

2.6.   Is there any justification for having a standard form for documents? If so, what is it?

2.7.   Why should the Software Requirements Specification be concerned with future changes in the proposed system?

2.8.   What is the difference between a development machine and a target machine?

2.9.   List some important resource limits to be concerned with in the Software Requirements Specification.

2.10. What is the purpose of the Introduction, General Description, and Specific Requirements sections of the Software Requirements Specification?

2.11. How can you specify the external interface requirements of a system?

2.12. What is a contract? What does a contract have to do with the Software Requirements Specification? With a software system?

2.13. How formal must a contract be?

2.14. Why is it difficult to specify software system requirements unambiguously in English?

2.15. What is the difference between a functional description and a structural description?

2.16. How useful is natural language as a means for specifying requirements? Structured English? Formal specification languages? Decision tables?

Exercises

2.1.   Propose a system that will require hardware, software, and manual procedures, and give a brief specification of each part.

2.2. Describe the difference in a Software Requirements Specification for a system in which the hardware is already in place, and a system for which the hardware must be acquired.

2.3. Write a specification for a parking garage ticket dispenser and entrance gate control.

2.4. In this chapter, one suggested requirement for a computer dating service was, "At least one match must be found." In another place, an example of a possible requirement was, "Matches are not guaranteed." The system can't fulfill both requirements. If both were in the Software Requirements Specification, what would you do?

2.5. The specification for the computer dating service requires a list of 40 questions. How are these questions determined, and where in the specification should they go?

2.6. Consider the client response categories for the computer dating service. Should they be scaled (e.g., strongly preferred, preferred, don't care, opposed, strongly opposed), or yes/no, or yes/don't care/no, or fixed categories (e.g., a xor b xor c xor d)? Who determines which it should be?

2.7. Write a user manual for a program that permits one or two players to play tic-tac-toe on a video screen.

2.8. Write a specification in structured English for a procedure to determine if three input values represent sides of a triangle, and if so whether the triangle is isosceles, equi lateral, or scalene.

2.9. Repeat exercise 2.8 but specify the problem with a decision table.

2.10. In Example 2.5, the decision table in Figure 2.8 was arrived at after several intermediate steps. These steps include:

- Combine the input states into a single rule.
- Determine the number of initial states (in this case 2 times 2 times 2 = 8).
- Determine which initial states are impossible.

Go through these steps to arrive at the decision table in Figure 2.8.

2.11. Describe the potential problems if acceptance criteria are not specified in a Software Requirements Specification Document for a software development project that promises an online system to do automatic translation of Russian to English and English to Russian.

References

DeMarco, Tom. Structured Analysis and System Specification. New York: Yourdon, 1979.

> An exposition and extension of the data flow methodology of Yourdon and Constantine. Excellent discussion of structured English.

Fox, Joseph M. Software and Its Development. Englewood Cliffs, NJ: Prentice-Hall, 1982.

> Discusses large project management, classifying system properties, and considerations of performance and tradeoffs.

Gehani, N., and McGetrick, A. D., eds. Software Specification Techniques. Wokingham, England: Addison-Wesley, 1986.

> Explores the controversy and range of recent research with a collection of 21 papers covering specification techniques, applications, case studies, and specification languages. More than 300 references are included.

Glass, Robert L., and DeNim, Sue The Second Coming: More Computing Projects Which Failed. Seattle, WA: Computing Trends, 1980.

> Collection of industrial stories, including several about the possible consequences of paying insufficient attention to the contract.

Institute of Electrical and Electronics Engineers. Software Engineering Standards. New York: Wiley-Interscience, October 1987.

> Includes "ANSI/IEEE Std 830-1984, Software Requirements Specifications," describing alternate approaches to good practice in the specification of software requirements. Also includes "IEEE Std 1016-1987, Software Design Descriptions," a description of documentation of software designs. Specifies the necessary information content and the recommended organization for a software design description.

Graves, Robert and Hodge, Alan. The Reader Over Your Shoulder, A Handbook for Writers of English Prose. Second Edition, Random House, 1971.

> Includes "From the Minutes of a Borough Council Meeting:" pp. 95-96

Meyer, Bertrand. "On Formalism in Specifications." IEEE Software 2, 1 (January 1985): 6-26.

> Analysis of errors in a natural language specification of a supposedly correct program demonstrating weaknesses of natural language specification and promoting formal specification.

Poston, Robert M. "Software Standards: Preventing Software Specification Errors with IEEE 830." IEEE Software 2, 1 (January 1985): 83-86.

> Recent experience shows that development costs have been dominated by testing effort. The cost of removing a bug increases progressively with life cycle phase. The use of a well-defined Software Requirements Specification can reduce the number of errors and hence the cost of testing and defect removal.

Turner, Ray Software Development Methodologies. Reston, VA: 1984.

> Extensive discussion of documentation standards for large and small projects. Read the discussion of how to select or hire team members in Chapter 13 before going on a job interview.

CHAPTER 3

SYSTEM MODELS

I will contend that conceptual integrity is the most important consideration in system design. It is better to have a system omit certain anomalous features and improvements, but to reflect one set of design ideas, than to have one that contains many good but independent and uncoordinated ideas.

- Frederick P. Brooks, Jr., *The Mythical Man-Month*

There was one who was famed for the number of things
He forgot when he entered the ship:
His umbrella, his watch, all his jewels and rings,
And the clothes he had bought for the trip.

He had forty-two boxes, all carefully packed,
With his name painted clearly on each:
But since he omitted to mention the fact,
They were all left behind on the beach.

-Lewis Carroll, *The Hunting of the Snark*

Software Life Cycle

Software Requirements Specification: Information model

```
        I. Software need
       II. Preliminary feasibility judgment
      III. Requirements analysis and feasibility study
       IV. Specification
        V. Preliminary software design and planning
       VI. Software development
               Detailed design
               Coding end unit testing
               Integration
               System Testing
      VII. Software maintenance
```

Project: Data flow diagram (or other high level description)

3.A. Introduction

Models provide an abstract way to represent complex systems. Models are useful because they may be inspected to determine whether any particular aspect of the system is consistent or complete. This inspection may be in the form of a **walkthrough** with the users. A walkthrough is a group effort to review a document or a product. It can be helpful in facilitating communication between users, analysts, and developers. (Walkthroughs are described in detail in Chapter 12.)

Building a model of a system to use in developing requirements is an iterative process. Usually the model building is associated with one or more methods of graphic representation of the relationships among system elements. After refinement, the diagrams and data definitions representing the model of the system are included in the Software Requirements Specification.

The information structure should be developed without prejudicing the design of the control structure. That is, the information model must define what is to be done in terms of how information gets from one place to another, but must not specify the basic algorithm for the source code to implement this structure.

The definition of the control structure is primarily the domain of software design, which comes later. First comes the specification of the requirements the system should satisfy. The tools required to do this may include data flow diagrams, data structure diagrams, data dictionaries, and perhaps others.

The key to using any of these techniques is to systematically employ the concept of abstraction. That is, the analyst needs to recognize the essential details and put them into a model while suppressing unessential details. Examples of unessential details include screen layouts, record formats, and error or exception handling and recovery.

In general, it is possible to build elaborations of the elements in a given model, modeling each element as another subsidiary model. In this way a hierarchy of models can be constructed at increasing levels of detail.

There are a number of modeling techniques, none of which is necessarily the best. The choice of methodology depends on several factors, such as the nature of the project, the standards in use by the software organization, and what information, if any, already exists about a project.

3.B. Data Flow Diagram

A **data flow diagram (DFD)** is a graphical tool for system representation. It differs from a flowchart for a program or algorithm in that it represents only the flow of information, whereas flowcharts represent the flow of control.

3.B.1. Diagraming Conventions

We look at a simple example to introduce the concept, and then show how to apply this idea to our project, the computer dating service. The data flow diagram shown in Figure 3.1 represents a system that generates student grade reports. Information used to determine grades comes from a file, indicated by a narrow box open on the right end and labeled *Grade_file*. This file contains scores from such things as quizzes and homework. Of course, these scores do not appear in the file by magic; they come from evaluations of student effort. The origin of this information is the students' work, which has been evaluated and has a score associated with it. This student work is referred to as a **source**, something outside the system we are looking at, and is indicated by a box in the diagram.

Transfer of information is indicated in a data flow diagram by a labeled arrow. In Figure 3.1 an arrow shows the transfer of scores and names from the student work by an unspecified process to the grade file. Another arrow indicates the availability of the name and scores contained in a student record to the averaging process.

Processes are represented by bubbles. Bubbles are round or rectangular with rounded corners. The latter design makes it easier to put text labels in the enclosed space. The design you use may depend on the tools available for creating the diagrams.

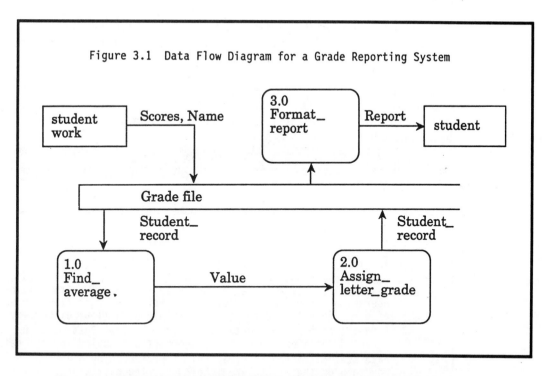

Figure 3.1 Data Flow Diagram for a Grade Reporting System

The averaging process bubble is labeled 1. This process consists of whatever arithmetic is necessary to get an average for each student. Note that the algorithmic details are left out of a data flow diagram. The next arrow indicates the transfer of the resulting average value, along with the associated name, to the next process. This process, bubble 2, assigns a letter grade for each average. The output of this process is the letter grade and associated name, which are transferred to the grade file.

The grade file contains the information used to generate grade reports. The necessary information, name and letter grade, are accessed by process 3, which formats a report sent to the student. The student, as a destination for the report, constitutes another entity that is outside the system. This type of entity is a **sink**. Like a source, it is indicated by a box.

Notice that the data flow diagram indicates the flow of information from one process to the next. Control is *not* indicated. Also note that each time data is transformed by the system, there is a **process**.

Several things of practical importance in the implementation of the system are not indicated on the data flow diagram. For instance, it is likely that the system looks at one set of scores at a time, and after each process goes back to the file to get another set. This looping process is not indicated on the diagram. That is a matter of flow of control. The information, that is, an individual item of information, does not loop. Similarly, branching is not indicated on a data flow diagram. A branch in a data flow indicates that the same data is used in multiple places.

One might object that this data flow diagram does not show enough detail with regard to the process of creating and reporting grades. The specific individual components of the grade are not clear, nor is the arithmetic process, which would include weighting factors, if any. Furthermore, there is no indication of the letter grades produced and the scores they correspond to. However, the data flow diagram does show the entire process. Algorithm details are not essential in this representation and *must* be left out of the data flow diagram.

This data flow diagram, while relatively simple, nonetheless contains all the components of any data flow diagram. These components are summarized in Table 3.1.

Table 3.1   Components of a Data Flow Diagram

1. **Bubbles** that must represent a process (not a place, person, or object, but a data transformation) and must be labeled with a process descriptor. For example, a bubble may represent arithmetic or logic operations to produce some result. Normally, data flows in and out of each process. There may be multiple data flows either way.
2. **Arrows** that represent data (information) flow. These must be directed (have one arrow head) and must be labeled for the data.
3. **Data stores** (stored information), represented by a narrow box open on the right, are labeled for the data store. They may represent physical files, files in mass storage, or a data structure in memory.
4. **Sources** and **sinks** of information, entities outside the system with which the system exchanges data. These are represented by boxes that are distinct from bubbles. These rectangles show where, in the universe outside the system, the information came from and where it is going.
5. **Description**, a caption for the entire diagram to indicate what it represents and its relation to other diagrams in a hierarchy, if any.

Before proceeding to another example, it is important to understand the difference between a data flow diagram and a flowchart. One is an information model; the other is a control structure. For comparison purposes, Figure 3.2 shows a data flow diagram and a Nassi-Schneiderman flowchart for a familiar process, that of finding the largest member of an array.

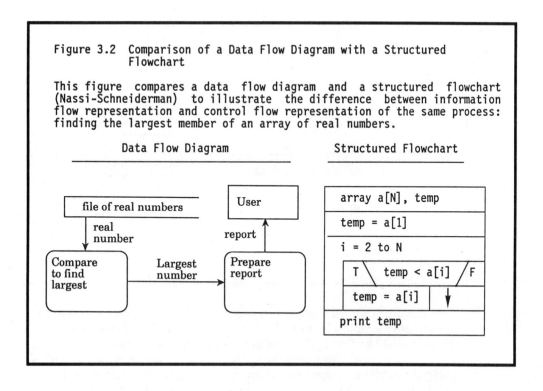

Figure 3.2 Comparison of a Data Flow Diagram with a Structured Flowchart

This figure compares a data flow diagram and a structured flowchart (Nassi-Schneiderman) to illustrate the difference between information flow representation and control flow representation of the same process: finding the largest member of an array of real numbers.

3.B.2. Stepwise Refinement

Stepwise refinement is a system development methodology in which data definitions and processing steps are defined broadly at first, and then modified, step by step, with increasing detail at each step.

Data flow diagrams are especially useful as high-level representations in system identification. Data flow diagrams may be used as tools for the presentation of the system description in a feasibility study or detailed investigation.

Using data flow diagrams, information flow can be represented for any system. Furthermore, data flow diagrams may be used to represent various levels of refinement of a system. Data flow diagrams are a powerful tool for top-down analysis. Each bubble may be further refined to show more details of the system, until a bubble represents a single module. A set of data flow diagrams can be used to provide both high-level and more detailed views of a system. What takes place within one bubble on a data flow diagram can be shown in detail on another, more detailed data flow diagram as a collection of subsidiary bubbles.

As an example of stepwise refinement, consider the problem of writing a computer dating system. At the highest level, the data flow diagram for the system could be as indicated in Figure 3.3.

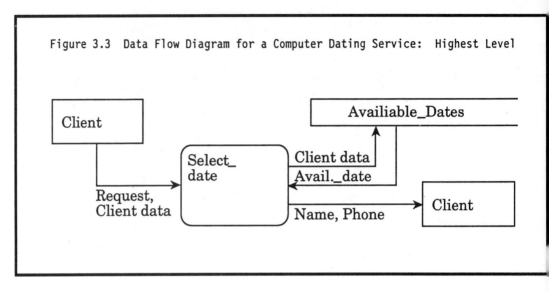

Figure 3.3   Data Flow Diagram for a Computer Dating Service: Highest Level

A request from a client is processed by *Select_Date,* along with information from the data file of available dates. Information about the client is
sent to the file. The *Select_Date* process sends names and phone numbers to
the client. This is the fundamental system model. However, this model is
clearly not detailed enough to support code design. We need to refine the
model. Stepwise refinement entails expanding one bubble at a time until a
sufficiently detailed model is reached.

Remember that a data flow diagram is a representation of a system
showing the processes and the data interfaces between them. It shows
processes and the flow of data among these processes. A data flow diagram
depicts information flow without explicit notation of control. It does not
indicate options, mutual exclusivity, or loops.

In the example of the dating service, the selection process is likely to
consist of doing comparisons on one case at a time from the file of available
dates. This will probably be implemented by a looping process, which is
not shown on the data flow diagram. Looping constitutes flow of control,
not flow of information.

The refinement in Figure 3.4 is a data flow diagram with two bubbles. In this case we have separated a process that adds the client information to the file of available dates if it is not already there. A code number is
used for this client throughout the system. The next step is to expand these
bubbles.

Stepwise refinement should always be done one bubble at a time. A
goal of stepwise refinement is to reach a level of detail such that a single
bubble (or possibly a collection of bubbles) represents a module of code.
This is accomplished by continuing to split the bubbles until each bubble is
at a low enough level of complexity. Ideally this means that each bubble

represents a task that could be implemented within some limit, such as 100
lines of code or less. Module size is discussed more fully in Chapter 7.

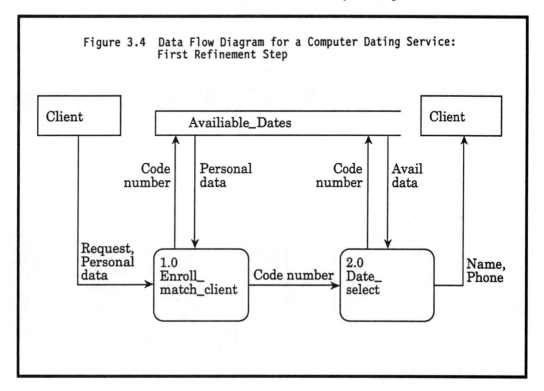

Figure 3.4   Data Flow Diagram for a Computer Dating Service:
            First Refinement Step

Another point to consider is the logical reorganization of the model.
There may be relations of processes that reflect policy details, not logical
system requirements. There may be alternative patterns of data flow that
could simplify the system. Because of organizational politics, some redundant data flows may be part of the requirements.

The final result is not predetermined. It may end up in one of several
different configurations, depending on the requests of the user and the
preferences of the analysts. The data flow diagram for the dating system
can be refined to any of several configurations.

Let us examine one possible way of expanding the *Enroll_match_
client* process of Figure 3.4. The *Request* coming in from the user is to indicate whether something is to be done with the client's personal data, or
whether the client wants a list of prospective dates. Figure 3.5 shows an
expansion of the first possibility.

Here the client has three choices: be added to the file if not already
there, be deleted from the file, or change (or view) information currently in
the file. An expansion of the *Add_Client* process is shown in Figure 3.6,
indicating that this process creates the client's code number.

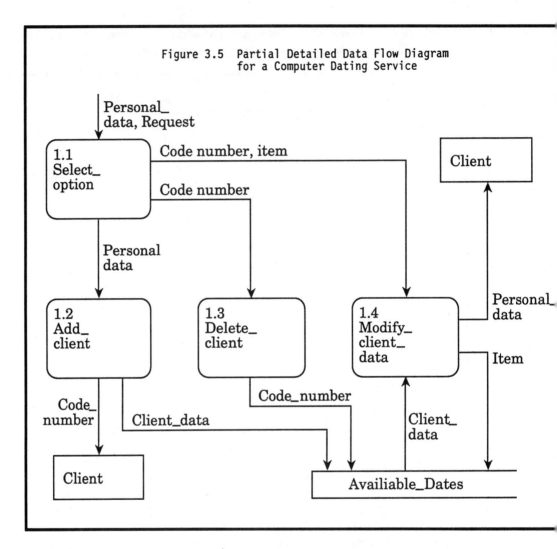

Figure 3.5   Partial Detailed Data Flow Diagram
for a Computer Dating Service

With a multipage diagram it is essential to have a rational indexing system to indicate the relation of a bubble on one page to another data flow diagram representing its expansion. Figure 3.5 shows an expansion of bubble 1 from Figure 3.4. The bubbles are numbered 1.1 through 1.4 to indicate their relationship to bubble 1. In Figure 3.6, bubble 1.2 has been refined into bubbles 1.2.1 and 1.2.2.

Similarly, in Figure 3.7, bubble 2 from Figure 3.4 has been refined into bubbles 2.1 to 2.4. A similar procedure would be used to further refine bubbles until the desired level of refinement was reached.

For clarity, a particular data flow diagram should not have more than about seven bubbles to conveniently fit on a page. It will usually be necessary to create a hierarchy of diagrams. A monolithic data flow diagram on a single page sacrifices readability of descriptors for data and processes to get it all on a page. Furthermore, such a diagram is difficult to incorporate in a document.

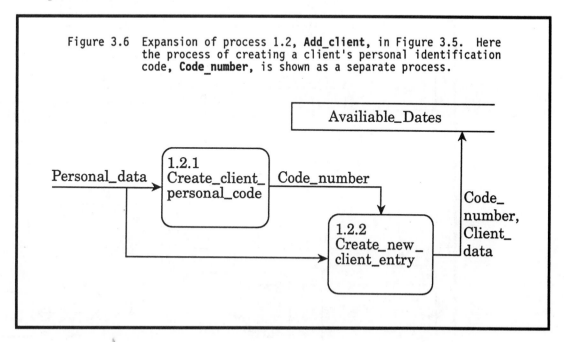

Figure 3.6 Expansion of process 1.2, **Add_client**, in Figure 3.5. Here the process of creating a client's personal identification code, **Code_number**, is shown as a separate process.

Table 3.2 summarizes guidelines that are useful in representing systems with data flow diagrams, beginning with a high-level data flow diagram and using stepwise refinement for a module-level representation of the system.

When creating a data flow diagram, the first layer should always be the fundamental system model. This may be a single bubble or a few bubbles, but should be the absolute basic system. All sources of information, primary I/O files, and information sinks should be carefully noted. The data flow diagram should clearly indicate where information has come from, and where it is going, from its source outside the system to its destination outside the system. Information generated by the system should be derivable from information outside the system.

All lines and bubbles should be labeled with meaningful names. The notation should be clear enough for someone who has not participated in the design process to understand.

Information continuity must be maintained. All information transfer should be clearly stated. Leaps of faith and flights of fancy are not appropriate to the design of a system. Again, someone who has not participated in the design process should be able to trace the flow of information through the system.

Figure 3.7 Expansion of process 2, **Date_select**, in Figure 3.4. This shows subcomponent processes to get and verify client's personal identification code, **Code_number**; searching file of available dates; flagging matches that are found; and reporting to the client the name(s) and phone number(s) of selected dates.

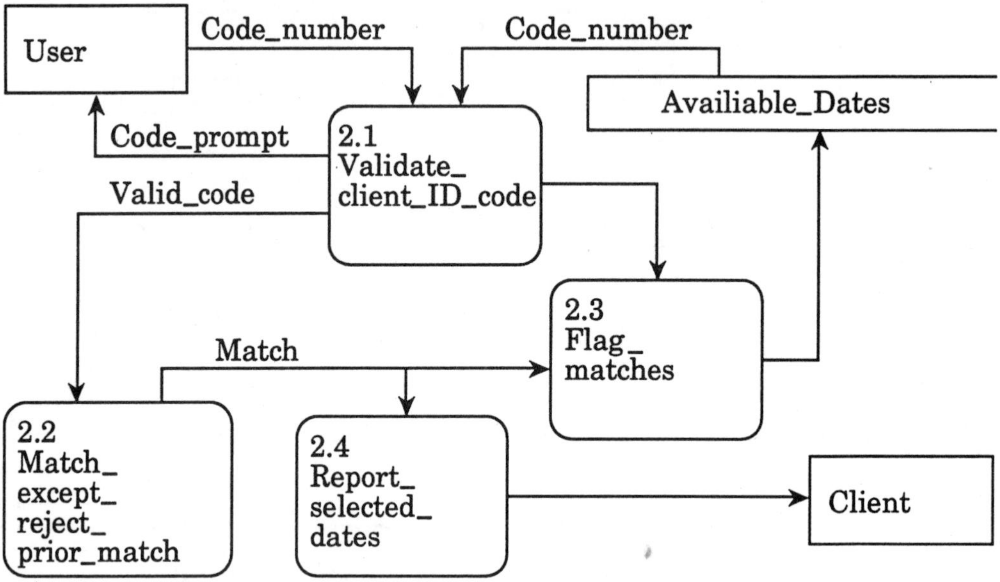

During stepwise refinement, one bubble at a time should be refined. This helps ensure information continuity and top-down development of the model. The model should be examined for possible reorganization to eliminate redundant data flows.

Data flow diagrams should be limited to a maximum of about seven bubbles on a page. If the final data flow diagram is too complex to fit on a single page, a higher level diagram limited to one page should be used, with further refinements indicated on separate pages. A numbering system indicating the relationships of the information and processes should be used.

The data flow diagrams must be confirmed as a system model by walkthroughs with users to evaluate their adequacy and completeness. If the user doesn't understand where something came from, where it went, or what it is for, these points must be resolved before continuing with the system. For example, if the user of the prospective computer dating system does not want to use code numbers for clients, it is better to find out now than after development of the system has started. Remember that it is not only easier, it is cheaper to modify a system at this stage than at a later one.

Table 3.2   Guidelines for Using Data Flow Diagrams

1. The first data flow diagram layer should always be the fundamental system model.
2. Sources, sinks, and primary I/O files should be carefully noted.
3. The data flow diagram should clearly indicate where information has come from and where it is going.
4. Each bubble must be evaluated to ensure that the outputs can be derived from the inputs.
5. All lines and bubbles should be labeled with meaningful names.
6. Information continuity must be maintained.
7. One bubble at a time should be refined.
8. The model should be examined for possible reorganization to eliminate redundant data flows.
9. Data flow diagrams should be limited to a maximum of about seven bubbles on a page.
10. The data flow diagrams must be confirmed as a system model by walkthroughs with users.

3.B.3. Analysis for Inconsistencies

An important use of the data flow diagram, or any other diagram representing a model of a system, is as a tool to analyze our current understanding of the system. A few general principles allow us to check for completeness and consistency.

Basically, we must presume that certain aspects of information are conservative. That is, the system's output must be derivable from its input. Hence, when we identify a class of output information, we must be able to trace back through processes that handle it to a source or sources. With the possible exception of pseudo-random number generators, every item of information has origins in some "externality" or source that supplies information to the system.

The usual problem is checking to see that all sources have been found and described. Sometimes we need to go back to the users with questions about origins. For example, suppose critical information is indicated as coming from an existing file. Natural questions are:

> How does the information get into that file?
>
> What else may affect the data in that file?
>
> Will our system's access needs conflict with other uses of that information?

Another detail to investigate is a file indicated as having only inputs. The question then is, why does that file exist? Similarly, if a file is indicated as having only outputs, the questions are, where does the information come from, and what determines its format?

Another aspect of checking the model is to examine the nature of transformations to see whether all necessary data flows are present to generate the required output. This sort of procedure leads to efforts to model processes in terms of more detailed data flows and subsidiary processes.

Producing graphic representations such as data flow diagrams is much easier if there are software tools to support their creation and modification. Not suprisingly they are becoming more popular now that Computer Aided Software Engineering (CASE) tools are available. CASE tools generally use a built in data dictionary system to perform consistency checks to prevent you from using data at one level which does not agree with the defined data flow at a higher level in the data flow model.

3.C. Data Dictionary Systems

A **data dictionary** is a database that identifies and describes all the data items pertinent to a system under analysis. It is an important adjunct to the use of data flow diagrams in structured analysis. This collection of information becomes the basis of defining all the data items and data structures used by a software implementation. However, in the analysis stage we are not concerned with physical data structures that programmers will create, but instead with the attributes and logical relations among the data.

We are deliberately avoiding a description that implies a specific physical implementation. In the not so distant past data structuring was dominated by punch card images. A card was a record, divided into fields and subfields, each of which contained a data item. It was natural to immediately link data relations into record formats. Now we have multiple file access methods to choose from, and languages that support complex data structures. In order to give the implementer the freedom to design internal and external storage formats, the analyst should define only the logical relations of the data items. The exception is when data is coming from existing files whose structure has already been specified.

A minimal structure to describe data in a system may consist of a three-layer hierarchy: data item, logical data structure relation, and a data flow with which it is associated. A minimal definition of a data item should include a **name** and a **description**. Individual data items should be grouped with other items, as appropriate, with a **group name** assigned to the logical data structure. A data item, group name, or a collection of these should be specifically associated with the particular data flow(s) in the system under study. Specific data flow or data structure diagrams should be referred to.

The naming conventions should be meaningful and unique. There should not be multiple items with the same name. If there are items with the same meaning but different names, the aliases must be referenced. Depending on the language choice for development, these names may be used directly in later software design. Hence it is reasonable to use naming conventions consistent with the software design and documentation standards that will be used in development.

Each data dictionary entry should also cross-reference related data in the system. The purpose is to include all descriptive information that will be required to specify the data items in software design. This includes data type and valid ranges or values.

Look again at the data flow diagram in Figure 3.1. Data items include *scores, name, letter_grade, and average.* These do not exist as independent entities; *name* must be associated with each of the others. We could create data items in pairs, such as:

A: name, scores

B: name, letter_grade

C: name, average

The last one in particular makes sense, since *average* is only used to convert *scores* into *letter_grade.* The first two, however, are associated in that they are components of the *grade_file.* It makes sense to create a data item that encompasses all associated values in the file. Instead of the above list, we might create these data items:

A: name, scores, letter_grade

B: name, average

Upon reconsidering the data flow diagram, we need a set of information to use for the student report. This is a subset of the file information, and we can give it a separate name. That could give us the data dictionary in Figure 3.8.

```
Figure 3.8  Data Dictionary for a Grade Reporting System

Student_Record
    name - 40 characters
    scores - array of seven real numbers (0.0 - 100.0)
    letter_grade - 1 character (A, B, C, D, or E)
Value
    name - 40 characters
    average - real number (0.0 - 100.0)
Report (this is a subset of Student_Record)
    name - 40 characters
    letter_grade - 1 character (A, B, C, D, or E)
```

Data dictionaries can be created at any step of the refinement process; for example, look at the relatively high level diagram for the com-

puter dating service in Figure 3.4. An associated data dictionary might look
like the one in Figure 3.9.

```
Figure 3.9  Data Dictionary for a Computer Dating Service

Client_data
     personal_data
          name - 40 characters
          phone_number - 10 characters
          code_number - 5 characters
               .
               .
               .
     request - Boolean [t - find match; f - just add to file]

Avail_data (this is a subset of Client_data)
     name - 40 characters
     phone_number - 10 characters
```

3.C.1. Organizational Uses

Once the data dictionary is set up it serves as a basis for uniform
definition of all data items for systems analysis, software development,
and maintenance. It provides a master cross-reference and index tool to
support the software. As such the access to the dictionary must be
restricted to read-only, except by an administrator with authority to update
it. Changes must be controlled and dated. This becomes crucial if there are
multiple versions of the software affected. As software is designed and
developed the dictionary entries for data items and data structures can be
annotated. This is to indicate specific code module file names, and data file
names that use data described in that dictionary entry.

The existence of a centralized data cross-reference is important. It
makes sure that a team of software professionals dealing with the system
have a single definition for any data item. By requiring the use of previously defined data names and data structures it is possible to limit the
tendency to propagate redundant data. This can eliminate many sources of
confusion for developers and maintainers. It also provides a baseline for an
analyst to evaluate elements of the system if the environment or business
conditions lead to a need for maintenance or replacement.

3.C.2. Automated Tools

A data dictionary may well be constructed on a deck of 3" by 5" cards
for a small project. However, it is becoming typical for development organizations to have an automated data dictionary system already in place.

For small software development organizations it is quite reasonable to set up such systems on a microcomputer or minicomputer using a database management system (DBMS). Once such systems are in place it is routine to begin integrating them with other software analysis and development tool systems. Such systems may be involved in software quality control audits, software configuration management, software test management, and software maintenance management (all to be discussed in later chapters).

3.D. Data Structure Models

Many computer applications can be directly modeled as a transformation of an input data structure (e.g., input data file) to produce an output data structure (e.g., report). Many business software systems, for example, fit this pattern. This has led to systematic approaches in systems analysis and design based on data structure models.

3.D.1. Data Structure Diagrams

A widely used notation in this area is the data structure diagram, introduced by C. W. Bachman. The data structure diagram is a graphic notation used to represent the relationships between the entities of a system. It consists of two symbols, the rectangle and the arrow.

A rectangle enclosing a name denotes an entity or record type that is dealt with in the system. Each record type (entity) is composed of data items (fields, attributes) but the names are suppressed in this description. There is a difference between a record type and an occurrence of a record type. We refer to the occurrence of a record type as a record.

Example 3.1

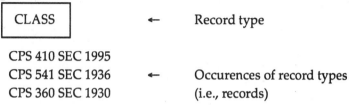

The other component in a data structure diagram is a directed arrow connecting two record types. The record type located at the tail of the arrow is called the owner-record type. The arrow directed from owner to member is called a set type and is named.

Example 3.2

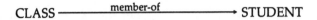

CLASS ——————————member-of——————————→ STUDENT

A set type named 'member-of' exists between CLASS (owner) and STUDENT (member). The existence of a set type is declared by naming it, stating its owner-record type (exactly one) and its member record type occurance. A set occurrence is one occurence of the owner-record type together with zero or more occurrences of each member-record type. This is shown for Example 3.2 in Figure 3.10.

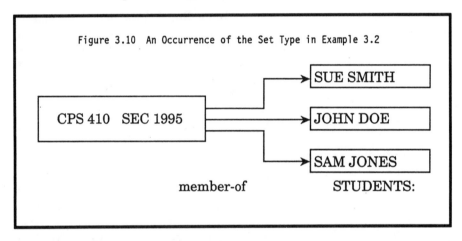

Figure 3.10 An Occurrence of the Set Type in Example 3.2

If we draw a data structure diagram to represent data in our system we imply that the following associations exist among the parts of a set occurrence:

- Given an owner record, it is possible for our system to process the associated member records of that set occurrence.
- Given a member record, it is possible to process the associated owner record of that set occurrence.
- Given a member record, it is possible to process other member records in the same set occurrence.
- A given member record may be associated with only one set occurrence of a given type.

One of the beauties of data structure diagrams is their ability to represent many-to-many relationships. To represent many-to-many relationships we define a third record type and use it to relate the two record types that are in a many-to-many relationship. A good example of many-to-many relationships is that of STUDENT and COURSE record types. A student takes several courses and a course has several students enrolled in it. One way in which this relationship could be represented using data structure diagrams is shown in Figure 3.11.

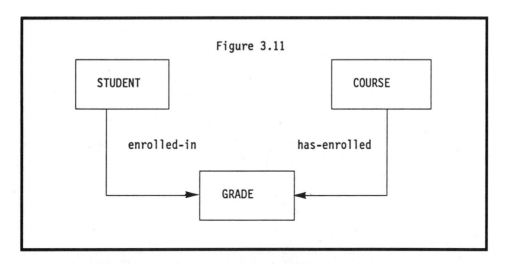

Figure 3.11

To find the classes and grades a student has, first find the grades for the student using the set type 'enrolled-in' and for each grade use the set type 'has-enrolled' to find the particular course. To generate a list of students who are taking a course, for the given course use 'has-enrolled' to get the grades and then for each grade us 'enrolled-in' to find its student.

The use of data structure diagrams in conjunction with data dictionaries forms a detailed system description. This representation of a system emphasizes the data items in the boxes and suppresses detail of the implied transformation processes required by the arrows. This is in keeping with the idea that a system model should indicate the function without specifying the algorithm

3.D.2 Jackson and Warnier-Orr Diagrams

The best known of the data structure models are the Jackson and Warnier-Orr techniques. An example is shown in Figure 3.12 using the Jackson style of data structure representation for a simple inventory structure. Each box represents a named data entity. If an entity is a set of other data entities, these appear below it and are connected by lines. A data item that has multiple occurrences is flagged with an asterisk. If an entity is one of several alternative values, it is flagged with a small circle.

The same example is repeated in Figure 3.13 in the Warnier-Orr representation. For the same data relations of Figure 3.12 the data relations are shown as a horizontal hierarchy from left to right. Note that repeated data entities have an extent or range indicator below the name. Alternative entities are indicated by an OR symbol, +, or EXCLUSIVE OR symbol, ⊕, as appropriate.

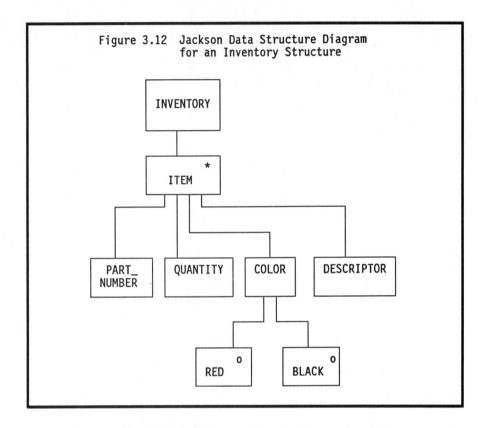

Figure 3.12 Jackson Data Structure Diagram
for an Inventory Structure

An associated data dictionary for the inventory structure might look like the one in Figure 3.14.

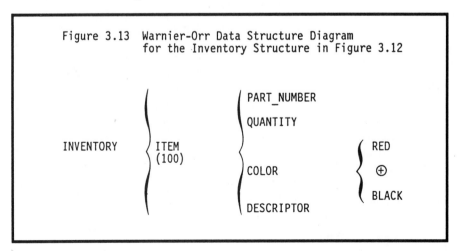

Figure 3.13 Warnier-Orr Data Structure Diagram
for the Inventory Structure in Figure 3.12

One might be tempted to specify these relations directly as code level data declarations with an array of 100 items, each item having the four subdivisions shown in the data dictionary. Such declarations, however, are likely to be unsuitable in a real application, since it may be that access to the DESCRIPTOR data might be needed less frequently and would not justify the space required to keep them in memory. The implementers might instead choose a physical implementation which used arrays in memory for some of the data fields, used a hashing function to get an array index from a PART_NUMBER, and stored the DESCRIPTOR data in a disk file. The specification of physical data structure implementation should be left to the code designers.

```
        Figure 3.14    Data Dictionary for Inventory Structure
                       in Figures 3.12 and 3.13

        part_number - integer
        quantity - integer
        color - character 1
        descriptor - character 64
```

The diagraming conventions employed in these methodologies are useful to analysts if it is understood that they are to be employed as a tool for the logical description of data relations, and not a prescription for the implementation of physical data structures.

3.D.3. Aspects of Data Structure

The basic data structure diagraming technique depends on the notion that there are four aspects of data structure, which are listed in Table 3.3. The first of these is hierarchical decomposition, which can be used in a method of designing a system by breaking down its components through a series of top-down refinements (stepwise refinement). The second is the nature of the alternation or selection conditions, the third is the ordering of the data, and the last is the number of repetitions in a group.

```
        Table 3.3  Aspects of Data Structures

        1.  Hierarchical decomposition
        2.  Alternation or selection conditions
        3.  Sequential ordering
        4.  Number of repetitions in a group
```

The data structure modeling techniques described above support these aspects. Jackson diagrams represent a vertical hierarchy of boxes with a data item name in each, whereas the Warnier-Orr representation shows a left to right horizontal hierarchy with levels indicated by braces. Both show sequence, alternation and repetition. The Warnier-Orr conventions are more explicit in defining numbers of repetitions and variant structures with varying numbers of repetitions. In the Jackson diagrams such details should be included in supplementary notations on the diagrams.

The use of data structure diagrams in conjunction with data dictionaries, Jackson diagrams, or Warnier-Orr diagrams forms a detailed system description. The data structure emphasizes the relationship between the data items, while the other model handles the more detailed data description. This is useful in situations where the relationship between data items is complex such as databases or information systems.

If there is a simple mapping from an input data structure to an output data structure, then it is reasonable to seek a systematic mapping from aspects of the data structure to the structured programming constructs necessary to do the transformation. These include sequential processing steps, iterative processing, and conditional branching. The principles of structured programming are reviewed in Chapter 7.

Whether or not the complexity of a given problem is conducive to directly synthesizing the system properties, the orderly approach to representing data structures can aid definition of data in the required data flows of a system. Hence a combination of diagraming methodologies is frequently used.

3.E. Decomposition Charts

A decomposition chart is a form of abstraction based on generating a hierarchy much in the same way as we outline material for writing. It is the most elementary hierarchical model of a system. At the highest level we have a descriptive functional title of the system. Next we identify the major subsystems which compose it. Each of these may in turn be viewed as being composed of sub-subsystems and so on.

An example is seen in Figure 3.15. It must be noted that such a decomposition is not unique. The viewpoint and concerns of the analyst determine what is the set of subdivisions. Depending on viewpoint, the subdivisions might be on the basis of processes (type of activity), functions (job category, type of equipment), data types, or even geographical location. What is an appropriate functional decomposition depends on the purposes for which the model is to be used. The mapping of these entities as processes which control the flow of execution leads directly to a modular structure of software to implement a system.

Figure 3.15   Conceptual Model of a Computer System
Based on Functional Decomposition

I. Computing Center as seen by Data Center Staff
   Operations Chief
         Systems programmers
         Clerical support
         Machine operators
         Terminal facilities managers
            Consultants
   Chief Budget Officer
         Research accounts manager
         Student accounts manager
         Accounting clerks

II. Computing Center as seen by Students
   A.   Terminal facilities
        1.   Video terminals
        2.   Printers
        3.   Plotters
        4.   Graphics terminals
        5.   Data communications
   B.   Computing hardware
        1.   Central processors
        2.   Mass storage
        3.   Memory
        4.   Network server
        5.   Microcomputers
   C.   Software support
        1.   Compilers
        2.   Editor
        3.   Utilities
        4.   Statistical packages
        5.   Database managers
   D.   Student computing accounts
        1.   Execution priority assignments
        2.   Resource limits
        3.   Cost of computing

Decomposition diagrams may be expressed in several ways. For example, as shown in Figure 3.15, they may be outline forms with structured indentation and/or systematic numbering and lettering. Another common method is graphical form as a tree with a box around each subdivision and branching lines to indicate the hierarchy. The control hierarchy of organizations is traditionally shown in this graphical form.

3.F. Algorithmic Models

Another model of a system that might be appropriate is the algorithmic model. Depending on the nature of a system it may be advantageous to use such a model. In fact for some computationally intensive systems this may be the only satisfactory model. If you are building a system to invert matrices the data flow is trivial and the algorithm all important.

3.F.1. Structured Flowcharts

Perhaps the first modeling technique used to represent software was the flowchart. Flowchart techniques have developed in parallel with computer languages. These flowcharts can be used to represent the control and sequence of execution in a system of software modules.

A structured flowchart is one that limits the types of constructs to sequence, branching, and looping. Some flowcharts, such as the Nassi-Schneiderman flowchart, illustrated in Figure 3.2, do not allow any other constructs. Other flowcharts, such as the ANSI standard, are not limited to these constructs. It is good practice to use structured flowchart conventions when a flowchart representation of high level control flow is required.

3.F.2. ANSI Standard Flowcharts

The structured flowchart is a relatively new development in program documentation. Flowcharts were originally used to represent an algorithmic description. This unstructured technique is rooted in the tradition of FORTRAN programming, and has been used to represent high level outlines of a procedure or to show algorithmic detail at the level of executable statements. Before source code documentation was routinely used, it was a useful technique for documenting an existing system. In fact, sometimes it was the only documentation.

Although the concepts of structured programming can be imposed on these diagrams, the diagraming convention does not require it. This nonstructured flowcharting was widely used in the past, and a great deal of code still in existence is documented with little else. Therefore, a familiarity with these conventions is likely to be helpful, sooner or later, when you run into a piece of software with a flowchart that is not necessarily structured.

These flowcharting conventions have been standardized by the American National Standards Institute (ANSI). Let us look at the ANSI standard conventions, and an example of an ANSI flowchart.

The ANSI flowchart conventions are depicted in Figure 3.16. The elements of these diagrams show conditional branching with diamonds, and sequences or sequential processes in boxes. The control paths are indicated by directed lines. An ANSI flowchart example is shown in Figure 3.17. These flowcharts are good at defining control flow sequence.

3.G. Course Project: System Model

In order to specify your system, you will need to build some kind of system model. Keep in mind that the purpose of this model is to represent the interrelationships of the parts of the system. This is partly to be sure that the system is internally consistent, and partly so that both users and developers can understand and review the system. It is important to be sure that the system being built will really solve the problem. When completed, the system model becomes part of the Software Requirements Specification.

In general, a hierarchy of data flow diagrams accompanied by a data dictionary is appropriate. It must be pointed out that either the diagrams or the dictionary by itself is an incomplete model of the system. While a data dictionary is essential, the choice of a graphical diagraming technique for the entire system or a part of the system may need to be chosen based on system characteristics.

There are many advantages to using data flow diagrams. One advantage is that they parallel object oriented design, described in Chapter 4. This is something with which you may already be familiar. The concept of flow of information is often difficult for many people who are used to dealing with the idea of program structure. However, it is an extremely important idea, and one that is necessary to understand in order to effectively use the concept of object oriented design. This methodology is widely used, especially among users of the Ada language.

Another advantage of data flow diagrams is that they can be used to model any system. A third advantage is that data flow diagrams are widely used, so you will be developing a marketable skill. Also, there are a number of tools available to develop data flow diagrams which may be available to your institution. These include Excelerator and DesignAid.

On the other hand, data flow diagrams are not the only way to model a system. It is possible that another model may be more appropriate for your particular project. A decision on which model to use needs to be based on such factors as your background and experience, the nature of the project, and the tools that are available to you.

Depending on the particular type of problem or application, a specific method or combination of methods may be used in a given software development organization. Some of the system modeling approaches have a particular emphasis or bias. Some focus on information transfer and transformations of information, others are focused on the detail of data structures, and still others concentrate on timing and control of events.

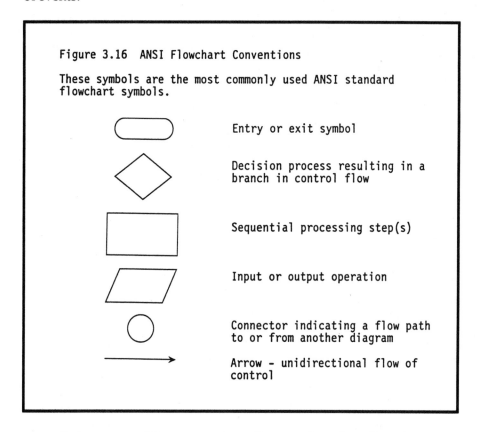

Figure 3.16 ANSI Flowchart Conventions

These symbols are the most commonly used ANSI standard flowchart symbols.

Entry or exit symbol

Decision process resulting in a branch in control flow

Sequential processing step(s)

Input or output operation

Connector indicating a flow path to or from another diagram

Arrow - unidirectional flow of control

It is not possible to unequivocally say that, for all applications, one approach is "best," although you may find adherents of one or another diagraming technique asserting such claims. If the system you need to build is heavily dominated by data structure and commercial data processing then a data structure modeling technique is probably best. On the other hand, if you must deal with a complex interactive environment, a data flow modeling approach may be superior. In other cases, particularly in real time process control, the time relations of many events may dictate a model that can express more directly the timing and control relationships. Many systems will be a mixture, and a combination of modeling approaches may be required.

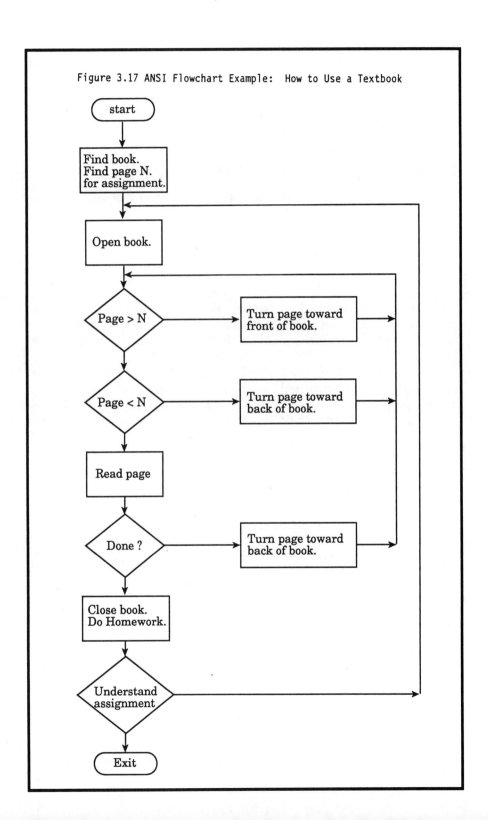

Figure 3.17 ANSI Flowchart Example: How to Use a Textbook

3.H. Beyond a Course Project: Other Techniques and Models

There are a very large number of modeling and refinement methods in use. We will mention here a few additional ones that are relatively widely used.

3.H.1. Variants of Decomposition Techniques

There are three main variants of the technique of decomposing system structure by refinement of data flow models. Each of these has been commercially promoted through professional seminars and various publications.

One collection of tools and techniques is a product of McDonnell-Douglas Automation, called Improved System Technology (IST). This methodology is based on the work of Gane and Sarson, and is the basis for the descriptions earlier in this chapter. The primary features include: emphasis on systematic numbering of processes, data flows for reference purposes, and the explicit use of symbols for externalities and material flows.

A widely used variety is that presented by Yourdon Inc. as Structured Analysis and Structured Design. They combine data flow diagraming techniques with the ideas of chief programmer teams, data dictionary use, and structure charts. The diagraming conventions include processes enclosed in circles instead of rectangles with rounded off corners, and files are indicated by a pair of parallel lines.

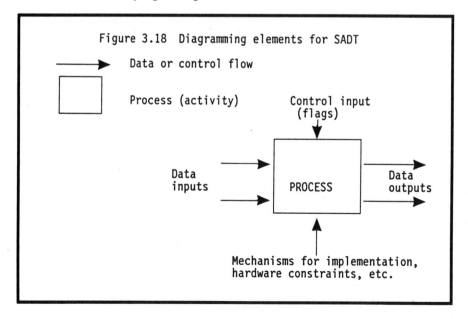

Figure 3.18 Diagramming elements for SADT

Data or control flow

Process (activity)

Control input (flags)

Data inputs

PROCESS

Data outputs

Mechanisms for implementation, hardware constraints, etc.

The third, and somewhat different variant is the data flow diagraming conventions of Structured Analysis and Design Technique (SADT), a trademark of SofTech Inc. As shown in Figure 3.18, their diagrams include data and control flows.

3.H.2. Other Models

Other representations of control flow include formal algebraic description, and finite state machines (described briefly in Chapter 2). The states of a finite state machine are segregated in the time domain. This makes the finite state machine particularly useful in describing event and timing dependencies in processes. The emphasis here is on tools for analysis, which should be usable in communication between users, analysts, managers and developers.

Summary

Most software systems are sufficiently complex that a good model must be built to ensure that the system is complete and consistent. The model must specify what needs to be done, but must not specify how to do it.

Data abstraction and stepwise refinement are essential to building a model. Data abstraction is the recognition of essential details and the concurrent suppression of nonessential details. Stepwise refinement means that data definitions and processing steps are defined very broadly, then modified step by step, with the level of detail increasing at every step until the level of detail is sufficient. It is sort of like going from this summary to the entire chapter.

Specific models include data flow models, data dictionaries, data structure models, decomposition charts, and algorithmic models. The most commonly used type of data flow model is the data flow diagram, a graphical method of portraying the flow of information, but not the flow of control. Data structure models include data structure diagrams, and the Jackson and Warnier-Orr techniques. Decomposition charts represent another type of abstraction and may be in outline or graphical form. One type of algorithmic model in wide use is the Nassi-Schneiderman structured flowchart. Another graphical type of algorithmic model is the ANSI Standard flowchart.

Keywords

ANSI Standard flow chart
abstraction
algorithmic model
data dictionary
data flow diagram
data structure model
decomposition chart
flow of control
flow of information
flowchart
fundamental system model
Jackson structure design
Nassi-Schneiderman flowchart
sink
source
stepwise refinement
structured flowchart
walkthrough
Warnier-Orr structure diagram

Review Questions

3.1. Why is it useful to build a model of a system?

3.2. What type of model best represents a system?

3.3. What is the difference between information structure and control structure?

3.4. What are the components of a data flow diagram?

3.5. What is stepwise refinement? How is it used in data flow diagrams?

3.6. How can a model be used to analyze a system for inconsistencies?

3.7. What is a data dictionary? What is it good for?

3.8. What is the difference between a data flow model and a data structure model?

3.9. Describe the Jackson technique; the Warnier-Orr technique.

3.10. What is a decomposition chart?

3.11. What is a flowchart? What is the ANSI flowchart? Why should you be familiar with it?

Exercises

3.1   Draw a data flow diagram showing how a personal checking account operates. Your model should cover making deposits, writing checks, cashing checks, and periodic statements.

3.2.   Produce a data dictionary for the system in Exercise 1.

3.3.   Draw a data flow diagram for a system to automate order processing for a fast food restaurant.

3.4.   Create a data dictionary for the system in Exercise 3.

3.5.   Construct a model of course registration for your college or university.

3.6.   From the Computer Dating Service example, Figure 3.7, produce a data flow diagram to expand the process of bubble 2.2, "Match, except reject prior match." What additional information might you need in order to do this?

3.7.   For the Computer Dating Service example, Figure 3.7, produce a data flow diagram to expand the process of bubble 2.4, "Report Selected Dates." Where would you expect a description of the form and content of the output to go in the Software Requirements Specification?

3.8.   Produce a Jackson diagram for a system to store and retrieve multiple choice examination questions where each questions may have five possible answers and an answer key.

3.9.   Produce a Warnier-Orr diagram for the problem in Exercise 8.

References

ANSI Standard X 3.5-1970, "American National Standard Flowchart Symbols and their Usage in Information Processing", American National Standards Institute, New York 1970

　　　The official description of what might now be called unstructured flowcharts representing flow of control.

Bachman, C. W., "Data Structure Diagrams," <u>Database</u> 1, 2 (Summer 1969)Introduces data structure diagram notation Brooks, Frederick P., The Mythical Man-Month, Essays on Software Engineering, Addison-Wesley Publishing Company, 1975, reprinted 1982

　　　Considered a classic of software engineering, Brooks presents the results of his experience as the project manager for the IBM OS 360. It is a clear exposition of the nonlinearity of manpower and project duration effects on software project management.

DeMarco, Tom, <u>Structured Analysis and System Specification</u>, with a Foreword by P. J. Plauger, Yourdon Inc., NY 1979

>An exposition and extension of the data flow methodology of Yourdon and Constantine. Excellent discussion of structured English.

Gane, Chris and Sarson, Trish, <u>Structure Systems Analysis: Tools and Techniques</u>, Prentice-Hall 1979

>Introduces systems analysis techniques. Emphasis is placed on building a hierarchical data flow model with an associated data dictionary. These authors invented the data flow diagraming conventions used in this book.

Gehani, N. and McGetrick, A. D., eds., <u>Software Specification Techniques</u>, Addison-Wesley, Wokingham, England, 1986

>Explores the controversy and range of recent research with a collection of 21 papers covering specification techniques, applications, case studies, and specification languages. More than 300 references are included.

Glass, R. L., <u>Modern Programming Practices</u>, Prentice-Hall 1982

>An account of industry practice based on applications in defense contracting with emphasis on real-time systems.

Jackson, M. A., <u>Principles of Program Design</u>, Academic Press, 1979

>Presents the Jackson data structure design methodology which is widely used in data processing applications development.

King, David., Current Practices in Software Development, A Guide to Successful Systems, Yourdon Press 1984

>A commentary and comparison of various methodologies in use by data processing system professionals. It does not introduce the details of the methodologies, but is an excellent description of industry practices. King advocates data flow methods for use in developing requirements, and shifting to Jackson methodology for software planning and design.

Korth, H. R. and Silberschatz, A., Database System Concepts, McGraw-Hill 1986

>A systematic presentation of hierarchical, network, relational and entity-relationship models of data bases. These approaches are important to consider if a system under study has a major information system component.

Leong-Hong, Belkis, and Plagman, Bernard K, <u>Data Dictionary Directory Systems</u>, John Wiley & Sons, Inc., 1982

>Primarily concerned with the management and use of data dictionary systems. The criteria to consider in the evaluation, selection and design of systems are also presented.

Martin, James and McClure, Carma, <u>Diagramming Techniques for Analysts and Programmers</u>, Prentice Hall, Englewood Cliffs NJ, 1985

>A compendium of definitions and examples of a large number of graphical presentation and modeling techniques, including data flow and data structure techniques.

McMenamin, Stephen. M. and Palmer, John. E., <u>Essential Systems Analysis</u>, Yourdon Press, New York 1984

>Presents requirements analysis with data flow modeling using Yourdon style data flow diagrams.

Nassi, I. and Schneiderman, B., "Flowchart Techniques for Structured Programming," <u>ACM SIGPLAN Notices</u> 8(8): pp. 12-26, August 1973.

> The definition of the Nassi-Schneiderman 'structured flowchart.'

<u>Nastec CASE 2000 DesignAid Reference Manual</u>, IBM PC Version, 4.0. Southfield, MI: Nastec Corporation, 1988.

> An automated CASE tool useful for production of data flow diagrams and data dictionaries for a system model.

Ross, D. T., "Structured Analysis (SA): A Language for Communicating Ideas," <u>IEEE Trans. Software Eng.</u> SE-3(1) (January 1977)

> Foundation reference for SADT.

Scanlan, David A., "Structured Flowcharts Outperform Pseudocode: An Experimental Comparison," <u>IEEE Software</u>, Vol. 6, No. 5, pp. 28-38, September 1989

> Description of experiments that indicate structured flowcharts increase speed and accuracy in solving some problems; recommends graphical descriptions of algorithms.

Taylor, Robert W. and Frank, Randall L., "CODASYL Data-Base Management Systems," <u>Computing Surveys</u>, Vol. 8, No. 1, March 1976

> Detailed description and history of data structure diagrams.

Van Duyn, J., <u>Developing a Data Dictionary System</u>, Prentice-Hall 1982

> Emphasis is on the design and implementation of a data dictionary system with a substantial case study example.

Weinberg, Victor, <u>Structured Analysis</u>, Prentice-Hall Software Series, 1980

> A mixture of practical details of systems analysis and the 'structured design' methods of Yourdon and Constantine.

Whitten, Jeffrey L.; Bentley, Lonnie D.; and Ho, Thomas, I. M., <u>Systems Analysis & Design Methods</u>, Times Mirror/Mosby College Publishing, 1986

> Systems analysis keyed to the use of "Excelerator," an automated dfd/data dictionary tool.

Yourdon, Edward N. and Constantine, Larry L. <u>Structured Design</u>, Second ed., Yourdon Press 1978

> Presents a systematic approach to structuring software design based on a data flow abstraction. Introduces data flow diagrams and methods to refine the model of the problem. Elements of the refined model are then used to specify modules of code to implement the software.

CHAPTER 4

SOFTWARE DESIGN AND PLANNING

Observe that for the [systems analyst], as for the chef, the urgency of the patron may govern the scheduled completion of the task, but it cannot govern the actual completion. An omelette, promised in two minutes, may appear to be progressing nicely. But when it has not set in two minutes, the customer has two choices - wait or eat it raw.

- Frederick P. Brooks, Jr., The Mythical Man-Month

Charles Babbage . . . died in poverty while trying to finish building the first computer, [and was] thus . . . the first systems designer to go over budget and behind schedule.

- Datamation, October 1981

Software Life Cycle

Preliminary software design

I. Software need
II. Preliminary feasibility judgment
III. Requirements analysis and feasibility study
IV. Requirements specification
V. Preliminary software design and planning
VI. Software development
      Detailed design
      Coding and unit testing
      Integration
      System testing
VII. Software maintenance

Project: System Plan - the high-level structure of the software; estimation and allocation of tasks, scheduling development and implementation.

4.A. Introduction

Software design is the process of defining the software architecture, components, modules, interfaces, test approach, and data for a system to satisfy requirements. We presume that decisions have been made about the allocation of the system elements between hardware, software, and manual procedures.

Up to this point, you have been concerned about defining the problem, understanding exactly what it is that the user wants. Now you will concentrate on finding a solution to the problem. You will need to specify a high-level structure for the system as a set of modules. In essence, **preliminary software design** is the art of choosing the architecture of a collection of modules and defining their relation to the system hardware.

Remember that the boundaries between various aspects of the software life cycle are often blurred. If you did a good job of specifying your system, with data flow diagrams that are satisfactory to your user, you will have come a long way in preliminary system design.

4.B. Object Oriented Design

One design method is **object oriented design (OOD)**. Object oriented design provides a means for the designer to group various state variables together into entities called objects. This allows the designer to create a balanced relation between the objects and the operations on them.

What do we mean by an object? It is a definable data entity or group of such entities in a system, each of which is named and has a "state" or value. An object or class of objects come into existence in a program by being declared as variables, constants, or groups of these (as in a data structure).

4.B.1. Methodology

The steps in an object oriented design methodology, summarized in Table 4.1, may be described as follows:

1. Identify general classes of objects and their attributes. For example, an object might be a stack of real numbers.

2. Identify operations on the objects and the relation between the objects. That is, what does the object do, or what is done to it? Establish the dynamic behavior of each object and identify time and space constraints. For example, in a stack, push and pop are the operations. The order of the pop operation is the reverse of the push operation, and each pop operation must be preceded by at least one push. An attempt to pop an empty stack must generate a warning of some kind. Furthermore, the push operation puts the next real number at the head of the line (top of the stack), and each pop operation deals with the real number that is on top of the stack.

3. Establish the visibility, or dependency, of each object in relation to other objects. What objects are related to this object, or what processes may know this object? This means that for each object (or class of objects) we must identify the other objects dependent on it and on which it depends. In the stack example, access to the stack depends on use in the system, but may be accessed by a recursive procedure. The stack may need access to an object that can check for stack underflow or overflow, or a control variable that will warn of an attempt to pop an empty stack.

4. Establish the interfaces. This involves deciding how the objects interact with one another and how much of one object another object can see. This is the boundary between the inside view and the outside view of a module. It involves creating a formal module specification in appropriate formal notation, which may be language dependent. In our stack example, the interface is likely to consist of a real number and a warning control variable.

5. Implement the operations. This step is language dependent.

Table 4.1 Steps in Object Oriented Design

1. Identify the objects and their attributes.
2. Identify operations that affect each object and
   the operations that each object must initiate.
3. Establish the visibility of each object in relation
   to other objects.
4. Establish the interface of each object.
5. Implement each object.

Booch, Grady. Software Engineering with Ada, 2d ed.
Menlo Park, CA: Benjamin/Cummings, 1986.

Let us go through another example of object oriented design. Consider the grade reporting system from Chapter 3, Figure 3.1, and its associated data dictionary in Figure 3.8. Those figures are reproduced here as Figures 4.1 and 4.2.

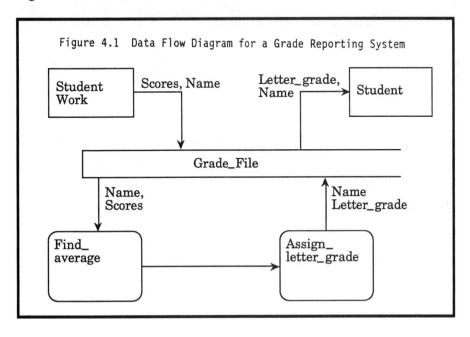

Figure 4.1 Data Flow Diagram for a Grade Reporting System

```
Figure 4.2  Data Dictionary for a Grade Reporting System

Student_Record
     name - 40 characters
     scores - array of seven real numbers (0.0 - 100.0)
     letter_grade - 1 character (A, B, C, D, or E)
Value
     name - 40 characters
     average - real number (0.0 - 100.0)
Report (this is a subset of Student_Record)
     name - 40 characters
     letter_grade - 1 character (A, B, C, D, or E)
```

The first steps in the object oriented design process are to identify the objects, their attributes, and the operations on them. For the grade reporting system, Table 4.2 shows one way of doing this.

Table 4.2   Objects, Attributes, and Operations for a Grade Reporting System

Object	Attribute	Operation
Student_Record	name scores letter_grade	input student work find average assign letter grade send report to student
Value	name average	assign letter grade
Report	name letter_grade	send report to student

The objects are the Student_Record, Value, and Report. The Student_Record has the attributes of name, scores, and letter_grade and is associated with the operations of input, average, assign letter grade, and send report. Value has the attributes of name and average, and is associated with the operation of assign letter grade. Report is a subset of Student_Record and is associated with a set of operations that is a subset of the operations on Student_Record.

The next steps are to establish the visibility of each object and the interfaces. These are given for the grade reporting system in Table 4.3.

Table 4.3 Interfaces and Visibility - Grade Reporting System

Process	Associated Objects	Visibility
input student work	Student_Record	name, score
find average	Student_Record Value	name, score name, average
assign letter grade	Value Report	name, average name, letter_grade
send report to student	Report	name, letter_grade

The visibility of each object refers to how much of it is needed for a specific process. The object associated with input is Student_Record, but that record includes a grade which is as yet unknown. Thus the parts of the object visible to the input process are the names and scores.

The averaging process is associated with the objects Student_Record and Value. Again, only the name and scores are visible. The grade part of the structure is not used here. For Value, both name and average are used.

In a similar manner, the data flow diagram and associated data dictionary for the computer dating service in Figures 3.4 and 3.9 are reproduced here as Figures 4.3 and 4.4. We will do another example of object oriented design on this system.

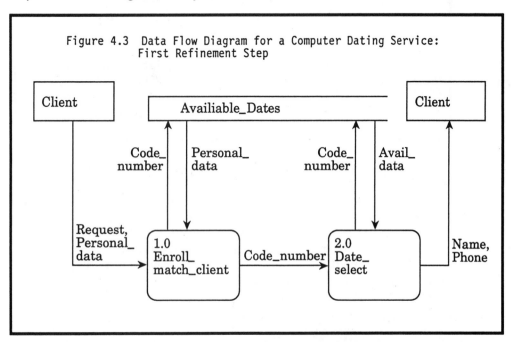

Figure 4.3 Data Flow Diagram for a Computer Dating Service:
First Refinement Step

```
Figure 4.4  Data Dictionary for a Computer Dating Service

Client_data
    personal_data
            name - 40 characters
            phone_number - 10 characters
            code_number - 5 characters
                     ⋮

    request - Boolean [t - find match; f - just add to file]

Avail_data (this is a subset of Client_data)
    name - 40 characters
    phone_number - 10 characters
```

The objects that we are interested in at this level of refinement are Request, Personal_data, Code_number, and Avail_data. These objects and their attributes and operations are shown in Table 4.4.

Table 4.4	Objects, Attributes, and Operations for a Computer Dating Service	
Object	Attribute	Operation
Request	request	input
Personal_data	name phone_number ⋮	input enroll_client
Code_number	code_number	match_client enroll_client date_select
Avail_data	name phone_number	date_select

The processes, along with associated objects and their visibility, are shown in Table 4.5.

The major difference between object oriented design and other design plans is that object oriented design puts more of an emphasis on software objects than on functional decomposition. If we are to successfully reuse software, we must indeed pay attention to software objects. However, object oriented design does not really involve stepwise refinement and hence for more than medium-sized projects should be used with a scheme that does.

Table 4.5   Interfaces and Visibility - Computer Dating Service

Process	Associated Objects	Visibility
input	Client_data	request personal_data
enroll_match_client	Client_data	request personal_data code number
date_select	Client_data	code number Avail_data

4.B.2. From Data Flow Diagrams to Object Oriented Design

If you understand the information that a system will process, you are on your way to a successful analysis of the system. The data flow diagram discussed in some detail in Chapter 3 is a graphical tool for describing the information flow characteristics within a system.

Object oriented design is closely related to data flow diagrams in that basically an object in object oriented design is a data flow in data flow diagrams. Both are concerned with the flow of information and the objects whereby information is handled. Thus data flow diagrams can be used as a tool in object oriented design. In a carefully refined data flow diagram, each data flow may represent a single object or group of objects.

Look again at the data flow diagram and data dictionary in Figures 4.1 and 4.2 and the list of objects and operations in Table 4.2. The objects correspond to the names on the data flow diagram arrows. The attributes are defined in the data dictionary. The operations include the processes and certain things associated with sources and sinks. In this example, the input of the name and scores is associated with a source. The output of a report containing a name and grade is associated with a sink.

Similarly, the visibility and interfaces in Table 4.3 may be derived from the data flow diagram and data dictionary. Note the relationships in the data flow diagram. For the process find average, the input information consists of the attributes of Student_Record and the output information consists of the attributes of Value. These constitute the interface. The visibility consists of the specific attributes of the object needed for the process.

The relation between data flow-directed design and object oriented design is apparent once it is recognized that an object in object oriented design is a data flow in a data flow diagram. Thus if we are careful to require that the diagrammed data flows are coherent data structures we can use data flow diagrams as a standard tool for object oriented design. For this purpose we must demand that every data flow be named and defined in our data dictionary. For each such entity to make sense as an object it must be composed of elementary data items that are logically related.

4.C. Specification of Modules

The next step in the design process, once the objects have been identified and the flow of information specified, is to decide on individual modules. Modules are the building blocks of software systems.

It is important to separate a module's external specification from a description of the module's logic. This way the logic of a module can change completely without affecting the other modules in the system. For this reason, any design criterion that might be subject to change should be localized to a module.

4.C.1. Partitioning the Software into Modules

The degree to which a Software Requirement Specification contains elements of preliminary or high-level design will vary considerably from one project to another and from one organization to another. In part this is because the commitment of resources often depends on the development and implementation costs. A reasonable or acceptable estimation of such costs may not be possible until at least a preliminary design has been done on which estimates of code size and complexity can be based. However, at the very least the specifications must have a working model of the proposed system in the form of its logical procedures and data flows.

The design of the control hierarchy must ensure that high-level modules are associated with clear functional properties of the system. In addition, a goal of the design is to minimize the number of control steps to carry out those functions that have critical performance constraints.

From an information model of the system as represented, for example, beginning with a set of data flow diagrams and using object oriented design, we may begin the task of designing an implementation. The goal is to build a hierarchical model of the relation of logical procedures in a top-down manner.

We must partition the set of relations of logical procedures and map them onto a set of functional physical procedures that will be embodied as modules of code in a control hierarchy. The result may be expressed as a hierarchy chart, described below, where each rectangle represents a code module.

4.C.2. Modularity Criteria: Size, Complexity

You probably already have some experience writing programs that consist of multiple modules. Your problem now is to determine what constitutes a module of reasonable size. Modules that are too large may be difficult to test; modules that are too small increase the amount of interfacing required, which increases the likelihood of errors.

One of the chief goals of modularity is to limit system complexity by partitioning the system. We will defer to Chapter 7 a detailed examination of software complexity metrics. For now, consider the complexity of an object (system or module) as a measure of the mental effort required to understand that object. In general it is a function of the relationships among the components of the object. Hence to minimize module complexity it is desirable to maximize the independence of the modules of the system. That is, we wish to segregate the problem of how modules interact from the problem of what the individual modules do.

Another important aspect of minimizing complexity is called **information hiding**. That means we seek to limit knowledge of particular information to the minimum locality that must have knowledge of it. For example, the only place where specific details of the physical record structure of a disk file record should be known is in the module that all other modules use to access the records on the disk. This allows us to stratify a system into levels of understanding by hiding unnecessary levels of detail. This kind of hierarchical view allows us to deal with large, complex systems in an intelligent way.

Another measure of complexity that software designers must be concerned with is the size of a module. In general, the larger a module, the harder it is to understand. As a practical matter, a module that is too large is difficult to read. This often leads to standards being set on the size of a module in terms of lines of code. Some organizations require limiting the amount of executable code per module to one screenful, or one page. These standards will vary from shop to shop and from language to language.

4.C.3. Code Size Estimation

One of the most widely used measurements of module size, and hence of general code size, is **lines of code (LOC)**. For any specific software system, an estimate needs to be made of time, machine and personnel resources, and other factors in creating the system. The cost of the project, and therefore a decision on feasibility and setting of deadlines, depends on the accuracy of these estimates. A major parameter in making these decisions is often an estimated total LOC.

However, there is little agreement on how to count lines of code. Many questions on methodology should immediately come to mind. Do you count executable lines of code only? Do you include comments? Do you count lines or statements? Do you count code written for another project and being reused? Is it worth the bother to count lines of code at all? The answer to any of these questions may be yes or no, depending on who you ask. Nonetheless, LOC is such a widely used parameter that that we will look at several factors to consider in its measurement.

First, the choice of language has a major effect on the number of lines of code. Assembly language programs typically have at least twice as many lines of code as their higher language counterparts. Job control language, on the other hand, typically is more compact in terms of lines of code.

There is no universal agreement on methodology, and lines of code for a given project can vary by a factor of 5 depending on how lines are counted. Therefore, some consistent means of counting must be established. At present, it doesn't matter too much what it is. Someone, somewhere, will agree with you and lots of other people will disagree. However, within a single group and if possible within a single classroom, there should be some specific criteria stated. Some of the questions that need to be answered are listed in Table 4.6.

```
Table 4.6  Factors to be Considered when Counting Lines of Code

Are you going to count:
     1. executable code only?
     2. data definitions?
     3. labels?
     4. comments?
     5. job control language?
     6. reused code from another module, macro, or library?
     7. lines or statements?
     8. temporary code (e.g., test drivers, stubs)?
     9. code that is suppressed in the delivered code,
        e.g., a trace system?
    10. tools and support programs?
```

Another important aspect to be considered when counting lines is the code that is going to be deleted. The additional code necessary for drivers and stubs for testing (described below) is critical to overall quality, but certainly won't show up in the end product. Also, an interactive execution trace system, such as the one described in Appendix B, is very useful in testing but may be suppressed in the delivered code. Yet no manager in his or her right mind would condone alternate methods of design that were less effective but produced more lines of code. Similarly, the use of text files for such things as menus and error messages enhances maintainability but reduces lines of code.

Most experienced programmers, given the algorithm for a module and a specified language, can do a good job of estimating lines of code, provided there is agreement on how to count. Since LOC is often used as a parameter of productivity, it is important to understand what is being defined and what it is being used for. One widely used industry standard is that the average programmer (whatever that is) should be able to produce 20 lines of code per day. This doesn't sound like much, especially if you have ever written several hundred lines of code in a sleepless, 30-hour fit of activity. However, the average level is presumed to refer to documented, tested, and debugged code, which, for the previously mentioned several hundred lines of code, could take weeks.

In summary, then, LOC is a useful parameter, but it must be clearly defined and then kept in proper perspective. It is absolutely necessary to document the counting rules employed whenever LOC is used as a measure of software size or productivity.

4.C.4. Hierarchy Charts

A **hierarchy chart** is a graphic method for describing a program's design. Hierarchy charts are used to indicate the software hierarchy of a system. They depict function and not procedure. Execution of the module represented by each box in a hierarchy chart can only be entered from the box (module) immediately above it and must return control to that box.

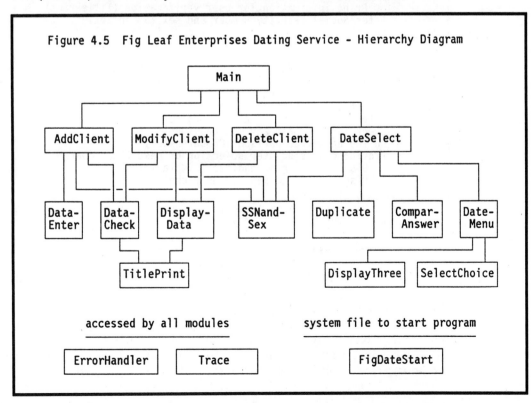

Figure 4.5 Fig Leaf Enterprises Dating Service - Hierarchy Diagram

Each box in the hierarchy chart corresponds to a module in the system. If a box appears more than once in a hierarchy chart it could be indicated, for example, by shading such boxes in the upper right hand corner. An example of a hierarchy chart is given in Figure 4.5 for a computer dating service.

Another method of representing the same hierarchy is shown in Figure 4.6. This method shows subordinate modules (modules called) clearly; it is harder to determine superordinate modules (modules called by). The level of each module is clearly indicated by the amount of indentation. There is space for more verbiage, with an indication of the module name that does not obscure its intended function.

```
Figure 4.6  Hierarchy for a Computer Dating Service

System file to start program: FigDateStart
Main Driver - Menu (Main)
    Add a client (AddClient)
        Enter information on the client (DataEnter)
        Check for correct data (DataCheck)
            Print information for user verification (TitlePrint)
        Enter Social Security number and sex (SSNandSex)
    Modify client data (ModifyClient)
        Check for correct data (DataCheck)
            Print information for user verification (TitlePrint)
        Enter Social Security number and sex (SSNandSex)
        Put the information on the screen (DisplayData)
            Print information for user verification (TitlePrint)
    Delete client (DeleteClient)
        Enter Social Security number and sex (SSNandSex)
        Put the information on the screen (DisplayData)
            Print information for user verification (TitlePrint)
    Select date (DateSelect)
        Enter Social Security number and sex (SSNandSex)
        Check for date already matched (Duplicate)
        Do the answer comparison (ComparAnswer)
        Provide choice of user selection or best three (DateMenu)
            Display top three choices (DisplayThree)
            Display all matches for user choice (SelectChoice)
Accessed by all modules:
    Execution trace system (Trace)
    Error handler (ErrorHandler)
```

The hierarchy chart in Figure 4.5 shows the level at which each module occurs. The connecting lines indicate which modules are subordinate to others and which modules are superordinate to others. This model shows the relationships more clearly but has less space for text information. Neither type of hierarchy diagram is inherently better than the other, since each emphasizes different things. Between the two methods, a reasonably clear picture of the system becomes available.

4.C.5. *Estimated Module Size and Interface Description*

Once a hierarchy chart of modules or some other high-level design of the system is available, the work can be partitioned among the team members. To effectively partition the work, much information is needed about each module. An estimate of module size, a list of module inputs and outputs, and a description of the interface with other modules is generally the minimum information needed.

The manner in which a module interfaces with the other modules of a system is of prime importance. To specify the interface we must specify three things:

1. Parameter list – This defines the number, types, and order of parameters passed to the module.

2. Input – This is an exact description of all inputs, whether from parameters, global variables, keyboard (user), or files. It must include a description of every input variable and a description of valid domains for each type of input. Languages that allow the user to define types help in this.

3. Output – This is an exact description of all outputs, whether to parameters, global variables, screen or other device, or to files. It must include a description of every output variable and a description of valid domains for each type of output.

All the data structures that the module operates on should be described together with valid domains. For example, files that the module operates on should be described.

All calls to other modules as well as the names of other modules that are called by the module must be mentioned. Any actions taken external to the system when this module is invoked should be mentioned. Some designers may want to include descriptions of the output generated when the input is invalid, although most would include it with the output description. Timing considerations should also be mentioned here.

It is also useful to have a systematic means of referring to the various modules, such as giving each one a number. This is also important later when modifications are being made and it is necessary to keep track of which is the most recent version of each module. This is called **configuration management** and is discussed further in Chapter 9.

An example of a list of modules with size estimates, input and output lists, interface descriptions, and programmer assignments is shown in Figure 4.7 for part of the computer dating service.

Figure 4.7   Example of Estimated Module Size and Interface Description

System Plan for Fig Leaf Enterprises Computer Dating Service
         Section 4: Module Descriptions; Inputs and Outputs

Global variable: Traceflag - array[1..17] of Boolean - index of array
                         corresponds to module number

Module Name: Main   Programmer: entire team
Module Number: 1   Estimated LOC: 45
Module Description: This operates the main menu, which will be in a text
file. From here, the user may ask to enter a new client, delete or modify
information on an existing client, or find a date match.
Module Inputs: Module Outputs:
   Menu - text file   ErrorNumber -integer
   Choice - character [1]   MenuList - array [1..8]
                                            of character [70]

Module Name: ErrorHandler   Programmer: Adams
Module Number: 2   Estimated LOC: 25
Module Description: This module accepts an error message number as a
parameter. It then reads a message from a text file, using the number to
determine the line of the text file to be read.
Module Inputs: Module Outputs:
   ErrorNumber - integer   ErrMessage - Character [80]
   ErrorMessages - text file

Module Name: Duplicate   Programmer: Brown
Module Number: 3   Estimated LOC: 60
Module Description: When a match is made for a Prospective date, this
module checks the Social Security number of the match to see whether this
pairing has already occurred. If it has, another match must be found. If
it has not, this module enters the Social Security number of the client
into the record of the match, in order to avoid repeating that pairing
later.
Module Inputs: Module Outputs:
   FigLeafData - file   ErrorNumber - integer
   SocSecNumMatch - character [9]   MatchFlag - Boolean
   SocSecNumClient - character [9]

Module Name: DisplayThree   Programmer: Corbin
Module Number: 4   Estimated LOC: 70
Module Description: This module takes the Social Security numbers of the
(up to) three best matches, and displays the name and phone number of each
of the prospective dates.
Module Inputs: Module Outputs:
   SocSecNum - character [9]   ErrorNumber -integer
   FigLeafData - file   Name - array [1..3] of character [30]
                                         PhoneNum - array [1..3] of
                                               character [10]

```
Module Name: SSNandSex              Programmer: Dallas
Module Number: 5                    Estimated LOC: 45
Module Description:  This module accesses the file that contains client
information.  For a new client, a record is created with the client's
Social Security number and sex. For an existing client, the name and sex
are retrieved from the file using the Social Security number as the key.
Module Inputs:                      Module Outputs:
    FigLeafData - file                  ErrorNumber - integer
    SocSecNum - character [9]            Name - character [30]
    Sex - character [1]                 Sex - character [1]
                                        CheckFlag - Boolean
```
```
Module Name: DateSelect             Programmer: Evans
Module Number: 6                    Estimated LOC: 65
Module Description:  This module functions as the supervisor for the
request for a match.  It accesses other modules in turn,  with the appropriate
record number from the file, which do the  actual comparisons,
selection, and checking for duplicates;  however, it must first verify
that the client is already in the system.
Module Inputs:                      Module Outputs:
    FigLeafData - file                  ErrorNumber - integer
    SocSecNum - character [9]            CheckFlag - Boolean
    Sex - character [1]                 FileNumber - integer
```

The programmer assignments may be extremely useful to know during various phases of development and maintenance. These assignments can be indicated graphically on hierarchy diagrams. The hierarchy diagram in Figure 4.5 is reproduced here as Figure 4.8 with programmer assignments indicated. An alternate method is color coding, if color reproduction is available.

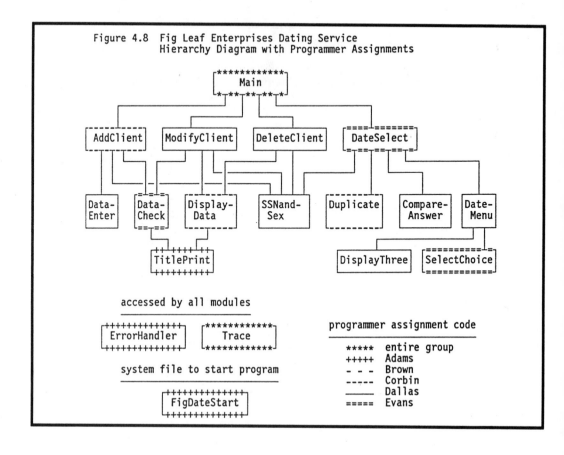

Figure 4.8 Fig Leaf Enterprises Dating Service
Hierarchy Diagram with Programmer Assignments

4.D. Identification of Critical Areas

Top-down design is a means of developing modules by successive refinement of a hierarchy chart. This permits the designers to focus on a single module at a time and to consider the connection between that module and its subordinates only. If the module under consideration does not perform a single function, its functions are divided among its subordinates. By using this approach, a large, complex programming task can be reduced to a set of subtasks, each of which is smaller and easier than the original task. We can proceed in this manner because each module is independent in function from its fellow modules.

Once the order for the completion of the many subtasks in a project has been chosen, we must consider the network of dependencies of these tasks. In any network of tasks for a software project, there must be some sequence of tasks in which each is dependent on its predecessor(s), determining the minimum time in which the project could be completed. Such a sequence, called a **critical path**, is described below.

4.D.1. Critical Path Management

Critical path analysis of a project is designed to tell us who must wait for what as the project is being developed and which activities must be completed on schedule to avoid delay. Of course we do not know in advance how long each activity will take. We usually have an estimated range of time for the activity, based on our knowledge of similar projects and events.

A number of project management tools deal with critical path scheduling techniques. One of these techniques, called the Critical Path Method (CPM), was developed at approximately the same time as PERT, described in the next section. All of these techniques have a number of things in common. They divide a project into tasks or activities. They then consider the questions listed in Table 4.7 for each of the tasks. We normally represent such information as either a directed graph or a precedence table.

Table 4.7 Questions Addressed by Project Scheduling Tools

- What other tasks must be completed before this task can be started? (What are the predecessor tasks?)
- How long will it take to perform the task once the predecessor tasks have been completed?
- If this task is late, what other tasks will be delayed?

4.D.2. PERT: An Example

PERT (Program Evaluation and Review Technique) is used for several things, but one of the most important is to evaluate whether specific deadlines can be met. A second use is determining which activities in a project are likely to be bottlenecks. These are the activities that will need extra effort to make sure they stay on schedule. A third use of PERT is to determine what the effect on the overall project will be if one part is changed. For example, one part of the project may take more time than was planned, or resources (such as machine time and/or programmer time) may be used for a different part of the project than originally expected.

The origins of PERT go back to 1958 and the Polaris Fleet Ballistic Missile program, a project that involved coordinating several thousand agencies and contractors. The PERT technique was developed and used for this project and was highly successful. One very important result was the completion of the project two years earlier than had been expected. Since then, PERT has been used by both industry and government agencies for the management of projects requiring the coordination of multiple interrelated activities. It is also well suited to the planning of large software projects. Let us look at an example.

4.D.2.a. Estimate of Minimum Time

Consider the example in Figure 4.9, which is a subset of the hierarchy diagram for the computer dating service. Let us first do an estimate of the minimum time in which this combination of modules is likely to be completed.

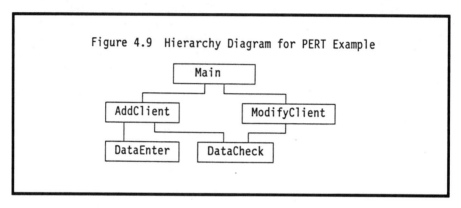

Figure 4.9 Hierarchy Diagram for PERT Example

We now enter these modules in a list with predecessor and successor tasks. This is based on the sequence in which the tasks are to be done. We also indicate an estimated **duration** for each task, shown in Table 4.8.

Table 4.8   Precedence Table

Task	Duration	Predecessors	Successors
A Main	3	none	B, C, D, E
B AddClient	5	A	D, E
C ModifyClient	7	A	E
D DataEnter	3	A, B	none
E DataCheck	2	A, B, C	none

For convenience, we will refer to the tasks by the letters A, B, C, D, or E, as shown in the task list in Table 4.8. The duration may be expressed in hours, days, weeks, or months, whichever unit is appropriate for a given project. For a course project, a reasonable unit might be days. Notice that in this example the tasks are listed in an order that is reasonable for them to be done.

Given a project begin time (Time 0), the **earliest begin (EB)** and **earliest finish (EF) times** can be computed for each task by the algorithm in Figure 4.10.

Figure 4.10 Algorithm to Compute Earliest Begin and
                Earliest Finish Times

1. If a task is not preceded by any other task, its earliest
   begin time is the project begin time.
2. The earliest finish time is the earliest begin time plus
   the duration.
3. The earliest begin time of a task that has predecessors is
   the largest of the earliest finish times of its
   predecessors.
4. The computed project finish time is the largest of the
   earliest finish times of those tasks that have no
   successor.

In our example, we begin at time zero. Earliest begin and earliest finish times are summarized in Table 4.9.

Table 4.9 Earliest Begin (EB) and Earliest Finish (EF) Times

Task	Duration	Predecessors	EB	EF
A Main	3	none	0	3
B AddClient	5	A	3	8
C ModifyClient	7	A	3	10
D DataEnter	3	A, B	8	11
E DataCheck	2	A, B, C	10	12

Since task A has no predecessors it has an earliest begin time of 0. The earliest finish time for A is 3. Tasks B and C have only A for a predecessor, so the earliest begin time for each is 3. Thus the earliest finish time for B must be 8 since its duration is 5, and for C it must be 10 since its duration is 7.

Now D has both A and B as predecessors, so its earliest begin time is 8, the larger finish time for those two. The earliest finish time for D must then be 11, that is, 8 plus the duration of D. Similarly, task E has A, B, and C as predecessors so its earliest begin time must be 10 and its earliest finish time must be 12.

Tasks D and E have no successor. The earliest finish time is 11 for D, and 12 for E. The largest of these is 12, the earliest finish time for E. This gives us an estimate of a minimum project finish time of 12. Of course, the accuracy of this estimate depends on the accuracy of the time estimates of the individual modules.

4.D.2.b. Estimate of Latest Begin Time

Let us look at another example based on the same hierarchy diagram. It might be specified that the project must be completed by a given time. We need to compute the very latest times that each task must be finished and begun so that we can tell whether the project will be finished by the required project finish time.

We compute the **latest finish (LF)** and **latest begin (LB)** times with the algorithm given in Figure 4.11.

```
Figure 4.11   Algorithm to Compute Latest Finish and
              Latest Begin Times

1. If a task is not succeeded by any other task, its latest
   finish time is the project finish time.
2. The latest begin time of a task is its latest finish time
   minus its duration.
3. The latest finish time for a task that has successors is
   the smallest latest begin time of all its successors.
```

Consider again our example, with information summarized in Table 4.10. Suppose we are given a required finish time of 15. We may use the above algorithm to compute the latest finish and latest begin times for each task.

```
Table 4.10   Latest Begin (LB) and Latest Finish (LF) Times.
             Required Finish Time:   15
```

Task	Duration	Successors	LF	LB
A Main	3	B, C, D, E	6	3
B AddClient	5	D, E	12	7
C Modify Client	7	E	13	6
D DataEnter	3	none	15	12
E DataCheck	2	none	15	13

We can see that D and E have no successors. The latest finish time for D and E must then be 15. It follows that the latest begin time is 12 for D and 13 for E.

Now C has E for a successor. This says that the latest finish time for C must be 13. B has D and E for successors, so its latest finish time must be 12, the smaller latest begin time of D and E. Its latest begin time is 7 (12 minus its estimated duration). Finally, A has B, C, D, and E for successors, so its latest finish time must be the smallest of the rest of the latest begin times, which is 6 for C. Then the latest begin time for A is 3.

This tells us that we can start no later than the third day if we expect to finish the project in the required 15 days. This example, it should be noted, does not necessarily correspond to the way real project schedules work.

4.D.2.c. Slack Time

With EB, EF, LB, and LF computed for each task, we may compute another quantity called **slack**. Slack indicates how much freedom we have between the earliest we can begin a task such that all of its predecessors are finished, and the latest we can begin it and still meet the required project finish time. The slack is LB minus EB for each task. This is indicated in Table 4.11 for our example, where the estimated minimum time is 12, and the deadline is 15.

```
Table 4.11   Slack Times

   Task              Duration   EB    EF     LF   LB   Slack

A Main                  3        0     3      6    3     3
B AddClient             5        3     8     12    7     4
C ModifyClient          7        3    10     13    6     3
D DataEnter             3        8    11     15   12     4
E DataCheck             2       10    12     15   13     3
```

Clearly, if the required project finish is earlier than the computed project finish there is a problem. The PERT chart can show where we can try to shorten the durations to make a new schedule that will meet the required project finish. To actually do this in a team project employing full-time people requires management skills that are beyond the scope of this book.

4.D.2.d. Critical Path

There will be at least one path from a task with no predecessor to a task with no successor such that every task along this path has a slack equal to the required project finish time minus the computed project finish time. This path is called the **critical path**. It is the longest path. That is the sequence of tasks that determines the length of the project.

This critical path has the smallest slack that occurs anywhere in the project. These are the tasks that must be controlled. The critical path for this example is shown in Figure 4.12.

Since the scheduled completion time is usually the same as the required deadline, most of the time this slack quantity will be zero. However, in our example, we are presuming that the project is scheduled to be completed three days before the deadline, giving us a minimum slack time of 3. The critical path is the one where the slack time is exactly 3 at every step.

```
        Figure 4.12  Critical Path

        Path       Slack
        A-B-D      3-4-4
        A-B-E      3-4-3
        A-C-E      3-3-3  ◄─── Critical Path
```

There is only one module with no predecessors, and that is A. There are two modules with no successors, D and E. Therefore, possible critical paths are A-B-D, A-B-E, and A-C-E. The slack times for each path are shown in Figure 4.12.

The difference between the estimated time (12) and the required finish time (15) in our example is 3. In only one path, A-C-E, are the slack times all equal to this difference. Therefore, this is the critical path, the one that must be watched most carefully as work progresses. Any increase in time for a module on this path will result in increased time for the entire project.

When we analyzed our hierarchy, we may have noted modules that are called by a number of other modules. Such a module may be a critical module. Other modules may be identified by anticipated difficulty in their algorithms. A critical module could cause us great problems. This must be considered in scheduling the order of module completion. If possible, such a module should be kept off the critical path.

A number of programs use PERT or other Critical Path Management techniques to aid in project management. They include shareware and public domain programs. There are also a number of tools for maintaining the system library and doing configuration management. Some of these are discussed in Chapters 9 and 11.

The method described above can be applied to a classroom project, to give an idea of some of the skills that will be required of project managers. However, note that the project in this example, and indeed any reasonable project for a software engineering course, is too small to appreciably benefit from PERT or any Critical Path Management. Nonetheless, major problems can arise if not enough time is allocated for a given task.

4.E. Development and Implementation Scheduling

We are now ready to organize the production and testing of the programs that make up the system. The actions planned for in this stage and carried out in the next are what most people associate with computer programming. Since most software projects are larger than can be reasonably done by one or two programmers, the success of a project may depend on how the work is organized.

Stages V and VI in our life cycle outline, **preliminary design and planning** and **software development**, are where the maximum number of people are likely to be involved in the project. A great deal of organizational skill is required during this time. The project manager has the responsibility of planning and scheduling the sequence of activities, coordinating the efforts of the members of a project team, and reorganizing if the plan is not adequate.

To successfully manage and control the development process various aspects of management, planning, and strategy must be considered. There is no one correct method. The most appropriate method may depend on such factors as the proportion of code available for reuse from prior projects, the experience of the team members, available tools, and other factors. We will present the following in the context of developing new software with a team with little prior experience. That, of course, is common in a course project.

4.E.1. Use of Drivers and Stubs

To be able to manage a project effectively there must be a testing program concurrent with design and implementation of the modules of the emerging system. In order to test modules individually or in small groups, generally special code must be produced to take the place of modules above or below the unit being tested in the hierarchy. These supplementary modules, referred to as the **driver** and **stubs**, are shown in Figure 4.13.

Figure 4.13 Unit Test

A hierarchy of software elements is shown for a test of a UNIT in isolation from the system. Higher elements of the system are replaced by the DRIVER while the lower elements of the system, which are called by the UNIT, are replaced by STUBS.

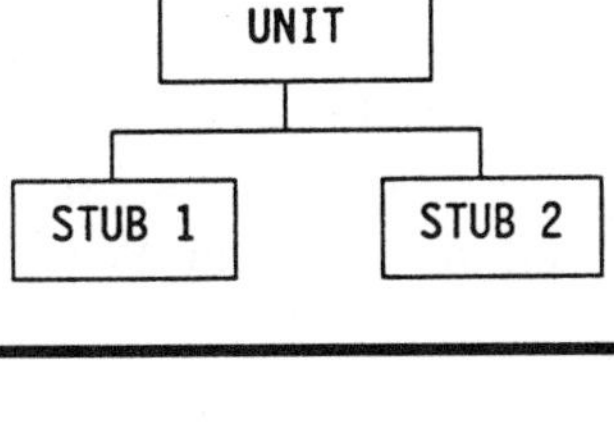

The driver executes calls to the unit under test and receives any results produced by execution of the unit. Depending on the design of the driver, the tests might be conducted in an interactive mode or as a batch process whose results might be captured in a file.

A stub replaces a particular lower level module called by the unit. The number of stubs needed depends on the system design; usually one stub is used for each module called directly by the unit. The data returned by a stub may be faked rather than computed, based on passed parameters. The essential feature is that the unit receives an appropriate response so that its execution may continue in the test. Stubs are frequently used to provide a means of testing a software module when the modules it must call are not yet available. Code examples of the use of drivers and stubs in testing are given in Chapter 8.

4.E.2. Development Strategies

The development strategy refers to the order in which modules of software in the hierarchy are designed and implemented. The ordering is **top-down** if you start with the top of the hierarchical pyramid and successively work down to the lower levels.

Conversely, a **bottom-up** approach starts with the lowest level elements of the hierarchy and systematically works toward the final completion of the highest module in the hierarchy. A strategy combining elements of both approaches is referred to as a **mixed** strategy. In any case a systematic stepwise strategy is required.

4.E.2.a. Top-down

In top-down development, modules are developed beginning at the top of the hierarchy diagram. Figure 4.14 gives a hierarchy diagram based on a subset of the computer dating service hierarchy diagram in Figure 4.8. Here we have replaced the module names with letters to simplify a discussion of the order of the module testing.

Top-down development means to start with the highest level module and add modules in the order of the calling hierarchy. This method has several advantages. One is that since the driver is created first, part of the system is always available as the driver for each added unit. This eliminates the need to write throwaway drivers. It also means that the driver and its accompanying stubs are available as the first step in a working prototype of the system (discussed in Chapter 6).

A top-down implementation will start with Module A, but where do we go from there? Going down the hierarchy can either be depth-first or breadth-first. In this example, depth-first development would take the modules in the following order:

A, B, J, F, L, C, G, D, E, H, I, K, M, N

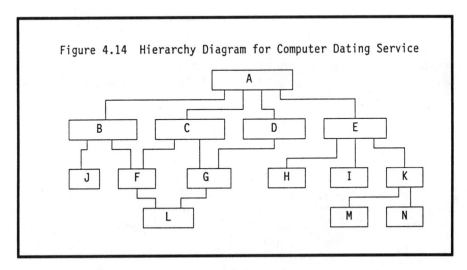

Figure 4.14 Hierarchy Diagram for Computer Dating Service

This technique has the advantage that a subtree of the hierarchy diagram will be completed before going on to the rest of the system. As a practical matter, this means that at least one feature of the system should be completely functional relatively early. This gives the software team something to demonstrate to the manager and, if necessary, to the user. It also means, in a classroom project, that at least one feature will be available to demonstrate. For that reason, we recommend this technique for course projects.

Although the top-down, depth-first technique is recommended for developing new projects, much of the time existing software is being modified. Therefore, we need to address other techniques. Top-down, breadth-first development in the example in Figure 4.14 would be done in the following order:

First level: A
Second level: B, C, D, E
Third level: J, F, G, H, I, K
Fourth level: L, M, N

In top-down development, the system driver is usually written first with stubs for modules that are not yet available. As modules become available, they are integrated into the system with further stubs created as necessary. Drivers need to be written for testing individual modules, but as the system is integrated, the existing system provides the driver for the additional modules.

4.E.2.b. Bottom-up

Bottom-up development, like top-down, may be done either depth-first or breadth-first. In bottom-up development, new drivers must be written as the system is integrated, but stubs are not needed.

Sometimes it is preferable to design using a bottom-up approach, beginning with the lowest levels of the design rather than the highest. This is often the case when we are attempting to reuse low-level code from a previous project or when our system was designed by a composition technique such as data abstraction rather than functional decomposition. The beauty of this method is that many high-level modules can share the same utility.

The danger of this method is that a high-level module may depend heavily on low-level algorithms or structure. The problem here is that there may be nothing that can be reasonably demonstrated until all the higher level modules are completed. That makes it difficult to produce believable progress reports for higher level managers. It also can be disastrous in a classroom project if the design doesn't work and the team doesn't realize this until the last week of the term.

4.E.3. Implementation

We now concern ourselves with implementing the system we have designed. No matter which design philosophy we follow we have the problem of putting together many modules into a working system. If we are following a bottom-up approach this may involve throwing many modules together that have never interacted as a system before. If we are following a top-down approach it involves replacing stubs with actual modules.

Testing, an integral part of the development process, is discussed in more detail in Chapter 8, and planning for testing is discussed in Chapter 5. We will refer briefly here to some of the aspects of testing, since it needs to be scheduled.

Let us consider a typical development situation. A module is completed and unit tested (as a single module). After all bugs have been corrected at this level it is entered in the program library. The programs in the program library are used to build an integrated system during integration testing.

The system's overall development plan has a lot to do with the timing of individual program development activities. If the top-down development approach is being used, the objective is to gradually build the complete system from top to bottom, testing each level as represented in the hierarchical structure chart. The details of test planning are described in Chapter 5, but it is important now to consider the allocation of time in the project schedule.

4.E.4. Scheduling

Two very important questions that customers will want answered are:

"How long will it take to develop the system?" and

"How much will the system cost?"

Answering these questions with any kind of accuracy requires a well thought out project schedule. A project schedule describes the software development cycle for a particular project. It breaks each project stage into a set of different tasks to be done. It also portrays the interactions among the tasks and estimates the time that each task or activity will take.

To manage development there must be scheduling to coordinate the efforts of team members and to monitor the progress of a project. The schedule is a reflection of management decisions as to how long the project will take and how resources are to be allocated over the time period. Building an actual schedule requires identifying a set of task dependencies, estimating task durations, and allocating resources. The dependencies arise from the development strategy chosen and the modular hierarchy design. The estimation of task durations depends on available resources.

4.E.4.a. Scheduling Methods

In order to set up an effective schedule, it is important to know the sequence in which things will be done and approximately how long each item will take. PERT charts are very useful in helping to prepare schedules.

One scheduling method, called a Gantt chart, shows things that are supposed to happen in a time sequence. An example is the Gantt chart in Figure 4.15 that shows a possible schedule for a top-down, depth-first development.

Another format for this schedule is given in Figure 4.16. This format tracks the work of individuals on the team, though it does not give the overall team progress picture as graphically as a Gantt chart. However, the format and the schedule are suitable for use by a small team on a small or prototype system, such as one that may be done as a course project.

4.E.4.b. Schedules as Tools to Monitor Progress

A schedule is divided into stages. Each stage is composed of steps, and each step is further subdivided if necessary. Some steps may be performed in parallel. Some steps must not be performed until other steps have been performed. Once a schedule has been completed we may use it to monitor the actual progress of the project. Monitoring the completion of tasks on the schedule is a means to evaluate the adequacy of the overall plan and the assumptions made about the costs of the project.

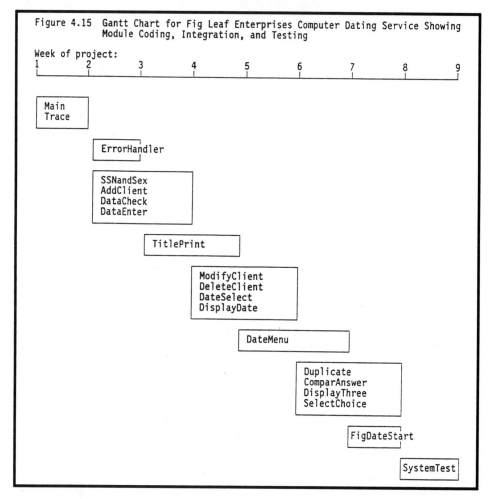

Figure 4.15   Gantt Chart for Fig Leaf Enterprises Computer Dating Service Showing Module Coding, Integration, and Testing

The schedule, if properly done, will enable someone to see the consequences if a particular step is being completed behind schedule. The effects could range from none at all if the step was not a prerequisite to any other step, to a major delay if the step was part of a critical path. Depending on the interpretation of such consequences it may be necessary to re-shedule and reallocate resources in the remainder of the project.

4.E.4.c. Milestones in Development

If we are to use schedules effectively for monitoring progress we must decide on certain milestones. A milestone is a clearly defined event in the schedule. Normally it is the completion of something that is deliverable.

```
Figure 4.16  Schedule for Development of Fig Leaf Enterprises
             Computer Dating Service.   Note that integration
             is done in a top-down, depth-first manner.
```

Programmers

	Adams	Brown	Corbin	Dallas	Evans
Week 1	Entire group - code, test, integrate, test driver and execution trace system				
Week 2	code,test int Error Handler	code, test, integrate AddClient	code, test, integrate DataEnter	code, test, integrate SSNandSex	code, test, integrate DataCheck
Week 3	code, test, Title Print				
Week 4		code, test, integrate Display Data	code, test, integrate Modify Client	code, test, integrate Delete Client	code, test, integrate DateSelect
Week 5	code, test, DateMenu				
Week 6		code, test, integrate Duplicate	code, test, integrate Display Three	code, test, integrate Compar Answer	code, test, integrate Select Choice
Week 7	code,test FigDate Start				
Week 8	Final integration and system test - entire team				

Milestones are particular points in time. An example of a milestone might be the delivery of a user's manual. Note the difference between the activity of developing the user's manual, which takes place over a period of time, and the milestone of the delivery of the user's manual, which is a particular point in time.

As another example, debugging may be perceived to be 95% done for more than half of the unit testing period, but this does not directly involve something deliverable. In contrast, delivery of a module that executes according to specification with expected results on all prespecified test data sets is a clear milestone.

4.F. Course Project: System Plan

The System Plan should include a narrative description; a hierarchy diagram of the system; a list of modules with module name and number, description, estimated lines of code, and interface description; a schedule for coding and testing; and a description of special resources needed, if any.

The narrative description in the System Plan should be a brief description of what the system is to do and the software and hardware that will be needed to run it. The System Plan should not reproduce the Software Requirements Specification; it should complement it. It is highly advisable to refer to parts of the Software Requirements Specification by section number in cross-references.

In the hierarchy diagram and schedule for the computer dating service, you may have noticed that an execution tracing system and an error handler were incorporated. Both of these are described in Chapter 6, and a sample trace system is given in Appendix B. The trace system is helpful in testing and debugging and the error handler is set up to use text files, which make maintenance much easier. Both are easier to incorporate in the planning stage than after development begins.

4.G. Beyond a Course Project: Plan for Future Reference

When writing the narrative description in the System Plan, do not assume that the reader will know what computer, operating system, and compiler are to be used. You may be inclined to assume that your instructor will know the intended hardware and support software and how to use it. This is usually true for a course project, but creating a document based on this assumption is a bad habit.

Consider that on the job the System Plan will usually be read by someone who needs to know which of several choices of hardware is to be used, quite possibly some of which is yet to be purchased. Furthermore, this System Plan may be read in later years for maintenance purposes, when the hardware you are now using has a new operating system. It is appropriate for you to get in the habit of recording all relevant information.

Remember, each aspect of a software system may be done by a separate team. You need to write your System Plan so that the information is sufficient for another team to develop the software system.

Summary

Once the problem has been defined in the Software Requirements Specification, we must find an appropriate solution. Software design involves defining the architecture, components, modules, interfaces, test approach, and data for the software system that will satisfy the requirements that have been specified.

Object oriented design is useful in the preliminary design of a system, especially when using object oriented languages such as Ada and Modula-2. Object oriented design is closely related to data flow diagrams and may be used in conjunction with them.

Top-down refinement of a system consists of splitting a system into appropriate subsystems until each subsystem represents a single module. Modularity is used to manage program complexity. Information hiding and measures of module complexity are addressed in detail in Chapter 7.

One common measure of module size is lines of code (LOC), although there is little agreement on how lines of code should be counted. However, once a set of criteria for counting is established, LOC may be used to estimate time, resources, cost, and deadlines for developing a software system.

Preliminary software design and planning are crucial to delivering a software project on time. The relationship of modules to each other may be shown in a hierarchy chart of modules. Each module needs to be described in detail, including inputs, outputs, interface description, and estimated size. This is used as the basis for programmer assignments. Each module must then be written, tested, and integrated into the system.

There are a number of development strategies that can be used, depending on various factors such as whether the project is to develop new code or modify existing code. For most class projects, top-down, depth-first development is recommended.

Scheduling is vital to software development and must be realistic. To a great extent, this is a management issue and as such is beyond the scope of this book. However, scheduling for a class project is not too complicated. Critical path management and identification of critical modules can be helpful in determining deadlines.

Keywords

attributes
bottom-up development
breadth-first development
configuration management
critical path
Critical Path Management (CPM)
depth-first development
drivers and stubs
earliest begin (EB) time
earliest finish (EF) time

hierarchy chart
information hiding
interface
latest begin (LB) time
latest finish (LF) time
lines of code (LOC)
module complexity
object
object oriented design
operations
PERT (Program Evaluation and Review Technique)
preliminary software design
process
project schedule
slack
top-down development
visibility

Review Questions

4.1. What is object oriented design? What is an object?

4.2. What is the relationship between data flow diagrams and object oriented design?

4.3. Name the steps in object oriented design.

4.4. Should the size of a module be limited? If so, why?

4.5. What factors need to be considered when counting lines of code?

4.6. What is an industry standard for an average programmer in lines of code?

4.7. What needs to be included in a complete description of a module (one that has not yet been written)?

4.8. What things must be specified for a module interface?

4.9. Why is it important to have a means of referencing individual modules in detailed design?

4.10. What can happen during development when some modules are modified, especially if this happens several times?

4.11. What is configuration management and why is it important in software development?

4.12. What is a critical path?

4.13. How do you compute the EB for a task? LB? EF? LF?

4.14. What is a predecessor task? A successor task?

4.15. What are drivers and stubs and where are they used?

4.16. What is the difference between top-down and bottom-up development?

4.17. What is an advantage of top-down, depth-first development?

4.18. When is it appropriate to use bottom-up development?

Exercises

4.1. Using object oriented design, define a procedure to establish and manage a queue of integer values.

4.2. Using object oriented design, define an electronic mail system.

4.3. Using object oriented design, define a procedure to establish and manage an automatic bank teller.

4.4. Use object oriented design to create a hierarchy diagram for the checking account system in exercises 3.1 and 3.2.

4.5. Use object oriented design to define a system for the fast-food restaurant in Exercises 3.3 and 3.4.

4.6. Produce by object oriented design a high-level representation of modules required to implement a small utility program. The program will dump the data in any file at 16 bytes per output line as hexadecimal and ASCII code representation. Each line is to begin with a **location**, which is the byte count from the beginning of the file for the first of the 16 bytes on the line. An example is shown below (report headings are not required):

LOCATION	16 HEX BYTE VALUES	16 ASCII CHARACTERS
0020	41 42 43 44 . 4F 50	ABCD ... OP

4.7. For the computer dating service, devise an algorithm to determine exact matching of a client and prospective dates.

4.8. For the computer dating service, devise an algorithm that will weight criteria so that a "closest match" can be found.

4.9. For the computer dating service, if the response categories are "a xor b xor c xor d," what should be the algorithm to find the closest possible match? What problems occur?

4.10. Use the information in Figure 4.9 and the information in Table 4.8 to associate the letters A - E with the modules in Figure 4.9. Also use the information for task durations from Table 4.8. Construct an implementation schedule to develop and integrate the modules   in this order: D, E, B, C, A.

(a) Characterize the type of implementation strategy this represents.

(b) Identify a critical path.

(c) In that schedule, when do the developers have confirmation that any specific high-level feature is functional?

4.11. What happens when a project cannot be completed on schedule?

References

Aron, Joel D. The Program Development Process, Part 1. Reading, MA: Addison-Wesley, 1974.

> The first volume discusses the individual programmer and includes a discussion of estimating programmer effort.

Aron, Joel D. The Program Development Process, Part 2. Addison-Wesley, 1983.

> The second volume concentrates on programming teams and various aspects of life cycle stages.

Booch, Grady. Software Components with Ada: Structures, Tools, and Subsystems. Menlo Park, CA: Benjamin/Cummings, 1987.

> Includes description of object oriented design and the relationship between data flow diagrams and object oriented design.

Booch, Grady, Software Engineering with Ada, 2d ed. Menlo Park, CA: Benjamin/Cummings, 1986.

> Good descriptions of software engineering principles and object oriented design as applied with Ada.

Bronikowski, Raymond J. Managing the Engineering Design Function. New York: Van Nostrand-Reinhold, 1986.

> Presents management aspects starting with product orientation. Includes engineering management and project control.

Brooks, Frederick P., Jr. "The Mythical Man-Month." Datamation (December 1974): 44-52.

> A widely reprinted excerpt from the book of the same title.

Brooks, Frederick P., Jr. The Mythical Man-Month, Essays on Software Engineering. Reading, MA: Addison-Wesley, 1975, reprinted 1982.

> Considered a classic of software engineering. Brooks presents the results of his experience as the project manager for the IBM OS 360. A clear exposition of the non-linearity of manpower and project duration effects on software project management.

DeMarco, Tom. Controlling Software Projects. New York: Yourdon Press, 1982.

> Emphasis on use of metrics with system models to provide a basis for cost estimation, planning, and control.

Hillier, Frederick S., and Lieberman, Gerald J. <u>Introduction to Operations Research</u>. San Francisco: Holden-Day, 1967.

> Chapter 7 includes a description of the origins and some early applications of PERT and CPM methods.

Jones, Capers. <u>Programming Productivity</u>. New York: McGraw-Hill, 1986.

> Thoroughly reviews multiple ways to count lines of code and the common failure to publish the rules used to generate published numbers of lines of code.

King, David. <u>Current Practices in Software Development, A Guide to Successful Systems</u>. New York: Yourdon Press, 1984.

> A survey of methods and practices used by data processing professionals. Data flow diagraming is in common use by analysts; Jackson design methods are most frequently used to design business software.

Parnas, David L. "On the Criteria To Be Used in Decomposing Systems into Modules." <u>CACM</u> 4, 12 (Dec. 1972): 1053-1058.

> Classic paper on modularity.

Putnam, Laurence H. <u>Software Cost Estimation and Life-Cycle Control</u>. Computer Society Press, 1980.

> A tutorial on the statistical models of project cost. Includes a bibliography and a collection of 17 reprinted papers. An excellent introduction to cost estimation models for large projects.

Reifer, Donald J., ed. <u>Tutorial on Software Management</u>, 3d ed. Washington, DC: Computer Society Press, 1986.

> This collection of 60 reprinted papers is divided into sections on planning, organizing, staffing, directing, productivity, and case studies.

Rosenaw, M. D., Jr., and Lewin, M. D. <u>Managing Software Projects</u>. Belmont, CA: Wadsworth, 1984.

> A readable introduction to software management. Good examples of critical path management technique are presented in Chapter 7, "Planning the Schedule".

CHAPTER 5

PLANNING FOR
SOFTWARE TESTING

In the Paleolithic Era of computer programming, when programs were small and rarely the product of more than a single mind, programmers discovered that they could not declare their programs to be complete until they had spent a fair amount of time removing the same bugs they had earlier implanted. . . .

The Neolithic Era of programming arrived during the early 1960s, with teams of programmers working on problems of greater scope and complexity. There were now tools to help cope with the new and greater problems: compilers, execution traces, and simple operating systems. However, programming continued to remain tantamount to debugging. . . The principal difference was that programmers could point accusing fingers at each other rather than have to accept the sole guilt of failure to reason correctly. . . .

Enter software engineering, with tools, techniques, and a disciplined approach to programming, and the modern era was established. Just in time, too, since the problems laid on today's programmers are a thousand-fold more sizable than the early ones, with the result that the ratio of bugs to problem size is no worse than it had been. However, the bugs that are resident in new code are often so concealed within the involutions of the program structure that up to half of all programmer labor-hours are expended in their removal.

  - Robert Dunn, <u>Software Defect Removal</u>

In examining conventionally scheduled projects, I have found that few allowed one-half of the projected schedule for testing, but that most did indeed spend half of the actual schedule for that purpose. Many of these were on schedule until and except in system testing.

  - Frederick P. Brooks, Jr., <u>The Mythical Man-Month</u>

Software Life Cycle

Software development: Test planning

I. Software need
II. Preliminary feasibility judgment
III. Requirements analysis and feasibility study
IV. Requirements specification
V. Preliminary software design and planning
VI. Software development
  Detailed design
  Coding and unit testing
  Integration
  System testing
VII. Software maintenance

Project: Plan testing and produce a test specification document

5.A. Introduction

Why, you may ask, is it necessary to plan for testing before the code is even written? Doesn't testing come after coding? Yes, but you must know what the code is supposed to do before you write it. Consider test planning as part of the specification of the code. Keeping in mind the tests that the code must pass will help you in the actual coding process.

You may have the idea that writing code is a creative endeavor. If so, now is the time to change that idea. From the standpoint of software engineering, the actual writing of code ideally should be done by drones. Since everything depends on everything else, especially in large projects, "creativity" in coding can actually be harmful. Code should be written to stated specifications.

Therefore, one of the documents that needs to be written before beginning software implementation is a test specification document. The purposes of a test specification document are to define a set of tests that will be adequate to verify that the system and its components perform according to the design specification, identify the test data to be used, and provide a schedule of tests and test reports to be produced. These purposes are summarized in Table 5.1.

Table 5.1 Purposes of Test Specification Documentation

- Identify the tests that will be carried out and the tasks required to complete the specific tests.
- Identify test cases, procedures and features to be covered, and pass/fail criteria.
- Document actual input values and expected outputs.
- Indicate the schedule of testing events and test reports that will be delivered.

5.B. Purpose of Testing

The primary purpose of testing is to uncover errors in the software and help ensure that the software does what it is supposed to do. However, testing and test design can also help in error prevention. Well designed tests can be a major factor in preventing errors. Programmers who keep in mind the testing criteria may be more likely to write code to meet the testing standards. This is beneficial to everyone, since an error that is prevented costs a lot less than one that must be detected and fixed.

It would be nice to think that a carefully tested software system is error free. Unfortunately, that is unrealistic. We have no absolute way to assure that a piece of software is bug free. As Edsgar Dijkstra has observed, "Testing can demonstrate the presence of errors, but not their absence." In most software systems, there are just too many possible ways that the system can be executed to test them all, as we shall see.

On the other hand, one should not be disturbed when a test uncovers an error. While test design should assist in error prevention, the goal of testing is error detection. When an error is found, the test has succeeded; it is the software that has failed and needs to be fixed.

5.B.1. Testing vs. Debugging

Although testing and debugging are closely related, they are actually separate and distinct activities. Testing is the process of detecting errors; debugging is the process of fixing them. Not all errors are necessarily going to be fixed.

Whether or not to expend the resources to fix an error is a management decision, which will depend on the nature and severity of the error, the number of other errors that have been found, the resources available, and the pressure to meet schedules and budgets. For example, an error that results in a minor deviation from the required output format may not be worth the time and effort to fix.

5.B.2. Types of Errors

When creating a test specification document it may help to keep in mind the types of errors that are likely to occur. There is no universally agreed-on method for categorizing errors, but one that will at least serve as a starting point is summarized in Table 5.2.

First we consider functional errors. Function-related errors are those caused by inadequacies in the requirements specification, design specification or testing. Specification of software requirements was addressed in earlier chapters. Testing may well find inadequacies in the design. Testing is itself prone to errors and should not be overlooked as a source of problems.

System errors include factors that are likely to be a problem when the system is transferred from the development machine to the target machine. Any aspect of the target machine that is not understood can cause problems, ranging from something as simple as an incorrect paging command to something as serious as insufficient memory. Other system errors involve internal interfaces. (This is discussed in more detail in Chapter 6.)

Process errors include errors in arithmetic, manipulation, initialization, control, sequence, and logic. They may be caused by mismatched types, erroneous type conversion, improper or no initialization, unreachable code, incorrect branching, missing steps, improper nesting, finding that a don't-care case does matter, or that an impossible case is possible.

Data errors include errors in specification, type, number, and initialization of values. No matter whether the data is used as a parameter or a control value (flag), errors can occur and must be considered. Data specification includes the data contents, structure, and attributes. The content is the actual bit string pattern; structure refers to its memory location and size (number of bits, whether on a word boundary, etc.); and attribute means the way it is interpreted (Boolean, floating point, integer, character, etc.).

```
Table 5.2   Summary of Categories of Errors

Function-Related Errors
   Specification - incomplete, ambiguous, or wrong
   Testing - tests are incorrect or inadequate
   Function - function is missing, wrong, superfluous
System Errors
   External interfaces - hardware, user
   Internal interfaces - I/O errors, parameter errors, wrong
      call sequence
   Hardware interface - address-generation error, I/O device
      not understood
   Operating system - O/S not understood, O/S error
   Software architecture - local setting of global parameters,
      global setting of local parameters, assumption that
      there will be no interrupts
Process Errors
   Arithmetic and manipulative - incorrect type conversion,
      improper comparison between types, ignoring overflow
   Initialization - failure to initialize; superfluous
      initialization of workspace, registers, data areas;
      loop control parameters; initialize to wrong format,
      data representation, or type
   Control and sequence - improper nesting, paths left out,
      bad loop-termination criteria, duplicated processing
   Static logic - improper layout of cases, improper negation
      of Boolean, improper simplification and combination
Data Errors
   General - declarations
   Dynamic data - bad initialization of shared structures
   Static data - bit-pattern anomalies, data not validated
   Information, parameter, and control - need validity check
   Contents, structure, and attribute - type errors
Code Errors
   Syntax - usually found by translator program
   Typographical - wrong variable, wrong logic
   Misunderstanding of Purpose - code written does not solve
      problem specification
Regression Errors - caused by fixing another error

Based on Boris Beizer, "A Taxonomy for Bugs," Software System
Testing and Quality Assurance. New York: Van Nostrand-Reinhold,
1984.
```

Code errors include practically anything that is in the code that isn't supposed to be there, often as a result of a typographical error. Syntax errors are usually detected by a compiler and you probably consider them merely a nuisance. However, there is one thing you should keep in mind about syntax errors, and that is that they may be an indicator of things to come. A very large number of syntax errors can indicate carelessness in programming and should be a red flag for logic errors. It is not uncommon that fixing a syntax error results in introducing an error of another type.

One study has shown a direct correlation between the number of compilations during creation of the code (for any reason) and the number of errors found in testing.

A regression error is one that is introduced in the process of fixing another error. Unfortunately, statistics show that the probability of this happening is about 50%. This is why regression testing, discussed below, is extremely important.

Considering ways in which the software could be in error can aid in devising tests to detect such errors. Chapter 8 discusses more aspects of carrying out and documenting the tests and the errors found.

5.B.3. Independent Test Teams

Ideally, the person testing software should not be someone who was involved in either writing the specifications or developing the software. One of the major problems in software systems is correctly specifying the requirements. This means not only making sure what the users want, but also writing it in such a way that it is clear and unambiguous to an outsider. Having an independent test team tests the requirements specification along with the software. Tests designed and executed by an independent test team are more likely to detect a failure to implement a specification.

Another source of errors is code designed by someone who does not understand the design specification. The code may do what the programmer wants, but not what was intended by the designer. This is one more reason why the code should be tested by someone other than the programmer.

The same argument holds for other types of errors. It is difficult for any of us to overcome the biases and blind spots relating to software we have written. An unbiased viewpoint produces more effective testing.

Philosophically, most people view writing code as a creative activity and testing as a destructive activity. It is hard to be destructive about one's own code. Thus there is an inherent conflict of interest in testing your own code. Having a test team that is separate from the programming team increases the motivation on both sides. The programmers are more likely to work hard to create a software system that will survive the most severe test, and the testers are likely to dream up every trick imaginable to bring the system down. The result of both activities will benefit the user, as the resulting system is much more likely to withstand abuse from the most incompetent (or devious) user.

5.C. Stages of Testing

Testing, like other parts of the life cycle, is not a linear process. As indicated in Figure 1.2, test results may require going back to any earlier stage of software development, up to and including revision of the requirements specification. This, in turn, may require revising the test plan.

The topics in this section are only an introduction to a very complex, time-consuming activity, which can take anywhere from 50% to 80% of software development effort. In the words of Boris Beizer(1984):

> *A dispassionate observer, a hypothetical person from Mars, might view programming as an activity dominated by testing with occasional lapses into design and documentation.*

We will look at several major types of testing: unit test, integration test, regression test, system test, and acceptance test. Please keep in mind, however, that several of these may be going on simultaneously in a particular project.

5.C.1. Use of Drivers and Stubs

In order to conduct a test on a subset of the system, it is generally necessary to have special pieces of code to run that test. That code consists of the test driver and stubs, as indicated in Figure 5.1. Creation of such drivers and stubs allows developers to plan and carry out tests on individual modules independent of the state of development of other parts of the system. When planning for testing we must identify the requirements for the test driver and stubs for each test scheduled.

Basically, test drivers consist of code that is written to substitute for a calling module. This driver may do nothing more than call the module being tested, pass appropriate parameters, and capture or display the results. Stubs are the converse; they represent modules that are called by the code being tested, and may do no more than execute a return. In essence a stub should be the minimum amount of code to permit the calling unit to continue execution.

Several examples of the use of drivers and stubs are given in Chapter 8. In addition, you may want to look at the Pascal example given in Figure 6.1. That example shows a main procedure that uses stubs for features not yet implemented. Although test specifications are to be written before actual coding is done, we feel that an actual code example may be beneficial to understanding the concept of drivers and stubs, which is important to writing good test specifications.

```
Figure 5.1  Hierarchy Diagrams for a System and a Unit Test
            of One of Its Modules, Module B.

In order to test module B in isolation, module A of the
system must be represented by a driver and modules D and
E may be replaced by stubs.
```

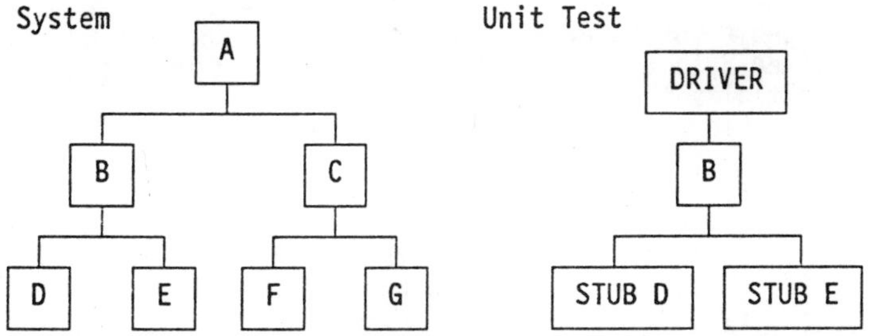

Figure 5.1 Hierarchy Diagrams for a System and a Unit Test of One of Its Modules, Module B.

5.C.2. Unit Test

A unit is a single, identifiable component of a software system, often a single module. Each module should be individually tested. If the unit under test is called by another procedure, the unit test will require a driver. If the unit calls other procedures, a stub will be needed for each such procedure.

Unit testing consists of verifying the execution of a unit by checking the interfaces, data structures, boundary conditions, and execution paths, described below. Table 5.3 summarizes the major areas to check.

Interface checks include parameters, global variables, and files. Parameter lists should be checked to see that the number and types are consistent. Global variables that are used should be noted, especially if they are altered in the module. Tests of file usage include opening and closing files, checking buffer size, checking adherence to file format specification, and checking any end-of-file conditions.

Data structure verification should check data types, initialization, and whether data structures have been accessed properly. This may well require a combination of source code review and examination of internal data during execution to see whether correct variables were used. In some languages, for example, only the first six characters of a variable name are significant. Such a language would not distinguish between VARIABLE1 and VARIABLE2. A specific check must be made to determine if data structures are properly initialized. Spelling checks on variables should include any truncation of variable name use.

```
Table 5.3  Checklist for Unit Testing

Interfaces
     parameters - match in number and type?
     global variables - used?  altered?
     file use - opened? closed? buffer size? EOF?
Data Structures
     types - consistent?
     mixed data types - conversion correct? truncation?
     initialization - in this module? elsewhere?
     variable usage - name correct? truncated?
Boundary Conditions
     conditions - correctly stated?
     arrays - first and last values checked?
     loops - control variable altered?  first, last values?
          is termination guaranteed?
Execution Paths
     path segment coverage
     locating 'dead' (unreachable) code
     exercising all possible exits
```

Data type conversions can introduce subtle problems. If your programming experience is dominated by Pascal, Modula-2, or Ada you probably will need to be very careful in working with languages that do not have strong data typing. Check particularly any time statements are evaluated using mixed data types. Default type conversion conventions are frequently the cause of problems. Consider the possible effects of roundoff or truncation in evaluating conditional expressions. If truncation has occurred by integer division, make sure the result is in accordance with program specifications.

If an improper initialization has occurred, its location must be found in the source code. Checking proper access to data structures may require special techniques for examination of data at run-time. This may mean using a source level debugging tool to permit setting breakpoints. (A breakpoint is a location in the object code that, when reached, results in an execution halt so that data may be examined before resuming execution.) If such a tool is not available, special code must be added to capture the needed data while tracing execution, such as the one described in Section G below and in Appendix B.

Boundary conditions cause a lot of subtle problems. A boundary condition is a state that occurs at the edge of a class of data values. A condition evaluation that works most of the time may fail at the boundary of the condition. For example, consider the condition:

$$if (x < y)$$

The boundary of this condition occurs in the neighborhood where x is approximately equal to y. An error here could be caused by roundoff or truncation, which is machine specific. Another possible boundary error would occur if the condition were supposed to be :

$$\text{if } (x <= y)$$

Then the condition will work fine except at the boundary; that is, the problem occurs when $x = y$.

It is important to execute boundary tests to catch problems like this. Other types of boundaries to check include array subscript ranges, loop limits, and control variables. Check first and last index values. This can be important, for example, if you are used to programming in a language in which index values start at 0 and you are now using a language in which index values start at 1. Loop limits need to be checked carefully. Not only should first and last values be checked, but look to see if the control variable is altered anywhere.

Execution paths are checked in a unit test of an individual module. This is **structural testing**, described in Section 5.D. Although it is not normally possible to check *all* combinations of paths, *each* execution path segment must be checked at least once. You don't want a program that has code you can't get to, as in the example in Figure 5.2. (Most unreachable code is not quite this obvious.) If such code exists, either it is unnecessary, in which case it should be deleted; or the module logic is in error and should be changed so that the path segment can be used. Consider also that the design of the set of test cases is in error and additional test case data may be needed to fully test the unit.

```
Figure 5.2   Pseudocode Example of Unreachable Code

         while x > 0 then
                   .
                   .
               if x = 0 then [action]
                   .
                   .
         end while
```

5.C.3. Integration Test

After each unit is tested, the units must be integrated into a coherent system. Integration consists of taking component parts of a system and linking them into larger, self-consistent elements. This should be done in a stepwise manner one unit at a time, testing after each linkage step. The process continues until we get a complete software system.

You might think that if each component is carefully tested, we should be able to wait until all the units are done and then link them all together into a working entity with no problems. For any system of significant size (more than a few units) it probably won't work. Integration testing is basically a test of the interfaces of the system components, which may or may not work together, even though they work individually. The point of stepwise integration is to systematically validate one unit interface at a time.

This is another aspect of the idea of modularity, based on the concept of "divide and conquer." It is not too difficult to eradicate one error at a time. However, it is extremely difficult to locate and fix a large number of simultaneous errors because the symptoms can become uninterpretable.

Integration testing does assume that each individual component has been tested and found to be working. We now need to demonstrate consistency and compatibility between the individual components of the system. The purposes of integration testing are summarized in Table 5.4.

Table 5.4 Purposes of Integration Testing

- Verify the architecture of the system.
- Verify that the interfaces and data structures are used correctly.
- Verify the overall system logic for normal execution and termination.
- Verify performance and functions against specification.

A major question to be addressed is that of the order in which the components are to be integrated. The two extremes in integration strategy are top-down and bottom-up. Each method has its proponents and critics. There are advantages and disadvantages to each. We feel that the advantages of the top-down technique make it more suitable for students who have never integrated a software system before.

The major advantage of top-down, depth-first testing is that as the code is integrated, an entire subtree will be completed before going on to the next phase of testing. This makes sure a minimal kernel of the system is actually working at a relatively early stage. Presuming that the module hierarchy represents a reasonable functional decomposition of the system, it also means completing features of the system one at a time.

Completing features not only improves programming team morale, it means that features are available to demonstrate to the user at an earlier time than if everything had to be done at once, at the end. This can be especially important in an introductory course where planning and scheduling are done by people with no previous experience. If there are serious problems in meeting the schedule, at least there will be something to demonstrate at the end of the term.

Bottom-up testing and integration are done in the opposite order. This has the advantage that stubs do not need to be written for integration, but it has the very major drawback that the entire system must be completed before it is known whether the design is valid. This means that there is very little on which to base estimates of how long testing will take. This makes the bottom-up strategy very stressful for developers and managers. It is useful primarily when an existing system is being modified.

One other "method" should be mentioned, and that is the method of putting all the elements together simultaneously. This has been referred to by some as the "big bang" method. It has the single advantage that if everything works right the first time you have saved some time. If the parts do not all fit perfectly together the first time, you have the very large problem of trying to figure out the source(s) of the errors.

This method is sometimes attempted in desperation by software engineering students who are getting uncomfortably close to the end of the term. We are very much aware of the pressure you are under. We are also aware that the pressure you will experience on the job is much greater, and the stakes will be higher.

5.C.4. Regression Test

Regression testing is done on previously tested code after a change has been made. Specifically, it means repeating tests that have been done before to be sure that the results have not changed except for elimination of a specific bug. If testing uncovers an error and debugging is done to fix the error, then regression testing must be done. It is incompetent to think that a code change to fix a bug will have no other effect on a system. The reasons for regression testing are summarized in Table 5.5.

Table 5.5 Regression Testing

Regression testing should make sure that:
- The change was correctly made.
- The problem was actually fixed.
- No new errors have been introduced.

Correctly changing the code depends on the source of an error being identified. Unfortunately, this is not always done easily. It is one thing to identify an error, that is, to define the circumstances under which software malfunctions. It is quite another matter, and often more difficult, to figure out why. And when the source has been localized, the fix may or may not work. In some software development houses, it has been found that the source of an error was correctly identified about half the time. Of these, the "correction" worked about half the time.

To make matters even more complicated, a fix that works may cause new problems. For example, there may have been compensating errors that showed up as a small problem. When one is removed, the other may manifest itself as a large problem. Unfortunately, the typical response is to panic and undo the first fix.

As another example, an error may have caused the system to fail. Fixing this error may open the path to additional, more severe failures. This does not mean that the fix was done improperly; it means there are more faults to be undone.

It has been found that errors generally tend to occur in clusters. This is something important to keep in mind when you are trying to decide whether it is worth the effort to do regression testing. Not only should you carefully redo tests that were previously done, you should also test nearby values, even when the fix appears to work. Be suspicious! If there was one error in that neighborhood, there are likely to be others.

The elimination of an error may well lead to increased use of a system that was previously hindered by that error. Thus code that was not adequately tested may now come into use, and its bugs will become apparent. This of course applies to a system that has been in use and is being modified.

The other purpose of regression testing is to see whether any new errors have come into existence. Eliminating an error causes the introduction of a new one about half the time. This is why you should never, never succumb to the temptation to put off regression testing until the "last" error has been fixed.

Regression testing is not fun to do, but it is extremely important. However, use some judgment in deciding how much testing needs to be repeated. For example, altering the help file to read 15 lines at a time instead of 25 may require relatively little regression testing. On the other hand, modification of a global data structure could require 100% regression testing.

Always keep good records of testing. Keep backup copies and keep track of versions. Granted, it is a lot of work, but it is even more work to completely reconstruct a test sequence.

5.C.5. System Test

System testing is the final level of test. Remember that the system is made up of more than just software. Programmers often neglect important details of the hardware. But it is there, and system testing is the arena in which all the component parts show whether they work together or not. With real-time and embedded systems, actual tests on the target machine are especially critical.

Recall the difference between the development computer and the target computer. Although in course projects they are likely to be the same machine, this is not the usual situation. During development, simulations are often run to see how the target system is supposed to work. Simulations are very useful, but they have their limits. We have a friend who is still fuming over the technician who tested his microcomputer when his brand-new hard disk was losing data. The technician announced that all was well, because he had successfully run a disk test . . . on a RAM disk (a virtual disk implemented in memory). Instead of repeatedly testing disk access he had loaded a file once and tested it a large number of times in memory. However, the actual hard disk access problem did not show up in the simulation and was still there. Unless a simulation reasonably represents the domain of the fault, the fault may never be observed.

Ultimately, a software system must be tested in the target environment. At that point any assumptions made in using a development environment for earlier stages of testing will be validated. Any incompatibilities due to environmental differences must be resolved before delivery of the software product. Some major considerations include checking the level of performance, recovery capabilities, and security.

5.C.6. Acceptance Test

The acceptance test is to assure the customer that the system actually does what it is supposed to do. The acceptance test procedure is usually specified by the user. This is where full performance must be demonstrated to the user. Usually this takes place in the user's domain, rather than in the development workplace, and must be done to the user's satisfaction. The acceptance criteria and evaluation standards are frequently set in a contract. Since the developers know what the test criteria will be, they will exercise the system against the acceptance criteria before submitting the system for the formal test.

Unlike previous types of tests, the purpose here is not error detection, but determination of whether the system performance is acceptable. If the system is declared unacceptable because of a major problem or a large number of minor problems, then it stays with the developers until debugging and regression testing are done (or the system is scrapped). If the acceptance test was specified by contract, there may also be penalty conditions for failing to pass the test by the scheduled delivery time.

It is possible for a system to be declared acceptable even though some errors are found, especially if the errors are relatively minor. This is because, as a practical matter, complex systems are extremely unlikely to be completely free of errors. The customer may prefer to accept a system with minor inconveniences rather than delay implementation. Phased implementation or planned upgrades to add features later are not unusual. This is why you will find descriptions of known bugs in user's manuals for delivered systems.

A successful acceptance test is followed by formal delivery of the system. Earlier in the history of the software business, acceptance tests were not generally done. At some point, the software was declared ready by the developer and turned over to the customer. This did not always create customer satisfaction.

A combination of professional ethics and competition have changed things. Now an acceptance test is normally specified in advance. The Department of Defense, for example, has mandated acceptance testing in their software procurement contracts.

5.D. Test Methods

Structural testing looks at the implementation details of the code. It tests logic paths and concentrates on such things as peculiarities of the language, programming style, control methods, and details of the hardware and operating system.

Functional testing treats the code as if it were a black box; that is, the details of the code are hidden. This is the way the system appears from the user's point of view.

Both methods of testing are important. In general, structural testing is used for unit tests and functional testing for integration and system tests. However, the boundaries between the two methods are not absolute, as functional tests of modules are actually structural tests of an integrated system.

5.D.1. Structural Testing

Structural testing, sometimes referred to as "white-box" or "glass-box" testing, is based on close examination of procedural detail. The idea of structural testing is to check all logical paths through a module. This kind of test can be designed only if the algorithmic detail has been defined. Ideally the module should be defined by some form of process description at the time the preliminary or high-level software design is done. If the module design is available as pseudocode, decision table, state transition table, or any other equivalent definition of the algorithm, the unit test can be designed. If that level of detail is not yet available, the definition of the unit test must be deferred.

Structural testing generally cannot test all possible paths for all combinations of logic, because for even a simple procedure there are too many paths. Consider a relatively simple procedure with a loop that is executed ten times. Inside the loop are four branches. A Nassi-Schneiderman chart expressing the algorithmic detail of this program is shown in Figure 5.3. This may not look very difficult to test, but examine what happens if we try to test for all possible combinations.

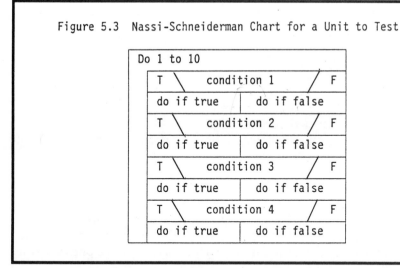

Figure 5.3   Nassi-Schneiderman Chart for a Unit to Test

For each branch, two possibilities need to be tested: true and false. If we test all possible combinations of just two branches, we have 2^2, or 4 combinations. For four branches, we have 2^4 or 16 combinations. To test all possible combinations, we need to check each order through all 10 loop executions. This means 16 possible combinations for each loop execution, which is 16^{10}, or more than a trillion combinations.

There are several problems with this. First, it is probably unnecessary. Second, it is not feasible. For the program above, how long would it take to run a trillion tests? (Remember, there are approximately 31.5 million seconds in a year.)

Although structural testing does not test all paths for all combinations of logic, each path should be executed at least once. Test cases are needed so that all logical conditions are executed for both true and false values. Loops should be executed over their entire range of values. The validity of internal data structures must be verified. For example, the value of all variables should be checked against their expected values. And everything should be checked at the boundaries.

Loops need to be tested at every execution, especially if there is a local variable that affects anything inside the loop. Testing should determine, for example, whether the local variable was properly initialized, what happens during the loop, and how it affects the status of things after the last execution.

5.D.2. Functional Testing

Functional testing is the verification that the externally observed properties of a software unit conform to specification, to determine whether the overall purpose has been satisfied. This is generally done without access to any internal variables of intermediate values and hence is often called "black box" testing. A set of inputs is supplied and the outputs are to be verified against the results expected under the terms of the specification. This testing focuses on the interface between the unit and some external entity such as a test driver.

Note that functional tests can be designed based on the software requirements and the interface specification of the modules. Thus functional tests to be performed during integration can be designed even if the algorithmic detail is not adequately defined to design a structural test of every module. Planning of functional tests at the module integration and system testing level should be done concurrently with the design of the software hierarchy and considered part of the design specification.

If a unit fails on some aspect of a functional test then it will be necessary to review the detailed design of the unit and perform additional structural tests to localize the fault. This is another instance when we find ourselves forced to return to an earlier phase for a rework of a portion of the system.

5.E. Test Specification Document

Now let us look at an example of a test planning document. First of all, the format must be specified. If your organization has a specified format, you should use it. Standard test documentation can facilitate communication by providing a consistent frame of reference, and can serve as a checklist for completeness. The use of standardized test documents also increases the manageability of testing.

The Test Specification Document we are using is based on ANSI/IEEE Standard 829-1984, Software Test Documentation. This is outlined in Table 5.6.

In the Test Specification Document, there should be specific reference to items in the Software Requirements Specification by section, subsection, and item number to indicate the feature or property being verified wherever possible. Many unit tests of single modules may not allow verification of specific specification items. But the identification of the unit should allow reference to documentation of the system architecture to clearly indicate what larger subunits of the system depend on it.

The test specification documentation may be revised several times during development, thus a clear marking of the test specification identification and version number should appear on every page as a standard header or footer. Later the resulting test reports should reference these for checks on compliance with the plan. An example is given in Figure 5.4 for the *Main* routine for a computer dating service.

The section of the test specification document for a unit test of a single module should include the module name, module type, and a list of all input and output parameters with the name and data types specified for each. For each parameter, the range of valid values should be specified. A set of specific values for each input parameter to be used in the testing should be listed. This should include both valid and invalid data items, along with the expected result for each. For invalid data the result should include an error message.

```
Table 5.6  Test Specification Document - Outline

1.  Test plan identifier (name, version number, date)
2.  Table of contents
3.  Introduction (narrative summary)
4.  A section for each test (unit, integration, or system),
    including:
    a.  Test identification
    b.  Features to be tested
    c.  Features not to be tested
    d.  Test data items
    e.  Item pass/fail criteria
    f.  Test deliverables
    g.  Testing tasks (noting any intertask dependence)
    h.  Environmental needs
5.  Responsibilities
6.  Schedule
7.  Approvals (place for supervisor's signature)
```

The document should include a specification of the environment for each test. This should include a description of any required driver or stubs. If a subset of the system is planned to be used as the driver, a brief description of the configuration and any necessary modifications should be included.

```
Figure 5.4  Sample Test Description for
            Fig Leaf Enterprises Computer Dating Service

Test Module: Main                   Date: June 23, 1990
Module Author: entire group         Version: 1.0
Test Environment: IBM PC (or compatible) with Turbo Pascal.
        One floppy in drive A is sufficient for this test
        This test is for the main driver and menu, which reads a
text file.  It is to test the keyboard response from the user
and to test  the file  commands  for reading  the menu  text.
Stubs are used for the add, delete, modify, find a match, and
help routines.  A temporary,  brief writeln statement is used
as a substitute for error messages to be integrated later.
        This test looks  for correct menu  display for  the main
menu.  It is to be displayed:
        (a) upon bringing up the system,
        (b) following erroneous user responses in the main menu,
        (c) following return from a feature.
        This test does not test the text file for error messages
called from the error handler.  A temporary message is written
directly from the  driver following erroneous  input.  After
testing,  this module will be tested for handling of that text
file.  Then it will be used as the driver for the routines to
be integrated.
Variables:      Type:           Description:
  ans           char            for input from keyboard
  menuflag      Boolean         to keep loop going until done
  promptflag    Boolean         for verbose or terse reply
  textline      string [65]     line of text from file

Files: Menutxt - text menu for command handler
       Menu    - local name for file
Test of variable 'promptflag': in reply to query
Test Input    Expected Result
_____  _____
 y, Y         terse prompts
 n, N         verbose prompts
 <cr>         verbose prompts
 1.5          verbose prompts
Test of variable ans: in reply to choice from menu
Test Input    Expected Result
_____  _____
 A, a          message from add client module
 D, d          message from delete client module
 C, c          message from modify client module
 M, m          message from find a match module
 H, h          message from help module
 Q, q          message to verify quit command, followed by
 Y, y              quit to operating system
 N, n              repeat menu, with message
 5, x              repeat menu, with message
 <cr>              repeat menu, with message
 0, 5, 2.3     repeat menu, with message
 b, B, $, !    repeat menu, with message
                 .
                 .
                 .
```

5.F. Design of Test Data: Triangle Classification Problem

Designing test data requires a certain mind set and a certain amount of practice. The emotional approach to testing is basically the opposite of programming. Writing code involves creating something; testing involves trying to destroy this creation.

In beginning programming courses, very little testing is done. It isn't that the programs are brilliant, it's that they have all been done so many times that the instructor knows exactly how the program is supposed to look and exactly what mistakes the novice programmers are likely to make. For example, is there a programmer alive who did not do a bubble sort in an introductory programming class? There are lots of places to make errors in one of these, but almost every introductory programming textbook gives an example of how to do it right. And every instructor knows virtually all the ways the students are likely to do it wrong.

With the development of new software systems, which is what software engineering is all about, there is no such guidance. You are now in the position of the first programmer who ever wrote a bubble sort, and you must test carefully to make sure it does what it is supposed to, and doesn't do anything it isn't supposed to.

We will introduce you to the world of test data generation by example. Let us look at a system addressing the problem of how to classify a triangle. We want to know what triangle type (scalene, isosceles, or equilateral) is represented by the values of the lengths of three sides. (Remember that an equilateral triangle has three equal sides, an isosceles triangle has two equal sides, and a scalene triangle has no equal sides.)

Our system expects as input three numeric values. As output, the user is to be told whether the three numeric values represent the sides of a scalene, isosceles, or equilateral triangle. The system needs to be carefully and adequately tested. We will assume that the system has been unit and integration tested, and we are doing system testing. We will therefore use functional testing methods.

Before you read any further, stop and take a few minutes to create a list of specific test data items which you think are adequate to determine whether the system functions properly. Then check the list of categories in Table 5.7. If you don't have sets of data for each category, there is a possible error in the code that could escape detection.

The idea of **equivalence classes** is important. If we imagine the complete space of input data we can divide that universe into a set of abstract domains. We want to identify a domain for each abstract category of valid inputs and a domain for each category of invalid data. These categories may encompass a very large number of values but share some identifiable abstract property. Having done this we can choose limited sets of data to represent each such equivalence class. In addition we can find test values to test the boundary conditions between the equivalence classes. In this way we can generate limited test data sets to cover the behavior of the system.

```
Table 5.7   Types of Test Data for the
            Triangle Classification Problem

Valid data:
     three categories: all equal, two equal, all different
     integer and real values
     positive numbers
Boundary conditions:
     numbers that test the upper limits of the machine
     values that approach zero
     values that create a triangle with no area
       (e.g., 4, 5, 9)
Erroneous values:
     negative, zero values
     too few values (0, 1, or 2)
     too many values (4 or more)
     nonnumeric values (character, letter O for zero)
     impossible combination for triangles
       (side a + side b < side c)
Note: In every category, values must be entered in multiple
orders in case the code is order dependent.
```

Table 5.8 gives sample test data with expected results. This data set does not include all possible conditions; can you think of any more? (As a start, what happens when you mix integer and real data input?)

It is essential to document in advance a collection of test data items with an explicit definition of the expected result for each set of values. This ensures that tests are carried out systematically. The documentation also makes it possible to inspect the test procedure and selected test data in advance for accuracy and adequacy. Later the test plan documents will also be necessary to be able to duplicate the test if the system is changed.

5.G. Interactive Tracing

The process of correctly identifying the source of an error may be tricky. It is helpful to know which part of the program was executing when something went amiss and what the value of the parameters and variables were at the time. Knowing these things can help solve problems ranging from an array subscript that was out of range, to a strange jump to an irrelevant module because a stack pointer was unintentionally changed. Such information can be made available for interactive systems through the use of an interactive trace system, such as the one described in detail in Appendix B.

```
Table 5.8   Test Data - Triangle Classification Problem

Test Data                 Expected Results


1, 1, 1                   equilateral
1.2, 1.2, 1.2             equilateral
1, 2, 2                   isosceles
1.0, 2.5, 2.5            isosceles
3, 4, 5                   scalene
1.1, 2.2, 1.3            scalene
1.0, 1.0, 0.000001        error message - boundary exceeded
                          (Note: This value will be system dependent)
1, 2, 3                   error message - boundary condition in
1.2, 2.3, 3.5                                  triangle size
0, 1, 2                   error message - zero value
1.5, 2.5, -2.1            error message - negative value
carriage return           error message - too few values
4, 5
1, 2, 5, 8               error message - too many values
10, 9, 9                 error message - letter O for zero in 10
one, two, three          error message - nonnumeric values
1, 2, 12                 error message - impossible combination
```

The best time to consider a tracing system is during the detailed design phase. If your language system has a source level debugger, plan to use it. Design your test plans around its capabilities. If you do not have access to such a tool then you need to construct a trace system by incorporating the necessary code for tracing as your system is designed. It is possible to add a trace system to existing code, but it is easier to do it as the code is written.

We recommend using an interactive trace system that enables the test team to turn the trace on or off for any individual module. The reason for creating the ability to turn flags on and off is so that selected sections can be analyzed.

It is possible to create a crude trace system that can be turned entirely on or off by simply putting a statement in each module of the type:

if (trace_flag = on) then . . .

However, in all but the smallest of systems one will soon be so overwhelmed with information that it is very difficult to sort it out. This can happen even with a system composed of as few as 40 to 50 modules.

It is also useful to have the system indent its trace comments for each module entered. This indentation feature enables the viewer to know whether an intermediate module was used with its flag turned off.

Even if you have to build it yourself, this system is well worth the effort. In the example in Figure 5.5 the trace system gives a message identifying the procedure on entering and leaving each procedure. The entry message also indicates parameters and key values. Note also that the level in the calling hierarchy is indicated by the amount of indentation.

```
             Figure 5.5  Sample Messages from Using an
                         Interactive Trace System

        Entering TraceFlag.  n = 5, Trace [5] = 1
            Entering ErrorHandler.  n = 5
            ERROR: Flag value out of range
            Leaving ErrorHandler.  n = 5
        Leaving TraceFlag.  n = 6, Trace [6] = 0
```

In the sample messages in Figure 5.5, the module *ErrorHandler* is called from *TraceFlag*, and an error message is printed while in that module. Then a message indicates leaving *ErrorHandler* to return to *TraceFlag*. This simple example demonstrates that trace output can be formatted to show by indentation the level in the calling hierarchy.

The code used for a system like this constitutes throwaway code in the sense that the user should not see it. However, whether it is deleted before the system is sent to the customer or simply turned off, its usefulness in testing is so great that the additional effort is well justified.

5.H. Verification and Validation

One phrase commonly used in discussions of testing and quality assurance is **verification and validation**. The terms are closely related. The ANSI/IEEE definitions indicate that verification is the process of checking during software development; validation is done at the end of development to assure that what was done was what was supposed to be done. The distinction has been put succinctly by Barry Boehm:

Verification: Are we building the product right?

Validation: Are we building the right product?

As a practical matter, the terms are almost always used together, often abbreviated as "v and v."

The concept of verification and validation is broader than just testing. It also includes review and analysis of the specifications, documentation, and details of the source code. Certainly it is important to ensure that execution terminates properly for all valid input data sets and without runtime errors. However, we must also try to ensure that all sets of correct input data produce results that meet the specifications. Furthermore, all incorrect data inputs should also terminate normally and generate the expected error messages or error codes. This topic is addressed in more detail in Chapter 6.

5.I. Course Project: Test Specification Document

Creating the Test Specification Document is dull, tedious work, but it can make the difference between a successful, excellent project and a mediocre or terrible one. Listing the values to be tested for each module forces the planner to systematically analyze the inputs and outputs of the module. This has many advantages. It helps to specify the module, making it clearer to the programmer exactly what is expected. The associated schedule establishes an order for modules to be completed, requiring that group members communicate effectively. And it prepares you for the realities of the job, where testing and related activities account for anywhere from 50% to 80% or more of development time.

There is also the possibility that test planning will result in an insight that some aspect of the system, as it is designed, is not going to work. This information may result in anything from a minor redesign to scrapping the project as unfeasible. But in any case, it is far preferable to proceeding with a faulty design.

It may seem to you that you are spending all your time specifying, planning, and preparing documents. You may be wondering when you are going to start actual development on the project. The answer is: just as soon as you get your initial documents approved. Are you concerned about how much time there is left to do the project? The actual writing of code, for a well-planned project, should only take about 15% of the time, at most. Time spent testing will inevitably be greater than time spent coding. Good preparation for testing will help keep the amount of necessary testing to a manageable level.

5.J. Beyond a Course Project: Test Data Generators

It would be nice if the creation of test data could be automated. Creating a suitable set of data that tests adequately is a monumental task. However, recall from our discussion of specifications that not everything can or should be automated.

The application under test may be a mathematical function or a numerical analysis system. In that case, the critical aspect of the testing may be a validation that the specified precision of values output is in fact obtained throughout the range of allowable inputs. That sort of test is especially appropriate to automate.

There are both positive and negative aspects of automated test data generation, and cost-effective use depends on the nature of the system to be tested. In many cases, if the system under development is similar enough to an existing system that the same test data can be used, then you may be reinventing the wheel. Unique and original systems usually require unique and original test data.

Some classes of systems need to be tested in similar ways. An example is a compiler. For example, if you are writing an Ada compiler, it must pass a set of standardized tests mandated by the Department of Defense in order to be validated.

Test data generators do exist, and they vary widely in both acquisition cost and usage cost. Such systems are frequently used in performance tests of systems. A large number of transactions may need to be created. Large data sets may thus be generated and stored in a test database. Such data sets may be used efficiently as special data generators to produce a population of values with prescribed ranges and statistical distribution. The data may be produced using simulation languages such as GPSS or SYMSCRIPT, or with programs using pseudo-random number generators written in a programming language.

At the present time, commercially available test data generators are few in number and language specific. If one is available for the system you are developing, you may want to try it.

An example of some of the limitations and drawbacks of test data generators, as well as some other aspects of testing, are illustrated in the following story that Edward Yourdon tells on himself in Nations at Risk (1986):

> At Digital Equipment Corporation I was told to write the math library for the PDP-6 computer. This included sine, cosine, logarithm, exponential, etc. Most of us vaguely recall from high school trigonometry that the sine of 0 degrees is zero, the sine of 90 degrees is 1, and the sine of 45 degrees is .7071 (square root of 2, divided by 2). But how could I tell whether my subroutine was generating the proper sine of 36.772 degrees? And did I have to test 36.773 degrees and 36.774 degrees too?
>
> My solution was to develop some automated tests. I remembered, for example, the old high school formula
>
> $$\sin^2(x) + \cos^2(x) = 1$$
>
> and I also remembered that the sine function could be computed using a simpler, less cumbersome formula than the one I had chosen. So it was easy to write a program that would generate millions of values of "x," and then test to see whether the "$\sin^2(x) + \cos^2(x)$" formula worked, and whether my algorithm matched the results of a different algorithm. The test program that I thus concocted used all computer resources on our test computer over an entire weekend. My boss was horrified, but impressed with the sheer volume of testing that I was carrying out.

Does this prove I was doing a good job of testing? Not really. Consider the following potential problems:

The testing sequence that I used might have had errors in it. It is certainly true for example that $\sin^2(x) + \cos^2(x) = 1$, but there is no guarantee that my testing program correctly computed that formula.

Testing the sine subroutine required the existence of other sub-routines - e.g., the cosine subroutine, or the alternative- algorithm version of the sine. What if those subroutines had compensating errors that offset the errors in my sine routine?

My testing program tried the various formulas and alternative calculations for sin(x) for an enormously large range of values. But what if I neglected to test carefully the boundary values, or if there were a bug in the part of my program that generated new test cases? In fact, the latter situation turned out to be true. I spent forty-seven hours of computer time repeatedly testing to ensure that my sin(x), cos(x), log(x), exp(x), atan(x) and sqrt(x) subroutines produced correct results for x = 0. I didn't have the courage to tell my boss.

Summary

Planning for testing should be done before the code is written. Testing is to ensure that the software does what it is supposed to do and to uncover errors in the system. However, it is normally impossible to certify that a software system is completely bug-free.

Testing, coding, and debugging are separate activities, generally done by separate teams. Errors found in testing need to be documented and often categorized. Testing, when properly done, is usually the most time-consuming aspect of software development.

Test planning involves specifying the test environment and configuration, including a description of the hardware needed and any required drivers and stubs. Unit testing is generally structural testing, and integration testing is generally functional testing.

Integration testing, like development, may be done top-down or bottom-up. We recommend top-down, depth-first integration for class projects.

Regression testing must be done after any error correction is done. The probability that a fix will uncover another error and/or introduce a new error is very high. System testing is especially important when the development machine and the target machine are not the same. Verification and validation are terms commonly used in relation to system testing. Acceptance testing criteria should be specified in the contract.

Design of test data is an art and must take into account all the ways that things could go wrong. Interactive tracing is a powerful testing technique. If a source level debugger is not available to you, guidelines for writing your own are given in Appendix B. Test data generators do exist, but are of limited usefulness.

Keywords

"big bang" method of integration
bottom-up integration
boundary conditions
debugging
errors
    code errors
    data errors
    function-related errors
    process errors
    regression errors
    system errors
equivalence classes
execution paths
independent test teams
interactive tracing
test data
test data generators
test driver and stubs
test specifications
Test Specification Document
testing
    acceptance test
    functional test
    data errors
    function-related errors
    integration test
    regression test
    structural test
    system test
    unit test
top-down integration
verification and validation

Review Questions

5.1. What is the purpose of testing?

5.2. What does it mean when the testing process uncovers a bug?

5.3. What is the difference between testing and debugging?

5.4. When might a bug not be fixed?

5.5. What are function-related errors? System errors? Process errors? Data errors? Code errors? Regression errors?

5.6. Why should the person(s) doing the testing be someone other than the person(s) who did the coding? Why should they be someone other than the person(s) who wrote the specifications?

5.7. What fraction of software development is usually spent on testing?

5.8. What is the difference between unit testing and integration testing?

5.9. Give some examples of boundary conditions and explain why they are important in testing.

5.10. In testing, should all possible execution paths be tested?

5.11. Describe the difference between top-down and bottom-up integration. Name an advantage and disadvantage of each.

5.12. What is regression testing and when should it be done?

5.13. When correcting an error, what is the likelihood of finding another error? Of introducing another error?

5.14. What is a systems test? An acceptance test?

5.15. What is the difference between functional testing and structural testing?

5.16. What is a Test Specification Document and what ANSI/IEEE Standard may be used when writing one?

5.17. How is writing code different from designing a set of test data to test that code?

5.18. What kinds of test data are included in a good test specification?

5.19. What are the advantages and disadvantages of test data generators?

5.20. What is interactive tracing and how is it used?

5.21. What are verification and validation?

Exercises

5.1. What is wrong with being creative when writing code?

5.2. If each team member develops one subtree of the system independently, what can go wrong when the team tries to integrate the system?

5.3. Consider a structural test of a small module with an attempt to test all possible paths when the code consists of a counted loop with index 1 to 16. Within that loop there is conditional logic with 16 alternative cases. How long would the exhaustive test take, if the loop execution time is 1 microsecond? (Hint: 2^{10} is approximately equal to 10^3, and 3.17×10^7 seconds is equal to one year.)

5.4. A mathematical function tan (x) is specified to be valid on the range of the input variable from 0.0 to pi/4.0 with a precision of 8 significant figures. Specify the test data to verify it.

5.5. A module selects valid input commands based on keyboard input of a 1 to 6 character string. Characters are assumed to be ASCII (7 bits). How many possible input strings are there?

5.6. You are given an object module for a routine that searches for real roots of an algebraic polynomial with real coefficients: $A(0) + A(1) * X + A(2) * X ** 2 + A(3) * X ** 3 = 0$. The module is to find R = ROOT (A(0), A(1), A(2), A(3), X). ROOT is a function that passes as parameters the real coefficients and a starting trial value. Specify test data and expected results sufficient to determine whether a root has been obtained within an assumed precision of 6 significant figures.

5.7. A module Get_Command is a function that returns a string from keyboard input. Valid inputs are Add, Modify, Select, and Quit. The system should accept the first letter or the entire command name. Write a set of test data to evaluate this module.

5.8. A module takes as input a 5 character string. It is proposed that the set of possible input strings should be tested exhaustively. How many are there? (Assume it uses the ASCII character set.)

References

ANSI/IEEE Standard 829-1983. Standard for Software Test Documentation. New York: Computer Society Press, 1984.

> Describes a set of basic test documents associated with the dynamic aspects of software testing and defines the purpose, outline, and content of each basic document.

ANSI/IEEE Standard 1008-1987. Software Unit Testing. New York: Computer Society Press, 1986.

> Specifies a standard approach to software unit testing and describes the software engineering concepts and testing assumptions on which the standard approach is based.

Beizer, Boris. Software Testing Techniques. New York: Van Nostrand-Reinhold, 1983.

> A thorough discussion of testing methods and rationales for test data generation. The problem of exhaustive testing of execution paths is explored and alternatives are presented to maximize the chance of detecting faults with modest test data sets. Test strategies based on test databases, decision tables, Boolean algebra, and state transition testing are explained.

Beizer, Boris. Software System Testing and Quality Assurance. New York: Van Nostrand-Reinhold, 1984.

> Includes the comment about a hypothetical person from Mars, quoted in Section C. Puts the test techniques in a broader context of reliability and quality of the system. Testing and test management are discussed at the unit, integration, and system levels. Also discussed are configuration, security, and performance tests.

Brooks, Frederick P. The Mythical Man-Month, Essays on Software Engineering. Reading, MA: Addison-Wesley, 1975, reprinted 1982.

> Considered a classic of software engineering. Brooks presents the results of his experience as the project manager for the IBM OS 360. A clear exposition of the non-linearity of manpower and project duration effects on software project management.

Brooks, Frederick P. "No Silver Bullet." IEEE Computer 20, no. 4 (April 1987): 10-19.

> Fashioning complex conceptual constructs is the essence; accidental tasks arise in representing the constructs in language. Past progress has so reduced the accidental tasks that future progress now depends on addressing the essence.

Deutsch, Michael S. Software Verification and Validation, Realistic Project Approaches. Englewood Cliffs, NJ: Prentice-Hall, 1982.

> Reviews several techniques and tools. Advocates systematic test planning and shows results of case studies at Hughes Aircraft.

DeMillo, Richard A., McCracken, W. Michael, Martin, R. J., and Passafiume, John F. Software Testing and Evaluation. Benjamin/Cummings, 1987.

> A comprehensive survey of the state of the art and current practice in defense-related projects. The 70-page bibliography is subdivided into several dozen topic areas.

Dijkstra, Edsgar W. "The Humble Programmer." CACM 15,10 (October 1972): 859-866.

> Contains "Dijkstra's Dictum" that testing can prove the presence of bugs but not their absence.

Dunn, Robert. Software Defect Removal. New York: McGraw-Hill, 1984.

>Defect removal is the goal of reviews and testing. The chapter on analysis of specification and design reviews is particularly appropriate to this chapter.

Evans, Michael W. Productive Software Test Management. New York: Wiley-Interscience, 1984.

>Planning and specifying testing are presented with a case study.

Glass, Robert L. Software Reliability Guidebook. Englewood Cliffs, NJ: Prentice-Hall, 1979.

>Surveys the state of software practices (1975-78) in defense and aerospace industries. Concludes with recommendations to improve software reliability.

Miller, Edward, and Howden, William E. Tutorial: Software Testing & Validation Techniques, 2d ed. Washington, DC: Computer Society Press, 1981.

>Reprints a collection of 36 papers with introductory sections by the editors. Extensive bibliography.

Myers, G. The Art of Software Testing. New York: Wiley, 1979.

>Presents the need for rational test planning and test data generation. Original description of the triangle classification problem.

Pfleeger, Shari Lawrence. Software Engineering, The Production of Quality Software. New York: Macmillan, 1987.

>An introductory text. Chapter 7 is on program testing, Chapter 8 is on system testing. Chapters have good exercises.

Pressman, Roger S. Software Engineering, A Practitioner's Approach, 2d ed. New York: McGraw-Hill, 1987.

>A survey of software engineering with thorough review of all phases of the life cycle and the management of software. The treatment of software design provides chapters on data flow, data structure, real-time, and object oriented design methods.

Yourdon, Edward, ed. Classics in Software Engineering. New York: Yourdon Press, 1979.

>Reprints of 24 classic papers; including Dijkstra's paper "The Humble Programmer," cited above.

Yourdon, Edward. Nations at Risk: The Impact of the Computer Revolution. New York: Yourdon Press, 1986.

>A readable account of the impact of computers on our world for computer professionals and a general audience.

Yourdon, Edward. Techniques of Program Structure and Design. Englewood Cliffs, NJ: Prentice-Hall, 1975.

>One of the first books on structured programming and testing to insist on the distinction between testing and debugging.

PART II

DEVELOPMENT

No scene from prehistory is quite so vivid as that of the mortal struggles of great beasts in the tar pits. In the mind's eye one sees dinosaurs, mammoths, and sabertoothed tigers struggling against the grip of the tar. The fiercer the struggle, the more entangling the tar, and no beast is so strong or so skillful but that he ultimately sinks.

Large-system programming has ... been such a tar pit, and many great and powerful beasts have thrashed violently in it. Most have emerged with running systems - few have met goals, schedules, and budgets.

- Frederick P. Brooks, Jr., <u>The Mythical Man-Month</u>

Part II deals with the actual development of a project. Some detailed design will be involved. The software life cycle is not strictly linear, as mentioned in Part I, Chapter 1. At any stage it may be necessary to go back to an earlier stage.

Because most course projects are interactive, Chapter 6 deals with various aspects of the user interface. Our recommendation is to write a rapid prototype interface first, along with an error handler and an interactive trace system.

Chapter 7 addresses some aspects of detailed design and development, including module complexity measures, cohesion, coupling, and information hiding. It would be nice to consider these during the planning phase. However, it is not possible to put everything first unless we label the entire book Chapter 1. This chapter also briefly reviews structured programming and describes proofs of correctness.

The next major phase of development, testing, is described in Chapter 8. Test reporting examples are given and a simple test report generator is described. Various types of errors are discussed and categorized.

Maintenance, strictly speaking, is not part of development. However, it usually represents a large fraction of the total life cycle cost of a software system. Therefore, it is in the best interest of a software system to be as maintainable as possible over its entire lifetime. Chapter 9 addresses this topic. Some historical aspects of maintenance are discussed; however, the primary objective is to encourage you to think about what happens to a software system after it is delivered. Some job aspects of maintenance and its unfortunate current low status are also addressed.

CHAPTER 6

USER INTERFACE AND ERROR HANDLING

No single component of an interactive program is more unpredictable in performance than the user interface. . . . The biggest surprises often occur when the programmer sits down with his first user to explain the operation of the program:

Programmer: Now that you've drawn part of the circuit, you might want to change it in some way.

User: Yes, let's delete a component. How do we do that?

P: Point at the menu item labeled CD.

U: CD?

P: It stands for 'component delete.'

U: Ah. Well, here goes .... hey, what happened?

P: You're in analysis mode: you must have selected AM instead of CD.

U: Funny, I was pointing at CD. How can I get out of analysis mode?

P: Just type control-Q.

U: [types C-O-N-T-R...]

P: No, hold down the control key and hit Q.

U: Sorry, silly of me ... OK, I'll try for CD again.

P: Maybe aim a bit above the letters to avoid getting into analysis mode - no, not that much above - that's better.

U: *Got it!*

P: *Now point to the component to delete it.*

U: *OK ... nothing's happening; what am I doing wrong?*

P: *You're not doing anything wrong; you've deleted the component, but the program hasn't removed it from the screen yet.*

U: *When will it be removed?*

P: *When you type control-J to redraw the picture.*

U: *I'll try it ... there we are; but only part of the component was removed!*

P: *Sorry, I forgot: you have to delete each half of the component separately. Just point to CD again.*

U: *Very well ... now what's happened?*

P: *You're in analysis mode again: type control-Q.*

U: *Control... where's that Q? There it is ... hey, why is the screen blank all of a sudden?*

P: *You typed Q, not control-Q, so the program quit to the operating system. I'm really sorry, but we've lost everything and we'll have to start all over again.*

U: *[groans] Could we postpone that until next week?*

William M. Newman and Robert F. Sproull

Principles of Interactive Computer Graphics

Much of the complexity that [the software engineer] must master is arbitrary complexity, forced without rhyme or reason by the many human institutions and systems to which his interfaces must conform. These differ from interface to interface, and from time to time, not because of necessity but only because they were designed by different people, rather than by God.

- Frederick P. Brooks, Jr., "No Silver Bullet"

Software Life Cycle

Software development: Coding

I. Software need
II. Preliminary feasibility judgment
III. Requirements analysis and feasibility study
IV. Specification
V. Preliminary software design and planning
VI. Software development
       Detailed design
       Coding and unit testing
       Integration
       System testing
VII. Software maintenance

Project: This chapter supports the design of a "crash-proof" interactive user interface, written as a rapid prototype and developed one feature at a time.

6.A. User Interface and Rapid Prototyping

6.A.1. Significance of the User Interface

The user interface is the first contact the user has with any interactive program. Its effectiveness can determine whether a program is considered wonderful, acceptable, or intolerable. Even if the system does what it is supposed to do and is the epitome of efficiency with regard to CPU time and memory, it may not be used if the user doesn't like it. Conversely, a system that is pleasant to use can conceivably offset some deficiencies in the system.

From the user's viewpoint, the major part of the system is in the "look and feel" of the interface. At the same time, end-users typically are not able to understand a formally defined specification of the required interface, and thus cannot give meaningful agreement to acceptance of the specification. In such circumstances a rapidly produced prototype of the system is an important tool in completing the requirements analysis. The prototype becomes a tool to help communicate with the users about the complete system requirements and how the system should anticipate their needs.

In building a prototype it is often appropriate to create a "do-nothing" system with a preliminary user interface that will provide prompts to the user and handle inputs. A prototype generally will not have extensive validation of input data. It should call appropriate functions for each response, but need not process any data. If necessary, precomputed data can be fetched from a file and displayed. Such a system constitutes a rapid prototype.

6.A.2. Rapid Prototyping: An Example

An example of a rapid prototype for Fig Leaf Enterprises Computer Dating Service is given in Figure 6.1. This introductory prototype permits users to request any of the four primary functions that were specified for this system. The text files used with the system, MENU1TXT and MENU2TXT, are shown in Figure 6.2. The form of this user interface is very simple and works on a dumb terminal. Obviously a nicer interface can be created if the terminal supports additional attributes. The use of text files is described below in Section 6.B.3.

```
Figure 6.1  A Simple User Interface Example in Turbo Pascal
            Showing a Command Handler with Stubs

   Display screens and error messages are generated by reading text
files. Also note that the user is given a choice of long (verbose)
or short (terse) prompts.
Program FigLeaf (input, output);
(****************************************************************
* An interactive computer dating service written for Fig Leaf *
* Enterprises, in  Turbo Pascal 3.0,  for an  IBM PC or       *
* compatible.  The program is assumed to be on a floppy disk  *
* in drive A: with data files contained on  drive B:.         *
*      It is intended to be executed by a trained operator,   *
* using forms filled out by an applicant with personal        *
* information and answers to 40 personal questions.  The      *
* options include entering a new client, modifying an         *
* existing client, deleting a client, and looking for a match.*
*_____*
* Files used: Help  - text file, for global "h" command       *
*             Menu1 - text file, for startup message screen   *
*             Menu2 - text file, for main menu                *
*             ErrorHandler - text file, error messages        *
*_____*
* Global variables  -   Data dictionary -                     *
*     answer:   character for reply from keyboard             *
*     menuflag: Boolean to repeat until answer is valid       *
*     promptflag: Boolean for short prompts                   *
*     textline: string                                        *
****************************************************************)
   var answer: char;
       menuflag, promptflag : boolean;
       Menu1, Menu2          : text;
       textline              : string [65];
```

```
procedure AddClient;
(***************************************************************
*  This is the procedure that adds a new client - stub only   *
***************************************************************)
begin (* AddClient *)
  writeln;
  writeln('You are in the procedure to add a client.');
  writeln('This feature is not yet available.'); writeln;
end;
procedure ModifyClient;
(***************************************************************
*  This procedure changes data on a client - stub only        *
***************************************************************)
begin (* ModifyClient *)
  writeln;
  writeln('You are in a procedure to change data on a client.');
  writeln('This feature is not yet available.');    writeln;
end;
procedure DeleteClient;
(***************************************************************
*  This is the procedure that deletes a  client - stub only   *
***************************************************************)
begin (* DeleteClient *)
  writeln;
  writeln('You are in the procedure to delete a client -');
  writeln('This feature is not yet available.');   writeln;
end;
procedure DateSelect;
(***************************************************************
*  This is the procedure to make a match - stub only          *
***************************************************************)
begin (* DateSelect *)
  writeln; writeln('You are in the procedure to make a match-');
  writeln('This feature is not yet available.'); writeln;
end;
(***************************************************************
*   MainDriver is the command handler :    Modules called -   *
*          AddClient, Modifyclient, DeleteClient, DateSelect  *
*        Modules called by - none                             *
***************************************************************)
begin (* MainDriver *)
(* Welcome user to system; ask about prompts; set flag *)
(* read from first text file here *)
assign (Menu1,'MENU1TXT'); (* assign name to text file *)
reset(Menu1); (* open existing file *)
writeln;
repeat
  readln (Menu1,textline);       writeln(' ',textline);
until EOF(Menu1);
close (Menu1);  (* close file *)
readln(answer);
if (answer = 'y') or (answer = 'Y')
  then promptflag := false
  else promptflag := true;
```

```
(* read from second text file here *)
assign (Menu2,'MENU2TXT'); (* assign name to text file *)
repeat (* repeating loop for duration of program execution *)
  menuflag := true; (* flag to terminate loop *)
  if promptflag
  then begin (* for long prompts *)
    reset(Menu2); (* open existing file *)
    writeln;
    repeat
      readln (Menu2,textline);     writeln(' ',textline);
    until EOF(Menu2);
    close (Menu2);  (* close file *)
    end
  (* for short prompts *)
  else writeln('A: add, C: change, D: delete, M: match');
  read (answer); (* get user's choice *)
  case answer of
    'A','a': begin
                AddClient;    menuflag := false;
             end;
    'C','c': begin
                ModifyClient; menuflag := false;
             end;
    'D','d': begin
                DeleteClient; menuflag := false;
             end;
    'M','m': begin
                DateSelect;   menuflag := false;
             end;

    'H','h': begin
                (* read help file - to be added later *)
                writeln;
                write('This will be the help file - ');
                writeln(' it is not yet available.');
                menuflag := false;
             end;
    'Q','q': begin
                writeln;
                write('Are you sure you want to quit? (y/n)');
                read (answer);
                if (answer = 'Y') or (answer = 'y')
                  then menuflag := true
                  else menuflag := false;
             end;
    else      begin
                writeln;
        (* This will be replaced by a call to ErrorHandler *)
                writeln('Invalid entry: please try again.');
                menuflag := false;
              end;
  end; (* case *)
until menuflag;
end. (* MainDriver *)
```

```
 Figure 6.2  Text Files Used in the Example in Figure 6.1
                         A. MENU1TXT
 *******************************************************************
 *                                                                 *
 *  Welcome to Fig Leaf Enterprises Computer Dating Service        *
 *                                                                 *
 *  This system is designed to be as helpful as possible.          *
 *                                                                 *
 *  If you are new to the system, we hope you will find our        *
 *     explanations helpful.                                       *
 *                                                                 *
 *  If you are familiar with the system, you may prefer to         *
 *    skip some of the explanations.                               *
 *                                                                 *
 *  Would you prefer the shorter prompts? (y/n)                    *
 *                                                                 *
 *******************************************************************


                         B. MENU2TXT
 *******************************************************************
 *                                                                 *
 *   Would you like to                                             *
 *                                                                 *
 *      A: Add a client to the files                               *
 *                                                                 *
 *      C: Change information about a client in the files          *
 *                                                                 *
 *      D: Delete a client from the files                          *
 *                                                                 *
 *      M: Select a Match for the client                           *
 *                                                                 *
 *      H: Read the Help file                                      *
 *                                                                 *
 *      Q: End the session (Quit)                                  *
 *                                                                 *
 *   Enter the letter of your choice and press Return              *
 *                                                                 *
 *******************************************************************
```

This prototype has several advantages. It is quick and easy to create, and provides a basis for verifying that the system under development is what the user actually wants. By demonstrating this skeleton to the user, the developer can determine whether the user interface is satisfactory and whether the functions to be invoked are in line with what the user expects. As development progresses, the stubs will be replaced with working code.

Another advantage of this setup is that if one or more features are not completely functional on schedule, the system will still be one that the user can operate. It should be sufficiently error free that the user will not lose control to the operating system even when accessing nonfunctional features. Under these conditions the user is less likely to be upset about a late system than if these same functions were partially working but the user couldn't stay in control.

We will return to this example throughout the rest of this chapter.

6.B. Error Handling

The user interface is probably the most unpredictable part of any interactive program. Things that can go wrong include invalid input by the user, invalid output by the system, and errors that are catastrophic to the system. Error handling must be used to check:

- input information, whether from the keyboard, files, or anything else
- output information to make sure that it is reasonable according to the user's standards
- the occurrence of internal system states that could cause termination, such as end-of-file conditions

When errors are detected, the user must be given information on what action to take. This is usually in the form of a text message.

The idea of constructing traps to detect potential errors is called **antibugging**. In practice, take the approach that program design is fallible. Consider building error traps to contain and identify any conceivable faults that might cause loss of execution control.

6.B.1. Goals of Error Handling

6.B.1.a. Detection of Invalid Data Entry or System Output

In an interactive system, the first goal of error handling is to retain control no matter what stupidity is inflicted on the system by the user. If the user can cause a reversion of control to the operating system through any sort of bad data entry, your system has failed. (This does not mean defeating the execution override control provided by the operating system, such as Control/C or Reset.)

Regardless of the time and effort put into designing the prompts and other information messages, sooner or later, the users will enter invalid responses. This is not necessarily due to incompetence on the user's part, nor to lack of clarity on the programmer's part. For example, our cat likes to stroll across our keyboard, producing strange error messages we might otherwise never see. An incorrect key may be pressed due to inattention to the screen. Or someone may rest an arm on the keyboard while reaching for a cup of coffee. The programmer must guard against all these possibilities, which means trying to think of anything and everything that can go wrong short of turning off the power to the system. The users must have confidence that "obviously wrong" data will be rejected or at least flagged by the system. They must be reasonably sure that output files or reports with detected errors will be flagged so that no invalid interpretations of the output will occur. To achieve these goals, the designers must find out what the users expect to do with the outputs and what they would recognize as bad data if they were to proofread the input or output. There may be context information that is not clear to the software professionals. For example, the users may know that Status Q is never found in Class C but can occur in Class A, B, or D. You do not need to know everything about Status Q or Class C, as long as you know that it is important to your user. Your system should detect errors that the users could see, so they won't need to look.

An example of a data entry error is the entry of a nonnumeric character when a numeric character is needed. For users who learned to type on typewriters rather than word processors, this is an especially common problem because many typewriters did not have the number one (1); the typist was expected to use the lowercase letter l. This can be a difficult habit to break. Also, since typewriters don't distinguish between zero and the capital letter O, some typists use them interchangeably. This is a simple problem to deal with, but it can make a great deal of difference in user satisfaction.

6.B.1.b. Notification to the User to Take Actions to Recover

Error messages should indicate not only what happened but also what to do about it. Try to give the user some idea of what went wrong, but in the briefest possible terms. A more detailed help file should be available if needed. For example, a helpful message for someone using the computer dating service in Figure 6.1 might be:

"Response must be A, C, D, M, H, or Q"

A good set of error messages should allow an average user to correct errors and recover without having to read the manual every time. The manual should have more detailed descriptions to help the novice user. If there are some obscure conditions for which the message cannot carry all required details these should be described in the manual. A message such as "ERROR 43" is not acceptable in a delivered product. "Cute" messages should never be used, such as "YOU DID IT AGAIN, JERK." A number of useful characteristics of error messages are summarized in Figure 6.3.

To facilitate error detection when numeric entry is required, the data should be entered as character strings and converted to numeric format. The conversion process will generate an error if anything nonnumeric was entered. The user can then be told of the error with an explanation and given a chance to enter the information correctly. The user should always be given the opportunity to verify that the entry was done correctly.

Figure 6.3 Error Message Recommendations

      Error messages should never:
- insult the user
- be ambiguous
- be unhelpful
- be just a number

      Error messages should always:
- clearly indicate the nature of the fault
- suggest actions to recover
- avoid jargon as much as possible
- classify the error, e.g., data entry, system software, hardware

---

Sometimes output verification is needed. One method is to require human intervention and confirmation, with perhaps an authorization code to permit completion of special cases. For example, if a weekly payroll program computes an individual paycheck larger than some maximum amount such as $10,000.00, the user may want this flagged for verification.

6.B.1.c. Detection of Invalid Internal System States

Another major task for error handling is to detect the presence of bad data at module interfaces and invalid data generated within a module. These represent events which, hopefully, will never be seen by the users. Examples include undefined states in a decision table that should not have occurred, internal or output data outside the expected range, and table or file index values that are out of range. One subtle cause of such problems in many programming languages is the fact that array subscripts are not checked for an out-of-range condition unless you do it yourself.

All module inputs and outputs should be checked where possible. This means not only the obvious parameter list, but also file inputs and outputs and data passed as global parameters.

Error traps for such events are much more critical in languages that have separate compilation and do not have strong data type checking, such as FORTRAN or C. On the other hand, applications in Pascal, Modula-2, or Ada benefit from compiler and runtime checks on data consistency. Separate compilation may provide advantages in reducing the number and duration of compiler usage in large systems. However, one penalty in FORTRAN or C is that the language system does not detect parameter errors at module interfaces that would be data type violations caught by the compiler in a language with strong type checking.

In any module the first place to put error traps is as close as possible to the entry point.   That is where the parameters received should be checked. This is critical, since bad parameter values will invalidate whatever the module does. In some languages, such as Ada, this is not a problem because the language system can provide data type and range checks at runtime. Still, even in Ada one must be careful to authenticate that the declared ranges of validity of data are appropriate.

In some languages the compiler does not check data types and there are no range of value checks at runtime. In that case, the only defense against an improperly constructed function call to the module is to thoroughly check the range of values of the parameter. This gives a good probability of detecting a bad parameter. For example, if the value of X should be a floating point number on the range 0.00 to 1.00, there should be a trap conditioned on $(X < 0.00)$ OR $(X > 1.00)$.

It is important to note that error traps on the range of data values should not be limited only to the modules that acquire the data item from a file or keyboard input. Conservatism dictates that every module check its parameters even if the data was supposed to have been checked in the module that sent it. Any range tests that are possible should be done on received parameters. Any possible validation of computed results in the module should also be done. By now, you should realize that it is generally unsafe to assume that any software module has been proven correct. Keep in mind Dijkstra's dictum, "Testing can show the presence of errors, but not their absence."

Many error traps may never be triggered after delivery of the system. However, they will be very useful in validating the specifications of the module during development and in regression testing after alterations are made during maintenance. For this reason, you should not remove an error trap put in to support development and testing unless there is objective evidence for the need to optimize the execution speed of a module. Time spent in that modification is essentially wasted. It is much better to support future retesting during the inevitable changes. If your compiler has a macro preprocessor or directives to support conditional compilation, use these to cause the compiler to automatically exclude many of the internal error traps in producing the final object code.

6.B.1.d. Recovery from Improper Internal States

Illegal data, control codes, or internal results will almost certainly occur during development. It is to be hoped that these events do not occur after delivery, but the system must be protected against that possibility. If such an event does occur after the system is delivered to the users, two things need to happen. A suitable message must be sent to the user, and suitable action needs to be taken by the system. (We are not considering the case of an embedded system, which is running independently of any human intervention. The handling of such a system is beyond the scope of this book.)

The messages should tell the user that the event is not something caused by data entry, and clearly indicate that the fault should be reported to the systems programmer. This means that the messages that are useful and appropriate for the developer probably will not be meaningful to the user for these internal errors and should be rewritten before delivery. The delivered system does not have to have user-understandable error messages for internal errors. A message such as:

*** Fig Leaf Dating Service INTERNAL ERROR 39 ***

REPORT TO SYSTEMS PROGRAMMER

may indeed be appropriate to properly inform the user of the Fig Leaf Dating Service program that this is an event that is not supposed to happen. The "INTERNAL ERROR 39" part of the message is for the benefit of the systems programmer.

In most cases recovery by the user from internal errors is not possible and will require that corrective maintenance be done. Under these conditions, proper response of the system to the detection of such an error should be to save whatever files or data may be appropriate, and abort execution after notifying the user of the event.

It is useful to have an error flag used to force the execution of a special abort routine. This routine could, for example, save temporary files that would be deleted in normal execution.

In most languages, it is possible to write routines to implement error handlers that intercept condition codes from the operating system. By using the intercepted condition code, it is possible to undertake recovery actions and print error messages for an event which would otherwise be a fatal error. This allows you to write error handlers for runtime errors.

In some cases, this facility is part of the language itself (Ada, Microsoft BASIC, and PL/I). In Ada, for example, the reserved words *exception* and *raise* are used to identify exception conditions, including errors, and indicate what action should be taken. Several exceptions are predefined in the language, including NUMERIC_ERROR to handle zero divide.

In other cases, one must use special system library routines that can communicate with the operating system (C/Unix V, Turbo Pascal 5.5/MS-DOS 3.+, and VAX FORTRAN 4.0/VMS 4.4). In C, for example, the term *signal* is used in reference to a condition code. A function by that name is used to examine the condition code and return a pointer to an appropriate error handler. The related function *raise* may be used to set the condition code.

In FORTRAN 77, the language standard provides support for I/O errors, but other runtime errors must be handled by special library functions associated with the operating system. In Turbo Pascal, a standard library procedure is supplied to handle runtime errors for use with graphics display hardware. The function GRAPHRESULT captures a condition code for the result of 24 different graphics output procedures. A user-written procedure can take alternative actions based on which of 16 possible return codes has been obtained. Other condition codes must be handled by user-installed "exit" procedures.

Figure 6.4 gives an example of exception handling in Ada. Consider the example of flagging a paycheck of over $10,000. The dollar amount is generated as an internal value. The code in Figure 6.4 shows how to use Ada's exception handling to flag this value. *large_check* is declared type exception. The raise statement calls attention to the exception, and the statements in the exception procedure tell what to do when this happens.

```
Figure 6.4   Example of Runtime Error Handling: Ada

procedure calculate_pay is
     paycheck:  float;
     large_check:  exception;
begin
     -- statements
     if paycheck > limit then
          raise large_check;
     end if;
exception
     when large_check =>
     -- statements for action to be taken
     -- for manual authorization
end calculate_pay;
```

Figure 6.5 shows a FORTRAN 77 example of intercepting an end-of-file or other I/O error. When the READ is executed, an end-of-file condition will transfer control to statement 100. Any other I/O error will transfer control to statement 200. ICOND2 is an integer variable that, after execution of the READ statement, indicates the I/O status by taking an integer value. The specific value or range of values is indicated in the manual.

```
Figure 6.5   Example of Runtime Error Handling: FORTRAN I/O

        READ (5, *, END = 100, ERR = 200, IOSTAT = ICOND2) X
            :
100     action to be taken if end-of-file occurs
            :
200     action to be taken if other I/O error occurs
            :
```

Figure 6.6 gives an example of intercepting a zero divide in Microsoft BASIC. The error handling statement (240 in this example) must execute before the point where a specific error might occur. This sets a pointer in an interrupt handler that is activated when an error occurs. In Figure 6.6, if statement 250 causes a zero divide error, control transfers to statement 300, presuming that no other error handling statement occurs between statements 250 and 300. Other ON ERROR statements may be placed in other locations in the program, with a suitable label, in the form

ON ERROR GOTO 'label'

In the event of an error, control transfers to the label specified by the most recently executed ON ERROR statement.

```
Figure 6.6   Example of Runtime Error Handling:
             BASIC Zero Divide

240   ON ERROR GOTO 300
250   X = A/B
        .
        .
300   action to be taken if zero divide occurs in statement 250
        .
        .
```

6.B.1.e. Provide Messages to Aid in Testing the System

The error handler may be used as part of instrumentation built in to test the system. The best policy is to ensure that the code required to test modules as units is still in place to test the module in the environment of the rest of the system. If at all possible these error traps should be left in place to support testing in whatever maintenance will be done later.

A special error message file may be kept for the maintenance programmer, with messages that are meaningful to the systems programmer but not to the users. Thus this message:

39: Error in SYS_PORT_2 on call from OUT_SET

might replace the cryptic message:

*** INTERNAL ERROR 39 ***

which might be seen by the user. The combination of a good set of error traps and coverage of the code structure by conditional output statements, as we discussed in the context of interactive tracing, should make it easy to do a systematic verification of the execution of the system. To this end the error handler should provide enough information to locate the specific error trap that has been triggered in the source code.

6.B.2. Separate Error Handler

6.B.2.a. Rationale

Any significant applications program is going to have many error messages. Many of these represent events which, to the system user, are equivalent. The user does not need to know if they arise in different contexts from the standpoint of the programmer. When different things happen that produce the same error from the user's viewpoint, the message should be same independent of where it comes from within the underlying code. In other words, errors from the same equivalence class should produce identical error messages. The easiest way to ensure that this occurs is to have all messages generated at one place even if they are invoked from many places within the software.

This has several benefits. One is that the message need only be written once. Also, from a maintenance standpoint, it is useful to have a single place where a message should be modified if the actual wording is not appropriate for the users and needs to be changed.

This viewpoint also dictates that the error messages should be in a text file, not coded as literals in output statements. The same disadvantages apply to strings coded as data initialization statements. Maintenance is easiest if it only requires the modification of a text file with whatever editor is available. Changing any error message embedded in source code requires recompilation, and should entail some testing to be sure that nothing else was inadvertently changed. The risk of inadvertent change is worst if the error messages are embedded at the point in the code where the error is detected.

6.B.2.b. Separate Error Handler Procedure

A good user interface is likely to have a large number of error messages, and for most systems it is reasonable to have them all handled by a single module. Even though this violates some principles that are recommended in the next chapter, the benefits tend to outweigh the disadvantages.

One of the major benefits of a separate error handler is that all error messages are in one place, preferably in a text file, and available for convenient inspection. This helps minimize duplication. A specific error message called from multiple places in the system will still be the same message and needs to be created only once. Another advantage is that it is relatively easy to review the error messages for consistency of style and for completeness. Furthermore, it is easy to add to the list at any time.

6.B.3. Use of External Files for Messages

Figure 6.7 shows the error handler procedure that can be used with the Fig Leaf Enterprises system in Figure 6.1. The error messages are put in a text file created with a text editor. Here we presume that there is one line (record) for each error message. The module is called with a single integer parameter, which corresponds to the record number. In Turbo Pascal it is possible to set the pointer directly on the desired record, but the method shown has more general application in other languages.

```
Figure 6.7  Example of an Error Handler That Uses a Text File

procedure ErrorHandler (number:integer);
(****************************************************************
*                                                              *
*   This is the procedure to find the appropriate error and    *
*   write it to the screen for the user,                       *
*                                                              *
*   Modules called - none                                      *
*                                                              *
*   Modules called by - all that use error messages            *
*                                                              *
*_____*
*                                                              *
*   Files used: Error - text file of error messages            *
*                                                              *
*_____*
*                                                              *
*   Data dictionary - number: integer for loop count           *
*                                                              *
****************************************************************)
var count: integer;
begin (* ErrorHandler *)
   count := 0;
   assign (Error,'ERRORTXT'); (* assign name to text file *)
   reset(Error); (* open existing file *)
   repeat
      count := count + 1;
      readln (Error,textline);
   until count = number;
   writeln(' ',textline);
   close (Error);   (* close file *)
end;
```

The general procedure is to open the file and read each error message until the desired message is reached. The desired message is then written to the screen.

The required error message is fetched by a sequential file access. This implies N-1 dummy read operations before fetching the record N, which we wish to write. You may ask, "Why not use direct access, since it is faster?" The answer is that you could, but why optimize a function that we know in advance will halt normal execution? For any reasonable system the access of error messages must be an exceptional event. These accesses will not contribute significantly to the runtime elapsed in normal execution. If uniformity of response time is an issue it is often possible to set the size of the buffer used for the read operation so that the message file is memory resident after the first access.

Also, some systems may require that the records in a random access file must be fixed length, which reduces our flexibility to modify and maintain the file with a text editor. Certainly you do not want to give up the flexibility before the system is ready for delivery, and probably not then.

Having the error messages in a text file, as with the menus, has enormous advantages. The flexibility of being able to modify and add to the list of messages without altering the code means you won't inadvertently introduce a problem into the source code. It also means you won't have to recompile to run the system with updated messages.

Multiple line messages are also possible and can be done in several ways. If each message is to be the same number of lines, that number of records can be processed with each iteration of the loop. More flexibly, one could ask for several messages. Using the error handler in Figure 6.7, the procedure would be:

ErrorHandler(22); ErrorHandler(5); ErrorHandler(12);

which would produce a three-line message.

Another advantage of using a text file is that you have a complete set of error messages in machine-readable form. Under these conditions it becomes trivial to add an exhaustive list of error messages to the user's manual. Perhaps some additional text might be put in the manual explaining implications or other actions that might be taken to recover from or to avoid recurrences of the error.

Sophisticated users will read the table of error messages to assess the limitations of the system. For example, in a particular application we wondered if there would be a problem if procedures became nested too deeply. The compiler language manual indicated that procedure return addresses were stacked, but did not say what the maximum depth was. There was no runtime error message for nesting depth. This led to a test with a recursive procedure to see how deep it would get before it failed. Fail it did at a depth of 20, but there was no appropriate error message. Control passed to the operating system, which gave various messages depending on what data happened to lie in memory beyond the stack area.

A set of error messages is also nice to incorporate into the maintenance programmer's manual. If the list is already in machine-readable form, this not only reduces the work needed to assemble the list, it also reduces the possibility of error in the manuals.

A text file of error messages is also extremely easy to show a user, to find out if the messages are as meaningful and instructive as the user would like. A user who can write his or her own error messages may be more interested in endorsing the product, and will certainly be less likely to complain when the message appears during use of the system.

6.C. Human Factors

A large part of the design of a user interface is in the domain of human factors. The study of the interactions of people with computers is still in its infancy. However, the goal must be to make the system pleasant to the user in order to help the user be more productive on the job.

The traditional concerns of human factors experts dealt with issues of safety and productivity in the workplace. It is unfortunate that it is now just becoming understood that care must be taken in the design of video workstations with regard to such things as proper seating and the adjustment of the keyboard height, video screen height, and viewing angle. If terminal users do not have these parameters adjusted properly they may develop muscle tension headaches or chronic problems in the back or neck. There are still users with superstitious fears that these symptoms are caused by "radiation" exposure, when they should be using such things as adjustable chairs, video display bases, and nonglare lighting.

However, while these things are important, they are beyond the scope of this book. Our concerns with human factors are with those that help us create user interfaces that will put the best possible face on our computer systems.

We do not yet have experimental studies to guide us as to the best display strategies for particular types of tasks. In the meantime the best guide may be the comparison of the characteristics of systems that have been very successful in the marketplace, in contrast to those which are not. Space permits examining only a few of these.

6.C.1. Communication Between User and Computer

A user interface, in general, is the set of communication channels between the user and the computing system. This usually includes the use of video screens and keyboards. In addition, it may include sound output from a terminal device. Other input devices include pointing devices (such as a trackball or a mouse), touch devices (graphics tablet, touch screen, or light pen), or possibly audio sensors (speech recognizers, tone detectors).

Some microcomputers give feedback to the user in the form of a click each time a key is pressed, to indicate that proper key contact has been made. This may be done in several ways. On one microcomputer we use, the speaker is in the keyboard case and is programmed to generate a click on a keypress. On other keyboards, key clicks emanate mechanically from the keys, rather than from a speaker. The presence of such an audio feedback system helps assure the user that information is being processed.

The mouse is another input device that is gaining in popularity as a means to produce user inputs. It is extremely useful as a pointing device to select items from menus, and is indispensable for drawing lines and curves in graphical input.

The hardware also exists now to generate speech output and to recognize simple spoken commands. These forms of communication with a machine open up new applications.

Some modes of communication between user and computer are summarized in Table 6.1. The provision of alternate input or output modes can extend the utility of a computing system. Various users may have preferences or limitations that make one type of I/O easier.

Table 6.1 Some Modes of Communication Between User and Computer

Information	Input/Output	Devices
text	input	keyboard, optical scanner/pattern recognition
text	output	video screen, printer
numeric	input	keyboard, keypad, bar code reader
numeric	output	video display, printer, numeric digit displays
logic state	input	keyboard, keypad, switch
logic state	output	screen, light
sound	output	speaker
graphics	input	mouse, light pen, digitizer, tablet
graphics	output	video screen, plotter, dot-addressable printer
speech	input	microphone/speech recognition system
speech	output	speech synthesizer/speaker
video	input	frame grabber

It is extremely important to choose modes of communication between the user and the machine that fit the user's environment. If, for example, you want to automate drafting, it will not be comfortable to the users unless you provide graphic input and output. As another example, if the user normally uses his or her hands continuously in another task, then speech input may be necessary.

6.C.2. Factors Affecting System Usability

A user's dialogue with the system can be divided into a series of subsidiary tasks. The number of these subtasks is a measure of the effort required to complete a task. Table 6.2 summarizes some types of component tasks involved in a user dialogue with a system, which should be considered when writing an interface. One aspect of designing the user interface is to explicitly decompose and model the dialogue with the user in terms of an identified collection of subtasks.

```
Table 6.2   Types of Subtasks in User-Computer Interaction

  • select an item              • position an object
  • orient an object            • define a path
  • quantify a parameter        • define text
```

The evaluation of user interfaces requires the consideration of a number of important human factors. Some of these are neither independent nor easily quantifiable. The evaluation of human factors may require experimentation with prototypes or observation of user activities as well as the usual interviews and surveys. Some factors to consider are listed in Table 6.3.

```
Table 6.3   Human Factor Concerns in Design and Analysis of
            User Interfaces

Primary concerns:              Secondary concerns:

  Task completion time           Learning time
  Accuracy                       Recall time
  Pleasure                       Short-term memory load
                                 Long-term memory load
                                 Error susceptibility
                                 Fatigue susceptibility
                                 Naturalness
                                 Boundedness
```

Note that some factors are readily measured while others are not. We have included "pleasure" in using the system even though that is not easy to measure. If a system is unpleasant to use, for whatever reason, it will be used as little as possible. If someone has to use it, the task will be inflicted on those who can't avoid it. Therefore designers must take pains to ensure that the users have a good feeling about the product.

Although our examples in this chapter consist of text-oriented communication with the user, you should choose the communication mode that is most appropriate for a specific application. If the interface concepts to be employed are new or if there is any reason to believe that there is risk in the design, it is wise to consider rapid prototyping.

Table 6.4 summarizes some general guidelines to consider in designing the system dialogue with the user to make the system easy to use. The dialogue should be designed to minimize user effort. This means that the designer must understand how the user will carry out tasks and what tasks normally occur together. A good system gives the user more information to help decide an action to select, if it is needed. The dialogue, however, should not force users to add steps that are perceived as unnecessary.

Table 6.4 Some General Guidelines to Ensure the
Ease of Use of an Interface

- The prompts must correspond to the normal language terms of users' tasks.
- All messages must be instructive. Error messages must indicate the steps necessary to recover. Teach rather than punish.
- All system messages must be polite and in good taste.
- It is desirable to have direct command entry for experienced users and also menu selection hierarchies for beginners.
- The system should sell itself to the user.
- The system must be supportive. Wherever the next step is not obvious, additional help should be available.
- The user's input should be validated wherever possible. The system should specifically recognize expected classes of errors.
- The dialogue structure should be designed to allow the user to perform routine tasks with minimum effort.
- The user should be given the option of moving the cursor to select menu items.
- Information needed for current operations should be kept on the screen. Irrelevant information should be deleted from the screen.
- The user interface should be field tested to ensure that it is easy to use (independent of rapid prototyping).

6.D. Aspects of User Interface Design

Some things to keep in mind while designing the user interface are summarized in Table 6.5. We will look at each of these items individually.

Table 6.5 Aspects of the User Interface to be
Considered During Design

- Design of a menu hierarchy
- Appearance of the screen
- Effective use of color
- Contents of the prompts and responses

6.D.1. Menu Design

Menu design covers several factors. If the number of commands or options available to the user is small enough, they should all be placed in a single menu. If additional submenus are needed then there is a tree of commands or menu hierarchy. In general a broader tree with less depth is preferable in limiting user effort. In addition, if the command structure is a multilayer tree, you must provide the means to a direct move to any sub-tree and back to the highest level menu.

Within a menu there are several ways to arrange the items: alphabetical order, functional grouping, or frequency of use. Experiments show that novices make selections faster from an alphabetical listing than from functional or random order. Expert users perform at about the same speed with either alphabetical or functional order, either of which is much better than random order. The menu items may be names or icons (pictures) or both. If only icons are used, take care that the icons are meaningful to the user.

Menus may be set up in a variety of ways. One way is to send the list of options to the screen from a text file and ask for a response, which will be entered following a system prompt such as a question mark. This response may be the entry of an initial letter or a number, or putting the cursor on the appropriate menu choice.

Menus are often written with lists of numbers or letters available for the user to enter. Mnemonics, or meaningful letters, are usually easier for the user to remember and make a system easier to use.

Q is used in many systems for the option to quit, as illustrated in Figure 6.1. If there is any chance that data might be lost by a premature exit to the operating system, use of this option should be followed by a verification. An example of this hazard is illustrated in our opening quote.

If the user is to enter the reply next to the system prompt, the menu should list exactly what the user is to type to get the option without using delimiters. In other words, a menu item of

A: Add a client to the file
is much clearer than

To add a client to the file, enter 'A'
where the user may try to type the quote marks as well as the letter. The system illustrated only accepts the first character, so entering a colon after the letter will not cause a problem. However, a response with an initial quote could make selection of an appropriate error message more complicated.

The user should always have access to the possible options for the requested response without seeking a written manual. These options may be printed above or below the prompt if space permits. Another technique is to write the options on a portion of the screen reserved for the menu. Or the options may be stored in a file that the user may request. This is especially useful if the user has opted to use a system with terse prompts. A common menu item is H for help files. Alternatively, a useful option for help files is ?.

An alternative method of menu selection is to highlight the current selection. Then a highlighted bar can be moved to successive items in the menu by arrow keys. A carriage return is accepted to select the item. A simple extension provides for moving the bar with a mouse and accepting an input selection when the mouse button is pressed.

In the case of multiple levels of menus, novice users may find a highlighted bar at each level easy to use. However, experienced users who already know the menu item they wish to select at each level may find this technique tedious. Such users will find it easier to use a mnemonic to access each successive menu level rather than moving cursor keys. It is even better if they can enter a sequence of letters that allows bypassing the menus. This gives them the fastest access to the system action they desire without actually reading all the menus.

To provide ease of use to diverse users, it is appropriate to support multiple response methods. This allows a user to choose the response mode based on his or her individual style. An example of a highly successful user interface that supports multiple response methods is the spreadsheet. The best known is Lotus 1-2-3. There are several products that have the same look and feel, that is they have essentially the same user interface in terms of command hierarchy and command entry even if the screen layouts are not identical. Thus once having learned to use one of them, it is easy to use any product that has those interface characteristics.

The example in Figure 6.8 shows a sequence of screen views from V P Planner Plus. This example follows a sequence of menu displays and selections that may be chosen by a novice user in selecting a spreadsheet file named **product.wks**. An experienced user who prefers direct command entry can enter:

/FRproduct

without looking at the menus, knowing that / starts a command and the sequence of first letters FR is a mnemonic for File Retrieve. Mouse users can move the highlight bars and make selections with a mouse button. Thus the same operation can be accomplished in several ways.

```
Figure 6.8  Menu Sequence in V P Planner Plus to Enter a Command to Load
            a Spreadsheet Workfile

  The sequence of screens follows a user through the steps in loading a work
file.  A command is  started by typing /.  Selecting the proper  command and
subcommand gets the user to the prompt for a filename.

Screen A:    V P Planner Plus opening screen.

        A       B       C       D       E       F       G       H
 1
 2
 3
 4
 5                      V P - P l a n n e r    P L U S
 6
 7                   Copyright 1985, 1986, 1987, 1988
 8              James Stephenson, David Mitchell, Kent Brothers
 9              Stephenson Software Inc. -- All rights reserved
10
11              Published by Paperback Software International
12
13
14                  Licensed for the exclusive use of
15                    Registered Single-User Licensee
16
17
18
19
20
 A1

1help 2edit 3name 4abs 5goto 6window 7data 8table 9recalculate 0graph
 43K                           9:51                                READY
```

Screen B: Highest level command menu. Secondary menu at the right shows the
options available for the highlighted item in the menu on the left.   The user
selects an item in the left menu by entering its first letter, or by moving
the highlight bar with the cursor keys or a mouse.   Selection is made by
touching a mouse button or the Return key.

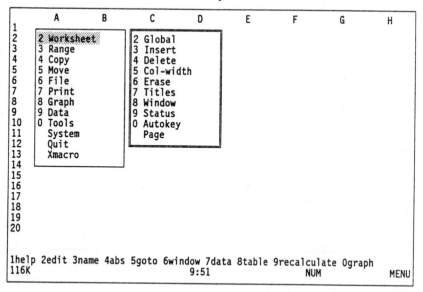

Screen C: Having selected F in Screen B, we see the options for file oper-
operations.   This menu has the first item highlighted and another window to
the right gives a brief description.   Pressing the Return key or a mouse
button selects the item.

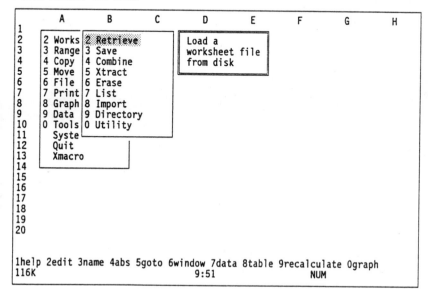

Screen D: We selected Retrieve from Screen C.   We are now presented with a
list of files from the current directory and a data entry line.

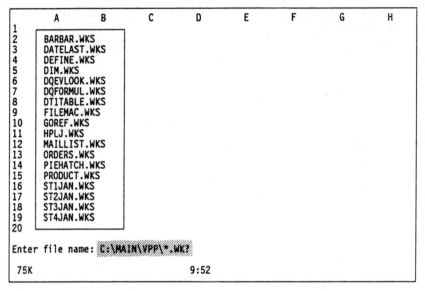

Screen E: At this point the user can select an existing file by moving the
highlight bar with the cursor keys or mouse and select the desired file.
Alternatively a file name can be typed in, at which point the directory list
vanishes and the name entered replaces *.wks in the data entry line.   On
entering a return character the file will be loaded (if it exists) or created.

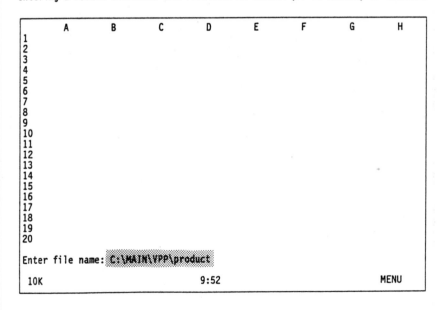

6.D.2. Tools for Creating Menu Systems

The problem of generating menus and help screens is one that recurs with each new system or major upgrade of an existing system. A menu generator, a standard tool for creating applications or prototypes, allows the creation or modification of menus and display screens by processing a text file as input. Such a system may be a compiler or an interpreter. Thus the creation process is reduced to a job with a text editor. Even if a menu generator has its own peculiar syntactic rules it is preferable to isolate the input/output operations from the functional and algorithmic details of the system as much as possible.

The purpose of the user interface is to translate what the user wants into a command in an internal (procedural) form convenient to the system. That command may be carried out by direct procedure calls, or it may select an executable program or initiate an operating system command file (batch file). Any of these may have parameters specified by keyboard input.

The use of a standardized menu generator makes the creation and modification of the menus and a command handler extremely simple. Many such systems are available commercially and a few are available as shareware or public domain software. It is good practice to use such a system rather than rewrite custom programs for each application.

One possible tool for prototyping an information system is a database management system (DBMS). A database product often provides an array of menu and screen design utilities to permit rapid prototyping, even if the final product will not be based on the DBMS. A database product like Ashton-Tate's dBASE III is also useful because it is an interpreter, which makes debugging easy during the prototyping process.

6.D.3. Screen Formatting

Screen appearance can have a major impact on the readability and acceptability of the user interface. Keep in mind the tremendous flexibility that is available in screen formatting.

If you are working with a color system, consider the impact of the color combinations. Use the highest possible contrast available for the most important menu items, as these will then be the easiest to read. This is especially important if there is any possibility that the system will be run with a monochromatic monitor. Graphics may enhance a computer interface if well done, but be careful not to clutter up the screen. Be sure to get the important information to the user first.

In creating screens for the user, be sure to leave adequate blank space. It is a good idea to put in blank lines between text lines. Use the entire screen width. A screen will usually handle more characters than you may be used to putting in a single line of text. But in terms of readability, one long line is often better than two short lines.

Finally, if information on the screen is not appropriate for the next transaction, or is not needed, it should be cleared from the screen. Information that is still relevant should be left in place. This can be done with control characters to move the cursor and clear specific portions of the screen.

Table 6.6 gives a list of some of the ANSI Standard Terminal Control Codes. Of course, not all terminals or microcomputer console devices use ANSI codes. On PC-DOS and MS-DOS microcomputers a standard install-able device driver routine (ANSI.SYS) is provided to make text I/O respond as an ANSI terminal. For other systems you may have to dig in the technical manuals to find the appropriate control codes or strings defined for screen control. A crude (and slow) alternative is to rewrite the entire screen with a suitable number of blank lines, and then rewrite.

By using terminal control codes you can reposition the cursor, which indicates where text entered from the keyboard will be displayed. By planning the layout carefully you can make it easy to clear data from the screen with the "clear to end of line" or "clear to end of screen" functions. This makes it possible to have fast screen updates even on dumb terminals. The key is writing or erasing the appropriate information in a limited area instead of painting the whole screen.

6.D.4. *Effective Use of Color*

Color can be used in many ways in menus. For example, it can add an additional redundant dimension to the organization of item groups. If items that are logically or functionally related are flagged by the same color, as well as grouped together in the same region of a screen, it reinforces the mental association of the item with the group. Such associations of a group with its color should be consistent on different screen displays in the system. In addition, other associations with a color can be exploited; for example, a red background box switched on for a warning or error recovery message can be effective in getting user attention.

Another factor to consider in creating color displays is to limit the total number of colors. While color can make a display screen more lively, humans can readily recall only a limited number of specific distinguishable states. If the goal is to associate a color with a function, there should be no more than seven for ease of recall.

As the color capabilities of display devices increase, it becomes possible to choose from a wide range of color combinations. However, the color perception capabilities of the human eye are not uniform across the spectrum.

```
Table 6.6  Some ANSI Standard Terminal Control Codes
           ANSI X3.64 (1979)

         ANSI Function                        ASCII Code Sequence
Set cursor at position row,col          Esc [ Row ; Col H
Clear screen and home                   Esc [ H Esc [ J
Cursor up n rows                        Esc [ n A
Cursor down n rows                      Esc [ n B
Cursor right n columns                  Esc [ n C
Cursor left n columns                   Esc [ n D
Save cursor position                    Esc [ s
Restore cursor position                 Esc [ u
Erase to end of line                    Esc [ K
Erase to bottom of screen               Esc [ 2 J
Report cursor position                  Esc [ n ; n R
Redefine a keyboard character           Esc [ ascii1 ; ascii2 p
      (the ASCII character defined by
      ascii1 is redefined to the ASCII
      character defined by ascii2)
Redefine a function key                 Esc [ 0 ; key ; "string" p
      key is defined as follows:
          F1 = 59, F2 = 60 ... F10 = 68
      string is a sequence of ASCII characters
Notes:
Terminal display screen coordinates for positioning a character are
   specified by row and column.   Home = 0,0 (upper left corner).
Esc = ASCII escape character, Control/[, or value 1B hex.
Row = number of a horizontal line on the screen in ASCII digit characters.
Col = number of a vertical column on the screen in ASCII digit characters.
n   = a parameter value in ASCII digit characters.
All other characters in the sequences are literals.   No blanks are in
   the sequences. Spaces are shown only for ease of reading.
```

The usual color system of a display monitor is based on mixtures of red, blue, and green (known as the RGB color system). The human eye has three kinds of receptors, also based on those primary colors. Other colors are seen as mixtures of these. However, the eye's receptors for blue are less sensitive than those for red and green. Your eye's depth of focus depends on the wavelength; that is, the eye focuses on red, blue, and green at different points. This is shown in Figure 6.9.

For a clear image of a picture that contains both red and blue, the eye must change the shape of its lens by muscle contractions to focus alternately between the red and the blue areas. The observer is not aware of these changes, but they can cause eyestrain. In this context, the worst possible color combination is red against blue. The best color combinations are yellow or green against black, and white or yellow against blue.

When creating a color system, remember that there is great variability from one model of monitor to another. A color system must always be tested on the target machine for an accurate assessment of the color portrayals.

Figure 6.9   The lens and cornea of the eye form a multi-unit thick lens system which has a focal length that vary with wavelength. Red rays have a shorter focal length than blue. Green is in between.   Light rays from a distant object, left, are bent to focus on the back wall of the eyeball.

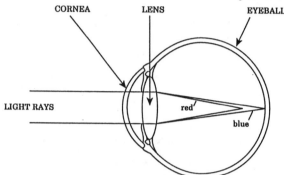

The inside of the back of the eyeball is lined with a very thin layer of nerve cells and photoreceptors. The lens is flexible and can change its shape to adjust the focused image for effects of distance and color.

Additionally, since many users may use the system with a monochrome display, you must consider their needs. Either make sure that the colors have distinguishable intensities on a monochrome monitor, or provide a user-selected optional display configuration for monochrome.

Color can greatly enhance users' pleasure in a system. Some guidelines for the use of color in screen displays are summarized in Table 6.7.

Table 6.7   Effective Use of Color

- Associate a specific color with a functional group on a menu.
- Limit the total number of colors in a display to seven or less.
- Avoid color combinations that produce eyestrain, especially red against blue.
- Use color combinations that are easy on the eye, especially yellow or green against black, and white or yellow against blue.
- Choose colors whose intensity differences are distinguishable if viewed on a monochrome display.

6.D.5. Contents of Interactive Prompts and Responses

Interactive prompts should be meaningful to the user. A prompt that is crystal-clear to you may mean nothing to someone whose expertise is in another area. Conversely, if the user wants a particular prompt that you don't understand, use it. Since it is the user who will be using (and paying for) the system, it is the user's terminology that should be used.

A system should be easy to learn as well as easy to use. Unfortunately, the very information that can help a user learn a system may also slow down an experienced user who has to wade through the information that he or she now finds obstructive rather than useful.

One solution is to write a system with dual levels, one for the novice and one for the experienced user. There are several ways of doing this. One way is by putting additional information into a separate screen section that can appear for the novice but not for the experienced user. This can be done by having the additional information appear after a time delay; that is, after there has been no keyboard input for a specified period of time.

Another approach is to give the user a choice of prompts, one verbose set for the novice and one terse set for the experienced user. The user interface in Figure 6.1 illustrates one way to do this, and gives the user the choice. Note that the experienced user can request the terse prompts, but the novice doesn't need to understand the question. Any answer other than Y or y, including an empty carriage return, results in the verbose prompts. This procedure consists of asking the user's preference before the command handler is used. This sets a global flag, which can be used anywhere in the program in an if..then..else structure to select the appropriate set of prompts.

For readability when writing interactive prompts, take advantage of upper and lowercase letters, and any other size that may be available in a graphics system. Use capitals and other large letters for emphasis.

The interactive response should be logical to the user. The menu given in Figure 6.2 for Fig Leaf Enterprises Computer Dating Service uses letters that are associated with the feature: A is used for adding a client, C for changing a client, and D for deleting a client from the file. For finding a match, the system could have used S for select, but not D for date. The letter M was used for match, and the corresponding word in the description was capitalized to help the user remember.

6.E. Design Constraints

When designing the details of a system, there are a number of things to keep in mind both from the standpoint of user convenience and programming approach.

6.E.1. From the User's Standpoint

The user should always have a convenient way out of every procedure, and should be able to terminate the system at any time. People on the job have multiple responsibilities, and a phone call can interrupt a program at any time. It should not be necessary for the user to have to wonder just where he or she is in the program, nor to have to go through a complicated, multistep procedure to save the work already done.

Another consideration that will make users happy is to keep a system flexible when it prints multiple screens of information. Be sure that the user has the option of pausing or conveniently terminating a procedure, as well as continuing until conclusion.

Users should be allowed the option of verifying their responses and given the opportunity to change them. Along with this, short verifications of the data being changed will assure the user that the correct data item is being changed.

6.E.2. From the Programmer's Standpoint

The design of input and output screens should be specified with sample screens represented with machine-readable files. Preferably these should be ordinary text files, which can be composed or interpreted with standard editors. Obviously these can also be printed as part of documents.

Some things to keep in mind when writing the program, which are not of interest to the user, can make a great deal of difference in program effectiveness, flexibility, and reliability. For example, when printing information from arrays, be sure to print only the information that has been initialized.

If there is a high probability that the user will address the same subroutine multiple times in succession, let the subroutine retain control until task completion. This reduces execution time.

Avoid using counted loops for data input. There is no satisfactory way to leave such a loop when the user is forced to terminate processing prior to completion of the loop count. Instead, use conditional loops such as while or repeat.

Before you conclude that these things should go without saying, ask anyone who has worked on a test team how often these errors cause problems (and then do your best to reduce that number).

6.F. Course Project: A Rapid Prototype

If your project is an interactive system, the first thing you might want to do is rapid prototyping; that is, construct a "do-nothing" user interface that calls stubs for each feature. Remember that a prototype is a simplified version, usually lacking the features of the finished product. It gives the user an idea of whether the system being developed is the system that is actually wanted. In the case of a course project, the entire project may itself be a prototype. In that case, the empty user interface would be a prototype of a prototype.

There are several good reasons for constructing this shell. One is that, as already mentioned, it can give the user the "look and feel" of the system under development. Another reason is that it gives the development group a morale boost. After all the time you've spent specifying and planning the system, it will feel good to see something actually working, especially if it performs the way you expect it to. If it turns out that it does not work the way you expect it to, some redesign must be done before going any further.

At this point, for most projects, you should also incorporate an error handler and an interactive trace system, possibly similar to the error handler described in this chapter and the trace system described in Chapter 5 and Appendix B. These features will be valuable in testing and debugging as you integrate your system.

From the standpoint of total development, the shell, error handler, and trace system are a relatively minor amount of the work and should not take long. The actual code for the rapid prototype will usually be about 5% of the code for most projects.

6.G. Beyond a Course Project: Performance Considerations and User Attitude

The display rate, or the rate at which information appears on the screen, can affect the user's attitude toward the system. As we have already indicated, many optimization and performance considerations are beyond the scope of this book. In this section, we describe some findings about aspects of user interfaces and system performance that have been found to influence user satisfaction.

If the display rate is slower than the user's reading speed, he or she may be annoyed at having to wait for the text to appear. On the other hand, if the rate of displaying a character stream is a little faster than a comfortable reading rate, the user will feel pressured to read faster and again will be annoyed. Interestingly, it has been found that if the display rate is much faster than the user's reading rate (1 to 2 seconds for a screen update) it is perceived as an instant screen change, and the user will scan the screen for the information needed without feeling compelled to read at the rate that information is appearing.

User satisfaction with a system may be influenced by the response time. Users have expectations about appropriate response from other devices such as typewriters. When entering text they expect the delay between a keypress and the appearance of the character on the screen to be within a normal reaction time, 0.2 to 0.5 seconds. If the characters are echoed by a time-shared system that is slowing down under a heavy user load, an increase in the delay to 3 or 4 seconds will be an aggravation. If a response time does not vary more than ±50% it will generally be tolerated. Greater variation can be much more aggravating than a slower system. This has led some system managers on time-sharing systems to slow system response artificially to reduce the variability of response time between slack and heavy usage times.

Generally, faster response time is better. There is an observable increase in error rates in user dialogues with the system when the response time is slower or irregular. There may be a relationship between this increased error rate and the negative user attitude toward these factors. This is especially true if error recovery is difficult. Delays greater than a few seconds and variable delays are a problem because of the limits of human short-term memory. Unexpected variations or longer delays make it easy to forget what you were planning to do next. Thinking "Did I enter that command incorrectly?" frequently leads to making an error on the next command. Long delays increase the probability that some detail of the current status will be forgotten because of distraction by noise or other event in the environment.

Users' anxiety at long response times can be mitigated by making something happen on the screen while they are waiting. It is reassuring to have a message appear after a few seconds, such as "Please wait, your file is being processed." During a long operation, a message with some information feedback could be printed such as:

Processing file, one star for every 1000 records.
*****

where a new asterisk appears after each 1000 records have been processed. This may slow the process slightly, but given information on the progress (and file size) the user can have faith that something is happening. We once had to sort several megabytes of data in a small machine. During the three hour process, a screen display counter alleviated anxiety over its progress.

Summary

The success of an interactive program depends heavily on how well the user interface works. The user interface represents the first contact the user has with the system, and judgment about the system may be based heavily on how well this interface performs.

One approach is to create a prototype of a system that does nothing in the way of data output, but produces the selection menus for the system. This is a good way to get feedback from the user as to whether the system you are developing is what the user actually wants.

Error handling must look at input from keyboard, files, and other modules. All incoming data should be checked. Output should be checked to see if it is in a reasonable range. The system should be protected from aborting suddenly because of a system error that is not the user's fault. Error handlers can also be used to facilitate testing and maintenance. In general, a system should be designed to be convenient for the user. Error handling should be done in a way that maximizes assistance to the user. As with menus, error messages are usually best put in text files. There are advantages to using a single module for error handling.

There are many possible modes of communication between user and computer. The modes selected result in the user's perception of the "look and feel" of a system. The methods chosen should be the user's preference. Menus in text files offer the greatest system flexibility. The subjective factors in this and other aspects of user perception are known as human factors.

Menu design is a major consideration in an interactive system. Menus may be set up in a number of ways. Tools are available to help with menu creation. The use of color should take into account aspects of human color perception.

Prompts in interactive responses must be meaningful to the user. Responses must also be in a form acceptable to the user. User satisfaction with a system can be affected by response time.

Keywords

ANSI Standard Terminal Control Codes
antibugging
display rate
error handling
error messages
error trap
exception handling
human factors
internal system state
look and feel
menu design
menu hierarchy
menu selection
mnemonics
performance
prompts
prototype
rapid prototype
RGB color system

response time
screen formatting
separate error handler
text file
user interface
user satisfaction

Review Questions

6.1. Why is the user interface unpredictable?

6.2. How important is the user interface? In what way?

6.3. What is meant by the "look and feel" of the user interface? How important is it?

6.4. Describe a prototype user interface.

6.5. What are the advantages of putting menus and error messages in text files?

6.6. What are the advantages of putting error handling in a single module?

6.7. What makes a good error message?

6.8. How do you create a system that can recover from invalid internal states?

6.9. Should error handling messages used in system development be deleted or left in delivered code? Why?

6.10. List human factors of concern in the work environment and in the user interface.

6.11. List different types of physical input and output devices that may be used in a user interface.

6.12. List at least five considerations of the user interface that don't apply to the rest of the system.

6.13. In menu hierarchies, which is preferable, a broad tree of a few menus, or a narrow tree of many menus? Why?

6.14. Compare the advantages and disadvantages of the following menu orders: alphabetical, functional, random.

6.15. Meaningful prompts are needed in menus. Meaningful to whom?

6.16. Cite at least one tool that is helpful in generating menus.

6.17. Is there any reason to worry about monochrome monitors when writing a user interface for a color system?

6.18. Describe some ways of enhancing readability in a user interface.

6.19. Why is it necessary to understand how the human eye perceives color in order to write the most effective user interface?

6.20. How can you write a user interface that is easy for the user to learn? Does this cause any problems for the experienced user?

6.21. What are the most important performance considerations from the user's standpoint?

6.22. What design constraints in the source code can affect user satisfaction, and why?

Exercises

6.1. Describe how a prototype can give a user the look and feel of a system.

6.2. Criticize the command set used in the CAD system in the opening quotation. Suggest an alternative command set.

6.3. Determine whether your compiler supports exception handling as part of the language or by special library functions.

6.4. For the language system you are using, write a code fragment to detect each of the following kinds of errors:
(a) division by zero
(b) read past end-of-file
(c) disk I/O error
(d) attempt to send output to an offline printer
(e) error in output to a graphics subsystem

6.5. Design a specific screen layout for the main menu of a computer dating system for a 25-line by 80-column video monitor.

6.6. Copy the table of error messages from your preliminary user's manual into a text file for use with an error handler. Write a sequential access procedure to access the messages by error number.

6.7. Write pseudocode for the movement of a highlighting bar in your main menu. Assume your terminal has appropriate ANSI Standard Terminal Control Codes.

6.8. Look at the user interface for some application software with which you are familiar. Describe the features that make it easy to use. Make at least one suggestion as to how it might be improved.

6.9. A proposed system menu consists of a screen with a light blue background and a red border. The light blue area is

divided into two regions. The larger region contains a
title and a list of eight major system functions, each of
which has its own distinct color. The other region will be
used for command entry and error messages. Criticize
the aesthetics of such a use of color.

References

Booch, Grady. Software Engineering with Ada, 2d ed. Menlo Park, CA: Benjamin/Cummings,
1986.

> Description of exception handling introduced in Chapter 6 and described in Chapter
> 17.

Borland International. Turbo Pascal Owner's Handbook Version 4.0. Scotts Valley, CA:
Borland International, 1987.

> Chapter 24 describes graphics error handling; Chapter 26 describes exit procedures
> that may be user-defined to provdie handling for runtime errors.

Brooks, Frederick P. "No Silver Bullet." IEEE Computer 20, no. 4 (April 1987): 10-19.

> Fashioning complex conceptual constructs is the essence of programming; acciden-
> tal tasks arise in representing the constructs in language. Past progress has so
> reduced the accidental tasks that future progress now depends on addressing the es-
> sence.

Card, S. K., Moran, T. P., and Newell, A. The Psychology of Human-Computer Interaction.
Hillsdale, NJ: Laurence Erlbaum Assoc., 1983.

> A case study and analysis of user interactions with a text processing system.

Cooper, Doug, and Clancy, Michael. Oh! Pascal! 2d ed. New York: W.W. Norton, 1985.

> Excellent introductory Pascal text. Includes antibugging and debugging in every
> new topic; also includes a chapter on software engineering concepts.

Digital Equipment Corporation. Guide to Programming on VAX/VMS (AI-Y503B-TE).
Maynard, MA: Digital Press, April 1986.

> A general reference to VMS environment and system support for various program-
> ming languages with specific examples in FORTRAN. Chapter 10 details the con-
> struction of exception handlers.

Dijkstra, Edsgar W. "The Humble Programmer." Communications of the ACM 15,10 (October
1972): 859-866.

> Contains "Dijkstra's Dictum" that testing can prove the presence of bugs but not
> their absence.

Foley, James D., Wallace, Victor L., and Chan, Peggy. "The Human Factors of Computer
Graphics Techniques." Computer Graphics and Applications 4,11 (November
1984): 13-46.

> A good comprehensive review of the state of knowledge of human factors in com-
> puter display techniques. Cites 77 references and gives an annotated list of 48 other
> reference sources.

Gehani, Narain. Advanced C: Food for the Educated Palate. Rockville, MD: Computer Science Press, 1985.

Chapter 7 provides a good introduction to exception handling in C.

Good, M. D., Whiteside, J. A., Wixson, D. R., and Jones, S. J. "Building a User-derived Interface." Communications of the ACM 27,10 (October 1984): 1032-1043.

A rapid prototype of an electronic mail system was used to test user-derived command structures. Synonyms for command actions were incorporated as alternative commands to permit the final system to recognize over 75% of naive user requests without training in command syntax.

Harrison, M. D., and Thimbleby, H. W. "Formalising Guidelines for the Design of Interactive Systems." In P. Johnson and S. Cook, eds., People and Computers: Designing the Interface. London: Cambridge University Press, 1985, pp. 161-171.

Discusses issues required in the specification of user interface. Lists numerous guidelines for design.

International Business Machines. IBM Ergonomics Handbook (SV04 0224 01). Armonk, NY: IBM, n.d.

A brief introduction to a range of workplace human factors concerns, including worker comfort and safety. Includes consideration of VDT height and viewing angle, keyboard height, and seating constraints.

Johnson, Peter, and Cook, Steven, eds. People and Computers: Designing the Interface. London: Cambridge University Press, 1986.

A collection of papers from the proceedings of the 1985 Conference of the British Computer Society specialist group Human Computer Interaction.

Lien, David A. The BASIC Handbook. 3d ed. CompuSoft Publishing, 1986.

A cross-reference for BASIC programmers. Indicates syntax variations among different versions of BASIC. Defines more than 600 commands, functions, statements, and operators and presents examples including "ON ERROR."

Miller, George A. "The Magical Number Seven Plus or Minus Two: Some Limits on Our Capacity for Processing Information." Psychological Review 63 (1956): 81-97.

Classic discussion of experiments on human memory. Included in Yourdon's Writings of the Revolution, described below.

Murch, Gerald M. "Physiological Principles for the Effective Use of Color." IEEE Software 4, no. 11 (November 1984): 49-54.

Introduction to physiological and psychophysical aspects of color vision applied to video displays.

Newman, William M., and Sproull, Robert F. Principles of Interactive Computer Graphics, 2d ed. New York: McGraw-Hill, 1979.

Introductory text on interactive graphics.

Rushinek, Art, and Rushinek, Sara F. "What Makes Users Happy?" Communications of the ACM 29,7 (July 1986): 504-498.

In analysis of a survey of over 4000 users, satisfaction with software was positively correlated with response time, size of local user community, function according to expectation, and aid to productivity (range +.32 to +.21). Running on a micro was +.6. Running on a mainframe had a -.18 correlation.

Schneiderman, Ben. "Response Time and Display Rate in Human Performance with Computers." Computing Surveys 16,3 (September 1984): 265-286.

> Reviews problem of error rates due to failings of human short-term memory if computer response times in task execution are too long. Preferred response times to permit best productivity are generally under 1 second. Long response times or highly variable response times are distracting and lead to user discontent and increases in error rates.

Schneiderman, Ben. Designing the User Interface: Strategies for Effective Human-Computer Interaction. Reading, MA: Addison-Wesley, 1987.

> An extensive discussion of human factors, user interface design strategies, performance, and implementation.

Smith, Michael J. "Human Factors Issues in VDT Use: Environmental and Workstation Design Consideration." Computer Graphics and Applications 4,11 (November 1984): 56-63.

> A review of field and laboratory studies of video display terminal users. Results indicate no significant radiation exposure but widespread occurrence of improper viewing angle, excess keyboard height, bad seating, and excessive glare.

Spenser, Richard H. Computer Usability Testing and Evaluation. Englewood Cliffs, NJ: Prentice-Hall, 1985.

> Thorough coverage of computers and software from a product usability standpoint. Includes user documentation, packaging, human factors, and marketing concerns. Discusses user interfaces from the outside looking in.

Yourdon, Edward. Techniques of Program Structure and Design. Englewood Cliffs, NJ: Prentice-Hall, 1975.

> Notable for having a chapter on antibugging.

Yourdon, Edward, ed. Writings of the Revolution, Selected Readings on Software Engineering. New York: Yourdon Press, 1982.

> Collection of major papers in software engineering, includes George A. Miller's "The Magical Number Seven Plus or Minus Two: Some Limits on our Capacity for Processing Information,"

CHAPTER 7

ISSUES IN DETAILED DESIGN AND DEVELOPMENT

Software development has become the malevolent genie that has escaped the computer hardware lamp and roams the world bedeviling the lives of systems developers everywhere.

> - Joseph M. Fox, <u>Software and its Development</u>

Software entities are more complex for their size than perhaps any other human construct because no two parts are alike (at least above the statement level). If they are, we make the two similar parts into a subroutine - open or closed. In this respect software systems differ profoundly from computers, buildings, or automobiles, where repeated elements abound.

> - Frederick P. Brooks, Jr., "No Silver Bullet."

Software Life Cycle

Software development: Detailed design and coding

I. Software need
II. Preliminary feasibility judgment
III. Requirements analysis and feasibility study
IV. Requirements specification
V. Preliminary software design and planning
VI. Software development
Detailed design
Coding and unit testing
Integration
System testing
VII. Software maintenance

Project: Design and code

7.A. Quality of Modules

One of the most important reasons for applying software engineering principles is that software systems have become too large for one person to understand entirely in detail. Ideally, software systems should be built of individual modules, each of which stands alone. Each module should be easy to test, and when necessary easy to fix. If the user wants a change, the appropriate module should be easy to modify without worrying about its effects on other modules. This ideal is seldom achieved, but it is a goal to keep in mind when designing a system.

In order to have a well-designed program, a program module should be a black box. This means that the module should be capable of being described in terms of its function rather than the procedure by which it performs the function. The three main elements associated with the black box concept are input, transform, and output. Input to a black box consists of data supplied to the module. Output from a black box consists of data generated by the module. In each of these cases the data may take many forms depending on the nature of the programming language used. Some of the more common forms are: parameters passed to a procedure, data in a file, or values of variables. The transform consists of the combined effect of the statements that make up the module.

In this section, we look at several aspects of modular quality. First, we look at the internal composition of a module. The relationships among the internal parts of a module are called *cohesion*. Next, we examine the interfaces between modules to see how strongly interconnected they are. This interconnectedness is called *coupling*. We also look at modular span of control and information hiding.

7.A.1. Cohesion

Cohesion refers to the internal function of a module; that is, to the parts that hold it together and are the reason for its being a module. Ideally, a single module should perform a single function, and all aspects of the module should relate to that function. A well-designed program should be made up of cohesive modules. How do we know when a module is cohesive?

There are several different categories of cohesion; some are preferable to others. There is actually a continuum of types of cohesion. For the purposes of this text we will label several points on the cohesion continuum from most to least desirable, as indicated in Table 7.1. This is not a linear scale. While we try for the top of the scale, the mid-range is often acceptable. The design of any module requires judgment and usually involves tradeoffs. Sometimes a less desirable type of cohesion is chosen to prevent the use of something even worse. The important thing is to understand the underlying concept and strive for the highest feasible level of cohesion.

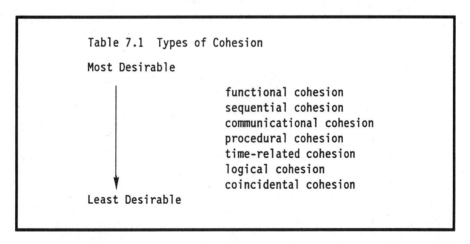

```
        Table 7.1   Types of Cohesion

        Most Desirable

             │                    functional cohesion
             │                    sequential cohesion
             │                    communicational cohesion
             │                    procedural cohesion
             │                    time-related cohesion
             │                    logical cohesion
             ▼                    coincidental cohesion
        Least Desirable
```

Let us look at the types of cohesion listed in Table 7.1, beginning with **functional cohesion.** It represents the most desirable form. A functionally cohesive module is a module in which every part is essential to the performance of a single, elementary function. It fits the description at the beginning of this section. It should be one that can be described in just a few words of English; for example, "Find the root of the function that lies on the interval [a,b]." However, some judgment needs to be used. For example, consider the module associated with the statement, "Process this month's payroll." This is too broad a statement for a module, just as a task such as "add two numbers" is too small to justify a module.

Sequential cohesion is when modules are designed on the basis of processing steps that occur in a specific order. For example, the output of part of the module becomes input for the next part. These operations must be done in the proper sequence. This usually is not a serious problem, but it should raise questions about whether the module is performing more than one function and should be split into two or more modules.

Another example of sequential cohesion is a module that combines initialization tasks with the first call to another module. This may be done because the programmer feels that there are not enough tasks to make up a "real" module. While it is true that adding another module means adding another interface to test, it is also true that single-function modules make testing and modification of a module easier.

Communicational cohesion describes a module in which several different processes are grouped together because they all use the same input data. This may be done for the convenience of having to use, for example, only one disk access. As another example, when the same information is going to be written on a report and stored in a file, it is very tempting to have both functions done by a single module. We are not telling you that it should never be done. That is a judgment call that depends on too many factors. But you should recognize it as communicational cohesion and document the module to note it.

Procedural cohesion occurs in modules that combine procedures. For example, there may be a grouping of items associated with a particular algorithm. Procedural cohesion often occurs when programmers identify the repeated performance of a series of steps. The danger lies in the steps not being related to a single function. For example, look at the hierarchy chart in Figure 7.1. The modules READ_PAY_RECORD, CALCULATE_PAY, and WRITE_PAY_CHECK may be part of a loop in the payroll program the figure represents. However, this is not a sufficient reason to put them in one giant module. The loop should not be the sole basis for module design. Instead, attention should be focused on the function performed and the amount and level of detail.

Another reason for putting related multiple functions in a single module is to ensure that they will occur in a specified order. Again, the decision to use a procedurally cohesive design is a matter of judgment. If used, it must be carefully documented. The distinctions between different types of cohesion are not always clear. The distinction between this example and the next type, time-related cohesion, can be somewhat fuzzy.

Time-related cohesion is based on a grouping of items that are associated because they occur together in time. One of the most common occurrences of time-related cohesion is in modules that perform initialization or termination. For example, such a module might open files and initialize variables. These things are done together because their relationship with each other calls for them to be done before certain other modules in the rest of the program are executed.

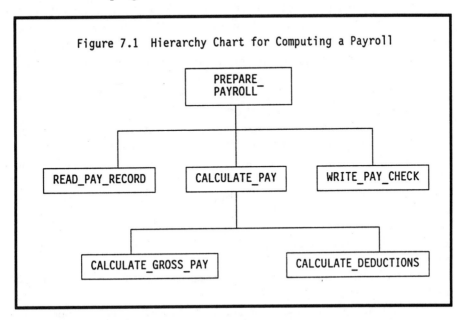

Figure 7.1 Hierarchy Chart for Computing a Payroll

Logical cohesion is based on a grouping of items that belong to the same broad class of logical functions. For example, the module may be generating several output items, related only by being in the same logical category of output. Which item in the class is dealt with may be set by a control variable received as a parameter.

This type of cohesion can lead to large, multiple-function modules. For example, a module may contain a case statement in which each option is a large collection of statements. It may be possible to change this into procedural cohesion by making sure that each case is handled by a call to a separate functionally cohesive module.

Coincidental cohesion occurs when a module contains otherwise unrelated functions; they just happen to be in the same module. Coincidental cohesion is not based on any rational grouping of items. In this case a module may look as if it consists of a more or less random collection of statements.

There is no universal agreement with regard to the exact nature of the continuum in Table 7.1. For a particular program, time-related cohesion might be preferred over communicational cohesion. Our recommendation is to follow a functional approach as your guide to program design.

In evaluating your own modules for cohesion, ask yourself some questions about each module, such as these:
- Does this module perform exactly one function? (If so, congratulations, you have functional cohesion.)

- If it performs more than one function, how are the functions related?
- Does one part use the results of another part? (sequential cohesion)
- Do all parts use the same information? (communicational cohesion)
- Are the parts put in one module because they need to be done in a specific order, perhaps to form a loop? (procedural cohesion)
- Is this module a collection of things that need to be done at the same time? (time-related cohesion)
- Are the parts somewhat related logically, e.g. all output, even though several different types? (logical cohesion)
- Is this module a catch-all for several things, perhaps each "too small" for its own module? (coincidental cohesion)

The level of cohesion to attribute to a module is the worst level observed. If any of your modules consist of any type of cohesion below functional, consider splitting the module into separate components. If you decide to leave the module as is, justify the use of cohesion in your documentation.

An example of how not to organize a software system is described by Edward Yourdon in <u>Nations at Risk</u> (1986):

> Several years ago I witnessed an amazing example of poor cohesion in one of the telephone operating companies in the Midwest. For traditional reasons, most of the software systems in this organization were divided into two major subsystems: "interstate processing" and "intrastate processing." In the system I examined, those two subsystems (or very large modules) probably had reasonably strong cohesion. But there was a third subsystem called "miscellaneous functions" that was much more dubious. And there was a fourth subsystem called "nonmiscellaneous functions" whose purpose I could never determine. On a ten-point cohesion scale, it would rank somewhere below zero.

7.A.2. Coupling

So far we have discussed what constitutes a good module. Equally important are the intermodular relationships. In this section we look at some aspects of modular independence. Remember that our objective is to build a system in which the individual modules can be understood, created, tested, debugged, and modified with a minimum of concern about other modules. We can do this when the modules are completely independent of one another. However, complete independence is not usually feasible since the modules need to work together. We want to make them as independent as possible.

Modules share interfaces and pass data and control across these interfaces. Two of the most common sources of coupling are parameters and global variables. When two modules share information and/or control, we have **coupling**. An important rule of good program design is that all kinds of coupling should be minimized.

Just as we placed types of cohesion on a continuum, we can place types of coupling on a quality continuum. It is usually impossible (and many times undesirable) to avoid all kinds of coupling. Types of coupling in order of decreasing desirability are listed in Table 7.2.

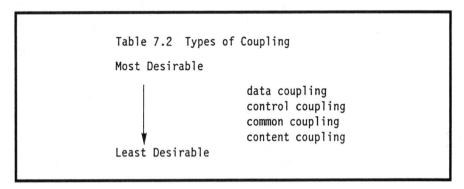

In **data coupling** the modules pass homogeneous data items between each other. These may be elementary data items such as integers, real numbers, or characters; or they may be data structures. An example is the standard parameter list passed between procedures in Pascal, PL/I, or FORTRAN. This is the most common kind of coupling and is at the low end of dependency; that is, it is the most desirable kind of coupling. It is practically impossible to create a software system without it.

In **control coupling** an element of control, often referred to as a flag or control variable, is passed between modules. The element of control may be passed in either direction. For example, consider a report generator that has the option of printing with or without a header. This decision is made by another module, which passes a control variable to the report generator at execution time to tell it to turn the header printing option on or off.

In **common coupling** the coupled modules share global variables. Data that is accessible by name, independent of module parameter lists, is global and hence produces common coupling wherever used. An example is the global flags used in the interactive trace system in Appendix B. Another type of common coupling is when several modules share data through access to a shared data file. As with cohesion, judgments need to be made in coupling as to whether the increased modular interdependence is worthwhile. In our experience, the usefulness of the trace system is so great that we have been willing to accept the common coupling involved in using it, even though this is near the least desirable end of the coupling continuum. A mitigating factor in common coupling is to restrict the use of a global variable such that only one module has authority to modify the common data while all other modules are restricted to read-only access.

Content coupling occurs when one module contains direct references to object code outside itself. An external reference to object code is the use of an alternate entry point of another module, for example, a GOTO used to transfer control to a label that is interior to another module. Or a reference might modify object code or data in the local environment of another module. When this occurs, modular independence is essentially destroyed. This is very bad, and usually the result of poor design.

Content coupling also occurs when a subscripted variable uses an index out of the declared range. Another example may involve arithmetic applied to generate a modified address pointer to access a data field instead of passing the additional item as a parameter. These instances are in the nature of bad programming practice. They cause defects that are very difficult to locate when the assumptions made about how memory is allocated in another module are invalidated by a change in that other module.

Modular independence is the ideal we want to achieve. As a practical matter, this is not always possible. However, we should strive to minimize coupling wherever possible. Only data, data structures, and control should be passed across modular interfaces. Ideally, we would pass only data. Thus, if the system can be partitioned in another way to reduce the total amount of coupling, that should be done.

If it is at all reasonable to reduce intermodular dependence, you should always do so. It may not seem to make much difference when considering a specific module or even a group of modules. But remember, the system is likely to increase in complexity and in concomitant interdependence. If your system is successful, it will be changed over time. A system that has a high level of modular independence will be much easier to change and, in the process, retain its independence level.

Finally, there is the matter of interfacing the software with the hardware. That topic is largely beyond the scope of this book, but it may be an important additional source of coupling.

If you have designed a system that has only data coupling, congratulations. You have accomplished something very difficult.

7.A.3. Span of Control

The **span of control** of a module is the number of subordinate modules it has. As a rule of thumb a span of control for a module should be bigger than 1 and less than 10. A span of control of 1 suggests either composite modules which should be separated, or the fact that there should be no subordinate module. A span of control of more than 10 suggests that the modules are too small and ought to be combined, or that the calling module should be subdivided.

The term **fan-out** is often used to mean the span of control of a module. For example, in Figure 7.1 the fan-out of the module PREPARE_PAYROLL is 3.

The opposite of fan-out is **fan-in**, which refers to the number of superordinates a given module has. For example, if a subroutine is called by 5 different modules, it has a fan-in of 5.

Note that a high fan-in often spells trouble. A high fan-in may seem desirable because it reduces the amount of code and allows the use of well-tested common functions. However, modules with high fan-in increase the risks associated with content coupling. Thus the coupling of any module with high fan-in should be carefully reviewed. To support testing and maintenance the fan-in of each module should be clearly documented.

7.A.4. Information Hiding

The basic question to keep in mind when evaluating a module is, "How much needs to be understood about other modules in order to work with this module?" The less outside information you need (from the standpoint of the individual module), the easier your job with this module will be. This includes design, coding, testing, debugging, and eventually incorporating changes that the user wants.

A module should be designed so that it keeps as much information to itself as it can. Anything that doesn't need to be known by another module is "hidden" in this one. This principle is called **information hiding**.

To understand this concept, it may help to think in terms of security precautions. Suppose you are working for a company that is developing an important product that it wants to keep secret. With a large number of people working on the project, one way of ensuring security is to let each person know only as much as he or she needs to know. You will be told only what you need to do your job and no more. This also reduces your chances of being kidnapped and tortured for information by the enemy. Your company is practicing information hiding.

The idea behind information hiding is to keep all knowledge of a particular data structure, device, or for that matter any resource, within a single module. Whenever this is done the independence among the program modules increases. Following this principle helps to make the individual modules cohesive and reduces coupling among modules. This makes it easier to work on an individual module, as it minimizes the amount of information that must be learned about related modules. By localizing knowledge of a specific design decision detail in a single module we increase modular independence.

In languages such as interpreted BASIC, which do not allow local variables or passing of parameters, it is very hard to achieve information hiding. Languages such as Pascal and C are somewhat better because of the ability to have local variables within a module. Modules in C are of course functions, and modules in Pascal are procedures or functions.

Ada and Modula-2 have even better constructs for information hiding, called packages and modules, respectively. Both Ada and Modula-2 provide facilities for making sure that all coupling is data coupling. They do this through enforced information hiding. Let us look at an example of the way Ada does it.

Suppose we want to implement a stack in Ada. We begin by using Ada as we would use Pascal. We might make the following data declarations:

```
MAX   : constant := 200 ;
STACK : array(1..MAX) of INTEGER ;
TOP   : INTEGER range 0..MAX ;
```

We might then write a procedure to push an element on the stack and a function to pop the stack, using the code given in Figure 7.2.

```
Figure 7.2  PUSH Procedure and POP Function in Ada

procedure PUSH( X : INTEGER ) is
    begin
        TOP := TOP + 1 ;
        STACK(TOP) := X ;
    end PUSH ;

function POP return INTEGER is
    begin
        TOP := TOP - 1 ;
        return STACK(TOP + 1) ;
    end POP;
```

The problem with these modules as written is that we cannot allow someone to use PUSH or POP without also giving them direct access to STACK and TOP. There is no way to enforce the stack protocol. In Ada we can rewrite these modules as a package, as indicated in Figure 7.3.

Note that this package comes with its own initialization procedure and that the user can only access the stack via the package's function POP and the package's procedure PUSH. Partial Ada code to use the package might look like that in Figure 7.4.

The use of information hiding to enforce limits on coupling is an important issue. If Ada and Modula-2 provided nothing else they would be worthy of consideration for this feature.

```
Figure 7.3  Package for PUSH Procedure
            and POP Function in Ada

package STACKPAC is
    procedure PUSH( X : INTEGER) ;
    function  POP return INTEGER ;
end STACKPAC ;

package body STACKPAC is
MAX   : constant := 200 ;
STACK : array(1..MAX) of INTEGER ;
TOP   : INTEGER range 0..MAX ;

procedure PUSH( X : INTEGER) is
begin
   TOP := TOP + 1 ;
   STACK(TOP) := X ;
end  PUSH ;

function POP return INTEGER is
begin
   TOP = TOP - 1 ;
   return STACK(TOP+1);
end POP ;

begin
   TOP := 0 ;
end STACKPAC;
```

```
Figure 7.4  Partial Code to Use a PUSH
            and POP Package in Ada

with STACKPAC;
procedure MAIN is
  use STACKPAC   ;
  M,N    : INTEGER ;
    begin

      .
      .
      .
      PUSH(M) ;

      .
      .
      N := POP() ;
   end MAIN ;
```

7.B. Structured Programming

7.B.1. Review of Principles

A structured program is a program whose modules consist entirely of three basic logic structures:

1.   seqence
2.   selection (branching)
3.   iteration (looping)

Programs which are structured are easier to maintain than those written without a formal structure. The three basic logic structures can be combined in a variety of ways to produce any required logic.

The onset of structured programming has led to a variety of new documentation aids. In this chapter we use structured flowcharts and hierarchy charts, which were introduced in Chapter 4, as aids. The hierarchy charts will be used to describe the relationships between modules and the structured flowchart will be used to describe how individual modules are implemented. Information such as what parameters are passed is contained in the structured flowchart that goes with each box in the hierarchy chart.

Structured flowcharts will be used to show how each module is implemented. One type of structured flowchart consists of boxes. Each box corresponds to a primitive action. To achieve sequence, boxes are stacked. In the following example ACTION A is followed by ACTION B.

```
┌─────────────────────┐
│  ACTION A           │
├─────────────────────┤
│  ACTION B           │
└─────────────────────┘
```

To achieve iteration the following construct may be used. (This is not the only construct that could be used. Many similar constructs have been proposed and used in the literature.)

```
┌──────────────────────────────────┐
│ DO WHILE ( condition )           │
│   ┌──────────────────────────────┤
│   │ Any sequence of valid boxes  │
└───┴──────────────────────────────┘
```

The box is interpreted as follows. First, a check of the condition is made. If the condition is true, each of the statements in the sequence is executed. When the sequence of statements has been executed the condition is checked again. The process continues in this manner until the condition is false.

To achieve selection the following construct may be used:

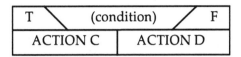

where ACTION C and ACTION D are any valid structured flow-chart boxes. If the condition is true, ACTION C is taken and ACTION D is ignored. The opposite occurs when the condition is false.

It should be clear that to write a structured program in any language, there must be a mechanism for implementing modules and a mechanism for implementing each of these constructs within the language. This is possible with most languages. Hence it is possible to write structured programs in any language even if the language is not specifically designed for structured programming. In the case of such a language, the structure is imposed from without by requiring adherence to programming standards that force the programmer to use the above constructs.

To illustrate the language independence of the structured programming constructs let us look at how we might implement them in a structured and an unstructured language.

In a structured language, such as C, the standards listed in Table 7.3 might be used.

```
Table 7.3  Standards That Might be Used in a Language Such as C

1. Modules will be implemented as functions.
2. Sequence will be implemented by placing statements on adjacent
   lines.  (No more than one statement per line.)
3. Selection will be implemented by the if-else construct.
4. Iteration will be implemented only by the while statement.
5. The main function will consist only of invocations of other
   functions.
```

A sample program written to these standards, which prints out the first 15 Fibonacci numbers, could look like the code in Figure 7.5. Note that having the main function consist entirely of invocations of functions is a common practice, which prevents the main module from becoming excessively large. In a simple program such as this it is only a matter of form.

```
         Figure 7.5   Structured Code to Find the First 15
                      Fibonacci Numbers in C

   main()
   {
        fibprint();
   }

   fibprint()
   {
        int first, second, third, count ;
        first = 1 ;
        second = 1 ;
        count = 3 ;
        printf("%d\n", first) ;
        printf("%d\n", second) ;
        while ( count <= 15 )
           {
           third = first + second ;
           printf("%d\n", third) ;
           first = second ;
           second = third ;
           count = count + 1 ;
           }
        return ;
   }
```

7.B.2. Imposing Structure in Unstructured Languages

Consider a similar program written in an unstructured language such as ANSI Standard BASIC. The standards listed in Table 7.4 might be used.

A program written with these standards to print out the first 15 Fibonacci numbers could look like the code in Figure 7.6.

Note that while it is possible to structure a language such as BASIC in this manner, there are still major problems caused by BASIC's lack of even primitive information hiding.

Table 7.4   Standards Useful for an Unstructured Language
              Such as BASIC

1. Modules will be implemented as subroutines and reached
   via the GOSUB statement.
2. Sequence will be implemented by placing statements
   directly after one another in the numbering sequence.
3. Selection will be implemented with the IF statement in
   the following manner:
       IF (condition) THEN GOSUB xxx ELSE GOSUB yyy
4. Iteration will be implemented with the WHILE and WEND
   statement.
5. The only module that is not a subroutine will be the
   driver module, which must consist only of GOSUB
   statements followed by an END statement.

Figure 7.6   Structured Code to Find the First 15
             Fibonacci Numbers in BASIC

```
10 REM The highest module contains only GOSUB statements
20 REM in this case it makes for a short driver.
30 GOSUB 50
40 END
50 LET FIRST = 1
60 LET SECOND = 1
70 PRINT FIRST
80 PRINT SECOND
90 LET COUNT = 3
100 WHILE COUNT <= 15
110        LET THIRD = FIRST + SECOND
120        PRINT THIRD
130        LET FIRST = SECOND
140        LET SECOND = THIRD
150        LET COUNT = COUNT + 1
160 WEND
170 RETURN
```

7.C. Complexity Metrics and Module Size

7.C.1. Divide and Conquer

We now consider a process by which structured modules that are
functionally cohesive can be designed, starting with the overall description

of the problem. This technique is called top-down design.

In top-down design you begin by identifying one module that describes the highest level function of the program. This module is partitioned into its main components. Each of these components is in turn partitioned into its main components. The process repeats until each module performs a single function. When we are done, each of the boxes of the hierarchy chart represents a single cohesive module.

Top-down design permits designers to concentrate on a single module at a time and to consider only the relationship between that module and its subordinates. This approach is often called divide and conquer. By using this approach, a large, complex programming task can be reduced to a set of subtasks, each of which is smaller and easier than the original task. We can proceed in this manner when each module is independent in function from its fellow modules.

7.C.2. Methods for Evaluating Complexity

There have been many attempts to quantify the modularity properties we have been discussing. We will look at some of these attempts. Remember that software engineering is in its formative years. Although most software engineers would agree that there is a quantitative relationship between the concepts we have discussed, few would agree on its exact nature.

We will look at two widely used metrics. McCabe's metric, generally referred to as V(G), is a measure of modular complexity based on the number of branching and looping structures. Generally recommended complexity is a V(G) no greater than 10. Halstead's software science is also used to measure software complexity, but is applied after the code is written.

7.C.2.a. McCabe's Complexity Measure, V(G)

McCabe's complexity metric, V(G), is a number that represents the complexity of a module. Recall from the example in Figure 5.3 (reproduced here as Figure 7.7) how each loop and branch in a module dramatically increases the number of paths to test. V(G) combines these structures in a single metric. The metric can be calculated from a graph of the control flow of a module's logic, or it can be done from source code or pseudocode. Let us look at the graphical method first.

McCabe defines his measure of program complexity in graph theoretical terms. In order to use V(G), we need a control flow representation of the program or module to which we are applying the measure. This representation must be in the form of a planar graph, such as the one in Figure 7.8. V(G) is based on the **cyclomatic complexity** of the graph, the number of regions into which the graph divides the plane. V(G) is found by counting these regions.

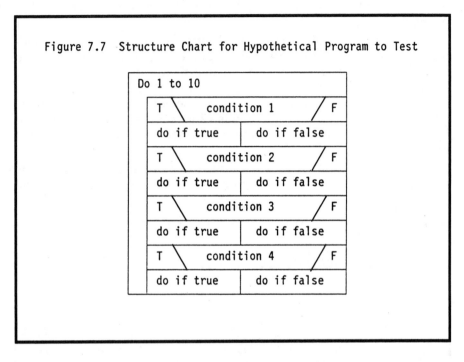

Figure 7.7   Structure Chart for Hypothetical Program to Test

A region is created any time there is a branch or a loop, whether or not the branches and/or loops are nested. In addition, there is the region of the plane outside the entire graph, which means any module has a V(G) of at least 1.

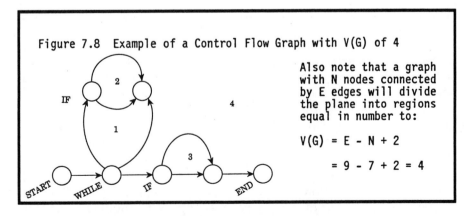

Figure 7.8   Example of a Control Flow Graph with V(G) of 4

Also note that a graph with N nodes connected by E edges will divide the plane into regions equal in number to:

V(G) = E − N + 2

= 9 − 7 + 2 = 4

The graph in Figure 7.8 represents a module with the structured programming constructs of sequence (which does not affect the metric), a branch nested within a loop, and another branch. The loop increases the metric by 1, as does each branch. Note that these areas are numbered on the graph. In addition, the rest of the plane is a region, in this case numbered 4. Calls to other modules, if any, are indicated in the graph as sequence and do not affect V(G).

V(G) can be evaluated from any control flow representation, including source code. We begin with the background region of 1 and add n-1 to it for each n-way branch. For example, an if-then-else construct is a 2-way branch and adds 2 minus 1 or 1 to V(G). A nested branch represents a separate 2-way branch, and each adds another 1 to V(G). A loop, usually implemented by while or do, represents a 2-way branch, and each adds 1 to V(G). A case statement with n alternatives is an n-way branch, and adds n-1 to V(G).

Look at Figure 7.9. This is a structure representation of the same module as in Figure 7.8, which shows this alternate way of calculating V(G).

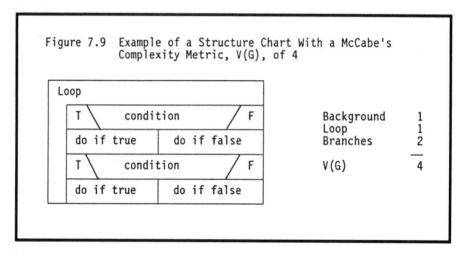

Figure 7.9   Example of a Structure Chart With a McCabe's Complexity Metric, V(G), of 4

Figure 7.10 gives another example, this time in pseudocode. The nested ifs each represent a 2-way branch, each adding 1 to V(G). The case statement is a 4-way branch, which adds 3. These plus the background value of 1 produce a V(G) of 6, a reasonable level of complexity.

For another example, one that uses source code, look at the fibprint module in Figure 7.5. This module includes sequence and one while loop, for a V(G) of 2. Now, go back and look at Figure 7.7, and see if you understand why it has a V(G) of 6.

McCabe's metric provides a good measure of testing difficulty and is a pretty good indication of ultimate software reliability. If you follow the development plans outlined in previous sections, V(G) should be small for each of your modules, generally less than 10. McCabe even suggests that his complexity measure be used in the top-down design process. He suggests that no module be allowed to exist as a single entity with a V(G) greater than 10.

```
     Figure 7.10   Example of Pseudocode with V(G) of 6

 If (condition) then
    If (condition) then
               .
               .
               .                      Background              1
            end if                    Ifs (2-way branches)    2
       else                           Case (4-way branch)     3
           case                                              ———
                   alternate 1        V(G)                    6
                   alternate 2
                   alternate 3
                   alternate 4
               end case
           end if
```

If the complexity of a module is too great, it is difficult to test adequately. Furthermore, a module that is too complex can be difficult to modify. Reasons for partitioning a module into two or more modules may be based on considerations of excess complexity, maintainability, improving cohesiveness, and/or reducing coupling.

7.C.2.b. Halstead's Software Science

The measures developed by Halstead are probably the best known of the many measures of software complexity. Halstead builds a theory based on certain metrics, which he defines.

Length of a program is the total usage of all operators and operands in a representation of a program. Operators include all arithmetic operators (such as +, -, etc.), logical operators (AND, OR, etc.), and syntactic elements of the language (such as IF, etc.). Operands essentially include all variables, named constants, and labels.

Length is somewhat tedious to calculate for a large program, so Halstead proposes the following approximation called the length formula, given in Equation 7.1.

$$\text{length} = n_1 \log_2 n_1 + n_2 \log_2 n_2 \qquad \textbf{Equation 7.1}$$

where:

n_1 = total number of distinct operators in an implementation

n_2 = total number of distinct operands in an implementation

According to experiments conducted by Halstead the values obtained from the length equation agree quite well with the values obtained by using the definition of length.

Other measures defined by Halstead are:

$$\text{Volume} = \text{length} \times \log_2 (n_1 + n_2) \qquad \text{Equation 7.2}$$

Volume is defined so as to factor out irrelevant differences in languages that might appear in the representation of a program.

$$V^* = (2 + n_2{}^*) \times \log_2 (2 + n_2{}^*) \qquad \text{Equation 7.3}$$

where:

V^* = potential volume

$n_2{}^*$ = number of input/output parameters

The motivation for V^* came from the notion that a program should have at least two operators (input/output) and there should be at least one occurrence of each operator and operand. Because of the $n_2{}^*$ term in the formula, V^* is truly language independent.

Another measure is the level of implementation of an algorithm. It represents the divergence from potential volume and is defined by Equation 7.4.

$$V^* = L \times V \qquad \text{Equation 7.4}$$

where:

L = the ratio of a program's potential volume to the program's actual volume

Since V^* is clearly a lower bound on V we know that L must be less than or equal to 1. Halstead proposes and validates an approximation for L of:

$$\hat{L} = (n_1{}^* / n_1) \times (n_2 / N_2) \qquad \text{Equation 7.5}$$

where:

N_2 = total number of instances of operands obtained directly from the source listing of a program

Using $\hat{L}$ you can define what is called the intelligence content of a program. It has been found by Halstead to be nearly invariant over representations of an algorithm in many different languages.

Halstead has proposed a measure of language level based on the measures we have seen so far:

$$\text{lambda} = L \times V^* = L^2 \times V \qquad \text{Equation 7.6}$$

Using this measure Halstead was able to show that the ranking of languages was to some extent intuitively correct. The results, as reported by Halstead, are given in Table 7.5.

```
              Table 7.5  Language Rankings by Halstead

              Language      lambda       variance

              English        2.16         0.74
              PL/I           1.53         0.92
              Algol 58       1.21         0.74
              Fortran        1.14         0.81
              Pilot          0.92         0.43
              Assembly       0.88         0.42
```

Halstead also proposes a measure of programming effort, which he defines as follows:

$$E = V^2 / V^*$$ **Equation 7.7**

If we combine this with Equation 7.6 we get:

$$E = (V^*)^3 / (\text{lambda}^2)$$ **Equation 7.8**

This shows an incredible effect of language level on effort. If one language is twice the level of another language, this equation seems to indicate that it will take four times the effort to program in the lower level language. The authors, having some experience in programming similar tasks in high-level languages and assembly language, tend to agree with this result.

7.C.2.c. Conclusion

Automated tools to compute both Halstead's and McCabe's V(G) measures are currently available. Because of the nature of the measures, V(G) can be used earlier in the design process than Halstead's. It looks as though V(G) will become a useful tool for program design while the Halstead measures will become effective tools for the classification and comparison of existent programs and languages.

7.D. Proof of Correctness

7.D.1. Introduction

In this section we look at two related problems: how to show **proof of correctness** and machine generation of programs to solve a problem. The first problem can be loosely stated as indicated in Figure 7.11. A statement of the second problem is given in Figure 7.12.

Figure 7.11   Showing That a Program is Correct

Given
    1. The desired results (postcondition)
    2. The initial conditions (precondition)
    3. A program segment

Show
    Starting with the initial conditions execution of the
    program segment always leads to the desired results.

Figure 7.12   Machine Generation of Programs to Solve a
              Given Problem

Given
    1. The desired results (postcondition)
    2. The initial conditions (precondition)

Find
    A program segment that when executed will produce the
    desired result whenever the initial conditions are true
    before execution.

It should be clear from the consequences of successfully achieving either goal for a real programming language that these are exciting areas of research in theoretical computer science. Both problems are difficult and may never be solved in general. Even so they are worth looking at because more and more of the software tools that a computer scientist will be expected to use will involve these concepts.

7.D.2. Basic Constructs

We will describe what a program segment does with a predicate describing the relationship between the values of program variables when a program segment stops, and their values before it is started. Such a predicate is called a **postcondition** of the program segment. Consider the following C program segment:

$$z = p / q ;$$ **Equation 7.9**

One possible postcondition of this program segment is:

$$p = z * q$$ **Equation 7.10**

This postcondition is a predicate that comes from the fact that z is the quotient of p divided by q. This postcondition is only one of many possible postconditions. There is another, more important problem. This postcondition alone is not enough to specify the behavior of the program. In the case of the program segment we are considering, q = 0 is illegal since division is not defined for divisors of zero. Such constraints will be expressed as predicates called **preconditions**. The combination of preconditions and postconditions allow us to say what a program segment does.

The notation

$$P\{S\}Q$$

where:

P and Q are predicates

S is a program segment

is read:

S is strongly correct with respect to precondition P and postcondition Q.

It means that if P is true when S begins executing then S will terminate and Q will be true. The example we have looked at could be written in our notation as:

$$(q \sim= 0)\{z = p\ /\ q;\}(p = z*q)$$

What the above says in plain English is:

If q is nonzero and the program segment z = p / q; executes, then p will be the product of z and q.

Note that the definition says nothing about what will happen if S executes when P is false. If P happens to be false, then Q does not have to hold when S terminates. Indeed, S does not even have to terminate. The postconditions can be viewed as promises about what our program segment will do. The promises only apply when the program segment is used as intended, that is, when the preconditions are satisfied.

Consider the C program segment S given in Figure 7.13.

```
Figure 7.13   Program Segment S in C

y1 = 0 ;
y2 = x1 ;
while(y2 >= x2 )
      {
        y1 = y1 + 1 ;
        y2 = y2 -x2 ;
      }
z1 = y1 ;
z2 = y2 ;
```

To prove the segment correct we must do *two* things: prove that the segment terminates and prove that the postcondition holds. In order to do this we may use the precondition and properties of the code segment.

7.D.3. *Methods of Proving Correctness*

We now tackle the problem of how to go about proving that a program segment with preconditions and postconditions actually satisfies those conditions. This is done using predicate transformation. We start with a postcondition Q and a program S. Depending on S, we then determine how to transform the predicate Q into the weakest predicate that if true before S is executed would make Q true afterward. "Weakest" is used here in the mathematical sense. A definition is given in Figure 7.14.

```
Figure 7.14  Definition

The weakest precondition of S with respect to Q,  denoted
wp(S,Q), is the weakest condition  that must be  true  in
order that  S terminates and that  Q be true  after S has
been executed.
```

How do we use this to prove correctness? If we are trying to prove P{S}Q we might consider first finding wp(S,Q) and then proving that P implies wp(S,Q). In fact this is the classic way of proving correctness.

We formalize proof of correctness by axiomatizing the weakest precondition for a number of small building-block computations and by defining composition rules, as indicated in Figure 7.15. In addition to the axioms we have a number of useful logical identities, given in Figure 7.16.

```
Figure 7.15  Proof of Correctness Axioms

1. Computation: Assignment
                    x = e ; where e is an expression

   Semantics: wp(x=e,R)=R with all occurrences of x
                       replaced by e

2. Computation: If-then-else
                    if (B) S1 else S2; where S1 and S2 are
                    statements and B is a Boolean expression

   Semantics:  wp(if(B) S1 else S2, R) =
               (B implies wp(S1,R) and NOT(B) implies wp(S2,R))

3. Computation: Sequences
                    S1; S2; where S1 and S2 are statements

   Semantics: wp(S1;S2,R) = wp(S1,wp(S2,R))
```

4. <u>Computation</u>: While-do
                          while (B) { S } where S is a statement
                          and B is a Boolean expression

<u>Semantics</u>: wp(while (B) { S } , R) =

                          there exists k such that k >= 0 and $H_k(R)$
                          where $H_0(R)$ = NOT(B) and R
                          $H_k(R)$ = (B and wp(S,$H_{k-1}(R)$)) or
                          (NOT(B) and R)
                          $H_k(R)$ is the weakest precondition that the
                          loop will terminate in k or fewer steps
                          and leave the computation in a state de-
                          fined by R.

Figure 7.16   Proof of Correctness Identities

1. No operation: wp(No Operation,R) = R
2. Exclusion: wp(S,False) = False
3. Implication: (Q implies R) implies (wp(S,Q)
   implies wp(S,R))
4. Intersection: wp(S,Q) and wp(S,R) = wp(S, Q and R)
5. Union: wp(S,Q) or wp(S,R) = wp(S, Q or R)

7.D.4. Some Theoretical Considerations

We could go on with examples of proofs, and with some practice you could develop a facility for proving small segments correct. But in real life we must prove large, complex programs correct. The problems involved in doing this are akin to the problems involved in writing large, complex programs. If proofs of correctness are to be of real use in programming they must be automated. When such tools do appear their successful use will depend on the ability of the user to set appropriate preconditions and postconditions.

The major weaknesses of proofs of correctness are the following. A proved program can still contain errors. Proofs are difficult to do by hand and have not yet been successfully automated for a real production language. Many of the constructs in production languages are not amenable to proofs. An elaboratation on these problems is found in the list in Table 7.6.

Despite these problems proofs of correctness do have some advantages. The process of framing preconditions and postconditions is a valuable way to express the specifications of a module. It is also a key to determine when an exception should be raised, for example, when the input conditions to a module violate the precondition. Proofs may detect bugs that might not have shown up in testing. And finally, the mere fact that a proof is going to be done forces the programmer to pay more attention to the specifications.

```
Table 7.6   Limitations of Proofs of Correctness

1. The program proof is only as good as the precondition
   and postcondition posed by the person making the proof.
   This will not change even if automated correctness
   proving becomes a reality.  If the postcondition or
   precondition is improperly stated the program can be
   proved correct while major errors remain.

2. If the proof is done by hand it will probably contain
   errors.  Expecting such a proof to be error free is
   like expecting a large program to be designed without
   error and run perfectly on first compilation.

3. Machine constraints such as roundoff errors and over-
   flow are usually not considered in proofs of correctness.
   Their consideration  greatly  complicates  proofs  of
   correctness.

4. Current proof techniques cannot successfully deal with
   input/output operations.  This is why we did not consider
   input/output operations in our examples.

5. Proofs do not detect side effects.  A correct program
   could easily change some important global variable.
```

7.E. Course Project: Detailed Design and Coding

You now have more information with which to evaluate the design of your system, including cohesion, coupling, span of control, information hiding, principles of structured programming, and McCabe's complexity metric V(G). You should now look at your preliminary design to see if it represents good design and coding practice, and modify it if it does not.

The principles described in this chapter are guidelines rather than rules. Some judgment is required for situations to which the guidelines do not apply. Such judgment comes with experience, and in general it would not be reasonable to expect you to make such decisions now. Therefore, our recommendation is that you follow the guidelines until you acquire enough experience to justify deviation from them. Some guidelines are enough experience to justify deviation from them. Some guidelines are summarized in Table 7.7.

```
Table 7.7  Guidelines for Developing Good Modules

1. A module should not exceed 50 lines of code.
   Normally it will be between 5 and 25 lines of code.
   (This will vary somewhat depending on language.)
2. The module should be describable in ordinary English
   without the use of a series of words such as "first,"
   "then," etc.
3. V(G) should not exceed 10.
```

Occasional deviations from these guidelines are not uncommon. For example, in the first guideline we state, "A module should not exceed 50 lines of code." However, remember that the number of lines of code depends on what language you are using and how you count. Code that can be written in 3 or 4 lines of C could take 20 lines of FORTRAN. If your module has 51 lines of code, hides its information, has reasonable fan-out and fan-in, and a V(G) of less than 10, don't change it. If your module has 300 lines of code, either change it or justify its length, for example, on grounds of information hiding and a V(G) of less than 10.

When you do feel an exception is justified, you should include an explanation as part of the documentation. Such exceptions will occur in your system if you follow our recommendations for error handling (described in Chapter 6) and a trace system (introduced in Chapter 5 and described in Appendix B). The error handler is called by every module, which represents very high fan-in. However, the advantages of using a text file for the error messages usually outweigh this drawback. The trace system not only has high fan-in, it uses global variables that represent common coupling. Again, the time and effort saved in testing, debugging, and maintenance justify this exception to generally recommended practice.

7.F. Beyond a Course Project: Other Linguistic Alternatives

Since the early 1980s there has been a movement away from procedural languages such as C, Pascal, Modula-2, and Ada toward nonprocedural languages such as RAMIS, MARK V, and CULPRIT. These languages, commonly called fourth-generation languages, share certain traits. They allow more dialogue between the user and the computer that is closer to English than procedural languages. They also allow solution of the problem by what amounts to a specification of the problem.

Currently such languages suffer from one major drawback: their domain of discourse is very limited. While they may do well at database applications, and indeed surpass procedural languages as a development tool for this environment, they lack the constructs for solving engineering problems in a nonprocedural way. Perhaps someday, just as database query languages grew into nonprocedural languages, simulation languages will grow into some kind of equivalent nonprocedural language for engineering applications.

Along the same line as fourth-generation languages we have applications generators. They are software systems that generate code for programs and systems from formal specifications of those systems. The more effective applications generators allow the programmer to specify the system in an interactive environment.

The distinction between applications generators and fourth-generation languages is somewhat blurred. Currently there are two major types of applications generators. One produces source code that can be modified by the user; the other produces object code for the application described.

At present the first kind is the most popular. This is somewhat of a shame, as one of the beauties of an applications generator should be that, because all the routines it produces have been thoroughly tested, much of the system design and test stages can be eliminated. This is, of course, in addition to the fact that it clearly reduces design and development activities. Perhaps when the second type really produces thoroughly tested code people will prefer it. To understand how close we are to making applications generators and fourth-generation languages as general purpose as procedural languages, consider the problems that were raised in the section on proofs of correctness.

Summary

Individual modules should have several important characteristics. They should utilize information hiding, maximize cohesion, and minimize coupling. The level of complexity should be such that adequate testing is possible.

Structured programming has considerable advantages in terms of readability and creating maintainable software. Structured code can be written whether the language used is structured or unstructured.

There are useful metrics for evaluating software. Two introduced in this chapter are McCabe's V(G) and Halstead's. V(G) is useful for evaluating module complexity. Halstead's software metrics are useful after code is written.

Proofs of correctness can sometimes be used, but their usefulness depends on the algorithm. However, stating pre- and postconditions can be valuable in expressing specifications.

Keywords

cohesion
    coincidental cohesion
    communicational cohesion
    functional cohesion
    logical cohesion
    procedural cohesion
    sequential cohesion
    time-related cohesion
coupling
    common coupling
    content coupling
    control coupling
    data coupling
cyclomatic complexity
fan-in
fan-out
Halstead's software science
information hiding
McCabe's complexity metric
postcondition
precondition
proof of correctness
span of control
structured flowcharts
structured program

Review Questions

7.1. What is structured programming? What is a structured language?

7.2. How do you write structured code in an unstructured language?

7.3. What is information hiding? Why is it important?

7.4. What is cohesion? What are the different kinds of cohesion and how desirable is each?

7.5. What is coupling? What are the different kinds of coupling and how much of a problem is each?

7.6.   What is a reasonable span of control for a single module?

7.7.   What problems are associated with high fan-out? With high fan-in?

7.8.   Describe Halstead's measures of software complexity. When are these measures most useful?

7.9.   How is McCabe's complexity metric found? What is a reasonable level for this metric?

7.10. How may proofs of correctness be used? What are some of their limitations?

Exercises

7.1.   List several programming languages that support structured programming, and several others that do not. Using an unstructured language, write a structured program to find the smallest and largest values in an array.

7.2.   Look at a program you have previously written. Look at each module and determine the number of lines of code. Cite specific examples of information hiding. If there aren't any, determine how the program should be rewritten. List each kind of cohesion and coupling represented. How would you rate this program?

7.3.   Look at the hierarchy chart in Figure 4.5. Give the span of control for each module. Cite examples of fan-out and fan-in.

7.4.   Look at a program you have previously written. Calculate Halstead's length, volume, and effort metrics.

7.5.   Look at a program you have previously designed. Write the flowchart for each module in graph form. Calculate $V(G)$ for each module. Do any of your modules exceed $V(G) = 10$? If so, how can you   restructure the program to reduce $V(G)$?

7.6.   The Department of Defense considers a "small" program to be one with less than 100,000 lines of code. Consider a program of 5,000 lines of code. How would you apply the principles of proof of correctness?

7.7.   Consider the incremental effect on McCabe's complexity for each statement that implies a branch in the underlying code when compiled.

GOTO	1-way branch
IF .. THEN	2-way branch

IF .. THEN .. ELSE	2-way branch
WHILE	2-way branch
IF (condition) 1,2,3	3-way branch on , =, (FORTRAN)
CASE STRUCTURE, N alternatives	N-way branch

What is the generalization for adding up McCabe's complexity on detection of a keyword associated with branching?

7.8. For a small program that you have written, count all the operators and operands and sum them to get Halstead's length metric. Also calculate length from Equation 7.1. What may influence the difference in results?

7.9. For a small program you have previously written, define the preconditions and postconditions for each module. Evaluate by hand the conditions for test data that are expected to lie at or near a boundary condition for an input parameter. Incorporate statements to test the pre- and postconditions into each module and run a few tests with boundary data.

References

Basili, Victor R. Tutorial on Models and Metrics for Software Management and Engineering, IEEE Catalog No. EHO-167-7. Washington, DC: Computer Society Press, 1980.

> Includes McCabe's original paper on cyclomatic program complexity, V(G), "A Complexity Measure," along with other models and metrics.

Booch, Grady. Software Engineering with Ada, 2d ed. Menlo Park, CA: Benjamin/Cummings, 1986.

> Good descriptions of software engineering principles and object oriented design as applied with Ada.

Brooks, Frederick P. "No Silver Bullet." IEEE Computer 20, no. 4 (April 1987): 10-19.

> Fashioning complex conceptual constructs is the essence; accidental tasks arise in representing the constructs in language. Past progress has so reduced the accidental tasks that future progress now depends on addressing the essence.

DeMillo, Richard A., McCracken, W. Michael, Martin, R. J., and Passafiume, John F. Software Testing and Evaluation. Menlo Park, CA: Benjamin/Cummings, 1987.

> A comprehensive survey of the state of the art and current practice in defense-related projects. The 70-page bibliography is subdivided into several dozen topic areas.

Fox, Joseph M. Software and its Development. Englewood Cliffs, NJ: Prentice-Hall, 1982.

> Discusses large project management, classifying system properties, and considerations of performance and tradeoffs.

Halstead, Maurice H. Elements of Software Science. New York: Elsevier North-Holland, 1977.

> Original work on Halstead's metrics.

McCabe, Thomas J. "A Complexity Measure." IEEE Transactions on Software Engineering SE-2 (December 1976): 308-320.

> Original paper developing the idea of cyclomatic program complexity, $V(G)$.

Pomberger, George. Software Engineering and Modula-2. Englewood Cliffs, NJ: Prentice-Hall, 1984.

> Description of software engineering principles applied in Modula-2.

Pressman, Roger S. Software Engineering, A Practitioner's Approach, 2d ed. New York: McGraw-Hill, 1987.

> A survey of software engineering with thorough review of all phases of the life cycle and the management of software. The treatment of software design provides chapters on data flow, data structure, real-time, and object oriented design methods.

Sahni, Sartaj. Software Development in Pascal. Fridley, MN: Camelot, 1985.

> Description of software engineering principles applied in Pascal.

Wulf, Wm. A., Shaw, Mary, Hilfinger, Paul N., and Flon, Lawrence. Fundamental Structures of Computer Science. Reading, MA: Addison-Wesley, 1981.

> General, intermediate level computer science with Formal Specification and Proof of Programs (Chapter 5) and Correctnesss of Data Representation (Chapter 11).

Yourdon, Edward N., and Constantine, Larry L. Structured Design, 2d ed. New York: Yourdon Press, 1978.

> Presents a systematic approach to structuring software design based on a data flow abstraction. Introduces data flow diagrams and methods to refine the model of the problem. Elements of the refined model are then used to specify modules of code to implement the software. Describes cohesion and coupling.

Yourdon, Edward, ed. Classics in Software Engineering. New York: Yourdon Press, 1979.

> Reprints of 24 classic papers, including "Structured Programming with go to Statements," by Donald Knuth, a description of when to (and when not to) use go to statements. Also includes "On the Criteria to Be Used in Decomposing Systems into Modules" by D. L. Parnas, original paper on information hiding.

Yourdon, Edward. Nations at Risk: The Impact of the Computer Revolution. New York: Yourdon Press, 1986.

> A readable account of the impact of computers on our world for computer professionals and a general audience.

CHAPTER 8

TESTING

The computer resembles the magic of legend. . . . If one character, one pause, of the incantation is not strictly in proper form, the magic doesn't work. Human beings are not accustomed to being perfect, and few areas of human activity demand it.

- Frederick P. Brooks, Jr., *The Mythical Man-Month*

You may seek it with thimbles - and seek it with care;
You may hunt it with forks and hope;
You may threaten its life with a railway-share;
You may charm it with smiles and soap!

For the Snark's a peculiar creature, that won't
Be caught in a commonplace way.
Do all that you know, and try all that you don't:
Not a chance must be wasted today!

-Lewis Carroll, *The Hunting of the Snark*

Software Life Cycle

Software development: Testing

I. Software need
II. Preliminary feasibility judgment
III. Requirements analysis and feasibility study
IV. Requirements specification
V. Preliminary software design and planning
VI. Software development
   Detailed design
   Coding and unit testing
   Integration
   System testing
VII. Software maintenance

Project: Coding and testing

8.A. Introduction

New programmers often do not view testing as a discovery process. Psychologically they view a critique of their program as a critique of their ability. To them, testing is a way of demonstrating that their program works. As a result they produce test data to show that the program works. Unfortunately the customer is not interested in knowing that the program works under certain ideal conditions. The customer wants the system to work properly under all conditions.

To help view the process of testing in the proper light, many software engineers adopt a strategy known as egoless programming. In this strategy a program module is viewed as a component of a larger system, not as the property of those who wrote it. The egoless programming team is concerned with finding errors and correcting them rather than on placing blame. However, even when a system is developed under an egoless strategy it is often difficult to remove personal feelings from the testing process. This is why it is good practice to have an independent test team.

Typically, the software engineering team doing a course project allocates a small amount of time to testing at the end of the term. This is a mistake. Recall the observation of Boris Beizer in <u>Software System Testing and Quality Assurance</u> (1984):

A dispassionate observer, a hypothetical person from Mars, might view programming as an activity dominated by testing with occasional lapses into design and documentation.

That is the way it will be on the job. You should start doing a good job of testing now.

Modules should be unit tested as soon as they are written. Integration testing can then proceed concurrently with coding and unit testing of other modules.

Sometimes it is extremely difficult to see why we need to go through all the tedious, boring effort of planning and documenting every single test when it is so much easier to sit at the terminal, try something out, fix the code, and try again. The reason is that most software systems are too large to deal with in this way. Unsystematic tests will miss many errors.

It is generally conceded that no large, complex system is likely to be completely error-free. This does not necessarily imply incompetence on the part of the developers. Rather, it indicates the level of complexity of the systems we keep trying to develop compared to the capabilities of humans, who are less than perfect.

All testing activities must be carefully documented. This is not a matter of placing blame, but of good practice. The most important reason for good record keeping is that when a test is successful and an error is found, debugging must be followed by regression testing. That is, the tests that were run before the error was found must be run again to ensure that new errors were not introduced in the correction process.

It is important to keep careful records on errors that are found during testing for other purposes, too. One purpose is to determine whether, and if so, when to fix the error. Also, in a well-organized software development team, test records can be used to assess several aspects of software quality. The records can be used to indicate the number and frequency of errors, the stage at which the errors were discovered, and the cost of fixing the errors. This information can be useful in estimating costs of future software systems. In extreme cases, test records may serve as a basis for deciding whether to continue with a system under development. If the system has so many errors that the project is way behind schedule and isn't likely to improve, it may be better to kill it.

Although systematic unit testing and integration tests are tedious, they are our best defense against the potential hazards of system testing. The worst defects to find and eliminate are those that involve subtle interactions of several modules. If there are many such defects, system testing can be extremely difficult and time consuming. Ideally, system testing should have relatively few defects to conquer and be primarily concerned with testing the system against the software requirements.

8.B. Documentation of Testing

The test planning document should be written before testing is begun, as part of the system specification. This was described in Chapter 5. In this chapter, we look at examples of testing and test documents. The bulk of such documentation is the log of the actual testing activity. These logs should contain a complete record of everything that happened during testing.

In this section, we examine several examples of modules under test. The source code for the examples is included, along with the drivers and stubs used for the tests.

8.B.1. Documentation Standards

The documents required to report the software testing include those listed in Table 8.1. This list is drawn from ANSI/IEEE Std 829-1983. The need for a test plan, test design specification, test case specification, and test procedure specification were introduced in Chapter 5. During testing there may be revisions to earlier efforts in these areas. The final test documentation is an accumulation of these documents, including a summary.

```
Table 8.1  Documents Required at the End of Testing

1.  Test Plan
2.  Test Design Specification
3.  Test Case Specification
4.  Test Procedure Specification
5.  Test Item Transmittal Report
6.  Test Activity Logs
7.  Test Incident Reports
8.  Summary of Testing
```

In a multiple team development organization there must be a formal transfer of each item to be tested from the development team to the test team. A **Test Item Transmittal Report** documents that event. It specifies exactly what the item is, who is responsible for it, locations of supporting materials, and a dated approval of the transfer.

In the following sections we describe many details of testing activities and some ways to systematically accumulate a log of those activities. Inevitably faults will be discovered that require that an item under test be referred back to an earlier stage of development for correction. In a multiple team environment it is necessary to fully document such an event for the transfer. That is the purpose of a **Test Incident Report**. In a small project this may be handled by annotating the source documentation and updating the configuration notes in supporting documentation. At the end of testing all the documentation must be accumulated and a summary prepared.

8.B.2. Example - Computer Dating Service

An example of testing done on the main routine for a computer dating service, written in Pascal, is given below. The program is based on the hierarchy diagram in Figure 4.5. The test is based on the test description document in Figure 5.4. The source code for the main routine and stubs for the test is given in Figure 8.1. Since we are testing in a top-down manner, no separate driver is required. Results of the test are given in Figure 8.2.

```
Figure 8.1  Source Code for Main Routine and Stubs

Program FigLeaf (input, output);
    type line : string [80];
    var answer: char;
        menuflag, promptflag : boolean;
        Menu                 : file of line;
        textline             : string [65];

procedure AddClient;
(****************************************************************
*                                                              *
*   This is the procedure that adds a new client - stub only   *
*                                                              *
****************************************************************)
begin (* AddClient *)
   writeln;
   writeln('You are in the procedure to add a client -');
   writeln('This feature is not yet available.');
   writeln;
end;

procedure ModifyClient;
(****************************************************************
*                                                              *
*   This procedure changes data on a client - stub only        *
*                                                              *
****************************************************************)
begin (* ModifyClient *)
   writeln;
   writeln('You are in a procedure to change client data.');
   writeln('This feature is not yet available.');
   writeln;
 end;
```

```
procedure DeleteClient;
(*****************************************************************
*                                                               *
*   This is the procedure that deletes a  client - stub only    *
*                                                               *
*****************************************************************)
begin (* DeleteClient *)
  writeln;
  writeln('You are in the procedure to delete a client -');
  writeln('This feature is not yet available.'); writeln;
end;

procedure DateSelect;
(*****************************************************************
*                                                               *
*   This is the procedure to make a match - stub only           *
*                                                               *
*****************************************************************)
begin (* DateSelect *)
  writeln;
  writeln('You are in the procedure to make a match -');
  writeln('This feature is not yet available.');
  writeln;
end;


(*****************************************************************
*                                                               *
*    This is procedure MainDriver, the command handler          *
*                                                               *
*    Modules called - AddClient                                 *
*                     Modifyclient                              *
*                     DeleteClient                              *
*                     DateSelect                                *
*                                                               *
*    Modules called by - none                                   *
*                                                               *
*****************************************************************)
begin (* Main *)

(* Welcome user to system; ask about prompts; set flag *)
writeln ('Welcome to Fig Leaf Enterprises Computer Dating');
   write ('Service');
writeln;
writeln ('This system is designed to be as helpful as');
   write   ('possible.');
writeln ('If you are new to the system, we hope');
   write (' you will find our explanations helpful.');
writeln ('If you are familiar with the system, you may');
   write (' prefer to skip some of the explanations.');
writeln;
writeln ('Would you prefer the shorter prompts? (y/n)');
readln (answer);
if (answer = 'y') or (answer = 'Y')
   then promptflag := false
   else promptflag := true;
```

```
    assign (Menu,'MENUTXT'); (* assign name to file *)
    repeat (* repeating loop for duration of program execution *)
       menuflag := true; (* flag to terminate loop *)
       if promptflag
       then begin (* for long prompts *)
          reset(Menu); (* open existing file *)
          writeln;
          repeat
             readln (Menu,textline);
             writeln(' ',textline);
          until EOF(Menu);
          close (Menu);  (* close file *)
       end


    (* for short prompts *)
    else writeln('A: add, C: change, D: delete, M: match');
    read (answer); (* get user's choice *)
    case answer of
       'A','a': begin
                   AddClient;
                   menuflag := false;
                end;
       'C','c': begin
                   ModifyClient;
                   menuflag := false;
                end;
       'D','d': begin
                   DeleteClient;
                   menuflag := false;
                end;
       'M','m': begin
                   DateSelect;
                   menuflag := false;
                end;
       'H','h': begin
                   (* read help file - to be added later *)
                   writeln;
                   write ('This will be the help file - ');
                   writeln (' it is not yet available.');
                   menuflag := false;
                end;
       'Q','q': begin
                   writeln;
                   write('Are you sure you want to quit? (y/n)');
                   read (answer);
                   if (answer = 'Y') or (answer = 'y')
                      then menuflag := true
                      else menuflag := false;
                end;
       else     begin
                   writeln;
           (* This will be replaced by a call to ErrorHandler *)
                   writeln('Invalid entry: please try again.');
                   menuflag := false;
                end;
    end; (* case *)
until menuflag;
end. (* MainDriver *)
```

```
Figure 8.2   Unit Test Document
             Fig Leaf Enterprises Computer Dating Service

Module: Main                         Date of Test: Dec. 29, 1989
Author: Entire team

Results: The error message and stubs for the four modules to
be called by the command handler performed as expected.
However, there was a problem with the menu. The text file,
when read, did not appear on the screen the way it was
supposed to.  This is because the file commands for a data
file were used.  These were replaced by the proper commands
for a text file, and then the driver performed as expected.

However, the menu appears in two places.  There is an
initial menu with questions, then the main menu which
reappears after each command sequence has been executed.
The testers feel that this violates the principle of putting
menus in text files, and recommend the creation of an
additional file for the first appearance of the menu.
```

This example illustrates two aspects of testing. First, an error was found: a logical error in the file handling, wherein the text file for the menu was not declared as text and hence by default was considered to be a nontext file. This was easily corrected. Second, the testers felt that one of the basic standards of the software organization creating the system had been violated, that of putting text into files so that they can be changed to suit user specifications without recompiling the system. Thus it was decided to put the opening message into another text file.

Both changes were implemented and tested, and then the code performed as expected. The corrected code was used in Figure 6.1 as an example of how to write an interactive prototype that reads a menu from a text file.

8.B.2. Example - Spies on a Grid

Let us look at another example, an interactive game called "Spies on a Grid." This is a very small program, easily understood by one person. In Chapter 9 we use it to illustrate several documents, including one for the complete source code. If you are interested, you can copy it, play it, and probably find several ways to improve it. For now, however, we will approach it as an example of incremental testing. The strategy is the same whether there are six or six thousand modules in the complete system.

We begin with the highest module in the hierarchy, main. You need to know what, if any, subordinate and superordinate modules main has. This will be in the test planning document. We show these relationships in the form of the hierarchy diagram in Figure 8.3.

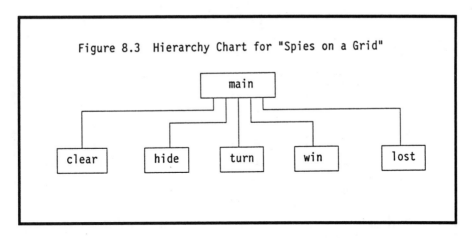

Figure 8.3 Hierarchy Chart for "Spies on a Grid"

First, we will do a unit test on the main module of the game. This is module main, which needs no driver, but needs stubs for the five modules it calls: clear, hide, turn, win, and lost. Since unit testing is structural, we need to see the source code for this test. This code, written in C, is given in Figure 8.4, complete with stubs for the five subordinate modules. Note that the C language requires that the highest level procedure be called main.

```
Figure 8.4  "Spies on a Grid"
            Source Code for Main and Procedure Stubs

#include <stdio.h>
main()
{
/****************************************************************
     This program is a game called SPIES ON A GRID.
The object of the game is to guess where spies are hidden on a
1 by 10 grid.      DeSmet C 2.51,     J. Student
****************************************************************/
int x[4], y[4], g, cturn;
char ans[256];
/****************************************************************

                    Variable Dictionary

   name  type              use
   ----  ------------      ------------------------------------
   x     integer array     holds x coordinate of the hidden spies
   y     integer array     holds y coordinate of the hidden spies
   g     integer           flag set to 1 to indicate a win
   cturn integer           holds current turn number
   ans   character array   answer to questions
```

```
                      Procedure Dictionary
      name              use
      -----             ------------------------------------------------
      clear             clears the screen
      hide              puts the four spies on the grid randomly
      turn              asks for a guess and checks to see how close
                          you were from each unfound spy.
      win               checks to see if you have won the game
      lost              prints out the locations of the hidden spies
                          if you have lost.

    ********************************************************************/

/* This is the main program
*/
 clear();
 ans[0]=NULL;
 while (ans[0]!='n' && ans[0]!='N' &&
        ans[0]!='y' && ans[0]!='Y' )
 {
     printf("Do you want to play spies? Answer Y or N.");
     gets(ans);
 }

 while(ans[0]!='n' && ans[0]!='N')
 {
     clear();
     g=0;
     hide(x, y);
     cturn=1;
     while (cturn <= 10)
     {
         turn(x, y, cturn);
         win(x, &g);
         if (g==1) break;
         cturn++;
     }
     if(g==0) lost(x, y);
     ans[0]=NULL;
     while(ans[0]!='n' &&  ans[0]!='N' &&
         ans[0]!='y' && ans[0]!='Y')
     {
         printf("Do you want to play again? Answer Y or N.");
         gets(ans);
     }
 }
}
/* Stubs begin here - to be replaced later with procedures */

clear()
{
     printf("clear\n");
}

hide(xcoord, ycoord)
int xcoord[], ycoord[];
{
     printf("hide\n");
}
```

```
turn(xcoord, ycoord, tn)
int xcoord[], ycoord[], tn;
{
     printf("turn\n");
}

win(xcoord, gg)
int xcoord[], *gg;
{
/*  This should be run with and without the next statement
    commented out.
*/
/*  *gg = 1 */
     printf("win\n");
}

lost(xcoord, ycoord)
int xcoord[], ycoord[];
{
     printf("lost\n");
}
```

A test report must be done for each test run. First, there should be a description of the test to be run, including the name of the module and any drivers or stubs. Then there should be a list of test conditions, followed by the actual test, with appropriate comments on the result.

It is much better to capture the actual results of a test than to simply make an entry in a notebook, such as "Test results - OK." An example of a test result report for main is given in Figure 8.5. Since writing down a long string of output is tedious, plan the test so that you can exploit the capabilities of your machine to capture the output. Many operating systems permit simple redirection of terminal output to a file. The figure, in fact, was created by appending the redirected output to the description and adding emphasis to distinguish the input.

```
Figure 8.5  Unit Test of Main Test Reporting Document
            Example - Spies on a Grid

Test Description:   The main routine is to be tested
  by running the driver with stubs for the procedures
  clear, hide, turn, win, and lost.

Test Conditions: The driver and stubs are to be run under
the following conditions:
    1. g set to 1 by win
    2. g not set to 1 by win
    3. User response at start: Y, y, N, n
    4. User response at end: Y, y, N, n
    5. Invalid responses at start: <CR>, 5, X, end
    6. Invalid responses at end: <CR>, 5, X, end
```

```
Sample Run (User input is highlighted):
    g not set to 1, response "y" at start, response "n" at end

                        Output:
clear
Do you want to play spies? Answer Y or N. y
clear
hide
turn
win
turn
win
turn
win
turn
win
turn
win
turn
win
turn
win
turn
win
turn
win
turn
win
lost
Do you want to play again? Answer Y or N. n

Test Result: as expected. No modification was made.
```

In this case the test results were satisfactory. This is not usually the case. The next example illustrates the more common result, finding an error.

We will unit test hide, one of the modules subordinate to the driver. Notice from the hierarchy diagram that hide has no subordinate modules. Therefore, a test of hide requires the use of a driver but no stubs.

The object of this module is to hide four spies on a 10 by 10 grid so that the player can guess their location. Although we have already tested the program's main routine, we don't want to use it for this test as it does too many things. We want an isolated test of hide.

All we want to know for this test is whether the part that actually hides the spies is working. Rather than hide the spies once, as an actual game would do, we decide to write a driver that hides them 20 times. The spies' hiding places are determined by a random number generator. The idea of this test is to see if the random number generator system works properly. This is a poor test design, as we shall see. The source code with a temporary driver is given in Figure 8.6.

```
Figure 8.6  "Spies on a Grid"
            Source Code for Procedure hide with Temporary Driver

#include <stdio.h>
main()
{
    int x[4],y[4],i,j;
    i=1;
    while (i <= 20)
    {
        hide(x,y);
        printf("Run %d ",i);
        j=0;
        while (j < 4)
        {
            printf("x = %d , y = %d ",x[j],y[j]);
            j = j+1;
        }
        printf("\n");
        i = i+1;
    }
}

hide(xcoord,ycoord)
/*****************************************************************
 This procedure hides the spies on the 10 by 10 grid.

                          Parameters

name      type            input/output    use
----      -------------   -------------   ------------
xcoord    integer array   output          x-coordinate
ycoord    integer array   output          y-coordinate
*****************************************************************/
int xcoord[],ycoord[];
{
/*****************************************************************
                     Variable Dictionary

name      type            use
----      -------         ------------------------------
i         integer         index for the coordinate arrays
*****************************************************************/
    int i,seed;
    double frand();
    char timeofday[9];
    times(timeofday);
    sscanf(timeofday+6,"%d",&seed);
    srand(seed);
    i=0;
    while (i <= 3)
    {
        xcoord[i]=10.0*frand()+1.0;
        ycoord[i]=10.0*frand()+1.0;
        i = i+1;
    }
}
```

The unit test results for hide are given in Figure 8.7. A first look at these results may cause panic. The places where the spies are hidden are all within the expected range but appear to be anything but random. However, upon reflection, it is not the program but the test that is at fault in this case.

```
Figure 8.7   Test Reporting Document Example
             Unit Test of Procedure hide, Driver ver. 1.

Test Description: The source code is to be tested by running
    procedure hide to check the random numbers generated.
Test Conditions: The procedure is to be run alone, with the
    four pairs of random numbers generated to be listed. It
    will be run 20 times to compare the outputs.
Test Results:
```

Run	x	y	x	y	x	y	x	y		Run	x	y	x	y	x	y	x	y
1	10	1	7	6	4	3	9	6		11	6	8	7	9	1	10	3	8
2	10	1	7	6	4	3	9	6		12	6	8	7	9	1	10	3	8
3	5	4	7	7	10	6	1	7		13	6	8	7	9	1	10	3	8
4	5	4	7	7	10	6	1	7		14	10	3	8	10	7	7	7	9
5	5	4	7	7	10	6	1	7		15	10	3	8	10	7	7	7	9
6	1	9	1	8	5	8	9	8		16	10	3	8	10	7	7	7	9
7	1	9	1	8	5	8	9	8		17	5	3	1	10	8	4	5	10
8	1	9	1	8	5	8	9	8		18	5	3	1	10	8	4	5	10
9	1	9	1	8	5	8	9	8		19	5	3	1	10	8	4	5	10
10	6	8	7	9	1	10	3	8		20	5	3	1	10	8	4	5	10

```
Comment: The places where the spies are hidden are all within the
expected range but are not random.
```

The explanation of the result is that the random number is seeded by the system clock. The test ran 20 times, but the tests were so close together that the clock seeding the random numbers did not have much of a chance to change.

In order to get test results closer to those obtained from a real play of the game, we decide to modify the driver for the test by adding a timing delay. The results obtained are given in Figure 8.8.

When a timing factor is added to the test, the results are satisfactory. The problem in the first test run will not be apparent when the game is played because people will not play the game in less than 1 second. This example illustrates how important it is to have good test design, as well as good code design.

We have already said that when it comes to integrating the entire system, it is not safe to assume that the integrated system will work just because each unit is working. However, unless each unit is working, there is no hope that the integrated system will do what we want. Therefore, testing each unit carefully and thoroughly is extremely important.

Figure 8.8   Test Reporting Document Example
Unit Test of Procedure hide Driver ver. 2

Test Description: The source code is to be tested by running procedure hide to check the random numbers generated.

Test Conditions: The procedure is to be run alone, with the four pairs of random numbers generated to be listed. It will be run 20 times to compare the outputs. A timing delay will be used between runs, since the system clock is used as seed.

Test Results:

Run	x	y	x	y	x	y	x	y	Run	x	y	x	y	x	y	x	y
1	8	7	4	7	10	5	6	10	11	5	4	6	1	5	8	8	2
2	8	9	4	8	4	7	4	10	12	6	6	8	3	7	7	5	4
3	4	1	4	10	8	8	1	8	13	1	10	7	4	8	4	7	5
4	9	6	3	10	7	5	10	7	14	10	1	7	6	4	3	9	6
5	2	6	5	8	5	2	8	6	15	5	4	7	7	10	6	1	7
6	4	1	3	7	10	5	4	5	16	6	8	7	9	1	10	3	8
7	7	9	5	6	2	10	7	4	17	10	3	8	10	7	7	7	9
8	1	7	2	5	8	7	3	3	18	2	7	6	9	3	1	5	10
9	10	3	6	3	2	2	1	1	19	7	9	8	8	4	3	7	9
10	1	9	8	1	10	5	2	1	20	4	1	6	7	6	9	10	8

Comment: As expected. No further modification was made.

After each module has been tested, an integration test needs to be run. The test conditions for this for the completely integrated system for "Spies on a Grid" are given in Figure 8.9, which is part of a test description document. The complete results of integration testing are too lengthy to be included here, but this example illustrates how to begin.

Figure 8.9   "Spies on a Grid"
Partial Test Description Document

This is a test of the entire system, functional testing only.

Test Conditions: The procedure is to be run under the following conditions:
1. Enter pairs of valid numbers at each request: 1, 5
2. Enter first numbers outside the allowed range: 0, 8
3. Enter second numbers outside the allowed range: 2, -5
4. Enter both numbers outside the allowed range: 11, 101
5. Enter nonnumeric values: A, B
6. Enter too few numbers: <CR> or 5
7. Enter too many numbers: 3 4 5

8.C. Test Report Generator

Tests are tedious, boring, and extremely important to run and document carefully. Each test report must contain a lot of information, including the name of the person testing, the date and time of the test, the name of the module tested, a description of the purpose of the test, a list of the input data, the test result, and commentary on the test result. Much of this is repetitive and can be automated. For example, the date and time can be taken from the system clock, which is not only easier, it is also likely to be more accurate. Let us look at an example of a unit test generator.

Recall the triangle classification problem from Chapter 5. Suppose we want to have a module called triangle to take as input the three sides of a triangle and determine whether the values represent the three sides of a scalene, isosceles, or equilateral triangle, or not a triangle. The unit test generator in Figure 8.10, written in C, can be used as a driver to test the module. The code for the module triangle is appended to the end of the driver in the source code shown in Figure 8.10. This source code and parts of the unit test generator specific to this module are **highlighted**.

```
Figure 8.10    Example of a Unit Test Generator in C

#include "stdio.h"
#include "math.h"
/************************************************************

    UNIT TEST DRIVER      =          UNIT.C
Takes input from the keyboard and generates a test report
which shows the test input items and results.  Optionally
the operator may  set the  trace/debug  flag  to show the
internal details  of execution,  where the output is made
conditional on the value of DEBUG. To capture a permanent
record of a test,  enter <Ctl/P> to the DOS prompt before
executing UNIT.       C. Sigwart, Northern Illinois Univ.

ver. 1.0  11/28/85  for C/80 compiler, CP/M 2.2, Kaypro 4
     2.0   2/14/87  mod. for DeSmet C 2.5, MS-DOS 2.2
     3.0   3/12/88  mod. for Turbo C 1.0, MS-DOS 3.2
     4.0   9/10/88
*************************************************************/
/*----------------------------------------
 * DEFINE GLOBAL DATA NEEDED         */

int debug ;        /* Debug flag,  0 -> OFF     */

/*----------------------------------------
 *  SUPPORT FUNCTION PROTOTYPES     */

void get_desc(char *);
int  input(char *, char *, int);
void put_header(char *, char *, char *);
```

```
#define NOT   !
#define OR    ||
#define AND   &&

int main()
{
char    comment[80],*com;  /* Test description line  */
char    response[80];      /* Query response         */
int     i,                 /* Iteration count        */
        E,                 /* Return code            */
        first;             /* Flag for first report  */
/*===========================================================
 *     DECLARATIONS SPECIFIC TO THE UNIT UNDER TEST         *
 *                                                          */
/* DESCRIPTORS OF MODULE & PARAMETERS PASSED TO UNIT:       */

static char    module[16]
                        = "triangle"; /* Name - test module */
static char    version[6] =  "1.00"; /* Version  'xx.xx'   */
static char    operator[32];         /* Person running test*/

static int     num_parm = 3 ;        /* No. of parameters  */
static char    parm_nam[10][15] =    /* Parameter names    */
                    { "side1", "side2", "side3" };
static char    parm_typ[10][15] =    /* Parameter types    */
                    { "float", "float", "float"  };
static char    parm[10][15];         /* Parameter  string  */
static double p[3];                  /* Parameter values   */

/* OTHER PARAMETERS, IF ANY REQUIRED :                      */

                        /*  NONE   */


/*===========================================================*/
/*-----------------------------------
 *  Set name of operator and prompt to
 *  set top of form.              */

printf(" UNIT TEST REPORT GENERATOR  prints a report\n");
printf(" for each test case used with unit under test.\n");
input( "\n THESE TESTS ARE BY (input tester name) : ",
    operator,50);
printf("\n     Did you use Ctl/P to turn on the printer?\n");
printf("If so, set Top of Form for printing reports.\n");
printf("You will be prompted for test cases and comments.");
input("\n\n Continue ? (Y/N)", response,30);

/*-----------------------------------
 *  Loop doing tests until    quit ->
 *  RESPONSE  NOT=  'y'                */

while( response[0] == 'y' OR response[0] == 'Y' )
    {
    put_header(module, version, operator);

/*----------------------------------------
 *  Get comments describing intent of test and
 *  any relevant detail of the environment. */

    printf("\n          DESCRIPTION of TEST: \n      ");
    get_desc(comment);
```

```
/*-------------------------------------------------
 *  Show input descriptors, get parameters.
 *  Add code to get additional parameters or
 *  to convert string representation to the
 *  data type needed for call to unit.        */

    printf
      ("\n\n        The parameters of function:  %s()   are:\n",
        module );
    i = 0 ;
    while ( i < num_parm )
        {
        printf("              %s as %s",
                &parm_nam[i][0],&parm_typ[i][0] );
        input(" ?:  ", &parm[i][0],14);
        p[i] = atof( &parm[i][0]);
        i++
        }
    printf ("\n        In main: %7.4f,%7.4f,%7.4f\n",
            p[0],p[1],p[2]);

/*-------------------------------------------
 *  Set debug flag(s) ?                 */

/*  set_debug();    NOT USED IN THIS TEST */

/*-------------------------------------------
 *   EXECUTE function under TEST -
 *   add any code required to do so */

    E = triangle( p[0], p[1], p[2] );

/*-------------------------------------------
 *   SHOW RESULTS
 *   add any code required to do so */

    printf("           %s returned the value: %d\n", module, E );

    switch( E ) /* Select case on value returned by 'triangle'*/
        {
    case 0 : printf("        Not a triangle \n");
             break;
    case 1 : printf("        Scalene, No sides equal \n");
             break;
    case 2 : printf("        Isosceles, 2 equal sides \n");
             break;
    case 3 : printf("        Equilateral, 3 equal sides \n");
             break;
    default  :printf("         ERROR, undefined return code \n");
        }

/*-------------------------------------------
 *  Prompt for comments on results  */

    printf("\n         COMMENTS ON RESULTS :\n         ");
    get_desc(comment);      /* Input until <CR> on empty line */
```

```
/*-----------------------------------
 *  Another report ?                     */
    input("\n        Do another test? (Y/N) ",response,79 );
    if( response[0] == 'y' OR  response[0] == 'Y' )
    continue ;
    else
    exit(0);

    }   /* end loop   */                                              }
        /* end DRIVER */

/*==========================================================*/
/*   APPEND  UNIT TO BE TESTED after separate compilation */
/*        done previously and syntax errors eliminated.    */
/*==========================================================*/


/*----------------------------------------------------
    TRIANGLE     A routine which accepts values of 3
    lengths of sides and determines whether the sides
    represent an equilateral, isosceles, scalene, or is
    not a triangle.

Return code, integer  :
    0 = Not a triangle
    1 = scalene, no equal sides
    2 = isosceles, two equal sides
    3 = equilateral, 3 equal sides

----------------------------------------------------*/
int triangde ( s1, s2, s3 )
    double  s1, s2, s3;
{
    printf ("        In triangle: %7.4f,%7.4f,%7.4f\n\n",
                        s1,s2,s3);

    if ( s1 == s2  AND  s2 == s3 )         /* 3 equal sides ? */
        {
        return 3;   /* Equilateral, 3 = sides */
        }
    else if ( s1 == s2 OR s1 == s3 OR s2 == s3 )
        {                                  /* 2 equal ? */
        return 2;   /* Isosceles, 2 = sides */
        }
                        /* If sum of any two sides not greater
                           than third side, it isn't a triangle. */
    else if ( (s1 + s2) <= s3  OR  (s1 + s3) <= s2
            OR    (s2 + s3) <= s1 )
        {
        return 0;    /* Not a triangle */
        }
    else
        {
        return 1;    /* Scalene. no equal sides */
        }
}
```

This unit test generator is designed to work on a microcomputer that directs its output to the printer as well as the screen. It sets a top-of-form for each unit test performed so that each test result begins on a new page.

Figure 8.11 shows the output generated by running this unit test generator with the triangle module for two sets of input data. In Figure 8.11 the page breaks are indicated by lines to save space. The information entered by the tester is indicated in **highlighting**. The first test checks three floating point numbers, and correctly produces the result, "Equilateral." The second tests nonnumeric data, which is incorrectly interpreted. The bug is described in the test result part.

```
Figure 8.11   Output from the Unit Test Generator
              in Figure 8.10, Used with Module Triangle

UNIT TEST REPORT GENERATOR  prints one page for
each test case used with unit under test.

  THESE TESTS ARE BY (input tester name) : G. Van Meer
      Did you use Ctl/P to turn on the printer?
      If so set Top of Form for printing Test Reports.
      You will be prompted for test cases and comments.

Continue ? (Y/N)y
-----------------------------------------------------------------

UNIT TEST REPORT       MODULE : triangle,      VERSION : 1.00
TESTED BY : G. Van Meer
TEST DATE/TIME : Tue Apr 04 10:17:40 1989
              -----------------------------------------------------

              DESCRIPTION of TEST:
                Three equal sides, floating point numbers

              The parameters of function:   triangle()  are:
                  side1 as float ?:  0.5
                  side2 as float ?:  0.5
                  side3 as float ?:  0.5
In main:  0.5000, 0.5000, 0.5000
In triangle:  0.5000, 0.5000, 0.5000
              triangle returned the value: 3
              Equilateral, 3 = sides

              COMMENTS ON RESULTS :
                Worked as expected

              Do another test? (Y/N) y
```

```
------------------------------------------------------------
UNIT TEST REPORT        MODULE : triangle,      VERSION : 1.00
TESTED BY : G. Van Meer
TEST DATE/TIME : Tue Apr 04 10:17:57 1989
------------------------------------------------------------
            DESCRIPTION of TEST:
              Nonnumeric data

            The parameters of function:   triangle()  are:
              side1 as float ?:  one
              side2 as float ?:  one
              side3 as float ?:  0.5
In main:  0.0000, 0.0000, 0.5000
In triangle:  0.0000, 0.0000, 0.5000
              triangle returned the value: 2
            Isosceles, 2 = sides

            COMMENTS ON RESULTS :
              Bug in program, should flag nonnumeric data

            Do another test? (Y/N) n
Null pointer assignment
```

If you do not currently have access to an automated test report generator, we hope you will find it worthwhile to use this one or to create your own in whatever language and style you prefer. Most of the code in a driver for report generation is generic and simply copied to make a driver for the next module to test. Obviously each unit test requires some effort to create a customized driver. These should be saved to support regression testing.

8.D. Interpretation of Test Results

When a test produces an unexpected result, the first reaction you are likely to have is "I found an error!" More realistically we must consider four cases in interpreting test results. Not only may the system under test be at fault, but also the test. We must validate the test as well as the object under test. An apparent error may be the result of a faulty test. Unfortunately there is also the possibility of an apparently correct result when there is an error in the system but it is masked by a faulty test. On the other hand just because no fault is found in the test environment it does not mean that the system is correct. Test results must be reviewed very carefully.

An error has occurred anytime there is a difference between what the software actually does and what we want it to do. Such errors can be classified in many ways other than the types we presented in Table 5.2. Here we look at some categories suitable for listing errors by type in a test report.

Errors can be put into the following major categories.

- software errors
- errors not caused by software (e.g. hardware error)
- things the user wants but didn't get

For the purpose of this chapter, we will look only at software errors. We first categorize software errors as private, public, or persistent. Then we look at a method of categorizing by severity of the consequences of the error as a basis for helping to decide whether or not to fix it.

8.D.1. Private, Public, and Persistent Errors

Private errors are the ones the programmer catches before anyone else sees the code, including errors that are caught before the code is written. In some software development organizations the prescribed unit test is the dividing line for private bugs. That is, the programmer debugs his or her module until ready to submit it to a documented unit test. When that test is run any errors found in that or later tests must be logged and categorized. Such bugs may, of course, still be private to the developers if the users do not get complete documentation.

Public errors, on the other hand, are the ones that the programmer's teammates and others are permitted to see. There is evidence that the average rate of public errors is one per hundred statements.

Since private errors usually are not documented, there are no statistics available on their frequency. However, Boris Beizer tells us in <u>Software System Testing and Quality Assurance</u> (1984):

> *I know how many private bugs I have: approximately 1.5 per statement. What is your ratio of private to public bugs? Does consideration of that ratio change your attitude toward bugs?*

The only way you can answer that question is to keep track of your own private errors for a while. It can be an eye-opening experience. Private errors that are not found become public errors, so if your ratio of private to public errors is high, it means you are doing a good job of finding your own errors. Of course a low rate of creating errors is even better.

Persistent errors are those that elude detection during testing, and surface when the software is operational. One study on persistent errors tabulated the first 100 such errors found in each of two embedded software systems. The frequency of each type of error found for each project is given in Table 8.2. Project A contains about a half-million instructions in the operational software and involved up to 150 programmers working together. Project B includes about 100,000 instructions and involved 30 programmers.

Table 8.2 Persistent Software Errors by Frequency of
           Occurrence (200 Errors examined, 100 on Each
           Project)

Project A: contains about a half million instructions in the
operational software, and involved up to 150 programmers
working together.

Project B: includes about 100,000 instructions and involved
30 programmers.

Category	Project A	B	Total
1. Omitted logic (existing code too simple)	36	24	60
2. Failure to reset data	17	6	23
3. Regression error	5	12	17
4. Documentation in error (software correct)	10	6	16
5. Requirements inadequate	10	1	11
6. Patch in error	0	11	11
7. Commentary in error	0	11	11
8. IF statement too simple	9	2	11
9. Referenced wrong data variable	6	4	10
10. Data alignment error	4	3	7
11. Timing error causes data loss	3	3	6
12. Failure to initialize data	4	1	5

13. Other categories of lesser importance (total 4 or less) -
    Logic too complex, compiler error, data storage overflow,
    expression incorrectly coded, pointer one off, dynamic
    allocation failure, data not included in checkpoint,
    microcode error, data boundary problem, macro error,
    multitasking synchronizing error, erroneous initialization,
    naming conventions violated, logic order incorrect,
    interface mismatch, data reset in error, parameter mismatch,
    inefficient code, data declaration wrong, bad overlay,
    statement label at wrong place, data clobbered.

    NOTE: An error was allowed to tally in more than one
    category. "Failure to reset data", for example, is almost
    always a specific instance of "omitted logic." So are "if
    statement too simple" and "failure to initialize data." Any
    error could also be a "regression error."

    NOTE ALSO: "Interface mismatch" and "parameter mismatch"
    errors are infrequent.

    Robert L. Glass, "Persistent Software Errors," Software
    Soliloquies, Computing Trends (1981).

The major types of errors that were found are defined in Table 8.3.
Note that interface errors and type matching errors, which are commonly
found in unit and integration testing, were not often present as persistent
errors. Note also that the single most frequent type of error was "omitted

logic," that is, the code was too simple to handle the complexity of the
problem it was supposed to solve.

Table 8.3 Error Definitions Major Categories of Persistent
           Errors Found

Category	Definition, Example
1. Omitted logic	Code is lacking which should be present. Variable A is assigned a new value in logic path X but is not reset to the value required prior to entering path Y.
2. Failure to reset data	Reassignment of needed value to a variable omitted. See example for "omitted logic."
3. Regression error	Attempt to correct one error causes another.
4. Documentation error	Software and documentation conflict; software is correct. User manual says to input a value in inches, but program consistently assumes the value is in centimeters.
5. Requirements inadequate	Specification of the problem insufficient to define the desired solution.
6. Patch in error	Temporary machine code change contains an error. Source code is correct, but "jump to 14000" should have been "jump to 14004."
7. Commentary in error	Source code comment is incorrect. Program says DO I = 1, 5 while comment says "loop 4 times."
8. IF statements too simple	Not all conditions necessary for an If statement are present. IF A < B should be be IF A < B AND B < C.
9. Referenced wrong data variable	self-explanatory
10. Data alignment error	Data accessed is not the same as data desired due to using wrong set of bits. Leftmost instead of rightmost substring of bits used from a data structure.
11. Timing error causes data loss	Shared data changed by a process at an unexpected time. Parallel task B changes XYZ just before task A uses it.
12. Failure to initialize data	Non-preset data is referenced before a value is assigned.

(Lesser categories are not defined here.)

Robert L. Glass, "Persistent Software Errors," Software
Soliloquies, Computing Trends (1981).

How can we find and eliminate defects such as those listed? The answer is to validate the system against the software requirements. System testing must include tests based on the requirements and the user documentation to make sure it does what the users expect it to do. This means checking the test plan and results against the design specifications and against the Software Requirements Specification.

We spend a great deal of time trying to break complex systems into relatively simple component parts. The results in Table 8.2 indicate that we also need to remember that large software systems are inherently complex. Effective error correction requires careful attention to detail at all stages of testing. There is no substitute for thorough reviews. Each stage of testing should be accompanied by a scheduled review process.

8.D.2. Classification by Severity

Another way to categorize errors is by the severity of the damage caused. This is not necessarily related to the difficulty of discovering or fixing the error. For example, a simple subscript out of range or incorrect flag initialization could have catastrophic results, but be trivial to fix.

Unfortunately, it is almost impossible to determine in advance how long and complicated debugging will be. Remember, on average, fixing one error results in introducing another half the time. Add to that the possibility that fixing one error will uncover another, and all the regression testing that implies, and your manager may have second thoughts about debugging. These second thoughts get stronger as the deadline approaches.

What is a reasonable basis for deciding whether to fix an error? From the user's standpoint, it is the impact of the error that counts. Trivial errors may be left in, with a description in the user's manual (thus implying a fix before the next version is released). It is not unusual for a large software system to have a published list of known bugs.

However, "trivial" is a relative term and decisions must be made on a case-by-case basis. As a guideline, see the list of possible consequences of errors, compiled by Boris Beizer, in Table 8.4.

8.E. Integration and System Testing

The goal of integration testing is to assemble the system of modules by linking them together and testing its interfaces. It is assumed that these modules have been individually tested. Integration testing is properly carried out in an incremental manner so that interfaces can be tested one at a time. This may be done in parallel with the coding and unit testing of other modules. The obvious advantage is that the next module added is more

Table 8.4 Consequences of Errors

1. Mild - The symptoms of the bug offend us aesthetically;
   a misspelled output or a badly aligned printout.

2. Moderate - Outputs are misleading or redundant. The bug
   has a small but measurable impact on the system's
   performance.

3. Annoying - The system's behavior, because of the bug, is
   dehumanizing. Names are truncated or arbitrarily
   modified. Bills for $0.00 are sent. Operators must use
   unnatural command sequences and must trick the system
   into a proper response for unusual, bug-related cases.

4. Disturbing - It refuses to handle legitimate transactions.
   The money machine refuses to cash your paycheck. My
   credit card is not accepted at the bookstore.

5. Serious - It loses track of transactions: not just the
   transaction itself (your paycheck), but the fact that
   the transaction occurred. Accountability is lost.

6. Very Serious - Instead of losing your paycheck, the
   system credits it to another account or converts a
   deposit into a withdrawal. The bug causes the system
   to do the wrong transaction.

7. Extreme - The above problems are not limited to a few
   users or to a few transaction types. They occur
   frequently and arbitrarily, instead of sporadically for
   strange cases.

8. Intolerable - Long-term, irrecoverable corruption of the
   data base occurs. Furthermore, this corruption is not
   easily discovered. Serious consideration is given to
   shutting the system down.

9. Catastrophic - The decision to shut down is taken out of
   our hands. The system fails.

10. Infectious - What can be worse than a failed system? One
    that corrupts other systems even though it does not fail
    itself; that erodes the social or physical environment;
    that melts nuclear reactors or starts wars; whose
    influence, because of malfunction, is far greater than
    expected, or wanted; a system that kills.

Boris Beizer, "The Taxonomy of Bugs." Software Testing
Techniques. Van Nostrand-Reinhold, 1983.

likely to be the source of an error when it is tested in the company of previously tested modules. This helps in localizing errors.

During integration the linking of separately compiled units is a fundamental activity. The integration process is inevitably interrupted as modules fail a test and are sent back to the design/code/unit test process to be corrected. This leads to a proliferation of versions of source and object code for modules. It is thus essential for everyone to be able to determine which version of each module is present. The required documentation and labeling with version numbers is called configuration management (this is described in detail in Chapter 9). Every integration test report document should indicate the specific versions of the elements of the configuration.

During integration it is easy to track and verify parameters that are explicitly passed in procedure parameter lists. We described some systematic ways of doing parameter tracing in Chapter 5 and Appendix B. Less obvious is that the use of globally defined data and data in shared files must also be tested. These may involve interactions that are not apparent from the hierarchy diagram. Thus it may take a lot of special code instrumentation to capture and verify data structures used globally in memory. Very often new test procedures, test data, and test designs may have to be created to localize and identify a fault that emerges during system testing.

One might presume that if each interface is verified and each element was separately verified, the completely integrated system is correct. We wish it were so. However, the problem of finding faults at the system level is so hard that we need to eliminate as many faults as possible with lower level testing steps.

System testing generally is more focused on the functional properties of the entire system. Thus each system test case should be tied to specific requirements. In addition, all the functional features and options described in the requirements documentation and the user documentation must be available and be shown to perform appropriately. The final testing summary should indicate a tabulation of which test validated each feature.

8.F. Course Project: Testing

No matter how carefully we have worked at creating error-free programs, we must still check to ensure that our modules are coded correctly. It is a common misconception to view testing as a demonstration that the modules perform correctly. In fact, this is the opposite of what testing is about. The goal of testing is to find errors. We test programs to discover the existence of errors. Once we have identified an error we may start the error correction process (debugging). This involves determining what caused the error and making changes to the system so that the error is removed.

Particularly in a course project, there may be a temptation to get bogged down in later stages of integration tests or in system tests. If there are severe problems which there is reason to believe are due to one or a few modules, it is better to backtrack to unit testing of those modules. The overhead of testing a module with multiple faults is excessive.

In a critical case it may be necessary for the team to thoroughly review the offending module(s). First review the unit testing that has been done for adequacy. Then design whatever additional tests may be required to ensure that it meets its specifications. Also consider the adequacy of the specifications.

To keep the overall development progressing, be pragmatic about using stubs for modules not yet available. You may have to reorganize and reschedule if you are behind schedule. The goal should be to restructure your effort so as to maximize the number of features of the system that can be completed. Hence if a module relating to a low-priority feature causes a severe problem it is sensible to abandon that feature. Make whatever code modification is required to avoid a patch of bad code and to keep the rest of the system running.

When a project gets behind schedule there are three possible management alternatives:

1.   Expend more resources and add more personnel.
2.   Extend the deadlines and reschedule.
3.   Deliver a subset.

The first alternative is usually the worst. Adding new people to a project requires that they learn about the software under construction. Furthermore, the more people that are working on a project, the more lines of communication are required. This can sometimes slow down a project. This is such a serious problem that Frederick Brooks has stated as Brooks' Law: *"Adding manpower to a late software project makes it later."*

Extending a deadline is not usually possible for a course project. As a practical matter, you probably can only choose the third alternative, delivering a subset. Therefore, do not let your schedule slip very much before seriously evaluating how you can choose an appropriate subset to maximize the deliverables in your project.

On the job there are serious ethical question associated with testing one's own code. It is very hard to admit to flaws in one's own work. Ideally, one team will test another team's code. At the very least, team members should test each other's code. It may be annoying to have another team member find a bug in your code. However, at least the team member wants to help ensure the quality of the product. This is preferable to having a user, who wants the perpetrator fired, find that bug. In a course project it is better to have a teammate find a bug than your instructor.

8.G. Beyond a Course Project: Limits of Testing Large Programs

A one-term course project cannot realistically prepare you for the magnitude and complexity of software projects that take years on the job. The typical software engineering student works on a project that is still small enough for one person to understand entirely. This is generally necessary because of time constraints and because we need to limit the scope of the software in order to explain the principles.

It is the principles that are important. These are what will make it possible for you to participate in a large project. Therefore, the principles should be applied rigorously, even when they are boring.

Consider acceptance testing. For a course project, acceptance testing will probably consist of you and your teammates sitting around a terminal, watching your instructor execute your program, while you hold your breath and worry whether anything unexpected will happen. This will probably occur during the last week of the course and take half an hour or so.

Contrast this with acceptance testing for a medium-size software system written for the Department of Defense. Acceptance testing is likely to take two to three months, and the documentation will probably run to several thousand pages. No one person can possibly keep more than a small fraction of a system this size in mind. This is why we need good software engineering techniques. This is why Edsgar W. Dijkstra said, as he recognized the essence of the problem back in 1965, "I have only a very small head and must live with it."

Summary

Testing can demonstrate the presence of bugs, as Edsgar Dijkstra has observed, but not their absence. Therefore, the purpose of testing is primarily to find bugs, rather than to demonstrate the conditions under which the program works. For this reason, it is advisable to have a test team that is independent from the programmers who wrote the code.

Testing (uncovering errors) is a separate activity from debugging (fixing errors). Whether an error is worth fixing is a matter of judgment. The decision depends on such factors as the severity of the error, whether the time and money for regression testing are justified, and whether the error was due to the source code, the hardware, the test design, or some other factor.

Errors may be caused by software, hardware, poor test design, or inadequate system specification. Software errors may be private (caught by the programmer), public (caught by the test team), or persistent (missed by the test team, found by the user).

Decisions on what to do about errors depend on a combination of the severity of the error and the level of complexity of regression testing that would be needed to assure that no new error was introduced.

It is very hard to overemphasize the importance of documenting all testing. The test report document must indicate each test that was run and its result. The test report document must also indicate whether the test was a unit, integration, or system test so that if and when debugging takes place, appropriate regression tests can be run. Good record keeping can save incredible amounts of time during regression testing. Since much of the work in testing is repetitious, some of it can be automated. An example of a unit test generator is given.

Keywords

    categories of errors
        software errors
        errors not caused by software
        things the user wants but didn't get.
    consequences of errors
        mild
        moderate
        annoying
        disturbing
        serious
        very serious
        extreme
        intolerable
        catastrophic
        infectious
    error correction
    independent test team
    test description document
    test design
    test report documentation
    test report generator
    testing
    types of errors
        persistent
        private
        public

Questions

8.1.   What are the goals of testing?

8.2.   What is the difference between testing and debugging?

8.3.   What are the advantages of independent test teams?

8.4.   What is regression testing and when is it used?

8.5.   What is the purpose of the test report document?

8.6.   Why should records be kept on errors once they are removed?

8.7.   What is the difference between the driver of an interactive program and the driver for a unit test?

8.8.   Name at least three different possible sources of errors other than the software.

8.9.   Do you know your rate of private bugs? Your ratio of public to private bugs? What are they?

8.10.   How are persistent errors detected?

8.11.   How can we reduce the complexity of large software systems?

8.12.   We have classified errors according to severity. In what other ways could errors be classified?

Exercises

8.1.   Keep track of your private errors the next time you write source code. What is your ratio of private to public errors?

8.2.   What is the significance of an error in a program? If a program contains an error, does that make the program wrong?

8.3.   Modify the test report generator in Figure 8.10 to run an integration test.

8.4.   What is the relative importance to a user of a bug that causes customer names to be misspelled and a bug that causes billing errors?

8.5.   Consider a program you have written. Have you ever had the experience of introducing an error by correcting another error? How do you know?

8.6.   Consider a program you have written and the errors you found. What was the level of severity of each error, based on Table 8.4? Have you ever worked on a program that produced errors in the last categories?

8.7.   How would you approach a test of your own code as
        opposed to a test of someone else's code? Describe how
        you would feel about the difference.

References

Beizer, Boris. Software Testing Techniques. New York: Van Nostrand-Reinhold, 1983.

> A thorough discussion of testing methods and rationales for test data generation. The problem of exhaustive testing of execution paths is explored and alternatives are presented to maximize the chance of detecting faults with modest test data sets. Test strategies based on test databases, decision tables, Boolean algebra, and state transition testing are explained. Also includes "Taxonomy of Bugs."

Beizer, Boris. Software System Testing and Quality Assurance. New York: Van Nostrand-Reinhold, 1984.

> Puts the test techniques in the broader context of reliability and quality of the system. Testing and test management are discussed at the unit, integration, and system levels. Also discussed are configuration, security, and performance tests.

Brooks, Frederick P. The Mythical Man-Month, Essays on Software Engineering. Reading, MA: Addison-Wesley, 1975, reprinted 1982.

> Considered a classic of software engineering. Brooks presents the results of his experience as the project manager for the IBM OS 360. A clear exposition of the non-linearity of manpower and project duration effects on software project management. Includes "Brooks's Law."

Deutsch, Michael S. Software Verification and Validation, Realistic Project Approaches. Englewood Cliffs, NJ: Prentice-Hall, 1982.

> Reviews several techniques and tools. Advocates systematic test planning and shows results of case studies at Hughes Aircraft.

Dunn, Robert. Software Defect Removal. New York: McGraw-Hill, 1984.

> Defect removal is the goal of reviews and testing. The chapter on analysis of specification and design reviews is particularly appropriate to this chapter.

Evans, Michael W. Productive Software Test Management. New York: Wiley-Interscience, 1984.

> Discusses management of testing, including countermeasures when projects get behind schedule and over budget.

Glass, Robert L. Software Reliability Guidebook. Englewood Cliffs, NJ: Prentice-Hall, 1979.

> Surveys the state of software practices (1975-78) in defense and aerospace industries. Concludes with recommendations to improve software reliability.

Glass, Robert L. Software Soliloquies. College, PA: Computing Trends, 1981.

> Collection of readable essays, including "Persistent Software Errors."

Institute of Electrical and Electronics Engineers. Software Engineering Standards. New York: Wiley-Interscience, October 1987.

> Includes "ANSI/IEEE Std 829-1983, Software Test Documentation," which describes a set of basic test documents associated with the dynamic aspects of software testing and defines the purpose, outline and content of each basic document. Also includes "ANSI/IEEE Std 1008-1987, Software Unit Testing," which defines an integrated approach to systematic and documented unit testing. Uses unit design and implementation information and requirements to determine the completeness of the testing. Describes a testing process composed of a hierarchy of phases, activities, and tasks.

McCabe, Thomas J. Structured Testing, IEEE Catalog No. EHO200-6. Washington, DC: Computer Society Press, 1983.

> Collection of papers on structured testing methodology. Describes measuring and limiting the complexity of program modules so they are more easily testable, and procedures and completion criteria applied in the process of testing. Includes McCabe's original paper on cyclomatic program complexity V(G), "A Complexity Measure."

Mills, Harlan D. "Structured Programming: Retrospect and Prospect." IEEE Software (November 1986): 58-66.

> First in a series called "Fundamental Concepts in Software Engineering," this article gives an overview of how structured programming changed programming practices over two decades. It also introduces some new ideas of how to alter current programming practices, such as eliminating the use of arrays.

Pfleeger, Shari Lawrence. Software Engineering, The Production of Quality Software. New York: Macmillan, 1987.

> Introductory text; Chapter 7 is on program testing, Chapter 8 is on system testing. Chapters have good exercises.

Pressman, Roger S. Software Engineering, A Practitioner's Approach, 2d ed. New York: McGraw-Hill, 1987.

> A survey of software engineering with thorough review of all phases of the life cycle and the management of software. The treatment of software design provides chapters on data flow, data structure, real time, and object oriented design methods.

CHAPTER 9

MAINTENANCE AND DESIGN FOR MAINTAINABILITY

The softness of software is an opportunity for the system synthesist, but it is a pitfall for the maintainer. The maintainer's chief skill, like the surgeon's, is not in making desirable changes but in avoiding undesirable ones. (Any fool can take out an appendix; the trick is to take it out without killing the patient.)

- G. Parikh and N. Zvegintzov,
<u>*IEEE Tutorial on Software Maintenance*</u>

Software maintenance is a crisis in itself: it is too slow, too tedious, too error prone, too boring, and too expensive. And it occupies too many of our software people: between 50 percent and 80 percent of the software people in the average software organization are involved in maintenance. The result . . . is that existing systems which were built ten or twenty years ago simply cannot be modified to meet the new demands of the government, or the economy, or the weather, or the fickle mood of the user. . . . [T]o the extent that software stagnates, the company or society served by the software will stagnate.

- Edward Yourdon, <u>*Nations at Risk*</u>

Software Life Cycle

Software maintenance

> I. Software need
> II. Preliminary feasibility judgment
> III. Requirements analysis and feasibility study
> IV. Requirements specification
> V. Preliminary software design and planning
> VI. Software development
> >Detailed design
> >Coding and unit testing
> >Integration
> >System testing
> **VII. Software maintenance**

Project: Coding, additional basis for refinement, testing.

9.A. Maintenance

Software maintenance is very different from hardware maintenance in that software does not wear out. IF statements do not need to be periodically replaced. However, software does sometimes need to be changed. It would be nice to think that once a software product is delivered, it will be used in the delivered form forever. This virtually never happens.

First of all, errors will probably be discovered. No matter how thorough the testing has been, as we saw in Chapter 5, it is not feasible to test all possible paths. The longer the system is in use, the more likely that additional paths will be exercised and errors will be found. For example, the original airline reservation system, SABRE, had been in use for some time before a strange error was found. It seems that attempting a reservation in which the names listed totaled 224 characters ending in "n" would crash the system. This was discovered when a reservation was attempted for the Boston Bruins hockey team. One can hardly fault the testing team for not checking that particular case (though it might be perfectly legitimate to criticize the design that resulted in the error).

Another source of required maintenance is a change in the environment in which the software is used. For example, the next version of the operating system for the machine on which the software runs could require changes in the software.

Finally, if the users like the software, they will probably think of other things they would like it to do. Addressing all these problems constitutes software maintenance.

9.A.1. Categories of Maintenance

Software maintenance consists of modification of a software product after it has been delivered. The various categories of maintenance are often referred to as corrective, adaptive, and perfective maintenance. **Corrective maintenance** consists of overcoming existing faults in the delivered software. **Adaptive maintenance** is done to make the software usable in a changed environment. **Perfective maintenance** is done to improve performance, maintainability, or other software attributes.

Successful software requires maintenance. The only software that doesn't need maintenance is the software that is so bad, it is never used. Maintenance is an essential, integral process in the life of a software system.

9.A.2. Impact of Maintenance

Software maintenance uses, on average, half of all resources expended on a software system, and in some cases as much as 90%. Since it has an impact on such a large part of the budget and resources of most software organizations, there is great motivation to try to reduce the time and effort that maintenance takes.

9.A.2.a. Historical Perspective

Once upon a time, programs were the product of a single person. That person usually stayed with one company and was available to do maintenance on his or her software product. As programs became larger and, simultaneously, programmers became more likely to change jobs, the work of maintenance began to fall to people who had nothing to do with the program's creation.

The challenge in doing any sort of maintenance is first to understand what it is that the software is supposed to do. In the past, this was incredibly difficult. You will appreciate this the first time you encounter a program that consists of a single module of 4000 lines of source code, with no documentation except perhaps, at most, an ANSI flowchart. And don't expect comments in the source code. When the program was written, it probably consisted of a stack of punched cards, and the programmer was not about to increase the weight of the cards that had to be carried around.

One of the major objectives of software engineering today is to create software that is maintainable. To do otherwise is suicidal. More than one software house has become "maintenance bound;" that is, so much of the resources had to be devoted to maintaining existing software that no new software could be created.

9.A.2.b. Does Software Ever Die?

Our life cycle model (Table 1.1) does not indicate a retirement section. This is not an accident. Experience has shown that implemented software is remarkably difficult to kill. However, eventually many programs do become unusable and are retired. This usually happens for one of several reasons. The program may be replaced. It may cease to be used because the need for it is past. Or it may fail to adapt to needed changes. Failure to adapt may be because so many changes have been patched in over the years that no one can make a desired change without causing undesirable side effects. Another possibility is that some aspect of the system, either hardware or software, has been changed in such a way that the program can no longer be run.

Some maintenance programmers would often like to hasten the retirement process. However, it is very expensive and time-consuming to create replacement software, so managers will try to postpone retirement. Sometimes a manager has other reasons for keeping a program going. This is illustrated by the following conversation between a maintenance programmer and a manager, which Edward Yourdon tells about in Nations at Risk (1986):

> Programmer: "This program is disgusting! It takes days to make the simplest modification, and then I have no idea whether it will work. If you would just give me a week, I could rewrite it completely."

> Manager: "I'm sorry. It's not in our budget."

> Programmer: "To hell with the budget. You'll save so much money with a new version of the program that you'll look like a hero. Why, I could write the program so that it would run three times faster and take seven times less memory."

> Manager: "The last time someone told me that, it took six months to rewrite the program, and the new version ran three times slower and took seven times more memory."

> Programmer: "Yeah, but this is different . . ."

> Manager: "That's what they all say. I just can't take the risk."

> Programmer: "Look, I'll do it on weekends, and at night; I'll do it on my own time. I'll give up my vacation. I'll do anything to get rid of this disgusting program!"

Manager: "Sorry. I just can't authorize it. Look, the program isn't really that bad. I should know: I was the lead programmer on the development project back in '68. Now if you have any questions about how it works, you just come ask me. . . ."

Programmer: "(Censored)"

9.A.3. Who Does Maintenance?

You are among the generation of software engineers who are being trained to write maintainable code so that the next generation of maintenance won't be such a nightmare. That's what this chapter is about. But first, let us take a brief look at who currently does the horrible job of maintaining older software.

Software maintenance has been viewed as the most difficult, most frustrating, least rewarding, and least creative aspect of software. And to whom do such jobs go? To the newest member of the team, of course. The chances are excellent that your first job will be in maintenance.

On the other hand, there are those who think that it doesn't make a lot of sense to assign the least experienced person to the most difficult job. The problem here is that maintenance is generally perceived as a low status job. Some companies have had the insight to try to alter this situation and find some way of getting their best, most experienced people involved in maintenance with concomitant increases in pay and status.

It is important for you to understand how things used to be and how fast they have changed. It is important for you to understand that a 10-year-old program whose documentation seems to you to be almost nonexistent may have been very well done for its time. This is something to keep in mind before you make a disparaging remark about a program and find out later that your boss was the one who wrote it, as in the conversation quoted above.

For now, however, it is important that you be able to write software that is maintainable, not only for yourself, but for the next generation of software engineers. Let us now look at some guidelines to help you do this. The commitment to devote the resources to design and implement software to support maintenance is a management issue. Doing it may cost more than the minimum cost to complete development.

9.B. Design for Maintainability

Many factors affect the maintainability of a software system. Some of them are summarized in Table 9.1. They include the type of application, the life of the system, the environment on which the system depends, whether the hardware is changed during the life of the system, and how much staff turnover there is during the life of the system.

Table 9.1   Factors Affecting Software System Maintainability

- Application type
- Life of the system
- Changes in system environment
- Changes in system hardware
- Staff turnover

Some of the problems associated with maintenance are listed in Table 9.2. They include, first and foremost, acquiring a basic understanding of the system. This is the most formidable obstacle to software maintenance and is exacerbated by limited documentation and high staff turnover. Not being able to find anyone who worked on the original system makes things harder. Another problem is the priorities of management, who would rather be building something new than modifying something in existence. This is reflected in the morale of the staff; it's not very rewarding to spend your time on something the boss isn't too interested in.

Table 9.2   Some Problems Associated with Software Maintenance

- User demands for enhancements and extensions
- Competing demands for programmer time
- Inadequate or nonexistent documentation
- Inadequate user training
- Difficulty meeting scheduled commitments
- Poor quality of the original programming
- Unreasonable user expectations
- Hard to understand what the system is supposed to do
- Can't find anyone who worked on the original system
- Management priorities
- Low status of job
- Morale problems

Perhaps the interest in modifying existing systems will never equal the interest in building new systems, but the amount of work and frustration for future maintenance can be reduced by using a variety of techniques when creating the software system in the first place. Good documentation is essential to solving the first problem, that of understanding what the system is supposed to do. A variety of programming techniques can help create more maintainable systems. Tools can be used effectively. Good configuration management can make an incredible difference. Users can be effectively involved with maintenance decisions.

9.B.1. Documentation for a Delivered System

One of the most important things anyone can do to make a system maintainable is to create the best possible set of documents that completely describe the system's design, development, and testing. In a well-done system, the documentation effort may equal the programming effort.

Documentation standards vary from one software organization to another. We have suggested one in Appendix A, and the examples in this chapter are consistent with that standard. However, on the job, it is important to find out what documentation standard you are expected to adhere to.

The first document we consider is the Software Requirements Specification (SRS), complete with any changes that have been made. Do not go back and rewrite the Software Requirements Specification as if the final version were the one you started with. Instead, include explanations for changes that were made. This will help prevent the maintenance programmers from going back to an earlier design that you already discovered wouldn't work. In this and in all other aspects of documentation, do everything you can to keep future software engineers from "reinventing the wheel" for this system.

In addition to the Software Requirements Specification, the set of documents produced for the system to be delivered should include a set of test reports, a user's manual, a description of the system design, and the documented source code. These may be a single document with separate sections, or separate documents, depending on the size of the project. Each document, and possibly each section of a large document, should have a table of contents.

9.B.1.a. Table of Contents

One of the simplest means of making things accessible in a set of documents is to provide a table of contents. No matter how good your documentation is otherwise, it needs to be well organized in such a way that things can be found. This is something that should go without saying, but the problem of overlooking the obvious is one that causes a lot of headaches for a maintenance programmer. One of the reasons a table of contents is often left out is that it has to be just about the last thing done, since you won't know the page numbers until the end. This means that it must be done when you are rushing to meet a deadline. One way of coping with this pressure is to create the table of contents in advance, leaving the page numbers to be filled in at the last second. Better still, if possible, use a word processing system that will automatically create it for you.

A sample table of contents for documentation for the "Spies on a Grid" game, described in Chapter 8, might look like the one in Figure 9.1.

```
Figure 9.1   Table of Contents for the Final Documents
             for "Spies on a Grid"

I. TEST REPORTING DOCUMENT
    A. Unit Tests                                    2
    B. Integration Tests                             7
    C. Final Tests                                  12
II. USER'S MANUAL
    A. Rules of the Game                            15
    B. How to Start the Game                        15
    C. How to Play the Game                         16
    D. Sample Game                                  17
III. SYSTEM DESIGN AND DOCUMENTED SOURCE CODE
    A. System Design Documentation
        1. English Description of Features          18
        2. System Data Flow Diagrams                21
        3. Hierarchy Chart of Modules               22
    B. Documented Source Code and Flowcharts
        1. Main Module                              24
        2. clear                                    25
        3. hide                                     26
        4. turn                                     27
        5. win                                      28
        6. lost                                     29
```

9.B.1.b. Test Reporting Document

Testing during maintenance is handicapped by the problems listed in Table 9.2. Machine time is limited, and maintenance testing is often given a low priority.

The major reason test documentation is needed during maintenance is so that regression testing can be conducted. In this, as with other aspects of creating maintainable software, the idea is that design and development work already done should not have to be redone. Without records of previous testing, the maintenance programmers would have to start from the beginning.

9.B.1.c. User's Manual

The basic contents of the user's manual are summarized in Table 9.3. The user's manual for the system should include a functional description, in English, of what the system does. It should also give the user a description of how to install the system and how to get started on the system once it is installed. There should be a reference section describing the facilities available, including, where appropriate, examples of how the system works. In some cases, depending on the software, there may be an operator's guide.

```
Table 9.3  Contents of the User Documentation

• Functional description of what the system does
• Introductory manual - how to get started
• Reference manual - facilities available
• Installation documentation
• Error messages and recovery techniques
• Operator's guide (depending on system)
• Index
```

A major problem of maintenance organizations is a combination of unreasonable user expectations and poor user training. The best defense against this is user documentation that is very clear about exactly what the product will and will not do. To maximize the chance that the users will figure out what they need to know, the manuals should be clearly written, well organized and well indexed. Not only should the necessary information be there, but it should be possible to find it through a combination of a table of contents, an index, and cross-references to other relevant sections or documents. Take advantage of the capabilities of a good word processor, which has special features to make it easy to create an index and table of contents.

The user's manual should also include information on what kinds of errors are likely to occur and how to correct them. A table of error messages and recommended recovery procedures should be included. An experienced user may judge the quality of the system by the range of error conditions checked (and by expected forms of errors that are not covered).

An example of a user's manual for the "Spies on a Grid" game is given in Figure 9.2.

Figure 9.2 User's Manual for "Spies on a Grid"

A. <u>Rules of the Game</u>
The game of "Spies on a Grid" is to be played on an IBM PC microcomputer. Four spies will be hidden on a ten by ten grid. You will have ten guesses to find the spies. If they are found within the ten guesses you win the game, otherwise you lose.

B. <u>How to Start the Game</u>
- Open the door of disk drive A.
- Put a system disk in drive A. (Holding the labeled end of the disk, insert it into the drive with the label facing up.)
- Close the disk drive door.
- If your computer is off, turn on the system unit switch and monitor. If the computer is already on, press the Del key while holding down the Ctrl and Alt keys.
- The disk will make noise for anywhere from a few seconds to a minute. You will be greeted by a message that will identify the operating system you are using. Beneath this message you should see the following:
  A>
- Take out the system disk.
- Put in the game disk.
- Close the disk drive door.
- Type spies and press the Return key. (The Return key has a picture of a curved arrow pointing to the left.)
- You are now ready to play "Spies on a Grid."

C. <u>How to Play the Game</u>
The computer will initially ask you if you want to play the game. Type Y if you do and N if you do not want to play.
Note: Any response beginning with y or Y will be considered a yes response and any response beginning with n or N will be considered a no response. Any other response will result in the question being asked again.
Once you have indicated a desire to play the game you will be given ten chances to find the spies. Your guess as to where a spy is should be a pair of numbers separated by one or more spaces. The numbers should correspond to coordinates on the ten by ten grid (i.e., they should be from 1 through 10).
At the end of each game, if you win you will be told, and if you lost, you will be given a list of the coordinates where the spies were hidden. Then you will be asked if you want to play again.

D. <u>A Sample Game</u>
Do you want to play spies? Answer Y or N. **y**
Turn Number 1 What is your guess ?4 1
Your distance from spy 1 is 6.324555
Your distance from spy 2 is 9.848858
Your distance from spy 3 is 6.708204
Your distance from spy 4 is 8.544004
Turn Number 2 What is your guess ?4 10
Your distance from spy 1 is 9.219544
Your distance from spy 2 is 4.000000
Your distance from spy 3 is 4.242641
Your distance from spy 4 is 3.162278
Turn Number 3 What is your guess ?8 8
Your distance from spy 1 is 5.385165
Your distance from spy 2 is 2.000000
Your distance from spy 3 is 1.414214
Your distance from spy 4 is 1.414214
Turn Number 4 What is your guess ?1 8
Your distance from spy 1 is 10.295630
Your distance from spy 2 is 7.280110
Your distance from spy 3 is 6.082763
Your distance from spy 4 is 6.082763
Turn Number 5 What is your guess ?5 5
Your distance from spy 1 is 5.385165
Your distance from spy 2 is 5.830952
Your distance from spy 3 is 2.828427
Your distance from spy 4 is 4.472136
Turn Number 6 What is your guess ?4 5
Your distance from spy 1 is 6.324555
Your distance from spy 2 is 6.403124
Your distance from spy 3 is 3.605551
Your distance from spy 4 is 5.000000
Turn Number 7 What is your guess ?5 4
Your distance from spy 1 is 5.099020
Your distance from spy 2 is 6.708204
Your distance from spy 3 is 3.605551
Your distance from spy 4 is 5.385165
Turn Number 8 What is your guess ?4 8
Your distance from spy 1 is 7.810250
Your distance from spy 2 is 4.472136
Your distance from spy 3 is 3.162278
Your distance from spy 4 is 3.162278
Turn Number 9 What is your guess ?3 9
Your distance from spy 1 is 9.219544
Your distance from spy 2 is 5.099020
Your distance from spy 3 is 4.472136
Your distance from spy 4 is 4.000000

```
Turn Number 10 What is your guess ?5 4
Your distance from spy 1 is 5.099020
Your distance from spy 2 is 6.708204
Your distance from spy 3 is 3.605551
Your distance from spy 4 is 5.385165
Locations of the hidden spies are
Spy 1 hid at (10,3)
Spy 2 hid at (8,10)
Spy 3 hid at (7,7)
Spy 4 hid at (7,9)
Do you want to play again? Answer Y or N. n

    I hope you do better at finding the spies than we did in
this example.
```

9.B.1.d. System Design and Documented Source Code

A table of contents for the System Design and Documented Source Code section for Fig Leaf Enterprises Dating Service is given in Figure 9.3. Note that the modules are listed in order by author.

```
Figure 9.3   System Design and Documented Source Code
             Fig Leaf Enterprises Computer Dating Service

                   Table of Contents
```

As part of the System Design document, an English description of the system should be included. This should give a discussion of the structure related to the intention of the designer and the relation of the structure to the design decisions that have been made. An example of this type of description of some features of the dating service is given in Figure 9.4.

Figure 9.4   System Design Documentation for the
Fig Leaf Enterprises Computer Dating Service

English Description of Some Features

I. General Overview
     This system is designed to be used by an operator for Fig Leaf Enterprises, and not directly by the client. It is an interactive system that facilitates learning for the novice operator by providing online information at several levels. It also provides text files for the command handler, a help file, date matching questions, and error messages for ease of update when required. Finally, there is an interactive trace system in place.

II. Online Information
     Information is available to the user at three levels. The first level is information that appears on screen with the prompts. Since this could be a nuisance for the experienced user, the operator is initially given a choice of terse or verbose prompts. The default is verbose; that is, the terse option must be explicitly chosen or the system reverts to verbose.
     The second level of information is an online help file. This may be selected at any prompt by entering 'H' (upper- or lowercase). This provides several screens of information read from a text file. At the end of each screen the user is given the option of continuing with the help file or terminating at that point.
     The third level is an explanation that is available at each prompt for the user who is in the terse mode. A question mark (?) entered at any prompt will cause the system to provide the information that is available in verbose mode.

III. Text Files

Text files are used in several places where changes are most likely to be wanted in the future. The use of text files means that the information can be modified with a text editor. Depending on the impact to the system, it may mean that no compilation is required to run the system after modification. This means that in some cases modification can be done by an operator who can use a text editor, but does not necessarily have any familiarity with programming. However, it is recommended that the modified text file be reviewed by a programmer for such things as appropriate line length and hidden commands (e.g., control-I for tabs).

The text files that are currently in place include the one for the command handler, which contains the main menu. Any rephrasing that may be of help to the operator can be done easily. However, any change in the options will require modification of the source code.

Another text file is the help menu. Modification here should not require any change in source code. The system reads one "page" at a time (20 lines) and then asks the user whether to continue. It is appropriate for readability to have each 20-line segment created with suitable paragraphing and page breaks.

The questions asked of a client are also in a text file, and correspond to the order in which they appear on the form the client fills out. The questions are weighted for the matching algorithm. Therefore, any changes to the system that involve adding questions at the end of the list can be done with relatively minimal programming change. Altering a question may require changing a weighting factor. Deleting a question could have a major impact on the system and must be done with care.

The error messages are in a text file. The line number of the file corresponds to the error message. The error handler is invoked with an integer, n, which is used to read n lines in the file. The nth line is written to the screen. It is recommended that any changes in the error handling system be limited to adding lines to the file, as the same messages are used throughout the entire system. Modifying existing messages in the text file could result in some strange error messages in some parts of the program, and could be counterproductive to the intent of helpfulness to the user.

IV. Trace System

An interactive trace system is in place, but is hidden from the operator. It may be invoked by the systems programmer by running the program normally, but selecting '*' as the option in the main menu. This is not listed as a choice for the user. Invoking this option will produce the message: "You have chosen the system trace procedure. This is not part of the computer dating service. If you do not want to be here, press the carriage return." This allows the operator to return to the system easily in case of getting there by accident. To actually operate the trace system, enter 'T'. This information is included in comments in the source code.

```
    The procedure allows you to operate the system normally,
but in addition to the usual information, you will get a
message as you enter and exit each module. It is a good idea
to refer to a copy of the hierarchy diagram as you use the
system.
```

Documented source code should be a direct copy of a source code listing. Do not try to improve the appearance of the source code. To do so can often cause problems. We have spent many hours trying to reproduce code from published listings that were inaccurate. In some cases, someone had tried to make the listing "look nice." In others, the author of the code decided to make "just one more change" and did not test the result. Sometimes the published code would not even compile. (We are making every effort to see that our source code listings are exactly the way they ran on our systems!)

Trying to alter the appearance of the source code in the document can cause problems in ways other than affecting reliability. If the listing in the document is different from the machine-readable version, it can cause confusion when the maintenance programmer tries to modify the machine-readable version. It is possible that a disaster could occur, such as a fire or something else that could destroy the machine-readable version of your system. In this case, the code might have to be reproduced from your document, and you want the listing to be accurate so as to not introduce more problems.

Of course, you want the source code to be as readable as possible. One way of doing this is with consistent internal documentation (comments in the source code). Each module should follow the same format. For example, it doesn't much matter whether data dictionaries are put in header or trailer blocks, but they should be in the same place in all modules.

For readability, each module should begin on a new page. An exception is the case of extremely small modules, when more than one can fit on a page, or extremely small programs. As an example, the documented source code for the "Spies on a Grid" game is given in Figure 9.5. Here the modules are all listed sequentially, rather than each on a new page. This is partly because the program is so short. However, for readability, there are several blank lines at the beginning of each module. The distinctive header block with the procedure description also helps locate module beginnings.

Figure 9.5 "Spies on a Grid" Documented Source Code

```c
#include <stdio.h>
main()
{
/****************************************************************
This program is a game called spies on a grid. The object of
the game is to guess where spies are hidden on a 10 by 10 grid.
DeSmet C  2.51
****************************************************************/
 int x[4],y[4],g,t;
 char ans[256];
/****************************************************************
                      Variable Dictionary

name  type              use

 x  integer array    holds the x coordinate of the hidden spies
 y  integer array    holds the y coordinate of the hidden spies
 g  integer          flag which is set to 1 to indicate a win
 t  integer          holds current turn number
ans character array  answer to questions
                     Procedure Dictionary
 name              use

clear           clears the screen
hide            puts the four spies on the grid randomly
turn            asks for a guess and checks to see how close
                   you were from each unfound spy.
win             checks to see if you have won the game
lost            prints out the locations of the hidden spies
                   if you have lost.
****************************************************************/

clear();
ans[0]=NULL;
while(ans[0]!='n'&& ans[0]!='N'&& ans[0]!='y'&& ans[0]!='Y')
    {
    printf("Do you want to play spies? Answer Y or N. ");
    gets(ans);
    }

 while(ans[0]!='n' && ans[0]!='N')
    {
    clear();
    g=0;
    t=1;
    hide(x,y);
    for(t=1;t<=10;t++)
        {
 turn(x,y,t);
 win(x,&g);
 if (g==1) break;
        }
```

```
        if(g==0) lost(x,y);
        ans[0]=NULL;
        while(ans[0]!='n'&&ans[0]!='N'&&ans[0]!='y'&&ans[0]!='Y')
            {
            printf("Do you want to play again? Answer Y or N. ");
            gets(ans);
            }
        }
    }

clear()
/***************************************************************
 This procedure clears the screen by printing 24 blank lines.
 ***************************************************************/
{
int i;
for(i=1;i<=24;i++) printf("\n");
}

hide(xcor,ycor)
/***************************************************************
 This procedure hides the spies on the 10 by 10 grid.

                        parameters

 name      type              input/output    use

 xcor      integer array     output          x-coordinate
 ycor      integer array     output          y-coordinate
 ***************************************************************/
int xcor[],ycor[];
{
/***************************************************************
                    variable dictionary

 name      type              use

 i         integer           index for the coordinate arrays

 ***************************************************************/
int i,seed;
double frand();
char timeofday[9];
times(timeofday);
sscanf(timeofday+6,"%d",&seed);
srand(seed);
for(i=0;i<=3;i++)
    {
    xcor[i]=10.0*frand()+1.0;
    ycor[i]=10.0*frand()+1.0;
    }
}

turn(xcor,ycor,tu)
/***************************************************************
This procedure plays a complete turn. It prompts the user for
a guess and then tells the user how far off from each spy the
guess was. It also tells the user if the spy was found. If a
spy was found its x-coordinate is changed to -1.
```

```
                    parameters

name    type            input/output    use

xcor    integer array   input & output  x-coordinate
ycor    integer array   input           y-coordinate
tu      integer         input           holds turn number
*****************************************************************/
int xcor[],ycor[],tu;
{
/*****************************************************************
                    variable dictionary

name    type        use

x       integer     x-coordinate guess
y       integer     y-coordinate guess
i       integer     used to index spy arrays


*****************************************************************/
int i,x,y,go;
double d,sqrt();
char thing[256];
go=0;
x=0;
y=0;

while (go != 1 )
    {
    printf("Turn Number %d What is your guess ?",tu);
    gets(thing);
    sscanf(thing,"%d %d",&x,&y);
    if( (x<=10) && (x>0) && (y<=10) && (y>0) ) go=1;
    }
for(i=0;i<=3;i++)
    {
    if(xcor[i]!=-1 && xcor[i]==x && ycor[i]==y)
        {
        printf("You have found spy %d\n ",i+1);
        xcor[i]=-1;
        continue;
        }

    if(xcor[i]!=-1)
        {
        d=(xcor[i]-x)*(xcor[i]-x)+(ycor[i]-y)*(ycor[i]-y);
        d=sqrt(d);
        printf("Your distance from spy %d is %f\n",i+1,d);
        }
    }
}

win(xcor,gg)
/*****************************************************************
This procedure checks to see if a win has occurred. If it has,
it prints a message and sets the contents of gg to 1.
```

```
                          parameters
    name    type              input/output        use

    xcor    integer array     input       x-coordinate(=-1 if found)
    gg      integer           output      set = to 1 for a win

    ************************************************************/
    int xcor[],*gg;
    {
    /************************************************************
                      variable dictionary

    name    type            use

    i       integer         index for x-coordinate array

    ************************************************************/
     int i;
     for(i=0;i<=3;i++) if(xcor[i]!=-1) return;
     *gg=1;
     printf("You have won\n");
    }


    lost(xcor,ycor)
    /************************************************************
    This procedure prints out the coordinates of the spies not
    found if you  have lost the game.

                          parameters

    name    type            input/output    use

    xcor    integer array   input    xcoordinate(-1 if spy is found)
    ycor    integer array   input    ycoordinate
    ************************************************************/

    int xcor[],ycor[];
    {
    /************************************************************
                      Variable Dictionary

    name    type            use

    i       integer         index to the coordinate arrays

    ************************************************************/
    int i;
    printf("Locations of the hidden spies are \n");
    for(i=0;i<=3;i++)
       {
       if(xcor[i]!=-1)
         printf("Spy %d hid at (%d,%d)\n",i+1,xcor[i],ycor[i]);
       }
    }
```

The modules should be in some sort of order: alphabetical; ordered according to a system on a hierarchy chart; or listed by primary author as in the example in Figure 9.3. Whatever system is used, there should be a table of contents so that the maintenance programmer can easily find the listing for a single specific module.

9.B.2. Programming Techniques to Enhance Maintainability

The techniques for design and coding, already described in previous chapters, generally apply to maintainability as well. These include such things as modularity, information hiding, and complexity metrics.

There are a number of ways to write source code to enhance maintainability. The use of meaningful variable names is one that should be familiar to you. Other things include structured coding, writing for readability, and the use of symbolic constants.

Some languages, such as Ada, enforce standards that make the code somewhat more tedious to write, but considerably easier to read. This is a recognition that effort put into designing and creating flexible, readable code pays off in reduced maintenance costs. Not all languages are so designed, especially the languages that were created before the recognition of the need to apply software engineering principles. However, as with the structured programming techniques described in Chapter 7, all these principles can be applied in any language.

9.B.2.a. Modularity

Limiting the size of a program module has already been described as a way of enhancing the understandability of a software system. Another advantage is that it can increase flexibility as well.

Software maintenance may involve adding features to a software system. However, as user needs change, it is also likely that the user will want modifications that involve deleting features. One approach to designing flexible systems is to explicitly define subsets and supersets of a system during design. Thus the designers should indicate clearly where any expected future enhancement should be inserted or attached. This should help the programmer to create independent modules that can be (relatively) easy to remove or add to.

One tends to think of maintenance as changing or adding modules (and this is indeed often the case). However, the idea of deleting modules should also be kept in mind. This makes it possible to remove features that are no longer needed, which might otherwise be difficult.

For example, consider a system that reads data items from a file, sorts them, and then processes them. Perhaps the time will come when data items will need to be read from another file with a different format or access mode. Perhaps the time will come when the sort feature is not needed. And of course the time will come when some previously unforeseen feature will need to be added. If the program is designed with modules that are sufficiently independent, the first modification can be done by changing a module, the second by deleting a module, and the third by adding whatever is needed. Each of these can be done easily if some thought is given to separating features into independent functional modules during design and development.

The matter of independence is particularly important to the success of system flexibility. That involves information hiding.

9.B.2.b. Information Hiding

One of the reasons for employing the concept of information hiding is to keep modules as independent as possible. When a module keeps all its essential information to itself, it can be deleted from a system or replaced with a functional equivalent without causing side effects. This is the ideal situation, of course, and seldom achieved. However, thinking in terms of modules as individual building blocks to be added, deleted, or modified should help to create systems that are more easily maintained.

Many programmers think in terms of adding features to a system; it is considerably trickier to think in terms of deletions. However, to do so will result in more flexible systems and hence lower maintenance costs.

9.B.2.c. Complexity Metrics

In keeping with the idea of making a system both expandable and contractible, it is a good idea to limit module complexity. McCabe's metric, introduced in Chapter 7, is one such measure. One major reason for limiting complexity is so that a module can reasonably be tested, as described in Chapter 8. An additional reason is so that it can be considered a single, independent block during system maintenance.

9.B.2.d. Symbolic Constants

Parameters used repeatedly throughout a system should be symbolic constants rather than numeric constants. This is done, for example in Pascal, using the *const* declaration. In other languages the compiler can recognize a preprocessor directive to define a constant as a macro. There are two reasons for handling constants in this way: giving the parameter a meaningful name, and maintaining ease of change.

When using a constant in a system, using a meaningful name rather than a numeric value will help the maintenance programmer remember what is going on. For example, suppose you are using the value of pi. Most of us recognize 3.14159 as a reasonable approximation of pi. However, declaring an exact value for a variable called pi (for example, pi = 4.0 x arctan 1.0) will not only help in recognition, but also make the calculations more precise.

The other reason for using symbolic constants is to make life easier when the value of the constant is changed. It's true that mathematical constants aren't likely to change, but virtually every constant in internal use by any company will, sooner or later, be changed. No matter how many years the company has used, let us say, the same cost/benefit ratio, it could be changed next week. Using symbolic constants means it will have to be changed in only one place in the software, no matter how many times and places it is used.

As a worst case example consider the maintenance problem caused when three different parameters happen to have the value of ten and their use is scattered throughout the system. If one of these parameters must be changed, all instances of the "hard coded" constant of ten will have to be examined. The likelihood of an update error and the problem of finding it is large. Thus the long-term costs of maintenance are reduced if parameters are symbolic and localized.

9.B.2.e. Restructuring Software

There is a problem of preventing the quality of the software structure from deteriorating under continued maintenance. This was observed in the maintenance history of some large software systems such as the IBM OS/360. It was seen that the fraction of the total number of modules that had to be changed for each new release continued to increase until it was retired. If the code is patched with unstructured methods the code will become less and less understandable over time. Naturally if the code is less understandable the likelihood of introducing a defect when making a change increases and the cost of adequate testing increases. Ultimately the software should be scrapped if the cost of upgrading it approaches the cost of starting over.

If there is an expectation that the system will be in service for many years, it is appropriate to invest effort in improving the structure while performing current maintenance. This means restructuring the code to maintain standards of module size, complexity, cohesion and the quality of coupling.

If changes require increasing the size of the module you should consider reorganizing the code and splitting out any functionally cohesive subsections to form new modules. This is also a reasonable tactic in a redesign effort triggered by problems in system testing. Remember, too, to update the relevant sections of all associated documentation.

Some organizations report that the cost of improving program structure and restructuring modules is small. Such restructuring has been advocated as a tool to improve understanding of the modules that need modification. The result of this practice is that the code may be improved over time rather than becoming harder to maintain.

Management willingness to commit to continuing enforcement of standards for good modularity can prevent the deterioration of software quality. Indeed, the maintenance history of some systems does show improvement in quality over time. Decreasing entropy does require planning and effort.

9.B.3. Use of Tools

Tools that are used in system design and development can also be used in system maintenance. Of course, maintenance tools need not be limited to design and development tools. The subject of tools is covered further in Chapter 11. However, a list of tools that are especially useful in maintenance, as well as design and development, is given in Table 9.4.

```
Table 9.4   Useful Tools in Software Maintenance

• Complexity calculator
• Cross-reference generator
• Data dictionary generator
• Debugging tools
• File comparator
• Split-screen editor
• Syntax-directed editor
• Pattern search utilities
```

Complexity calculators generate complexity metrics and help keep the logic of a module within bounds. Cross-reference generators and data dictionary generators help reduce the tedium and increase the accuracy of good internal documentation. Debugging tools are useful at every step of any process in creating code.

File comparators may be most useful in telling you where two versions of a file differ, which can be crucial in configuration management (discussed below). Some experimental work has been done with large screens (62 lines by 160 characters), which permit visual review of a larger portion of the source code at one time. In conjunction with this, the same screen can be split into two 62-line by 80-character screens to permit simultaneous viewing of two files. This allows review of two related files or two versions of the same file (for example, source code and flowchart).

Source code and text editors go together, but syntax-directed editors, which are language-specific, can save a lot of time and effort both in modifying the code and avoiding syntax errors. Pattern search utilities can be invaluable in locating all references to a particular variable, constant, or function.

You are well advised to find out what tools are available to you and how to use them. As a software engineer, you should be constantly on the lookout for additional tools. The effort used to learn a new tool will be rewarded, not only with reduced tedium when the tool is applied, but with expanded knowledge and ability on your part.

Software tools range from indispensable to useless. Don't be discouraged when you occasionally run into one of the latter. And remember, there is no single all-purpose tool in software any more than there is in carpentry. Can you imagine trying to build a house with just a hammer and a hand saw? It could be done, but no one would want to. That would be comparable to trying to create a million-line software system with just an editor and a compiler.

No one tool will create, compile, compare, cross-analyze, debug, and configuration manage every program you write. But there are a lot of tools that will make life much easier. This topic is discussed in detail in Chapter 11.

9.B.4. Configuration Management

Configuration refers to the arrangement of a computer system, in terms of hardware or software or both. **Configuration management**, then, is the process of identifying and defining the configuration items in a system, controlling the release and change of these items throughout the system life cycle, recording and reporting the status of configuration items and change requests, and verifying the completeness and correctness of configuration items. This includes, but is not limited to, keeping track of the modules of a system and their state of development and keeping track of how many versions there are of each. This is why it is useful to have a systematic means of referring to the various modules, such as giving each one a number. It is especially important when modifications are being made and it is necessary to keep track of which is the most recent version of each module.

9.B.4.a. Document Configuration

Good configuration management is essential to every aspect of the software life cycle, including maintenance. Let us assume that a software system is extremely successful and multiple versions are released over a period of years. Configuration management is essential to keep track of the features of each version. Especially for a product with multiple versions in service, it is essential that all items of software and related documents identify the version easily.

Good configuration management practices established during design and development will help all concerned identify what version of an item they are dealing with. It is essential to the maintenance programmers to figure out exactly what has already been done. Also, having good practices already established means not having to "reinvent the wheel."

Configuration management during maintenance should provide the answers to the questions listed in Table 9.5. For the initial release, there should be a version number (probably Version 1.0) and the necessary documentation to answer questions about features and hardware requirements. It will be helpful for maintenance if the original configuration management is set up with the idea of eventually answering questions about multiple releases.

```
Table 9.5   Questions That Good Configuration Management
            Should Answer

• How many different versions have there been?
• How many of these are still in use?
• What are the similarities and differences between versions?
• When will the next version be available?

For each version:
      • What hardware is required?
      • What documentation is available?
      • What is the revision history?
      • What errors have been corrected?
```

Because of the large volume of documentation that (ideally) accompanies a software system, some organizations use loose-leaf notebooks, especially for user's manuals. That way, when a new version is released, a subset of the manual can be modified for the new version, rather than reproducing an entire document. Of course, it is important to indicate on each new page what version is represented and which pages are being replaced.

9.B.4.b. Introduction to make

In managing development projects and in maintaining systems, a very important aspect is making sure that changes to a module are included in the latest system version. This can be accomplished with tools that automatically build the current version from a special configuration file. An example of a utility for doing this is called **make**, available in UNIX and other operating systems. This utility was originally designed to help automate the building of C programs. Derivatives of **make** are now used to create and maintain software in other languages.

The interfile dependencies and the commands that must be executed to create files are specified in a file called the **makefile**, which is written by the user of the tool. Through its rule-processing capability, **make** can infer, without being explicitly told, the files on which a file depends and the commands that must be executed to create a file. Some rules are built into **make** and some the user must specify within the **makefile**. Rules simplify the task of writing a **makefile**: a file's dependency information and command sequences only need to be explicitly specified in a **makefile** if this information cannot be inferred by the application of a rule.

Make has a macro capability. A character string can be associated with a macro name, and when the macro name is invoked in the **makefile**, it is replaced by its string.

The main function of **make** is to make a target file "current." To do this it must examine the date and time stamps maintained by the operating system for all the related files. A file is considered current if the files on which it depends are current and if it was modified more recently than its prerequisite files. To make a file current, **make** makes the prerequisite files current; then, if the target file is not current, **make** executes the commands associated with the file, which usually recreates the file.

As we can see, **make** is inherently recursive. Making a file current involves making each of its prerequisite files current; making these files current involves making each of their prerequisite files current; and so on.

Make is very efficient; it only creates or recreates files that are not current. If a file on which a target file depends is current, **make** leaves it alone. If the target file itself is current, **make** will announce that fact and halt without modifying the target.

When **make** starts, the first thing it does is to read an input file, the **makefile**. This file contains dependency entries defining interfile dependencies and the commands that must be executed to make a file current. It also contains rule definitions and macro definitions. These are text entries created by the user.

A dependency entry in a **makefile** defines one or more target files, the files on which the targets depend, and the operating system commands that are to be executed when any of the targets is not current. The first line of the entry specifies the target files and the files on which they depend. The line begins with the target file names, followed by a colon, followed by the names of the prerequisite files.

After the definition of the file and its dependency information are command lines. The first character of a command line must be a tab; **make** assumes that the command lines end with the last line not beginning with a tab. Also, **make** assumes that the files are C files, where a source code file has an extension of **.c** (such as myfile.c) and the corresponding object code file has the same name with an extension of **.o** (such as myfile.o). The final, linked system will have an extension of **.com**, such as program.com.

For example, consider the following dependency entry:

    prog.com: prog.o sub1.o sub2.o
            link -o prog.com prog.o sub1.o sub2.o -lc

This entry says that the file **prog.com** depends on **prog.o, sub1.o,** and **sub2.o**. It also says that if **prog.com** is not current, **make** should execute the link command. **make** considers **prog.com** to be current if it exists and if it has been modified more recently than **prog.o, sub1.o, and sub2.o**.

The above entry describes only the dependence of **prog.com** on **prog.o, sub1.o,** and **sub2.o**. It does not define the files on which the .o files depend. For that, we need either additional dependency entries in the **makefile** or a rule that can be applied to create .o files from .c files.

For now, we will add dependency entries in the **makefile** for **prog.o, sub1.o,** and **sub2.o**, which will define the files on which the object modules depend and the commands to be executed when an object module is not current. Then, we will modify the **makefile** to use **make's** built-in rule for creating an .o file from a .c file.

Suppose that the .o files are created from the C source files **prog.c, sub1.c,** and **sub2.c**; that **sub1.c** and **sub2.c** contain a statement to include the file **defs.h**; and that **prog.c** does not contain any file inclusion statements. Then the rather long-winded **makefile** given in Figure 9.6 could be used to explicitly define all the information needed to make **prog.com**.

The **makefile** in Figure 9.6 contains four dependency entries: for **prog.com, prog.o, sub1.o,** and **sub2.o**. Each entry defines the files on which its target file depends and the commands to be executed when its target is not current. The order of the dependency entries in the **makefile** is not important.

Figure 9.6 Example of a `makefile`

A file whose dependency is defined has a following list of filenames on which it is dependent, separated by a colon. Such a file dependency list may also be followed by lines with rules (commands) that are to be used in creating the file from the predecessor files. Note that link invokes a linkage editor, and cc invokes a C compiler.

```
        prog.com: prog.o sub1.o sub2.o
                        link -o prog.com prog.o sub1.o sub2.o -lc

        prog.o: prog.c
                        cc prog.c

        sub1.o: sub1.c defs.h
                        cc sub1.c

        sub2.o: sub2.c defs.h
                        cc sub2.c
```

We can use this **makefile** to make any of the four target files defined in it. If none of the target files exist, entering will cause **make** to compile and assemble all three object modules from their C source files, and then create **prog.com** by linking the object modules together.

Suppose we create **prog.com** and then modify **sub1.c**. Then telling **make** to make **prog.com** will cause **make** to compile and assemble just **sub1.c** and then recreate **prog.com**.

If we then modify **defs.h** and tell **make** to make **prog.com**, **make** will compile and assemble **sub1.c** and **sub2.c** and again make **prog.com**.

We can tell **make** to make any file defined as a target in a dependency entry.

A **makefile** can contain dependency entries for unrelated files. For example, the following dependency entries can be added to the above **makefile**:

```
hello.exe: hello.o
    link hello.o -lc
hello.o: hello.c
    cc hello.c
```

With these dependency entries, we can tell **make** to create **hello.exe** and **hello.o**, in addition to **prog.com** and its object files.

We can see that the **makefile** describing a program built from many object files would be huge if it had to state explicitly that each object file depends on its source code file and is made current by compiling that source file.

This is where rules are useful. When a rule can be applied to a file that **make** has been told to make or that is a direct or indirect prerequisite of it, the rule allows **make** to infer, without being explicitly told, the name of a file on which the target file depends and/or the commands that must be executed to make it current. This allows **makefiles** to be compact, just specifying information that **make** cannot infer by the application of a rule.

Some rules are built into **make**, but we can define others in a **makefile**. Here we describe the properties of rules and how we write **makefiles** that use **make's** built-in rule for creating an **.o** file from a **.c** file.

A rule specifies a target extension, source extension, and sequence of commands. Given a file that **make** wants to make, it searches the rules known to it that apply to a file with the same extension as the target file. It also checks the existence of predecessor files with appropriate extensions and their dates and times of creation. It then applies the specified rules in the order found. An example of a rule built into **make** is that for converting **.c** files into **.o** files, as given in Figure 9.7.

```
Figure 9.7  Built-in make Rule for Converting C Source Files into
            Object Code Files

An object file having extension .o depends on the source file having
the same name, but with extension .c.  To make  such an .o file
current, execute the compile command:
                          cc x.c
where x is the name of the file.
```

The ".c to .o" rule allows us to abbreviate the long-winded **makefile** given in Figure 9.6 as follows:

```
prog.com: prog.o sub1.o sub2.o

    link -o prog.com prog.o sub1.o sub2.o -lc

sub1.o sub2.o: defs.h
```

In this abbreviated **makefile**, a dependency entry for **prog.o** is not needed; using the built-in ".c to .o" rule, **make** infers that **prog.o** depends on **prog.c** and that command **cc prog.c** will make **prog.o** current. It also says that both **sub1.o** and **sub2.o** depend on **defs.h**. It does not say that they also depend on **sub1.c** and **sub2.c**, respectively, or that the compiler must be run to make them current. However, **make** infers this information from the ".c to .o" rule. The only information given in the dependency entry is that which **make** could not infer by itself: that the two object files depend on **defs.h**.

On occasion we do not want a rule to be applied; in this case, information specified in a dependency entry will override that which would be inferred from a rule. For example, the following dependency entry in a **makefile**,

```
add.o:
    cc -dfloat add.c
```

will cause **add.o** to be compiled using the specified command rather than the command specified by the ".c to .o" rule. **make** still infers the dependence of **add.o** on **add.c** using the ".c to .o" rule, however.

We will not explore the more advanced features of **make** here. You should examine the documentation for **make** or whatever software configuration management tool that is available to you. In particular, you should examine how macros may be used, what built-in rules exist, and the conventions for building a **makefile**. As a final example we show an abbreviated command syntax for **make** in Figure 9.8.

Figure 9.8 Command Line Syntax and Parameters for **make**

make [-f makefile] [options] [file1] [file2] ...
where:

The parameters file1, file2 ... are the names of the files to be made. Each file must be described in a dependency entry in the makefile. They are made in the order listed on the command line.

The other command line parameters are options, and can be entered in upper- or lowercase. Their meanings are given below:

-f If no -f option is present, a file named **makefile** is expected as the makefile. A file name following the -f will replace that default filename. If a makefile name is given as -, the standard input is taken. More than one -f option may appear.

-d Debug mode. Print out detailed information on the files and times examined.

-i Ignore error codes returned by invoked commands.

-k If a command returns nonzero status, abandon work on the current entry, but continue on branches that do not depend on the current entry.

-n Trace and print but do not execute the commands needed to update the targets.

-p Print out the complete set of macro definitions and target descriptions.

-q Returns a zero or nonzero status code depending on whether the target file is or is not up to date.

-r Do not use the built-in rules.

-s Do not print command lines before execution.

-t Update the modified date of targets, without executing any commands.

File extensions recognized by built-in rules in **make:**

.c C source file
.e Efl source file
.f FORTRAN source file
.l Lex source grammar
.o Object file
.r Ratfor source file
.s Assembler source file
.y Yacc-C source grammar
.ye Yacc-Efl source grammar
.yr Yacc-Ratfor source grammar

9.B.5. *Importance of Users*

What do users have to do with software maintenance? Usually they are the ones who are asking for the modification, repair, or enhancement to a system. In other words, users are the major source of maintenance requests. And the typical user hasn't the least idea of the time and cost involved in a system change, much less the nature and extent of the effort.

As with system design, a better understanding between software people and users can benefit everyone. Some efforts have been made to increase user participation in maintenance by having users help set priorities and schedule modifications. Results have been highly satisfactory.

We strongly recommended increasing user involvement in the design and development process. This has advantages that are described in Chapter 10, and also lays the groundwork for a closer liaison between users and software people when maintenance is needed.

9.C. Course Project: Occam's Razor and the KISS Principle

Most of the principles that apply in creating maintainable programs also apply to other aspects of design and development. However, one reason for considering maintenance is to convince you that these things really are important and will become more, not less important as time goes on.

Sometimes the sheer magnitude of a problem to be solved by software will seem overwhelming. This is the nature of software, and there aren't many ways to make it easier. Typical software systems are too large for one person to understand, which is why it is important for you to work as part of a software team. The best thing we can do is carefully document everything so that someone trying to understand our part of a system will be able to figure out what is going on.

Many people have tried to figure out ways to make software simpler. Brooks, on the other hand, has pointed out that complexity is inherent to the very nature of software. In his article, "No Silver Bullet," he points out that software is not like a werewolf. A single silver bullet cannot solve the problem.

Sometimes scientific researchers use a principle known as **Occam's razor**. This is an excellent principle to know about, but one must use great care in exercising it when it comes to software.

William of Occam was a fourteenth century English philosopher and Franciscan who believed in the Aristotelian principle that "entities must not be multiplied beyond what is necessary." Using Aristotle's idea, Occam developed the principle known as Occam's razor: that a problem should be stated in its basic and simplest terms. The scientific application of this principle is that given a choice of more than one theory that fits the facts of a problem, the simplest should be selected.

The basic idea of Occam's razor can sometimes be applied to program modules and other aspects of software system development. Thus, if there is a simpler way to code a module, it is preferred. This has been succinctly rephrased in what has come to be known as the **KISS principle (Keep It Short and Simple).**

As a caveat, however, let us remind you that in Chapter 8 we reported the findings of a research study that showed the most common type of persistent software error was found where the software was simpler than the problem to be solved. Given a choice between two designs (or code structures, or documentation methods), either of which will solve the problem, by all means choose the simpler. Just be sure that it actually does solve the problem and that it does not introduce another problem.

9.D. Beyond a Course Project: Current State of Maintenance

Software maintenance is a process with its own rules and techniques. The art of software maintenance, while an important part of software engineering, requires many skills beyond those described in this book. That is because maintenance today includes work being done on programs that were written ten or twenty years ago, often without using the software engineering techniques that you are learning.

These programs, including such things as payroll systems and compilers, are large enough and widely enough used to be worth maintaining. But to do so requires understanding of the methodologies and the languages in use at the time the software was written.

Maintenance done on unstructured software, such as the single-module, 4000-line program described earlier, is a subject in itself, which we can do no more than introduce here. With unstructured code, it is difficult to figure out completely what the program does; or sometimes, even what it is supposed to do. It is often impossible to do regression testing because there are no records of previous tests. Sometimes, the only thing available for a system that needs maintenance is the object code.

Several things can be done to bring order out of the chaos of unstructured programs. To begin to understand what a program does, sometimes users can be interviewed. This usually will not give you complete information, and responses from users may even seem to be contradictory. But it is a start.

It is appropriate to create flowcharts and hierarchy diagrams. Data dictionaries are useful and can often be created with the assistance of tools. Sometimes just reformatting the source code can make it more comprehensible. This means putting the source code in a form that indents for such things as levels (as in nested if-then-else statements or their equivalents) and separate program segments. Automated tools, usually called "pretty printers," are available to do this. Modifying a portion of the code so that it goes into a separate module is often a good idea. This not only helps the maintenance programmer to understand the software, it makes the program more easily maintainable in the future.

Anything that is done during maintenance should be carefully documented. This includes any mistakes that are made. Don't try to hide a mistake; document it so the next maintenance programmer won't waste time going through the same process and making the same mistake you did. Try to think in terms of prolonging the life of the software, because whether you want it or not, the software is likely to be around for a long time.

Summary

Maintenance is done on software systems after they are delivered. It is done to fix errors, to adapt to a changed hardware system, or to add enhancements. These areas are often referred to as corrective, adaptive, and perfective maintenance, respectively.

Maintenance currently takes from half to more than 90% of all resources expended on a software life cycle. Therefore, it is important when creating new software to facilitate future maintainability in any possible way.

Maintenance has usually been viewed as the least rewarding, least interesting, and most undesirable aspect of software engineering. Often maintenance jobs are assigned to the least experienced and least qualified persons.

To create maintainable systems, it is important to provide adequate documentation, including the Software Requirements Specification, Test Reporting Document, User Manual, System Design and Documented Source Code. An internal trace system can be invaluable. Coding practices that include modularity, information hiding, limited modular complexity, and the use of symbolic constants and meaningful variable names are also helpful. Some useful tools are available both for developing maintainable systems and for doing maintenance on older systems. Good configuration management will help with everything. An example cited is **make**. Users should be involved in maintenance.

When doing software maintenance, the first thing needed is an understanding of what a system is supposed to do. This can be difficult, especially in the absence of adequate documentation. Users are often a valuable source of information about a system. Anyone who has worked on the system, if available, can also be helpful.

Keywords

complexity metrics
configuration management
information hiding
internal documentation
KISS principle
maintenance
    adaptive
    corrective
    perfective
maintenance bound
maintenance programmer
maintenance requests
maintenance testing
make
modularity
Occam's razor
software maintenance tools
    complexity calculator
    cross-reference generator
    data dictionary generator
    debugging tools
    file comparator
    large and/or split screen
    syntax-directed editor
symbolic constants
unstructured software

Review Questions

9.1. Why is maintenance needed on software?
9.2. What software needs no maintenance?
9.3. What is meant by corrective, adaptive, and perfective software maintenance?
9.4. What fraction of resources is consumed by software maintenance? Why?
9.5. What can be done to reduce the cost of software maintenance?
9.6. Does software ever die?
9.7. Who does software maintenance?

9.8.   How do you feel about taking a job that requires you to spend most of your time doing software maintenance?

9.9.   How do you design a software system so that it will be maintainable?

9.10.   When you are given a software system that needs maintenance, how do you determine what the system is supposed to do?

9.11.   What documents might be useful for software maintenance?

9.12.   How much regression testing needs to be done during software maintenance?

9.13.   What programming techniques do you use that would make a software system more maintainable? What are some other techniques?

9.14.   What software tools do you have access to that are useful for software maintenance?

9.15.   What is configuration management? How is it used in maintenance?

9.16.   What kind of tool is **make**? How is it useful for maintenance?

9.17.   How can users be helpful in software maintenance?

9.18.   If an error is introduced in software maintenance, why should it be documented?

Exercises

9.1.   In Figure 9.2, the user's manual for "Spies on a Grid," Part A, "Rules of the Game," is very limited. Examine the rest of the documetation and the source code (Figure 9.5), and rewrite "Rules of the Game" in a more complete, detailed manner.

9.2.   In Figure 9.2, the user's manual for "Spies on a Grid," Part D, "A Sample Game," does not give any indication of the number of correct guesses made. Suppose the user asks to have this feature added. Write the necessary specification and documentation.

9.3.   The "Spies on a Grid" game has been written using text only so that it can be played on any system with a suitable compiler. How would you change the game into one that worked on a color monitor with graphics? What type of maintenance would this be?

9.4.   An inexperienced maintenance programmer was once given the job of dividing a 4000-line monolithic program into

50-line modules "in his spare time." His response was to take the source listing and draw a red pencil line after each 50 lines of code. Do you see any problem with this? Do you see any merit in his procedure?

9.5. Look at a program you have previously written. How could you improve the documentation to make the program maintainable in the future? Assume the maintenance programmer is someone who will never meet you and who has not used the system your program runs on.

9.6. Examine an existing small program and consider translating it to another language with which you are familiar. How will the program have to be reorganized? Will it be easier to translate than to recreate the program from its specification? Why might the new program be larger or smaller?

9.7. What is the risk in ignoring configuration management in a project involving 10 programmers compared to the risk in a single programmer project?

9.8. Compare and contrast a configuration management plan you would produce for an evolving software tool used within your company with a configuration management plan for a software product used by many customers on several kinds of computers.

9.9. Users are complaining that an existing application maintained by your organization is inefficient. What should you do to evaluate potential changes to be proposed as perfective maintenance tasks?

References

Arnold, Robert S., ed. Tutorial on Software Restructuring, IEEE Computer Society Catalog Number EH0244-4. Washington, DC: IEEE Computer Society Press, 1986.

Intended not only for the modification of existing nonstructured programs but also for the development of new software. Includes criteria for recognizing good and bad structure, horror stories of origins and effects of poor software structure, and models for calculating time frame and payoffs of software restructuring.

Arnold, Robert S., and Martin, Roger J. "Software Maintenance, Guest Editors' Introduction." IEEE Software 3, no. 3 (May 1986): 4-5.

Brief overview of history and current state of maintenance, with a brief introduction to the rest of the articles in the issue.

Brooks, Frederick P., Jr. "No Silver Bullet," IEEE Computer 20, no. 4 (April 1987): 10-19.

Fashioning complex conceptual constructs is the essence; accidental tasks arise in representing the constructs in language. Past progress has so reduced the accidental tasks that future progress now depends upon addressing the essence.

Eschoff, J. L., and Marcotty, M. "Improving Computer Program Readability to Aid Modification." <u>CACM</u> 25 (August 1982): 513-521.

> Advocates systematic reorganization of relevant sections of source code to improve readability as a first step in a cycle of maintenance activity. This was based on experience in improving software quality during maintenance at General Motors. The authors' experience was that this was a small but extremely productive cost.

Feldman, S. I. "MAKE - A Program for Maintaining Computer Programs." <u>UNIX Programmers Manual</u>, Version 7, vol. 2 (1983): 291-300.

> An introduction to the make utility by its creator. The makefile used to create make itself is presented as an example.

Glass, R. L., and Noiseaux, R. A. <u>Software Maintenance Guidebook</u>. Englewood Cliffs, NJ: Prentice-Hall, 1981.

> Presents a broad introduction for managers and software engineering students.

Institute of Electrical and Electronics Engineers. <u>Software Engineering Standards</u>. New York: Wiley-Interscience, October 1987.

> Includes ANSI/IEEE Std 828-1983, Software Configuration Management Plans, which is similar to Std 730-1984, Software Quality Assurance Plans, but limited to software configuration. Provides a means by which the steps in the software are recorded, communicated, and controlled.

Lientz, B. P., and E. B. Swanson. "Problems in Applications Software Maintenance." <u>CACM</u> 24 (November 1981): 763-769.

> Report of a survey of 487 data processing organizations, asking respondents to rate the severity of 26 categories of maintenance problems.

Parikh, Girish, and Zvegintzov, Nicholas, eds., <u>Tutorial on Software Maintenance</u>, IEEE Catalog No. EH0201-4. Washington, DC: IEEE Computer Society Press, 1983.

> Based on the premise that maintenance is essential in the life of a software system, maintenance is a process with its own rules and techniques, and that the era of mature software (in use and likely to stay that way, such as payroll systems) is here.

Pfleeger, Shari Lawrence. <u>Software Engineering, The Production of Quality Software</u>. New York: Macmillan, 1987.

> Introductory text with a chapter on maintenance, with good exercises.

Price, Jonathan. <u>How to Write a Computer Manual, A Handbook of Software Documentation</u>. Menlo Park, CA: Benjamin/Cummings, 1984.

> Introductory description of how to write user documentation for a nontechnical audience. Includes writing a step-by-step tutorial and a general reference.

Spier, Michael J. "Software Malpractice - A Distasteful Experience." <u>Software Practice and Experience</u> 6 (1976): 293-299.

> A cautionary tale about how optimization tricks and incompetent maintenance caused the progressive failure of a software system.

Yourdon, Edward. <u>Nations at Risk: The Impact of the Computer Revolution</u>. New York: Yourdon Press, 1986.

> A readable account of the impact of computers on our world for computer professionals and general audience.

PART III

THE REST OF THE PICTURE

According to the Genesis account, the tower of Babel was man's second major engineering undertaking, after Noah's ark. Babel was the first engineering fiasco.

The story is deep and instructive on several levels. Let us, however, examine it purely as an engineering project, and see what management lessons can be learned. How well was their project equipped with the prerequisites for success? Did they have:

1. *A clear mission? Yes, although naively impossible. The project failed long before it ran into this fundamental limitation.*

2. *Manpower? Plenty of it.*

3. *Materials? Clay and asphalt are abundant in Mesopotamia.*

4. *Enough time? Yes, there is no hint of any time constraint.*

5. *Adequate technology? Yes, the pyramidal or conical structure is inherently stable and spreads the compressive load well.*

Clearly masonry was well understood. The project failed before it hit technological limitations.

Well, if they had all of these things, why did the project fail? Where did they lack? In two respects - communication, and its consequent, organization. They were unable to talk with each other; hence they could not coordinate. When coordination failed, work ground to a halt....

The Tower of Babel was perhaps the first engineering fiasco, but it was not the last. Communication and its consequent, organization, are critical for success. The techniques of communication and organization demand . . . as much thought and as much experienced competence as the software technology itself.

- *Frederick P. Brooks, Jr., The Mythical Man-Month*

The topics in these chapters need to be considered in every project on the job. Chapter 10, Systems Analysis, discusses the vital work to be done when a determination has to be made about whether a project is feasible, whether a company has the resources to do it, and whether one wants to take on the job. One topic which may be needed at the beginning of the course is how to interview a user.

Chapter 11, Software Tools and Environments, is an introduction to the subject. Students' backgrounds vary widely, depending on their experience and the resources of their institutions. Not every college or university will have access to many of the tools that will be available on the job, but it is appropriate for students to start to think in terms of automating any aspect of a software engineering project for which automation is feasible.

Chapter 12, Quality Assurance, is a topic that should be incorporated into every software engineering project from Day 1. However, the complexities and subtleties in this area make it extremely difficult to explain to anyone who is new to software engineering. Therefore, it is appropriate to first understand a little of the general nature of software engineering projects, in order to gain some appreciation for the magnitude of the headaches that quality assurance and software evaluation can save you.

Chapter 13, Software Protection, Security, and Ethics, is something that also needs to be considered in every software engineering project. Considerations range from making backup copies of everything to legal protection. In the dating service example, security is a very important consideration, especially if the users are entering information directly into the system. It is extremely important to protect the privacy of clients from someone who tries to tiptoe through the data files.

In almost any student project, the question may arise as to who owns the copyright to the work. And any project that is done for an outside organization must include legal considerations. For example, the company that wrote the compiler used for project development in an academic setting may have a claim on the product.

The one common theme underlying all these topics, as indicated in our opening quote, is that they are all very communication intensive. This is perhaps one of the hardest things to learn to do effectively.

CHAPTER 10

DEFINING THE PROBLEM: SYSTEMS ANALYSIS

The hardest single part of building a software system is deciding precisely what to build. No other part of the conceptual work is as difficult as establishing the detailed technical requirements, including all the interfaces to people, to machines, and to other software systems. No other part of the work so cripples the resulting system if done wrong. No other part is more difficult to rectify later. . . .

Complex software systems are . . . things that act, that move, that work. The dynamics of that action are hard to imagine. So in planning any software design activity, it is necessary to allow for an extensive iteration between the client and the designer as part of the system definition.

- Frederick P. Brooks, Jr., "No Silver Bullet"

I said it in Hebrew - I said it in Dutch -
I said it in German and Greek:
But I wholly forgot (and it vexes me much)
That English is what you speak!

- Lewis Carroll, <u>The Hunting of the Snark</u>

10.A. System Identification

The software life cycle begins with the recognition of a need for a software system. This leads to the second phase, preliminary feasibility study. Someone must make an analysis to determine what, if anything, should be done about the perceived need. This activity is part of systems analysis. Systems analysis is the work of investigating a system to analyze a problem, determine its scope, evaluate the feasibility of alternatives, and specify the characteristics that will be necessary and sufficient to solve a problem. This is an art. It requires a substantial amount of experience to do well. The practitioners of this art come from backgrounds in software engineering, hardware engineering, and application areas.

The actual development of software, even with all the vagaries of problem solving and testing, is much simpler. In the development arena we always have the immediate satisfaction of seeing the product run. Systems analysis has to deal with the broader problem of identifying and satisfying the goals of the user organization. These goals will not always be stated clearly by the users. For example, the problem may be stated as: "We need to automate." It is the job of the systems analyst to figure out just what that means.

So it is that, beginning with an imprecise problem, the analysts must build an abstract model of the system and produce an unambiguous definition of a solution to guide the development and implementation of required software. You may feel (probably correctly) that the analyst's job is beyond the level of expertise needed for a project for this course. However, it is essential that those who are to practice software engineering understand the origins of the specifications that guide their work in development. This may give some basis for being patient with your managers when, as is inevitable, you are suffering through specification changes in the middle of a project. At the same time, the developer must understand that he or she generally cannot individually change any specification. To ensure successful production of a system, the specifications must be a basis for evaluating the product when produced by the collective effort of many professionals.

In recent years much research and effort have gone into the problem of proving the correctness of programs (discussed in Chapter 7). In general this rests on the foundation of an assumed correct specification upon which the design of the software implementation is based. An equally fundamental problem is that of assuring the validity of the underlying specifications. It is a nontrivial task to assure that the system specified is the system that meets the needs of the user community.

We do not have a theoretical method of proving that the systems analysis of any real problem is correct. We do, however, have a collection of methodologies which experience has shown are helpful. These include functional decomposition, data flow models, data structure models, data dictionary systems, and standards for documenting requirements.

Another example is a systematic strategy to involve users in the process of analysis and design.

When a need is stated as, for example, a "need to automate," there is enormous potential for misunderstanding just exactly what needs to be done. It is an incredible amount of work to develop the necessary familiarity with the user's terminology and to get the users to state exactly what is wanted in clear, concise terms.

10.A.1. Establishment of a Need

The origin of a software system is a statement of a software need presented to the software professionals who will consider how it might be met. This may also be referred to as the concept exploration phase of the software life cycle. In most cases the statement of need is brief. Usually it will also be vague and imprecise; for example, "We need a billing system for Nocturnal Aviation's new Overnight Delivery Service." A slightly more detailed example is given in Figure 10.1 for another company.

```
Figure 10.1   Example of a Statement of a Software Need

                              INTERNATIONAL WIDGET CORP.

MEMO TO:  John Doe, Director, Systems Analysis Group
FROM:     William Smith, Vice-President, Operations
DATE:     June 13, 1986
SUBJECT:  Backlogs in widget production and quality control

John,

   Production supervisors are blaming periodic failure to meet
their production quotas on the requirement that the line
workers must manually fill out quality control report forms
for each widget on the line.  They want to schedule more
overtime for line workers.
   Would it be reasonable to automate reading the sensors and
tabulating the quality assurance reports?  What will it cost?
   Please consult with Jane Johnson on background details.

                                            Bill

cc: Jane Johnson, V.P. Manufacturing
```

The apparent need for software creation may arise in many ways. A few of these are summarized in Table 10.1. Usually the need is associated with change. Sometimes this involves the creation of an entirely new system, but more frequently it is associated with changes in an existing system. Often the expression of the need arises from problems encountered in dealing with the existing system.

```
Table 10.1  Some Origins of a Need to Create Software

• Inability of a manual system to handle an increasing
  workload.
• Creation of a new environment, new business, new process,
  or product.
• Failure of an existing software system due to accumulated
  faults introduced in maintenance.
• Changes in the information  environment to which the old
  software is not easily adaptable, such as new incoming data.
• Changes in technology, such as new computers, introduction
  of networks, new peripheral equipment, or a new competing
  product.
```

It is also possible for the expressed need to be unfounded, counterproductive to other organizational goals, economically unjustified, or even technically unfeasible. An example of this is a request such as, "Make sure the new billing system will ensure that customers pay their bills promptly."

It is crucial to recognize that detecting the existence of a problem does not mean that the nature of the problem is understood. There is often a real possibility that introducing a "solution" to the perceived problem may cause other, worse problems due to side effects.

As software professionals, we must be sure to expend our efforts creating solutions for the correct problems and within the bounds set by the resources required to implement the solutions. Ultimately we must adhere to ethical standards of professional conduct, as well as satisfy those who pay us.

10.A.1.a. The Systems Analyst

The person who typically is responsible for investigating the feasibility of proposed computer projects and beginning their design often has the title of **systems analyst**. He or she may also be called a system designer, software engineer, system engineer, or even programmer-analyst. Whether these functions are a specialized full-time job responsibility or one part of the job of a software engineer assigned to a project, we will use the term systems analyst or analyst.

Often the person with the responsibilities of systems analyst is a person who has experience on a variety of projects and familiarity with the software organization's goals, resources, and the technology relevant to the problem(s) at issue. The systems analyst may also have the skills summarized in Table 10.2.

Table 10.2 Some Skills Needed by Systems Analysts

- Ability to understand the user's environment and needs.
- Ability to recognize the relation of a system to the organization's goals.
- Ability to create abstract models of systems.
- Ability to recognize essential substructures of a system while ignoring unessential detail.
- Ability to design software elements to implement substructures of a system.
- Ability to sort out conflicting or inconsistent data on needs for proposed systems.
- Ability to communicate well with managers, users, and developers.

Systems analysis may be carried out by senior people in a software development organization, or by people in a separate organizational unit devoted to systems analysis and planning. In any event the systems analysts must have considerable experience with the area of application of the system and the software and hardware technologies that could be applied. Many of the systems analysts will have had prior experience as software engineering professionals.

10.A.1.b. Organizational Structures

In general, software engineering is a group endeavor and is carried out in an organizational context. Those involved with getting software to solve the needs of the user organization may be spread among several distinct parts of an organization. In some organizations they are split according to the software life cycle phase they work with and they have various titles. These might include Systems Analysis group, Software Development group, Software Evaluation group, Data Processing group, and Software Maintenance group. In other organizations there may be multiple groups dealing with software, organized by the area of application of the software, such as the Accounting Systems group, Process Control group, or Management Information System group.

The formal recognition of a software need is usually associated with a contractual commitment to expend resources to investigate the feasibility and dimensions of the proposal. This must be approved by a person in the organization who has authority to commit the resources. The initial, tentative consideration of a software need may be in the form of a request for a proposal (RFP) or simply a memo to the systems analyst requesting a preliminary judgment. An example is shown in Figure 10.1. In other cases the initial recognition of a need may come from the software people and be a solicitation to a manager to approve a project they are proposing. In any event there must be a preliminary judgment of feasibility and approval of the next step, Requirements Analysis.

10.A.1.c. Preliminary Feasibility Judgments

Software is the embodiment of a solution to a problem. In order to consider the creation of software we must first understand the nature of the problem it is supposed to solve and the environment in which the problem exists. Not all problems are best solved by creating software. In fact, some problems may not be possible to solve with software. It is not necessary to automate absolutely everything; anything that can be done better by humans than by machines should be left to humans. However, many things are better done by automation, and it is the purpose of software engineering to address methodologies that will produce a satisfactory product.

Usually the first step is for a systems analyst to make a preliminary judgment of both the feasibility of the proposal and the order of magnitude of the resources required. Such a judgment, whether formal or informal, is usually required because the person who has the power to commit the resources does not have the expertise to make the judgment. This preliminary judgment might be like the example in Figure 10.2, which is a response to the request in Figure 10.1. This step is important, since there are many more ideas about "needs" for software than resources to satisfy them.

The management task is to be sure that the resources available are used for those projects that will produce the greatest benefits to the organization and the least risk. To support these decisions, the manager needs to know a probable cost, the expected benefits, and estimates of resources and time requirements. Also needed is an assurance that there are no immediately obvious technical flaws in the idea that make it unfeasible.

The experienced systems analyst can make a judgment as to whether a proposition is reasonable. Such a person should know the resources of the organization in personnel, areas of prior experience, existing software applications, software tools, computing systems, and budgets. The preliminary analysis may require such input as discussions with key personnel and preliminary calculations based on educated guesses at some of the parameters of the problem.

Basically, what is required is a determination as to whether the proposal is reasonable and important enough to justify expenditure of the resources required to fully analyze the problem and produce a detailed set of requirements and proposed specifications for a system design.

```
Figure 10.2  Example of a Preliminary Feasibility Statement

                                  INTERNATIONAL WIDGET CORP.

MEMO TO:  William Smith, Vice-President, Operations
FROM:     John Doe, Director, Systems Analysis Group
DATE:     June 16, 1986
SUBJECT:  Quality control automation to reduce production
          backlogs

Bill,

    At your suggestion I reviewed the situation and it appears
that automating data acquisition and quality control report
generation is both feasible and likely to be cost effective.
The current situation is that the widget production line
requires a 6% increase in wage costs when production is above
75% of capacity.  Marketing projects a need for 87% of capacity
over the next 24 to 36 months.
    The estimated cost to complete the analysis and preliminary
design is $14,000 and would take 6 weeks.
    Estimated total system costs are:
                                  cost        time required
        Analysis and design    $ 14,000        6 weeks
        Development              18,000         9 weeks
        Test                     25,000         9 weeks
        Hardware                250,000
                               _____        _____
        Total                  $307,000        24 weeks

The system could be implemented in 6 months, and we have the
technical staff to support it.  It might produce a one-month
delay in bringing up  the new version of the Master Inventory
Control System currently in development.  After implementation
the estimated annual costs, based on a 5-year amortization at
a 10% interest rate, are:
        amortized, annual system cost   $ 77,000
        annual system maintenance         10,000
while the annual overtime labor costs of continuing the present
system are about $200,000.  This indicates a possible savings
of about $113,000/yr. if production stays above 75% of
capacity.

                                                  John


cc: Jane Johnson, V.P. Manufacturing
```

   A proposal that is given a preliminary judgment of feasibility includes an estimate of the costs. This includes the cost of conducting a
formal analysis of the proposal and the development cost if implemented.

In the case of a commercial product a preliminary estimate of market factors is also essential. The analyst then estimates the cost in dollars, person-hours, and computing resources required to determine software requirements and proposes specifications of software and hardware. An estimate of total development cost is, of course, very crude at this stage. However, management needs to know at least an order of magnitude figure for development before committing funds to the requirements analysis and preliminary design.

Feasibility has many dimensions. All the costs must be considered, and some may not be monetary. Something may not be feasible for many reasons. A task may be technologically feasible but not feasible for a particular organization because it must be done within a particular time frame. If necessary resources are not available at that time, the project is not feasible even if unlimited financial support is available. The fact that there are people with the required skills or that required software tools exist elsewhere is irrelevant if the organization cannot get them for the project.

It is important to know the factors that are considered and any assumptions that are made in rendering a statement of feasibility or unfeasibility. Some of these factors are listed in Table 10.3. If the judgment on the feasibility of a project is to be considered a professional judgment rather than a political judgment, the reasons must be explicitly stated.

Table 10.3 Factors Influencing Feasibility of a Software Project

- Availability of sufficient money to cover costs.
- Availability of computing capacity to support development.
- Availability of adequate software tools.
- Availability of skilled personnel.
- Availability of suitable algorithms.
- Availability of sufficient time for development.

Because there are usually many alternative ways to satisfy a set of needs it is normal for there to be multiple proposals under analysis. Ultimately it is a management decision to choose which, if any, of a set of proposals will proceed to further development.

10.A.1.d. Outlining Requirements Analysis

Requirements analysis includes both the process of studying user needs to arrive at a definition of system or software requirements, and also the verification of these requirements.

It is extremely important to properly identify the characteristics of a proposed system, its environment, and the real problem. This analysis task is made difficult by the usual circumstance that the initial information available is probably incomplete, contains some irrelevant information, and may contain false information and/or requirements.

A false requirement, in this context, usually means one that is not necessary to the implementation of a system. Requirements should not overspecify by stating unnecessary implementation details specific to hardware or software. If the system could be implemented in a different way and satisfy all purposes of the system, then the requirement is considered false.

If a requirement imposes unnecessary limitations on the developer, it is also a false requirement. For example, a requirement to use a feature of IBM 370 OS/VS would be a false requirement if all the purposes of the system could be satisfied by an alternate implementation within, for instance, a Digital Equipment VAX 11/780 VMS environment. When a requirement is false, it doesn't necessarily mean that there isn't a genuine requirement; it means that it is unnecessarily constrained. In the above example, the requirement to use the feature is genuine. It is the limitation imposed by specifying the IBM 370 OS/VS that makes it false.

Our challenge is to maintain a suitable level of skepticism while gathering enough information to sort out a coherent, self-consistent, and valid definition of the problem whose solution will satisfy the apparent need. Once the problem is understood we can determine a set of requirements that will define a solution.

The process of doing this may be difficult. It may require a lot of investigation. The information is likely to come from numerous sources. Some of the information will probably be misleading or wrong. Other required information may be hard to find. Worst of all, there is no guarantee that the needs of different groups of users will not be mutually contradictory. And the investigation must be done without giving any of the participants false expectations of what they will get from the results, if possible.

Dealing with unreasonable expectations can be a problem. An example from the authors' experience is the manager who promised the clerical personnel that "once the wonderful new automated system is in place, all you will have to do is push a button and any report that is needed will come out." The problem here was that no mention was made by the manager of the need to enter into the machine the last five years of data that the clerical staff had routinely put onto paper forms (thereby requiring that this work all be done over again). The analyst who needed the clerical workers' input in order to specify the data entry system was not well received.

As soon as there is authorization to proceed with a detailed analysis of a problem (feasibility study), the specific tasks to be done to carry out the systems analysis must be planned and organized. The strategy and methods for accumulating the necessary information must be planned and documented. The staff assignments and budget allocations must be made.

Authorizations to access various sources of information must be obtained. Lists of user contacts must be drawn up and permission obtained to interview them. The major jobs of the analysts during a feasibility study are summarized in Table 10.4.

```
Table 10.4   Tasks of a Feasibility Study

1. Gather information to define the problem, its context, and
   the bounds of the software need.
2. Build a conceptual or informational model of the system
   and evaluate it and possible alternatives.
3. Produce software requirements specification documentation
   for one or more solutions, or report feasibility problems.
4. Review and evaluate  costs, benefits, and validity of
   previous work.
```

10.A.2. Sources of Information

Sources of information should be classified carefully in order to judge their reliability and importance in the analysis. One of the primary sources of information about the requirements of a software system is the user community. When the system is installed they are the ones who will have to live with it. And they will have to do any tasks that their organization needs done which are not included in those done by the software.

Additional information pertinent to an existing system and the unmet needs of the community can often be found by analysis of other sources. These include existing system documentation, archived historical data on system operation, error reports, maintenance records, or direct observation of operating personnel.

10.A.2.a. Data Acquisition from the User Community

One thing the users know is what their needs and priorities are. They may not understand the implications of those priorities for software development, but they know how their jobs relate to organizational goals. As a result, the systems analyst has to get their views on aspects of the proposed system.

In addition, the users' view of the importance level of each potential requirement must be determined. To make the decisions as to which features are included in a system, a balance must be struck between the needs and priorities of different groups of users. Thus it is essential to get statistics on the priority ratings for subsets of users, clearly identified with their position in the organizational hierarchy. The analysts must screen every possible requirement for potential impact. A scale such as the one given in Table 10.5 is appropriate to use.

Table 10.5   Priority Scale for Potential Requirements Factors

Factor	Interpretation
Essential	Inclusion is mandatory to the success of the system.
Very desirable	Requirement would support many users.
Useful	Useful to some users but not necessary.
Extraneous	Frill, might be nice to have.
Detrimental	Conflicts with an essential requirement.

Another aspect of the difficulty of the systems analysis task is that it often may be carried out in a complex environment, involving the diverse needs, wants, priorities, and egos of a large number of people. Many problems are beyond the scope of understanding of any single individual, and collective information from various people who do not necessarily have similar priorities must be sifted through.

Therefore, in addition to defining the complex goals of the user organization, the requirements analysis team must determine the potential and extent of multiple, possibly conflicting vested interests. For example, the needs and priorities involved in computerizing a medical facility could be perceived very differently by laboratory technicians, nurses, doctors, clerical staff, and patients. Ultimately the analysts must negotiate a system specification that will fit the needs, wants, and resources of a heterogeneous group of users and, in addition, the constraints of the available resources of the software developers.

The investigation of the needs of the user community must be done in a top-down manner, from the top of the user organization hierarchy chart to the lowest level of users. Those users at the highest level must be approached first, because they have the most clout. Keep in mind that the production of a new system or revision of an existing system is a political process as well as a technical one.

Optimally there should be direct participation of the user community in the analysis team. This facilitates communication and promotes cooperation. Participation is also a measure of commitment of the user community to the success of the new system. This commitment might be part-time or full-time, but should be associated with release from regular duties. Such a commitment makes it a joint project instead of "us" against "them."

Software professionals should be trained to be sensitive to the users' viewpoint. It is all too easy to declare that the users don't know what they want, so we will decide for them. However, the users know things that the analysts don't, just as the developer knows things that are not of concern to the user. A summary of some of the relative strengths and weaknesses of users and analysts is indicated in Table 10.6.

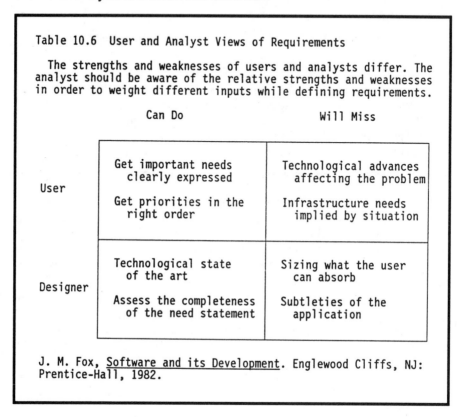

Table 10.6 User and Analyst Views of Requirements

The strengths and weaknesses of users and analysts differ. The analyst should be aware of the relative strengths and weaknesses in order to weight different inputs while defining requirements.

	Can Do	Will Miss
User	Get important needs clearly expressed Get priorities in the right order	Technological advances affecting the problem Infrastructure needs implied by situation
Designer	Technological state of the art Assess the completeness of the need statement	Sizing what the user can absorb Subtleties of the application

J. M. Fox, <u>Software and its Development</u>. Englewood Cliffs, NJ: Prentice-Hall, 1982.

10.A.2.b. Data Acquisition from the System

Another potential source of information is a currently existing system. The documentation from the original Software Requirements Specification (if one exists) may be available. Examine it for the rationale and details of the existing features and characteristics, and the needs that they were intended to fill. Specific requirements that have become obsolete can then be enumerated with new, additional needs.

Other details of the operation of the system may be gleaned from studying the collection of written documentation that may exist for it. In particular, a study of system usage logs may be helpful in determining how the system has performed over time and how it handled peak load conditions. Patterns of usage may be important in some performance requirements. The ways in which the system is inadequate may be seen in the records of error/problem reports kept by maintenance programmers. An examination of system changes that have occurred in maintenance programming may also be revealed by records.

Table 10.7 lists some documents that, if available, could be useful when analyzing a current system.

Table 10.7 Some Forms of Existing Documentation That May be Useful in Analysis of the Current System

- System requirements specifications
- System development plan
- Test documentation
- Documentation of the current source code and structure
- Maintenance history records of any corrective changes, adaptive changes, and enhancements
- Maintenance records of any fault/error reports from users
- Logs of system usage
- Documents of a prior investigation of proposed system changes
- Memoranda associated with any system failures

10.A.2.c. Serendipity

Although it is necessary to carefully plan the process of gathering data for the requirements analysis, we must always be on the lookout for information that could alter our initial notions about the system. Serendipity is the exploitation of information that is uncovered by chance while looking for something else. For example, while systematically looking for details on how exception handling is done, one may discover that what was thought to be a rare event is a regular task that should be covered by the system.

It is important to verify in an existing system that the procedures and processes in the official documentation do correspond to actual practice. Important elements of the current system may not be documented. Or it may be discovered that some occasional event, which would require enormous labor to automate; might be better done manually.

10.A.3. Interviews and Their Pitfalls

Interviews are perhaps the most common method of information collection. The potential is enormous but so are the pitfalls. Interviews can be rendered ineffective if there is a lack of communication or cooperation, or if there is hostility to the interviewer.

The major problem with interviewing users is that of managing communications. The interviewer must be able to communicate in the users' language and be able to establish rapport. This is not easy without considerable planning and some training in interview technique. Conversations with users require an understanding of their viewpoints and terminology, otherwise discussions can be reminiscent of Alice's conversation with the queens in Lewis Carroll's Through the Looking, Glass:

> The Red Queen began again. "Can you answer useful questions?" she said. "How is bread made?"
>
> "I know **that**!" Alice cried eagerly. "You take some flour-"
>
> "Where do you pick the flower?" the White Queen asked. "In a garden or in the hedges?"
>
> "Well, it isn't **picked** at all," Alice explained: "it's **ground--**"
>
> "How many acres of ground?" said the White Queen. "You mustn't leave out so many things."

To help ensure the cooperation of an individual user it is essential to have the approval of the user's superior before approaching him or her. It is possible that a manager may become uncooperative and make it difficult to get access to his or her subordinates or to the information in his or her domain. Since this could result in an incorrect or incomplete system specification, it then becomes necessary to get specific authorization and directives from such a person's superior. Resistance may, of course, be covert, so systems analysts must carefully note such things as patterns in canceled interviews and delays in producing requested information.

The whole process is time consuming for all concerned and may pose substantial difficulties in scheduling. Furthermore, scheduled interviews may be canceled, posing rescheduling problems.

To get reasonable amounts of information, the interviewer must have a well-thought-out set of questions prepared in advance. At the same time, however, the interviewer must be prepared to listen to the user's opinions and concerns regarding the proposed system.

Sometimes there may be significant details that the users won't think to mention, since to them, these things are trivial and/or obvious. In some cases it may be necessary for a systems analyst to essentially live with the users in their job environment to observe and learn what it is all about.

Furthermore, for the analysis to succeed, the users must have a sense of participation. If the systems analyst does not respect the area of expertise of the users, and projects the attitude that "we are going to decide what the users need and inflict it on them," the users are not likely to be cooperative.

Sometimes users will treat this as an adversary process. They may fear that the new system will eliminate their jobs. Or users may be opposed to changing the status quo if it will require changing their environment and/or force them to retrain. In these circumstances they may give misleading information, omit as much information as possible, or be reluctant to participate.

On the other hand, a user who truly wants to sabotage your system may try to appear helpful. It is important to try to ascertain a user's attitude and note whether he or she is in favor of, neutral, or opposed to the proposed system.

Because there is always a political or sociological impact from a new system, the analysis team must be aware that some requirements that are being sought may not be justified. There must be careful consideration of the political versus the technical reasons associated with any requested system requirement. The goals of a particular user subgroup may not be completely in the best interests of the organization as a whole.

It must be emphasized, however, that in many circumstances requirements can be negotiated to gain the support of a particular group. Some requirements may be present only as a concession to a particular segment of the user community that has the clout to get it done their way. This is not inherently bad as long as there is no significant performance or cost penalty that compromises the overall goals of the organization. Some of the major considerations for interviewers to keep in mind are summarized in Table 10.8.

```
Table 10.8  Guidelines for Interviewers

Interviewers MUST:
• avoid leading the users to believe that the new system
  will do everything they can conceive of.
• develop a sense of the users' environment.
• note any bias of users - whether positive, negative, or
  neutral.
• expect different users to have contradictory views.
• get users to rate priority of different system goals.

Interviewers MUST NOT:
• assume that users are technically competent.
• use technical jargon; they must speak users' language.
```

The users collectively know what is needed; however, the problem is that usually no single user has the whole picture. It is the systems analyst's job to construct a composite picture from the pieces extracted from various users. The hardest task for the systems analyst is to develop an understanding of the environment and situation of the user so that the right questions will be asked. Some combination of interviews, surveys, and observation is useful.

Surveys sometimes get information that would not be revealed in interviews. A good survey can cover a larger population and produce statistics that may reveal subcategories of users and needs. However, survey design requires considerable expertise, and an in-depth discussion of the topic is beyond the scope of this book.

Table 10.9 summarizes some of the pros and cons of the various information-gathering methods.

```
Table 10.9   Some Advantages and Disadvantages of Different
             Sources of User Requirements Information

INTERVIEWS
        scheduling problems
        time consuming
        easily biased by analyst
        provide freedom to explore issues
        require care to structure
SURVEY QUESTIONNAIRES
        difficult to design
        easy to analyze for bias
        simplify analysis of results
        means for anonymous complaints
OBSERVATION
        can validate accuracy of reports
        can find undocumented aspects of system
        requires special sensitivity by observers
```

10.B. System Realities

10.B.1. Current System Modification

Analysis must begin with a current situation. If there is an existing system, manual or automated, it must be explored. First determine what it does. What does it do well? And what does it do badly or not at all? To aid in exploring the system you should build a data flow model of the existing system, adding and correcting details as information becomes available.

In the case of an existing manual system it is important to understand exactly what it does, because a faulty system that is merely automated only makes mistakes faster. Also, the answer to all problems is not necessarily automation. There may well be aspects of a system which deal with specialized and rare events that are better handled manually.

In the case of an automated system already in place, the analysts must quickly familiarize themselves with the current state of the system. Usually this means reviewing any existing documentation of the current system - its original requirements specifications documentation, the development documentation, its maintenance history, and any documentation of recent disasters or other events pertinent to the proposal for a new system.

Analysis of the available description is critical to understanding the nature of proposed changes. Possible documents that may be available are summarized in Table 10.7. As part of the analysis it must be determined if current actual practice is at variance with the requirements documented for the system. This could be essential in understanding problems.

One of the most important aspects of systems analysis is to determine the cost and benefit consequences of proposed requirements. This is essential to a rational decision as to what features of system operation should be supported by software, machines, or manual operations.

10.B.2. Introduction of a New System

In the event that a wholly new system is being created it is essential to get available information on similar systems that may exist elsewhere. To do otherwise is known as "reinventing the wheel."

If the system really has no precedent, then the risks involved in specifying it may be high. Invention cannot be scheduled. Thus any part of a development that will require an invention is a gamble. Obviously many large organizations take such gambles, but usually the critical developments are funded as research, or as research and development projects, which are not done in direct support of critical and current goals of the organization.

10.B.3 Acquisition versus Development

One of the alternatives to consider when system requirements have been defined is whether to develop or acquire a system. This may mean contracting for the development to be done outside the organization. In that case the requirements analysis is essential to evaluate contract bids and to assure that the contracted software will meet the needs.

Acquisition may also mean recommending the purchase of existing software. Purchasing existing software eliminates development time and usually is much cheaper. The major analysis problem then becomes determining whether the available software will satisfy the organization's requirements. In some cases the organization may find it economical to change its practices to conform to the software. In other cases it may be economical to modify purchased software.

10.C. Planning and Managing Systems Analysis

A primary responsibility of the conceptualization phase is to carefully identify the operational and long-term goals of all the constituents of the relevant user communities. The goals of different groups may not be consistent. Organizational politics may lead groups to seek system characteristics that enhance their status at the expense of others. In some cases this will result in proposals for features that are not "required" by any technically justified need. However, all that a systems analyst can do is to determine the costs and allow the managers and the competing spheres of influence to determine how the organization is willing to spend its resources.

The requirements definition methods must be well defined and documented. A clear, written statement of the method and sources of requirements may force any political contention over requirements specifications to be settled before development proceeds. A particular advantage of getting user representatives directly involved in requirements definition is specifically to mitigate political problems that might result from misunderstandings. With user involvement there is usually much better communication and a reduced chance of failing to cover significant user needs. In addition, traceability of the origin of requirements may become especially important in the event that a specification change is negotiated during development.

The phases of the software life cycle rarely proceed as linear, non-overlapping activities. With the best of efforts to define and freeze the specifications, very likely there will still be specification changes throughout development. For this reason, it is important to have a designated requirements manager throughout development. Proposed changes must be reviewed and formally approved or rejected after their impact has been assessed and justified.

The requirements manager has the responsibility for initiating communication between users, managers, analysts, and developers if and when specification changes are requested and approved, so that real needs are expressed in the requirement. He or she must also protect the developers by restraining users from asking for frivolous features or unjustified changes. This job may require intense activity initially and optimally reduce to the minimal efforts of liaison and clarification as the development phase proceeds.

Some guidelines for managing requirements analysis are listed in Table 10.10.

```
┌─────────────────────────────────────────────────────────────┐
│                                                             │
│   Table 10.10      Guidelines for Managing Requirements Analysis │
│                                                             │
│   • Define requirement definition methodology.             │
│   • Review existing system documentation first.            │
│   • Build a top-down data flow model of the system.        │
│   • Systematically identify and define all data in the system. │
│   • Give analysts access to real users, not surrogates.    │
│   • Requirements not written down and not available don't exist. │
│   • Keep users' personalities out of requirements.         │
│   • Define quality assurance criteria for the project.     │
│   • Have a requirements manager throughout development.     │
│                                                             │
└─────────────────────────────────────────────────────────────┘
```

10.D. Planning for Quality Assurance

Quality is not a system attribute that can be added on later. For a given system the criteria that will be used to regulate the quality of the project and its development must be defined. These criteria are essential to a quality assurance plan. Such a plan should be considered as part of the requirements.

Often specific guidelines for quality assurance plans are used. One example is the ANSI/IEEE Standard 730-1984, Software Quality Assurance Plans. In order to assess quality, the requirements must include a definition of the review processes, documentation, and standards for verification of compliance with the quality criteria defined for the project. At a minimum there should be a definition of the standards to be employed in various phases of the project, what documentation is required, and a definition of what reviews will be conducted. These are all discussed in Chapter 12.

Summary

Systems analysis involves analyzing a problem to specify the requirements for a solution. For our purposes, usually this solution will be a software system. Finding a solution means identifying and satisfying the goals of the user organization. This can be extremely difficult. The systems analyst, by whatever title, needs to be someone with broad experience.

The initial statement of need may be vague or detailed, formal or informal. A feasibility study needs to be done to see whether solving the problem is technologically and economically feasible. If there is a judgment of feasibility and if it is approved, the next step is requirements analysis.

Requirements analysis means defining the requirements of a system and verifying those requirements. Initial information may or may not be complete and/or correct.

Sources of information include users and any existing system. Users should be included in the analysis at every step, as they are the ones who know what they need and expect from the system. Interviewing users requires considerable planning and skill. Questioning a user is very different from asking questions in a classroom. Instructors can usually be counted on to be knowledgeable and helpful. Users are concerned with their own interests, which may or may not be served by your proposed system.

System requirements will usually be based on an existing system, whether manual or automated. The creation of a totally new system is risky.

Provision must be made for long-term consistency during the life of the software system. One way of doing this is to have a requirements manager whose job is to keep track of any changes that are requested from anyone involved, and to communicate among all concerned. The factors that will be important in quality assurance should be specified as part of the requirements.

Keywords

concept exploration phase
false requirement
preliminary feasibility judgment
requirements analysis
requirements manager
request for proposal (RFP)
serendipity
systems analysis
systems analyst

Review Questions

10.1.   What is systems analysis?

10.2.   List some problems that cannot be solved with software.

10.3.   What is a requirement? A specification?

10.4.   Think of an example of a false requirement.

10.5.   Why would you want to involve users in systems analysis?

10.6.   What does a systems analyst do? What are some other commonly used titles for this job?

10.7. How is a software need likely to be stated initially?

10.8. What is involved in a preliminary feasibility judgment?

10.9. List some reasons why a project may not be feasible.

10.10. What is requirements analysis?

10.11. List some methods of collecting information on a proposed system.

10.12. What is the difference between creating a new system and modifying an existing one? Which is likely to be easier?

10.13. What does a requirements manager do?

Exercises

10.1. How could an information system application give a company a competitive advantage in its industry?

10.2. Consider a proposal to make it possible for your company's customers to access your current inventory status on the products they may be interested in ordering. What are the advantages and disadvantages to the company in doing this?

10.3. Outline a strategy to survey potential clients of a computer dating service to determine what criteria would define an adequate match of preferences and characteristics. What questions should be asked?

10.4. What criteria would you assess in determining a cost/benefit ratio for a set of proposals for modifications to an existing system?

10.5. A manager in your company notes that sales clerks cannot complete any sales transactions when the mainframe computer is down. You are asked to consider the problem of upgrading point-of-sale terminals to microcomputer-based terminals that communicate with the mainframe. What do you do?

10.6. It is proposed that the subscriber mailing list management system of a monthly magazine publisher be moved to a desktop microcomputer. A subscriber is currently defined by a text record with 150 characters. To fit the application into a machine with 640 kilobytes of RAM and 10 megabytes of disk space, it is proposed to adopt binary codes for state, zipcode, expiration date, subscriber ID, and some other fields. This could reduce the stored subscriber record to 120 bytes. Discuss the merit of this proposal.

10.7. Your company is engaged in integrated circuit manufacturing. Each IC layout is composed of hundreds of modular elements including many types of elements. Each element is rectangular, with many inputs and outputs. Your boss wants you to write a program to optimize layout geometry to produce maximum usage of space on the surface of the silicon and minimize the length and number of signal lines between non-adjacent elements. Consider a simpler problem of interconnecting 64 square, 1 x 1 elements into an 8 x 8 array where we have a table of interconnections from each element to a subset of the other 63 elements. Each element has 4 possible orientations. How many ways are there to interconnect them? What are the implications of the number of computations and comparisons if we do them exhaustively to find the optimal solution?

10.8.   What are the differences in planning required between the installation of software to support credit card transactions on a network of 1000 point-of-sale terminals and the installation of software to provide an online calender and daily work scheduler for 1000 users ?

References

Aron, Joel D. The Program Development Process, Part 2. Reading, MA: Addison-Wesley, 1983.

> The second volume concentrates on programming teams and various aspects of life cycle stages.

Bronikowski, R. J. Managing the Engineering Design Function. New York: Van Nostrand-Reinhold, 1986.

> Presents management aspects starting with a product orientation and includes engineering management and project control.

Brooks, Frederick P. "No Silver Bullet." IEEE Computer 20, no. 4 (April 1987): 10-19.

> Fashioning complex conceptual constructs is the essence; accidental tasks arise in representing the constructs in language. Past progress has so reduced the accidental tasks that future progress now depends on addressing the essence.

DeMarco, Tom. Structured Analysis and System Specification. New York: Yourdon, 1979.

> An exposition and extension of the data flow methodology of Yourdon and Constantine. Excellent discussion of structured English.

DeMarco, Tom. Controlling Software Projects, Management, Measurement & Estimation. Englewood Cliffs, NJ: Yourdon Press, 1982.

> An outline for establishing quality assurance practices and managerial perspective on project management. Includes a Foreword by Barry W. Boehm.

Fox, Joseph M. Software and its Development. Englewood Cliffs, NJ: Prentice-Hall, 1982.

> Large project management, classifying system properties, and considerations of performance and tradeoffs.

Gilb, Tom. Principles of Software Engineering Management. Reading, MA: Addison-Wesley, 1988.

> Description of practical approaches to engineering and management technology.

Glass, Robert L. Software Soliloquies. State College, PA: Computing Trends, 1981.

> Collection of essays on software engineering, light reading style with some profound observations.

Institute of Electrical and Electronics Engineers. Software Engineering Standards. New York: Wiley-Interscience, October 1987.

> Includes "ANSI/IEEE Std 730-1984, Software Quality Assurance Plans," concerned with legal liability. It is directed toward the development and maintenance of software that concerns safety or large financial or social implications. Also includes "ANSI/IEEE Std 830-1984, Software Requirements Specifications," a guide that describes alternate approaches to good practice in the specification of software requirements. "ANSI/IEEE Std 983-1986, Software Quality Assurance Planning," explains the contents of a software quality assurance plan. Directed at the requirements in Std 730-1984. "IEEE Std 1016-1987, Software Design Descriptions," is a description of documentation of software designs. Specifies the necessary information content and the recommended organization for a software design description.

Kendall, Penny A. Introduction to Systems Analysis and Design, A Structured Approach. Dubuque, IA: Wm. C. Brown, 1989.

> General introduction to systems analysis with Yourdon methodology, strongly oriented to business applications.

Lucas, H. C., Jr. Analysis, Design, and Implementation of Information Processing Systems. New York: McGraw-Hill, 1981.

> General introduction to systems analysis with case studies and emphasis on user input to the analysis and design process.

Pressman, Roger S. Software Engineering, A Practitioner's Approach, 2d ed. New York: McGraw-Hill, 1987.

> A survey of software engineering with thorough review of all phases of the life cycle and the management of software. The treatment of software design provides chapters on data flow, data structure, real time, and object-oriented design methods.

Weinberg, Gerald M. The Psychology of Computer Programming. New York: Van Nostrand-Reinhold, 1971.

> The first attempt to systematically describe the subject; its anecdotal style makes it highly readable.

Weinberg, Gerald M. Rethinking Systems Analysis. New York: Dorset House, 1982.

> Discussion of many pitfalls of analysis and project management. Several humorous fables are presented to emphasize particular topics.

CHAPTER 11

SOFTWARE TOOLS AND ENVIRONMENTS

Compared with other fields of study, computer science is a very young discipline. It has had its revolutions, which roughly parallel what we call the generations of computer hardware, each made possible by the tools of the computer architect. These tools include the vacuum tube, the transistor, and now the integrated circuit. However, ... the capability of our hardware tools has grown to far exceed our ability to manage them.

Our computers make some things more efficient and have opened areas of application that were previously impossible to solve. Correspondingly, we have developed software tools such as programming languages to help us solve problems and control our machines, but many of these tools still do not help us cope with the complexity of our solutions. Thus, software development is no longer a labor-saving activity but is labor intensive instead.

- Grady Booch, Software Engineering with Ada,

The availability of automated support tools helps the programmer and systems analyst concentrate on the truly creative part of the job and spend less time worrying about the mundane parts of the job.

- Edward Yourdon, Nations at Risk

11.A. Software Development Environment and Productivity

In one sense, the history of software development methodology is the history of software tools. Programmers have always looked for ways to get the computer to take over any development task that has become drudgery. In the beginning the rigors of creating even small programs in machine code led to the development of assemblers and compilers. As the size of programs grew, the development of text editors was stimulated to reduce the effort required to produce source code to feed to the language translators. The development of complex operating environments with multitasking and multiuser capabilities required the development and evolution of operating system services to carry out the details of managing system resources for the users, including programmers.

From another viewpoint, the idea of software tools has come to mean the use of a large number of specialized utility programs to carry out specialized tasks. It is possible to use a standard, general-purpose software tool to carry out almost any particular task. However, it may be much more efficient to use a specialized program to do that task. For example, a text editor might be used to manually convert a text file from double-spaced lines to single-spaced lines. That is reasonable if the task is to convert a 50-line file. But if you need to reformat 50,000 lines in many files, the manual labor required to use the text editor might be outrageous, while a specialized program used to automate the process is reasonable.

11.A.1. Traditional Software Tools

The traditional tools of software development are the text editor, compiler, assembler, linker, and debugger. These software tools are adequate for small programs. However, they are not adequate to develop, test, and maintain the software systems with more than a million lines of code that are now being created.

The traditional development tools for software are analogous to hand tools. They presume that the individual developer is responsible for a large proportion of the information management required to design, create, test, interpret, locate, and modify elements of the software. But the increasing complexity and size of software systems requires us to become adept at using power tools in place of hand tools.

11.A.2. Classes of Software Tools

Software tools may be divided into four broad classes: editors, translators, monitors, and resource managers. Within these classes are traditional software tools. As software has become more complex, additional tools have come into use. A brief list of some of the most common software development tools is shown in Table 11.1.

Table 11.1 Classes of Software Tools

Class	Traditional Tools	Others of the Class
text editor	line editor full-screen editor	text formatter syntax-directed editor report generator filter
translator	assembler compiler	interpreter cross-assembler cross-compiler
monitor	assembly debugger	profiler file dump memory dump source-level debugger
resource manager	linker	database manager library manager configuration manager

In general an **editor** is a software tool that permits the creation or modification of text or data. Text may be used as the input for a translator.

A **translator** is a software tool that converts text (source code) into executable machine code (object code). You are probably familiar with compilers for one or more high-level languages and the assembler for at least one machine language, which you have used to translate source code into executable programs.

A **monitor** is a software tool to examine and trace the execution of programs. This class includes various utilities to analyze how our programs execute for the purpose of debugging or efficiency analysis.

Last, the **resource manager** assists us in using the facilities of the machine. One of these facilities is the linker (or linkage editor). This is used to build executable load modules by combining the object modules created by our translators and object code from system libraries to form actual programs. Other resource managers are used to build and maintain files of reference data for specifications, design, source code libraries, object libraries, and specific system configurations.

After completing several courses in computer science you probably have heard of all of these and have had experience using many of them. Software tools may be quite complex and have attributes of several of these classes, or organize the application of several different tools.

11.A.3. Operating Environment

Another way of viewing a collection of software tools is to consider the way in which they are used. The operating characteristics of software tools depend on the environment established for them by a combination of the hardware and the operating system. Each software tool must exist in a particular environment and be adapted to that environment. This means that most software tools will be closely linked to particular hardware or a particular operating system, and may be specific to a particular programming language.

Software tools may also be described by the class of operating environment in which they function. These operating environment classes include batch, interactive, concurrent, and distributed. A major difficulty is that a different instance of each type of software tool may be required for each class of operating environment. This leads to a proliferation of software tools. Being able to coordinate the tools to support software is a growing concern. One approach to this problem has been to develop workstation environments, where one or a few users share a set of software tools.

A recent trend has been the development of coordinated sets of tools that support different stages of the software life cycle. Various tools have emerged under the name of Computer Aided Software Engineering, or CASE. These tools have mainly supported system design with data dictionaries and data flow diagramming. New tools are emerging to extend these design representations as a basis of code generation.

11.B. A Look at Some Specific Software Tools

11.B.1. Text Editors

For a programmer, the first software tool is the text editor. Its minimum list of features might be those described in Table 11.2. The editor used may be a general-purpose word processor with many other features for document preparation, or it might be integrated with a compiler. In any event you should be adept in using the basic features and be on the lookout for features to minimize any burdensome text processing operations. There are many source code and documentation tasks for which one specific text editor is a better tool than another.

Table 11.2   Features of a Programming Text Editor

- text creation
- text review
- search for a text pattern
- text replacement
- move/copy a block of text
- window to another file

- text insertion
- text deletion
- read text in from a file
- copy block to a file
- macro definition facility

11.B.2. Compilers

Table 11.3 Features and Options of Compilers

- diagnostic syntax error messages
- warnings on usage that may be bad programming practice
- line-numbered source listing
- summary of space usage for data and code in object code
- summary list of all symbols used (variables, labels)
- directives to control page format of listings
- directives to control conditional compilation
- macroprocessor directives
- produces header on listing identifying compiler, version, date
    and time of compilation, host environment, and so on
- production of a complete cross-reference table
- optional initialization of all data space to zero values
- optional choice of optimization: none, space, speed, or both
- optional dump of object code in hexadecimal
- optional dump of intermediate assembly language code
- optional inclusion of symbol table
- optional automatic inclusion of code to produce trace of the
    execution path by procedure or by line number
- optional generation of a profile of execution time as a log at
    runtime by procedure or by line number
- optional generation of dumps and diagnostics on runtime error
    detection

The compiler is, of course, a programmer's central software tool. For this reason large numbers of features and options beyond the fundamental task of language translation have been developed. Table 11.3 gives a list of some of the features of a typical compiler. For a specific application, you need to consult the documentation for the particular compiler you are using. Usually you will find a large number of features beyond those presented in your programming courses.

The various compiler features are there because professional developers find them useful. Learn to use these additional features. Cross-reference tables, trace data, log files, and dumps frequently can help solve problems with defective code if you learn to read them carefully.

11.B.3. Linkers

The linker is a software tool that tends to be ignored. It has to be there, but it may be automatically invoked by the compiler (or by a procedure file that is also setting compiler options). As shown in Table 11.4, the linker may have some options you may wish to use. Some control of space usage and space optimization may require setting option parameters for the linker. The linker may also produce optional memory maps of the executable program, which may be needed in interpreting a trace of execution at the machine or assembly language level.

```
Table 11.4   Features of a Linker

 • build executable load modules from object modules
 • extract support functions from library modules
 • exclude any library modules not required
 • type check calling parameters of modules
 • produce reference memory map of executable file
 • allow specification of executable file name
 • select memory model/operating environment
 • optionally include symbol references for debugging
```

11.B.4. Debuggers

A debugger is a software tool to monitor and trace program execution. You may have encountered an assembly language debugger when you learned to write assembly language programs. There are also source-level debuggers that permit reference back to the source code file in a high-level language. Typical debugger features are listed in Table 11.5. Source-level debuggers require the cooperation of the compiler and linker to preserve a symbol table to do this. Some of these functions can, of course, be implemented by adding statements to the code for any program, but a separate debugging/tracing tool is much easier to use. Debuggers are machine and language specific so they are not always available. But if one is available you will not regret the time required to master it.

```
         Table 11.5   Features of an Interactive Debugger

       • display source code
       • set breakpoints
       • show resulting values during execution
       • trace execution path
       • step through code
```

11.B.5. Interpreters

An alternative to the debugger in testing and debugging is an interpreter. An interpreter is a language translator that converts and executes source code one line at a time. It is generally not useful for production programs because it has inherently poor execution efficiency. However, if you are using a language for which both an interpreter and a compiler are available, it is very effective to use the interpreter for coding and testing modules, reserving the compiler for integration, system testing, and production of the final system. Why? Interpreters usually let you modify code while executing and testing it. That makes it easy to try out and test code corrections. Language interpreters are also very good for novice programmers because they provide quick feedback on syntax errors. Both interpreters and compilers exist for many languages, including APL, BASIC, C, and Pascal.

11.C. Environment and Life Cycle Concerns

Future improvement in the productivity of software designers, implementers, and maintainers requires that the software tools and techniques of all phases of the software life cycle must be coordinated into a recognizable software support system. In many cases today, the coordination is poor. This can be caused by a lack of standard interfaces. For example, if one system does not produce a file format that is compatible with another system, those systems will not be used with a common set of files unless someone can produce a file format translator.

In other instances systems of programs become difficult to use in practice. They may have commands and procedures that are completely different and it is too tricky for the typical user to learn to coordinate them. This has led to considerable effort to develop rational software development environments that automate the coordination of many standardized tasks.

The goals of such environments are to enhance software productivity and to improve the quality of the software produced. If a tedious task can be automated, it is likely that the product quality can be improved by eliminating human errors. These goals are summarized in Table 11.6.

Table 11.6   Goals of a Coordinated Software Support Environment

- store results of analysis
- central specification access
- online document store
- improve reliability
- improve portability
- promote software reusability
- centralize data dictionary
- store test plans/data/results
- configuration management
- improve productivity
- promote standardization
- improve maintainability

11.C.1. UNIX: An Example of Coordination

An early and major example of coordinating a set of tools for software support was developed with the UNIX operating system as The Programmer's Workbench. As originally described, this was the idea of using a separate machine with an environment tailored to software development and support. This machine was independent of the target machines dedicated to running production software.

Some features of The Programmer's Workbench are described in Table 11.7. This was really the foundation of the idea of workstations, which are common today. The original concept represented a transition from an era of keypunch input and batch processing to a new era of time-shared computing with interactive video terminals. The UNIX software tools are still very important and form the basis of many workstation software environments today. The term "Programmer's Workbench" is still current as the name of a specific software tool set marketed separately from UNIX operating system software.

Table 11.7 Programmer's Workbench goals and early tools: The concept
of the 'workbench' anticipated today's workstations.

1. Support analysis and design activities - generation, modification,
   and production of specifications and other supporting documents.
2. Create, edit, and control source code and test data.
3. Compile, execute, and debug programs, either as terminal to host/
   target or independently.
4. Generate, integrate, and install systems.
5. Support regression testing and load testing of subsystems and systems.
6. Provide analysis and reduction of test results.
7. Track changes to the system, problem reports, and enhancement requests.
8. Evaluate and monitor system performance, system modeling, and simulation.
9. Convert databases and load the host for operation.
10. Produce lists, statistics, and reports for management of maintenance.

Based on E.L. Ivie, "The Programmer's Workbench - A Machine for Software
Development." CACM 20,10 (November 1977).

The UNIX approach may also be summarized as a strategy of supplying a development environment rich in software tools, and the means to
coordinate those tools. Many of the software tools may be "unfriendly"
individually, but it is easy to create procedure files that combine component tools. These can then be used to perform a sequence of subtasks to
complete a job. Such user-created procedures encourage the evolution of
new, compounded software tools. The UNIX system also fosters an attitude of seeking or creating tools to automate new forms of drudgery as
soon as they are recognized. This has been elegantly described by Brian
Kernighan in his various writings on the UNIX programming environment. In practice, users create many very small command files combining
various standard tools, selecting the options needed for their tasks.

11.C.2. Workstations

The first workbench implementations used minicomputer technology to support an independent development platform for mainframe computers. The advantages of doing this included cost savings based on:

- Centralized implementation of software tools.
- Standardized program developer training.
- Centralized documentation management, with a single standard
  and environment for documentation.
- Minimizing the pain of system conversion by making software
  tools and host upgrade schedules independent.

- Allowing an independent choice of target equipment without the necessity of compromise between production needs and development needs.

These advantages were achieved at a time when the typical environment was primarily a multiuser minicomputer system, time shared by dozens of programmers. Much of the work was batch oriented and involved remote job entry (RJE) access to other computers.

The software tools available in 1977 were of course more limited than those available today, but they included:

- Compilers in various languages.
- Version control system for programs and documents.
- File system support to manage test data and results.
- Documentation tools such as an editor, spelling checker, print spooler, text formatter, table formatter, and macroprocessor.
- Test driver, an emulator for IBM 3270 cluster controller.
- Electronic mail, providing group communication support.

Current workstations use more sophisticated network services and a wider array of tools. Also, since the price of hardware has declined, the number of people sharing one workstation's computing power has also declined. Software to achieve all the goals of The Programmer's Workbench concept are now being used in many development organizations.

11.D. Integrated Software Tools

Recently there have been many efforts to integrate several traditional software tools to create highly coupled environments. The traditional development environment involves the use of several separate software tools whose execution is determined by the programmer issuing commands to the operating system. The bulk of the development activity thus was a cycle of edit, compile, link, and test, repeated until a correct program module had been produced. The commands and decisions might be represented by the pseudocode of Figure 11.1. A lot of the programmer's time would be spent waiting for compilation or some other job step to be done, and then entering the command to use the next tool.

The operating system command language usually provides the means to put a sequence of commands into an executable file. Thus good programmers can automate repetitive command sequences. Most operating systems also support this by permitting programs, including standard software tools, to report a condition code so that the next job step can be conditionally executed. A PC-DOS example of this is shown in Figure 11.2, in which a development cycle is automated. This still is quite crude since it requires the programmer to find the place in the source that should be modified each time it is necessary to return to the edit step.

Figure 11.1 Commands and Decisions to Create a Program.

The following is a simplified pseudocode procedure defining a major part of the effort to develop a software module. This sequence can be converted into a PC-DOS batch file to get the PC-DOS command inter-preter to automatically cycle through the steps, as shown in Fig. 11.2.

```
1.  EDIT ..                 Create or modify source language text
2.  COMPILE ..              Translate source code to object code
3.  IF compile error           -> syntax error
         THEN  GOTO 1 ..    correct syntax errors
4.  ELSE  LINK ..           Fetch library modules, build load module
5.  IF  link error          -> unknown module names or parameters
         THEN  GOTO 1 ..    correct the source code
6.  ELSE  RUN program  ..   execute test
7.  IF  execution error ..  on a functional or logic error
         THEN GOTO 1 ..     correct the source code
8.  ELSE  success ..        run more tests and document program
```

Figure 11.2 A PC-DOS Code Development Environment

PC-DOS or MS-DOS, the operating system for IBM PC compatible microcomputers, allow the creation of batch command files, which cause the execution of conditional sequences of PC-DOS commands. Such files are recognized by the filename extension .BAT. This example shows the listing of a batch command file, CODE.BAT, which implements the pro-cedure of Fig. 11.1. This example assumes that an editor is used named EDIT, that the compiler is F77, and the linker is named LINK. The procedure uses a filename following the name of the procedure on the command line.   This parameter is inserted as a macro expansion when executed by the PC-DOS command interpreter. The token used to indicate where to insert the first parameter after the command name is %1.

The condition code returned by an executing program when it termin-ates is known to the batch procedure as the value of ERRORLEVEL. Also note that a line beginning with : is a label indicating a target for a GOTO, and a line beginning with rem is only a comment.

```
rem                 Check if filename given, else go give usage prompt
rem                 Equal only if filename was missing
IF  "NULL" = "NULL%1"  GOTO NOFILE
rem                 Start loop for edit/compile/link/run
:START
rem                 Pause prompts and waits for key entry
rem                 Guarantees screen not cleared before reading
rem                   any messages from previous program
PAUSE  " FORTRAN,   CTL/C to QUIT, any key to continue"
rem                 Edit the filename given on the command line
EDIT  %1.FOR
rem                 Then compile the program that has been edited
rem                 Compiler input 'name.FOR' -> output 'name.OBJ'
F77   %1.FOR
```

```
rem                     Compile error -> errorlevel =1, go edit
IF   ERRORLEVEL  1  GOTO START
rem                     If no compile error then build load module
rem                     Linker input 'name.OBJ' -> output 'name.EXE'
LINK  %1.OBJ
rem                     If linker error, go back to editor
IF   ERRORLEVEL  1  GOTO START
rem                     Successful link, so we execute program
%1.EXE
rem                     If program returns error  go edit, else quit
IF   ERRORLEVEL  1  GOTO START
rem                     Terminate batch procedure, normal exit
EXIT
rem                     Prompt user if invalid command line.
:NOFILE
ECHO      Usage:    CODE  name
ECHO                Do not include the file extension '.FOR'
```

When using the editor much time would be spent looking for locations in the source code corresponding to each error found by the compiler, linker, or at runtime. This can also be automated if the editor and compiler are integrated to share a symbol table that references each variable assignment and each decision point in the object to the corresponding point in the source code file. With that information, one could get back to the appropriate point in the source code in the editor automatically, without searching the text by variable name or by line number.

11.D.1. Example: Turbo Pascal

An early example of the integration of a compiler and editor was Turbo Pascal by Borland International. The first version of that microcomputer Pascal compiler appeared in 1983. That integration permitted the detection of syntax or runtime errors to result in an automatic jump back into the editor. The programmer was presented with the error message, while the cursor pointed at the location of the error. The basis of this action was a symbol table shared by the compiler and editor. This increased the productivity of programmers substantially. Other Pascal compilers at the time were stand-alone tools and typically produced error messages such as "ERROR 047 at line 132."

Since then Turbo Pascal has continuously evolved. By Turbo Pascal version 5.5, the environment expanded to include the integration of a full-screen editor, a faster compiler, a linker, a configuration management tool, and a source-level debugger. A summary comparison of these two versions of Turbo Pascal is given in Table 11.8. Similar environments were developed by several vendors for several languages and for many different computers in the 1980s.

```
Table 11.8  Features of Turbo Pascal Environment
            (TM Borland International)

Features of the Turbo Pascal programming environment, version 1.0, 1983:
• integrated full screen editor
• Pascal compiler
• Pascal language extensions:  string data type, support functions,
     operating system function access
• English error messages
• use syntax/runtime error to position cursor in source
• compiler directives to control I/O modes, select optimization options,
     select error check options, provide file inclusion, and provide
     inclusion of inline assembly code
Additional features in Turbo Pascal, version 5.5, 1989:
• integrated MAKE facility
• integrated source-level debugger
• integrated linker
• context-sensitive help for Pascal syntax
• access to DOS without leaving editor
• menu bar with pull-down windows with submenus
• facility to customize environment at any time
• environment remembers parameters including where you were the last
     time the editor was used
• separate windows for error messages/output/source
• compiler directives to support conditional compilation
• language extensions:
     more data types and type checking, graphics support of functions
     and device drivers, separate compilation of modules, arithmetic
     coprocessor support, object oriented programming support of static
     and dynamic objects, inheritance, static and virtual methods, object
     constructors and destructors, object constants
• overlay manager
```

11.D.2. Syntax-Directed Editors

Another approach to the integration of the compiler with an editor has concentrated on the problem of syntax errors. With these, the syntax is checked as program statements are entered. This way the programmer is given immediate feedback so that incorrect code is less likely to be written. This procedure is referred to as syntax-directed editing. Early examples of this approach were used in editors for LISP. Later it was applied to Pascal and Modula-2.

Although syntax-directed editing speeds the production of syntactically correct code, it does not ensure that the correct program has been written. There are many different syntactically correct programs that do not solve a specified problem. Only the testing and validation of programs can ensure that the program written does satisfy the specification of the intended application.

11.E. Standardization and Portability

Many programming environments depend on a specific language, operating system, and system display hardware. Thus a new version of the environment often must be produced for each workstation and language. On the other hand, the conventional text editor and compiler can be more easily moved to another processor because the individual components may be less complex and less machine dependent.

Portability of programs between various machines has been a goal since the first FORTRAN and COBOL language definitions. However, software has always had limited portability. Those who wish to maximize the performance of a program are likely to use any machine-specific detail to get a performance gain. This limits the portability of the programs. In recent years substantial interest has emerged in improving program portability. Such efforts have been fostered by new language standards.

For example, the Department of Defense has decreed that all Ada compilers must pass the same certification tests and that there will be no subsets of the language. Thus any machine with an Ada compiler can be a target for all Ada programs.

As another example, the ANSI C Standards Committee has made great efforts to support portability of programs. This has included recognizing the problems of handling the I/O interface with library functions. These interfaces are being standardized.

Standardization has even included setting conventions for handling alternate character sets for many languages so that strings can be handled in a uniform way. These and other similar efforts will increase the potential for portability of program source code across different machine environments.

11.F. Software Tool Evaluation

11.F.1. Criteria for Software Tool Evaluation

Development organizations generally have limited resources, so the costs and impact of a decision to adopt a new software tool must be analyzed and justified. In particular, the potential benefits and the goals of an organization must be given priority ratings to decide which potential software tools will be most effective.

Before adopting a new software tool, several factors should be considered. These are summarized in Table 11.9. Indirect costs must also be considered. In addition to the acquisition cost, there will be costs associated with training staff in the use of the software tool. There may also be the costs of modifying other software to achieve compatibility with new software tools and systems. Compatibility is an important consideration since the cost of modifying software or the cost of data file format conversion could well outweigh the benefits of the software tool in its primary use.

Table 11.9   Factors to Evaluate in Adopting a New Software Tool

- priority of need
- compatibility with other tools
- productivity gains
- availability
- language independence

- functionality
- ease of use
- other benefits
- cost of tool
- training cost

In doing an evaluation, keep in mind that the suppliers of a given software tool tend to overestimate the potential productivity gains attributable to it. Finally, if a proposed adoption is for a software tool that is not commercially available, the cost of in-house development must be justified.

11.F.2. Training and the Learning Curve

The adoption of a new software tool implies that the users will have to learn how to use it. How much time and effort will be required may be strongly dependent on its inherent functionality and ease of use. The time characteristics of the effort to put the software tool into service is referred to as its **learning curve**, illustrated in Figure 11.3.

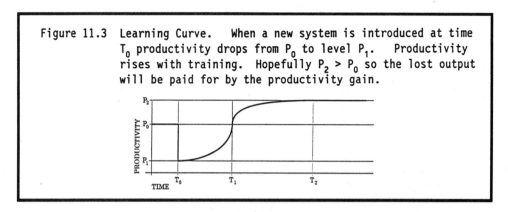

Figure 11.3   Learning Curve.   When a new system is introduced at time T_0 productivity drops from P_0 to level P_1.   Productivity rises with training. Hopefully $P_2 > P_0$ so the lost output will be paid for by the productivity gain.

The time and effort required to put the software tool into use, including training, are part of the cost of acquisition. Clearly if one software tool can do the necessary tasks with less training or user effort in learning, it may have a smaller total cost of introduction, even if the software purchase price is higher.

11.G. Where Do We Get the Needed Software Tools?

Once a software tool has been identified as necessary but not presently available within your organization, its acquisition must be planned. Basically there are three options:

- Buy the exact software tool needed.
- Modify another software tool.
- Build it yourself.

Clearly the choice depends on a number of cost, resource, and benefit factors, so that this becomes a managerial decision.

An analysis should be done to generate a formal specification of the needed software tool. Planning the acquisition and support of the tools for a software project should be a standard part of the planning process. A significant factor in the feasibility or technical risk of a project may depend on the creation of a software tool. For example, consider a contract to deliver a project written in the Ada language, when the Ada compiler for the target machine is still under development. Your project may be in serious trouble if the compiler vendor does not deliver the Ada compiler on schedule.

11.G.1. Buy

Generally, if a needed software tool is available commercially, it will be cost effective to purchase it. However, the supposed benefits should be verified by testing the software tool. Unfortunately not all claimed benefits of new tools and methods are realized.

11.G.2. Modify

If an available software tool, whether a commercial product or one previously created in your organization, has some of the needed characteristics, then the needed tool may be produced by modifying an earlier one. Frequently a needed tool is an extension of the concept of another tool. The needed capabilities may be achievable by patching or adding on to a previously used software package. The cost of such modifications becomes a cost attributable to the current project.

11.G.3. Build

In some areas of application a software tool needed is not commercially available. In many cases developers have decided that the only reasonable way to do a project is to use particular software tools that are to be developed within the organization.

What else can be done with the tool once it is developed? Perhaps the organization can justify the cost of producing a software tool by selling it to other developers. However, there may be concern about keeping proprietary software tools within the limits of trade secrets. There are Department of Defense regulations requiring contractors to deliver all required tools along with project software. This has led to instances of companies refusing to bid on such projects because they wished to retain rights to their specialized tools.

Even if all the needed software tools are available, there should be an analysis to determine the effort needed to customize any of the software tools for a specific project. The resources necessary to support the software tools must be considered in the overall resources allocated for a given project. A large project may have a specific subgroup dedicated to production of software tools if it decides to create the software tools in house rather than buy them.

11.H. Examples of Software Tools and Tool Building

11.H.1. Filters and Pipes

A **filter** is a utility program that processes files using standardized input and output interfaces, and performs a cohesive operation on the input stream. Filters are important because they lead to the solution of data processing problems by organizing a set of operations based on existing software tools rather than writing and compiling new programs. This is particularly important for prototyping or for limited jobs where optimization is not significant.

The usual requirement for a filter is that input will come from **standard input** and that output will be sent to **standard output**. These input and output streams are managed by the operating system, not by the program. The usual default is that standard input comes from the keyboard and that standard output goes to the terminal screen. However, either of these streams can be **redirected** by specifying an alternate input or output file name on the command line, as indicated in Figure 11.4.

In addition to supporting standard input and output, a filter may also have parameters that modify the function performed. For example, for a sort operation one might have the choice of alphabetical order, reverse alphabetical order, or sort starting with column N. The default is likely to be to sort in alphabetical order starting with column 1. Such parameters or option flags follow the name of the command and precede any redirection indictors. Typically the special symbol indicating such a parameter is / (slash) or - (hyphen). The latter is typical for UNIX systems; the slash is most common for MS-DOS or PC-DOS.

```
Figure 11.4  Redirection of Input and Output

   For the UNIX, MS-DOS, and PC-DOS operating systems the  symbol used
to direct an input is <.  The symbol > will cause the output to be
redirected, and >> will cause  redirected output to be redirected and
appended to the file  indicated.   The example below uses a common text
filter,  sort, which sorts a file of text records:
                sort <source.dat
The above causes the input file source.dat to be sorted and sent to the
screen (which might be done to check whether the default sort parameters
are okay.)
                sort <source.dat  >result.dat
Now we are sorting source.dat and sending the output to result.dat.
                sort <more.dat >>result.dat
We may also append a redirected output to an existing file, so the sorted
contents of  more.dat will appear added to the end of result.dat.  This
last file is now sorted.
Finally, if you had a word list in some arbitrary order on  paper and
wanted it sorted, you might enter the list and have the computer create
a sorted file.
                sort >ordered.lst
Input (one word per line) is entered at the keyboard.   The  only trick
is in terminating the input file.  (For MS-DOS or PC-DOS, an end-of-file
mark is the <Control/Z> character.)
```

As an example using filters, consider the following problem. We have a large data file, **our.dat**, in which each value is an ASCII text record. We need to get a frequency distribution of the values of the data items. We have available the common filter utilities such as those shown in Table 11.10.

Let us assume for this problem that the count field is a constant number of digits. We can get the needed frequency distribution by executing the commands:

```
sort < our.dat > temp1

uniq -c < temp1 > temp2

sort < temp2 > freq.dat
```

The utility **uniq** will find and count the multiplicity of records, where the **-c** parameter says to put the count before each unique record. However, for this to work, the multiple copies of records must all be adjacent. Hence we first need the **sort** as a preliminary step. The last sort puts the records in the order of the frequency counts. The **freq.dat** file is also a text file.

Filters are made even more powerful when the operating system can automatically create and manage temporary files between processing steps. This service, called a **pipe**, was introduced in UNIX and was copied by Microsoft in MS-DOS and PC-DOS. A pipe permits several filters to be sequenced. The output of one filter in the sequence automatically becomes the input of the next filter. The symbol | is used to tell UNIX or PC-DOS to set up a pipe to carry output from one process to another. Thus we can command the creation of a frequency distribution for the example above in a more compact form:

    sort < our.dat | uniq -c | sort > freq.dat

This gives the same result, but doesn't leave temporary files, since the operating system automatically creates and deletes them.

Another important filter used to find the locations of patterns in text is **grep**. The syntax of the **grep** command is indicated in Figure 11.5. By using a special descriptive language, the **regular expression,** we can represent any construct that a language compiler could recognize. That means that a search can be made to recognize an element in a document or in a source code file based on the context rather than just as a literal string.

```
Table 11.10  Some Common Text-Processing Filter Utilities

Name   Function and Applications

DIFF   Show differences between two files
       Useful in debugging and maintenance to locate the differences
       between two versions of a file.
FIND   Find character string in a file
       A  PC-DOS or MS-DOS  filter that finds a literal string in a
       file for debugging or maintenance.  (Not to be confused with
       the UNIX command to locate a file in a directory tree.)
GREP   Find pattern by a general regular expression
       A powerful pattern-matching search utility.  GREP  is very
       useful in analysis, debugging, and maintenance.  Options per-
       mit counting occurrences, showing filenames and line number.
HEAD   Output file header
       Makes it easy to display a header block for a source file.
MORE   Output screenful at a time
       A PC-DOS or MS-DOS specific utility that pauses for input
       after each 23 lines of text.
SORT   Sort text records
       Useful in manipulating data sets.
TAIL   Display end of file
       Allows easy use of standard trailer block in documentation.
UNIQ   Output unique lines
       Makes it easy to strip adjacent duplicate records from a file
       Optionally one may output only records that are duplicated, or
       the repetition count for records.
WC     Count characters, words, lines
       A simple but useful metric to compare files.
```

```
Figure 11.5   Usage of the GREP utility

Usage:   grep [option] pattern filelist

where option is one or more of the following letters
              preceded by a - (hyphen):
   c  Only show count of matches
   f  Show file names with match
   i  Ignore case in making match
   l  Show only file names with a match
   n  Show line numbers at beginning of matched lines
   v  Show only lines that do not have a match

pattern is a  pattern to be searched  for specified as a
        regular expression. (See Table 11.11 for special
        characters  in such  patterns.)   Pattern may be
        quoted to escape operating system interpretation.

filelist is a list of file names to be searched for pattern
```

To represent patterns with regular expressions we need a number of special symbols, as described in Table 11.11. Note that a means to escape from interpreting a character that is not intended to be a special character is provided with a \ (backslash). These symbols allow us to search for either general or specific items while ignoring irrelevant included portions of the file.

Table 11.11 Special Characters Used to Form Regular Expressions

These characters are used in forming regular expressions to represent a text pattern. A regular expression may be used to identify the syntax of a line in a text file.

^   Matches column 1. A following pattern must start in column 1.

$ Matches end of line.   ^$ matches an empty line.

.   Matches any character except newline at end of line.

*   After an expression, means 0 or more repetitions of the expression are also accepted. Hence ..* is any one or more character string.

[string] Matches a character to any of the characters in 'string' and no others. [Aa] matches a or A.

[^string] Matches any character **not** in string but not the terminal newline.

\   Denotes escape from interpreting following character as a special character. To use any of the special characters ^$*.[]\/ as a literal in a pattern, precede it by a \. To match a FORTRAN comment marked by C or * in column 1, use '^[*C].*'

/   used as begin or end marker for a regular expression.

The concatenation of regular expressions is itself a regular expression. A character not specially defined is a regular expression matching itself.

11.H.2. Command Interpreters

To build useful procedures from a collection of filters and other programs, we need a facility called a **command interpreter** to build abstractions and name them as new commands. The operating system of any significant computing system does this by allowing a stream of commands to be redirected, so that command input is taken from a file. The terminology for these command files varies depending on the system. Examples are **proc file, JCL file, batch file**, or **shell script**. Whatever they are called, the fact that we can create a sequence of commands and give it a name means we can create and name new software tools. Users are spared the need to know the internal details and only need to know the shorthand name for their own customized procedures to carry out the desired task.

Studies of groups of UNIX system users have shown that the way they use the system is to create many more shell scripts than compiled or assembled programs. Most shell scripts are short. They may be the names of operations familiar to the user from some other computing system and may contain the local equivalent command (alias) with options. Hence users can customize their environment to reduce the number of commands to remember, especially when dealing with multiple systems.

11.H.3. Batch Editing Using sed

Many document preparation and software maintenance tasks require tedious repetition of some operations. It is more accurate and reliable to do these tasks with an automated software tool. Although many text editors and word processors have search and replace commands, their pattern-matching capability is generally limited to simple string matching. Since it is onerous to manually examine and identify a large set of candidate replacements, you should consider a batch editing tool.

Some text editors can have their input redirected so that a list of edit commands and insertion texts can be prepared and stored as a file (script file). To create a script file you must be able to specify a complete list of commands that will perform the required editing operations. The script file can then be used for processing one or more text files. The UNIX editors, **ed ex**, and **sed**, or the PC-DOS editor, **edlin**, are examples of such a tool. If you use a normally interactive text editor for a batch editing job there are a few guidelines to consider:

- Operate only on files that have backup copies.
- Be sure you have included a command to save the results.
- Be sure there is a command to end the edit session.
- Test your command script files carefully.
- Validate that the intended file modifications occurred.

In the following paragraphs we will concentrate on **sed**, because of its powerful pattern matching. **Sed** is a derivative of **ed** and **grep**. In addition, it can perform text substitution and other operations on selected lines. Using a file of commands (script file), several different operations can be performed in one pass through an input file. The location at which the editing operations are to be performed can be defined by line numbers. The appropriate lines can also be defined by pattern recognition of the contents of the line, or operations can be done on a sequence of lines identified by recognizing a pattern to start a block and another pattern to end the block of lines (line number range).

Sed differs from other editors used in batch processing in that it only makes one pass through a file and never goes back to an earlier part of the file. If a script of operations is provided, every operation will be applied to each line of the target file. With other editors you need to specify operations to move around in the file. In such editors many commands may be needed to move the file line pointer, but there is no restriction preventing moving back to an earlier portion of the file in a sequence of editing steps. With **sed**, processing is only done sequentially in the order of the lines of the file. If an operation must be done on an earlier part of the file, a separate batch process will be required. Note that **sed** can export lines, copies of lines, or portions of lines to another file. A major advantage of the sequential processing is that **sed** can work on files of arbitrary length. Also, because it only works on a small buffer, **sed** is small and fast.

This is a sophisticated batch processing tool that can take a command from the command line or access a file containing a script of commands. Commands are applied to each line of an input file according to the line or block address directives. **Sed** automatically reads the input file a line at a time, processes, and then writes an output line. It repeats this process until end-of-file on the input. After current command(s) have been completed the modified or unmodified line is written to output and the next line is read from the input. **Sed** does not modify the input file. The output file is a new, modified version of the input file. Since it only operates on one line at a time, **sed** is a small program that can process very large files efficiently.

Sed is a standard software tool in a UNIX environment, but it is also available to run on IBM PC and PC-compatible microcomputers under PC-DOS or MS-DOS. There are some usage differences due to the fact that MS-DOS and UNIX differ in how the command line is interpreted.

UNIX allows arguments to be quoted to avoid command interpretation; MS-DOS does not. Since one normally would not want a **sed** operation on the command line to escape the actions of UNIX, you will find that examples in UNIX texts always have single quotes around the **sed** operation. Therefore any **sed** command in a PC-DOS or MS-DOS environment that contains blanks or newlines must be put in a script file.

If you type in **sed** with no arguments it gives a prompt:

Usage: sed [-n] [-e script] [-f sfile file ...]

This is not too helpful for the novice, so some examples may clarify the usage. First, look at the usage description in Figure 11.6.

Sed input is by default from standard input (keyboard), and output is by default to standard output (screen). The input or output may be redirected from or to a file or logical device by the standard redirection syntax. Examples for MS-DOS or PC-DOS:

>prnsends output to the printer device

<myfile.txt input from a file: MYFILE.TXT

>newfileoutput to a file named NEWFILE

What are the sed commands? Table 11.12 gives a summary of the command operations. **Sed** commands are line oriented and follow the syntax of the UNIX line editor, **ed**. Table 11.13 gives the special characters used by **Sed**.

An operation may have 0, 1, or 2 line numbers (decimal) before it. If no line number is indicated, the operation applies to all lines of input. With only one line number that is the line to which the operation applies. With two, they must have a separating comma; line1 is the first line and line2 is the last line of a block to which the operation is applied. For example, to delete lines 3 through 10 of **file** as copied to **out**:

```
sed -e 2,10d <file >out
```

A line number may also be determined by a pattern match of a regular expression to the text of the input line. Such a line number is called a context address. Such patterns are regular expressions using the special symbols described above for GREP in Table 11.11.

For **sed**, each pattern must begin and end with a / as a delimiter. For example, as a single line reference,

```
/^DEBUG/
```

will be valid for any text lines beginning in column 1 with the string DEBUG. As another example, a range of lines

```
/begin/,/end/
```

will define that an operation following it is to apply starting with a line containing **begin**, and succeeding lines including one containing **end**.

```
Figure 11.6   Usage of the Stream EDitor (SED)

Usage:  sed [-n] -e command [<infile] [>outfile]
    or  sed [-n] -f sfile file1 [file2] ... [>outfile]

where command is a valid command string of the form:

        [line1 [,line2]] operation [arguments]

        and line1 or line2 may be decimal values or
        regular expressions matched to the line, or
        to the starting and ending line of a range.

-n          Copy to output only the lines specified by the
            print operation when used with the -e or -f
            options described below.  When used alone
            only unmatched lines are also copied to out-
            put.

-e          Edit.  Copy from input to output and apply the
            command following this option.

-f          sfile file1 [file 2 ...]  Take a sequence of
            commands from sfile and apply all of them to
            each line of file1 and any other file listed.
            Write results to standard output.

Sed operations are summarized in Table 11.12.  Regular
expressions to recognize target text lines or patterns for
replacement within a line use special symbols listed in
Table 11.11, and text replacement patterns use special
symbols listed in Table 11.13.
```

Table 11.12 Some SED Command Operations.

Note that operations are single letters. Some operations may have arguments. The first column indicates the maximum number of line numbers or
context address patterns that may precede it. This list is not complete;
see the original description by McMahon listed in the chapter references
for more operations.   The first column below indicates the maximum
number of line numbers or context addresses.

Number	Operation	Description
0	:label	Label marks destination of control transfer by b or t operation. A label is 1 to 8 characters. A nonunique label produces an error prompt.
1	=	Output current line number (as a separate line). Count from beginning of first file.
1	a\	Append - the following text line to output after text writing the designated line to output. This is a single-line command because \ hides the embedded newline. This may be done in a script file. (The MS-DOS command interpreter will not accept an embedded newline.)
2	b label	Branch to the command after :label.
2	c\ text	Change - replace the designated line with the text that follows. See append above.
2	d	Delete the indicated line(s).
2	g	Get - replace current input line buffer with contents of hold buffer.
2	h	Hold - copy current line buffer to the hold buffer. This replaces the prior hold buffer data.
2	i\	Insert - output following text line before output of text current line. See append.
2	l	List - output showing any nonprinting characters with markers.
2	p	Print - send indicated line(s) to output.
1	q	Quit - after processing the indicated line.
2	r file	Read - include file at indicated line(s).
2	s/old/new/option	Substitution - check line for the pattern old and replace with new, and output according to option(s). (0 or more allowed.)

old = search pattern (regular expression)   [see Table 11.11]
new = replacement text, <u>not regular expression</u> [see Table 11.13]
option: none = apply to all lines
         g   = replace all occurrences of pattern
         p   = print after substitute at first occurrence
       w file = write to file

| 2 | t label | Test - if any successful substitution has been made, branch to label and take the next operation. |
| 2 | x | Exchange - swap content of current line buffer and the hold buffer. |

Sed is not very friendly in many respects. However, the power of
the pattern matching in substitution and in finding lines to edit by pattern
recognition make it well worth the effort to master a few of its commands.

Table 11.13 Special Characters Used in the Replacement
             Text of the **sed** Substitute Command

In the replacement text of a substitute operation, the
special characters for patterns defined in Table 11.12
do not apply. Replacement text is not a regular expression. Instead the following special characters may be used.

&   A place holder and position where the character or
     string that was recognized by the search pattern is
     to be copied into the replacement text.

/d   Where d is a single digit, indicates that the d th
     match of the search pattern is where the replacement
     text is to be inserted.

/   Either & or / can be used as a literal character in
     the replacement text, if it is preceded by a /.

Sed can make it easy to do some editing tasks on large sets of files which
would require either much more work with less efficient editors or writing
special programs to do the text processing.

Figure 11.7   Batch Edit to Reformat a Document to Remove a String
              of Blanks at the Left Margin Throughout a Text File

You have a 140-page user's manual in a text file that uses 380 kilobytes.
It is noted that most lines have 10 blanks at the beginning.   You need
to shrink the file to fit onto a 360-kilobyte diskette.   Using a word
processor, it will take 1 sec./line in a global search and replace, but
it will also unformat tables and uncenter section headings, which would
would have to be fixed manually.   The estimated time to do this with a
word processor is 3 hours.   The following simple **sed** command takes 10
minutes on an IBM PC-XT microcomputer.

```
  sed -f margin  man  >man1.txt
```

where **margin** is a file containing: s\^   \\

Interpretation: Take a command from file MARGIN. Read a line from file
MAN.TXT. For each line, substitute (starting in column 1, for a string
of 10 blanks) (replace with a null string). Copy each modified line and
any line which doesn't fit the pattern to the output file MAN1.TXT.   We
use the **-f** option because MS-DOS would interpret the command arguments
as indicated by the underlines below. On keyboard input, MS-DOS command
arguments are delimited by white space.

```
  sed  -e s\^            \\ <M1 >MAN1.TXT
```

As a result **sed** emits the error message: "command garbled :   s\^"
because MS-DOS gives it only part of the argument. It works properly
when **sed** reads its commands from a script file.

One drawback is that there is no support for documenting script files with comments. It is appropriate to build script files by stepwise refinement. An application should be built by adding only one or two lines at a time to a script file and testing its execution with a suitable small test input file. Be sure to enter a carriage return at the end of the last line in a script file. A command line not terminated with <CR> is ignored.

Another reason to use a script file in a PC-DOS environment is to prevent the PC-DOS command interpreter from misinterpreting the command line. An example is shown in Figure 11.7. In a UNIX environment a command string can be enclosed in quote marks to prevent the command interpreter from processing a string to be passed to a program as an argument.

A few examples show some of the kinds of manipulations of source code or other documentation that are easy with batch editing. Consider first the task of collecting all macro definitions, putting them in a separate header file, and inserting a file inclusion directive, as shown in Figure 11.8. By using a batch editing script it is possible to do this efficiently on a large number of files.

Batch editing is also useful in handling text files that are part of system documentation. In some cases you may wish to reformat files for printing. A very common task is the addition of white space to the left margin before printing. On the other hand if all the documentation has been stored in the form of page images with top, bottom, and side margins already added, this increases the file size substantially.

The example in Figure 11.7 is one we encountered. The manual, with lots of white space, was 10% too large to fit on a floppy disk, which was the medium we wished to use to distribute the file. We noted that every text line had a left margin of 10 blanks. The solution was to use **sed** to selectively take out the leading blanks.

As another example, consider the task of stripping all the commentary and all the quoted strings from source code. This is illustrated for Pascal in Figure 11.9. This might be required as a preliminary step to produce temporary files to use in generating software metrics. The purpose we had in mind was to make it easier to count lines of code. The resulting file still has some "empty" comments. Those can be removed by one more filtering with another set of patterns.

You may ask, why tinker with a two-pass filter solution to solve this problem? The alternative is to write a program to do the job. Such a program will be many times longer than the required script of **sed** operations and take many times longer to write, debug, and adequately test. (We will concede that if you already happen to be an expert in a pattern matching language like SNOBOL, ICON, or AWK, a program in such a language may be competitive.) In essence,if you have a specialized problem such as text pattern manipulation, use a pattern-manipulation tool rather than an unsuitable language or word processor.

```
Figure 11.8   Batch Edit to Collect Macro Definitions and
              Put Them in a Separate Header File
```

We have several source code procedures, each of which has directives to define constants. We wish to put all these definitions into one header file and have a directive to include that file at the top of a single source file. The command line and a file of **sed** commands to do this are shown below.

Command to start **sed** below and script file, MAKE-H, right

```
    sed -f make-h prg1.c prg2.c >prg.c
```

```
1i\
#include <macro.h>
/#define/w macro.h
/#define/d
```

Interpretation: Commands for **sed** are read from MAKE-H. Input is from the files PRG1.C and PRG2.C. Output is to PRG.C. A literal string #include <macro.h> is sent to output before line 1. Each input line is examined, and if it contains #define it is sent to file MACRO.H and not to the output file (deleted). Otherwise all lines are output to PRG.C. Sample files are shown below.

Input files: PRG1.C   PRG2.C

```
#define TRUE  1             #define N  4
#define FALSE 0             next(p)
main() {                    int p; {
int x;                      int i;
if (x == TRUE)              for(i=0;i=N;i++)
    puts("yes");               puts("x");
else next(x);               return;
}                           }
```

Output files: PRG.C   MACRO.H

```
#include <macro.h>          #define TRUE  1
main() {                    #define FALSE 0
int x;                      #define N  4
if (x == TRUE)
    puts("yes");
else next(x);
}

next(p)
int p; {
int i;
for(i=0;i=N;i++)
   puts("x");
return
}
```

11.H.4. Execution Profilers

A software tool that analyzes the execution profile of a program is often called a **profiler**. Typically two types of profile may be produced:

- execution counts, or
- cumulative execution time.

These counts or times may be referenced to line numbers of the source code, or alternatively to code modules.

```
Figure 11.9   Batch Edit to Remove All Comments from
              a File of Pascal Source Code

For purposes of processing source code for complexity  metrics it makes
the task simpler if there are no keywords or variable names in comments.
To do this we must find comments that are embedded within a single line
and  multiline  comments.   We assume that comments  start with  (* and
terminate with *).  Thus we have four patterns to recognize:

        1. lines containing an entire comment
        2. lines on which a comment starts and does not terminate
        3. lines on which a comment does terminate but didn't start
        4. lines that occurred after a start of a comment but before
           the line on which the comment terminates

In each of these cases we wish to remove the commentary text.
A script file which does this is:

        s/(\*.*\*)//
        /(\*/s/(\*.*$/(\*/p
        /.*\*)/s/^.*\*)/\*)/p
        /(\*/,/.*\*)/d

The first script line replaces a within-line comment with a null string.
The second recognizes a beginning of a comment and replaces it with a
null string, but leaves the (*.  The third script line detects an end
of comment, replaces from the beginning of the line to the comment mark
with a null string, and leaves the end comment mark, *). The second and
third lines have the p option so they are passed to output immediately.
The copy of an input line in the line buffer is modified by each succes-
sive command in the script.  The last line identifies all lines from the
beginning line of a multiline comment to the last one and deletes them
from the buffer.  Any line not matching any of the patterns is copied to
output.
```

Execution time profiles are essential to performance evaluation. They are the hardest to produce. These require support by the hardware and the operating system to capture the timing measurements. The basic problem is that one needs to capture time data that relates solely to the execution of the element under study. It must exclude other tasks in a multitasking environment and operating system overhead tasks in any system.

Counts of the execution of lines or procedures are a lot easier and are feasible in any computing system. Such profiles are of more limited use in performance evaluation, but are still important. Such counts can be valuable in locating "hot spots" in a system that account for major parts of the execution time. This information is needed in order to make rational decisions about where to expend effort on optimization or performance improvement.

A profiler should also be considered an important debugging and testing tool. Profiler output should be a standard part of your testing suite. Why? Because it is much easier to evaluate and validate loop execution with the profiler. A profiler can eliminate the need for special instrumentation of the source code to capture counts of the execution of each path segment in the code. For a given test case you should know how many executions of each loop should occur. The profiler output easily tells you whether they occurred.

Validation of line or procedure counts in a test case can sometimes reveal problems that have not been detected in examinations of system outputs. Bentley has described several cases where "hot spots" involving large execution counts have led to locating invalid code when it had not previously been recognized that the system was slower than it should have been.

Another class of problem is when attempts to correct a defect or the addition of an enhancement leads to another defect. Such defects may be revealed by changes in the loop counts or relative counts of alternative paths in two versions of the code when exercised by the same test case. These analyses require that:

- The test case data is documented and preserved.
- Execution profile data of resulting tests is retained.
- Results of tests are systematically compared.

11.H.5. Preprocessors and Macroprocessors

If you do not have a profiler option on your compiler or a stand-alone profiler utility, you may need to insert code into the programs under development to capture the execution counts. If you have to do the code insertion, you may wish to selectively instrument path segments rather than introduce a counter for every line of the original code. Such code insertion may be helped with a **preprocessor**.

A **macroprocessor** is a software tool that recognizes a defined character string and performs a text substitution. Often this is just a matter of substituting one string for another. In other cases a macro is a symbol name followed by a list of one or more arguments to be inserted into a substitution string, as shown in Figure 11.10. A macroprocessor may be a stand-alone utility such as the C PreProcessor (CPP), or it may be a standard part of a language. C, PL/I, assembler, and operating system command interpreters include macroprocessors. Macro directives normally are executed as a preprocessing step before compiling or interpreting the source text. Stand-alone macroprocessors can be used with the source code for any language.

Figure 11.10   Conditional Compilation to Insert Code for Assertion
               Checking Using the C PreProcessor (CPP)

The macro assert (A) is expanded to several statements to insert a test
of an assertion about the correctness of the data received by a module.
The macro definition is conditional. If ASSERTION is defined the macro
will be expanded. If the macro ASSERTION is not defined, the assert
macro will be replaced by nothing, i.e., it's deleted. Directives to the
preprocessor all begin with #. Such lines are interpreted by the preprocessor and discarded.

Directive	Meaning
#define macroname replacement_text	Define a macro
#ifdef macro2	Interpret IF macro2 defined,
..	include text or directive(s),
#else	ELSE if macro2 not defined,
..	include text or directive(s),
#endif	End of conditional clause.

Example source with macro definitions and macro reference:

```
#define ASSERTION 1
#define NULL      0
#ifdef  ASSERTION
#define assert( A )    if( !( A )) { printf(\
        "Assertion failed in file: %s, at line %d\n",\
                  __FILE__ , __LINE__ ); exit(1); }
#else
#define assert( A )
#endif

int Search( value, table,  n )
    int value,    /* integer value to be searched for */
    *table,       /* table of integers to search */
    n ;           /* size of table, count.    */
{
    int errcode =0;
/* Assertion placed after local declarations.  A NULL value
for table (a pointer to an array) would indicate bad data.
An error message should be printed and execution halted.  */

assert( table != NULL );

/* body of code module */

return errcode;
} /* End Search */
```

The result of expanding the assert macro above also shows how CPP
uses the predefined variables __LINE__ and __FILE__ to reference the
current line number and file name.   Note that while expanding the
macros, CPP also stripped all directives and comments from the source
code.

```
int Search( value, table,  n )
    int value,
    *table,
    n ;
{
    int errcode =0;
```

```
if( !( table != 0  )) { printf(
        "Assertion failed in file: %s, at line %d\n",
        "search.c" , 21 ); exit(1); };
   .
   .
   .
return errcode;
}
```

Macroprocessors written in the language C have migrated to every machine that supports a C compiler. Examples include the UNIX macroprocessors **m4**, CPP (C PreProcessor as a stand-alone program), and the macroprocessor from Kernighan's Software Tools. Using such a software tool can reduce the work of code modification in a language that does not include a preprocessor facility. An example might be the insertion of code for assertion checking or execution tracing in Pascal or FORTRAN by using CPP. Here is another example where software tools developed for one language can improve productivity by migrating to tasks in another language environment.

One of the reasons for interest in batch editing is that many of the tasks that might be performed by a macroprocessor or a language preprocessor can also be done by a batch editor, in some cases without using a separate macroprocessor. This is true if the pattern-recognizing capability of the search and replace facility is adequate. That is one reason why editors that support regular expressions as the basis for pattern matching are important software development tools.

11.H.6. Documentation Tools

Figure 11.11 Documentation Tools

Print formatter	A printing utility to set margins, add headings, page numbers, line spacing, page length; some recognize directives in the text.
Pretty printer	A filter to automatically adjust indentation of block structure for a target language.
Uniq	copy only unique lines. Useful to strip extra blank lines if you know that there are no other adjacent duplicate lines.
Spelling checker	Never deliver a document without using one. Check your add on dictionary for correctness.
Index generator	Use it to sort index items and build an index, check for and eliminate irrelevant citations.
Table of contents generator	Use it to make sure the page numbers cited are correct.

Finally, a few words on documentation tools. Undoubtedly you have made good use of word processors. However, do not neglect other text manipulation tools when preparing documentation. A list of some common documentation tools is given in Figure 11.11.

For example, if a pretty printer is available, don't waste time tinkering with indentation format of source code. There are many other tasks that should not be done by "hand" with a text editor. Note that several of these documentation tools may be included in full-featured word processors. Automate as many tasks as possible to minimize mistakes. Spend more time editing. That means reviewing and improving the content of the documents. Use software tools wherever possible to make systematic changes to the appearance.

Of course, you should be skeptical of what happens to the text, so be sure to read it before submitting the result. (We know someone who has added two alternative misspellings of the same word to his personal dictionary.) Your work will be judged by the quality of the details as well as its appearance.

11.I. Conclusions

The idea of the development workstation contained in Ivie's description of a programmer's workbench has become the norm for today's software professional. This has been achieved by a combination of improved hardware technology and software development. While many software tools exist to support code development, and CASE tools have recently appeared to support analysis and design activities, the coordination of tools is still a major challenge.

The advent of personal workstations has tended to decentralize development efforts. The technology to support centralized repositories of software support information exists. Although networks and distributed computing are available, the software links to ensure coordination and configuration management are not yet in wide use.

The search for new software tools will continue. The problem is that we have no theory yet to define the best approach. Every proponent of a new software tool or method tends to overgeneralize its benefits. New methods have costs as well as benefits. It is essential that we measure the actual costs and benefits so that we get progress and not just change.

Summary

The major classes of tools are editors, translators, monitors, and resource managers. Within each class are found the traditional tools of text editors, compilers, assemblers, linkers, and debuggers. Operating characteristics of tools depend on the hardware and operating system with which they are used. In order to manage large software systems, it is important to have appropriate, coordinated tools.

An early example of coordinated tools was the concept of The Programmer's Workbench, the forerunner of today's workstation. This included compilers, a version control system, file system support, documentation tools, test drivers, and electronic mail.

More recent tools include the integration of a full-screen editor, compiler, linker, configuration management tool, and source-level debugger. Syntax-directed editors and pretty printers are especially useful for documentation. Execution profilers may be used to evaluate either the time or the execution counts of software. These and/or preprocessors and macroprocessors are useful for testing and debugging.

Tools may be bought, modified from existing tools, or built. A cost/benefit analysis must be done. One cost is the time needed to become proficient with the new tool. Tools must be tested, as they don't necessarily live up to their advertisements.

Some examples of tools that can be used to build tools are filters and pipes. The **sed** editor is an example of a small, efficient editor that works quickly on large files.

Keywords

assembler
batch editing
command interpreter
compiler
debugger
documentation tools
editor
filter
grep
index generator
integrated software tools
interpreter
learning curve
linker
macroprocessor
monitor
pipe
preprocessor

print formatter
profiler
Programmer's Workbench
redirection
regular expression
resource manager
sed
shell scripts
software tools
spelling checker
sort
syntax-directed editor
table of contents generator
text editor
translator
uniq
UNIX
workstations

Review Questions

11.1.   What is the purpose of software tools?

11.2.   Describe the difference between general purpose tools and specialized tools. Give an example of each.

11.3.   List the four major classes of software tools. Give an example of each.

11.4.   List the major characteristics of text editors, compilers, linkers, and debuggers.

11.5.   What is the difference between a compiler and an interpreter?

11.6.   What is coordinated software?

11.7.   What is the relationship between UNIX and a workstation?

11.8.   What is meant by "Programmer's Workbench"?

11.9.   Give an example of an integrated software tool.

11.10. What languages use syntax-directed editors?

11.11. What advantages are there to standardized software tools?

11.12. Explain the learning curve.

11.13. When you need a software tool, how do you go about evaluating one? Where do you get one?

11.14. Give an example of a filter. Explain how it is used.

11.15. Give an example of a pipe. Explain how it is used.

11.16. What is the purpose of redirection of input and output? Give an example of how it could be useful to you.

11.17. Explain a command interpreter and the benefits of batch processing.

11.18. How does **sed** differ from the text editor you have been using? Cite a use in which **sed** would outperform your text editor.

11.19. What are the two major types of profilers? How are they useful for testing and debugging?

11.20. What is the difference between a preprocessor and a macroprocessor?

11.21. Which documentation tools are available to you? Which would you like to have?

Exercises

11.1.   Examine the documentation for a compiler that you use and compare it to the features list in Table 11.3. What features are available that are not in the table? Which features in the table are not available?

11.2.   For your operating system, if standard input for a filter is from the keyboard, how do you enter an end-of-file to terminate input?

11.3.   Assume that your programing language requires that every variable must be declared by name before use.

What is the significance of a variable listed in a cross-reference table that appears exactly once in the program?

What does it mean if a variable appears exactly twice? (Can you construct an example in your programming language that would not be anomalous?) These are useful checks that can be done while desk checking code. Some compilers notice such anomalies and issue a warning, but most do not.

11.4.   Write regular expressions for a **grep** command to match text patterns in the following situations:

The word "the" whether or not capitalized.

/* Any C comment within one line . */

Any array reference: identifier [index], where you may assume that the syntax is valid, square brackets always refer to an array element, and square brackets enclose a refer to an array element, and square brackets enclose a legal array index. Note that a bracket is a special character.

11.5.   Write a **grep** command line to find every procedure statement in a Pascal program, PROGRAM1.PAS, with their line numbers. One of those lines could be:

> *procedure NumberString (N: integer; var S : string);*

Assume that the keyword **procedure** and a pair of parentheses are mandatory.

11.6.   Consider a file of data records. There are a small number of different values and we want the frequency of each. The data has been sorted so all identical values are adjacent. We produced a work file with 'uniq -c' to get the counts of the unique records:

Note that the counts are either one or two digits. To sort this file into a frequency distribution we need a leading zero added to one - digit values. Write a script file for batch editing such a file.	75: apple 1: orange 3: peach 21: pear

11.7.   Use **sed** to copy a file and add seven blanks to the left margin of all nonblank lines of the file. This is a useful filter to print source code. The margin lets you punch three holes and/or bind it. Put the commands in a file. Put the **sed** invocation line in an MS-DOS batch file with an appropriate name.

11.8.   Write a sed script file to convert a multiline statement,

while ... wend		while () begin ... end
while (...)	to	while ( ) begin
. . .		. . .
wend		end;

11.9.   Write a set of commands for a batch edit of a file that has already been processed with **sed** with the script of Figure 11.9. The file has "empty" comment blocks: a begin comment mark on one line followed by an end of comment mark at the beginning of the next line. Remove the empty comments.

11.10.   Consider building a line count profiler for code modules. One approach would be to create a file with a counter array declaration to be inserted near the beginning of the target module, and a file of sequential statements that increment successive counter array elements. Preprocessing involves merging the file of counter statements and the target code, reading from the target code and counter statements alternately.

Also insert a statement to save the array of counters to a file just before each possible exit from the module. Design procedure(s) to carry out the instrumentation of code modules to get an execution count for each executable line of the target code module. Estimate the executable lines of the procedures necessary to set up your profiler.

11.11. What is the difference between a macro and a subroutine in terms of runtime space usage and execution efficiency?

11.12. Write macros to insert statements to:

- print a message indicating what procedure is executing.
- write the procedure name and current time to a file.
- convert a function call to inline code.

References

Bentley, Jon. "Programming Pearls: Profilers." CACM 30 (July 1987): 587-592.

> Profiler output is discussed with examples showing methods of debugging and performance evaluation.

Booch, Grady. Software Components with Ada: Structures. Tools, and Subsystems. Menlo Park, CA: Benjamin- Cummings, 1987.

> Includes description of object oriented design, and the relationship between data flow diagrams and object oriented design

Booch, Grady. Software Engineering with Ada, second edition. Menlo Park, CD: Benjamin-Cummings, 1987.

> Good descriptions of software engineering principles and object oriented design as applied with Ada.

Campbell, Joe, Creating C Tools for the IBM PCs. Englewood Cliffs, NJ: Prentice-Hall, 1986.

> System programming tools and techniques for the IBM PC are presented with extensive examples in assembly and C programming. Areas covered include access to DOS services, keyboard, video access, interrupts, and serial communication. A source code disk is available from the author.

Hunt, William J. The C Toolbox. Reading, MA: Addison-Wesley, 1985.

> Hunt gives C programmers a description and analysis of a number of common utilities to support assembly and high level language programming. He includes file display, sorting, indexed files implemented with B trees, terminal emulators, and IBM PC environment support. Code examples are available on disk from the author.

Ivie, Evan L. "The Programmer's Workbench - A Machine for Software Development." CACM 20,10 (November 1977): 746-753.

> A classic paper describing the use of a minicomputer under UNIX as a workstation for software development. Describes the essence of a set of coordinated tools for life cycle support of software.

Kernighan, Brian W., and Mashey, John R. "The UNIX Programming Environment." IEEE Computer 14, no. 4 (April 1981): 12-24.

A general discussion of the UNIX development environment based on experience with early minicomputer applications.

Kernighan, Brian W., and Pike, Rob. The UNIX Programming Environment. Englewood Cliffs, NJ: Prentice-Hall, 1984.

Introduces the UNIX operating system, batch programming using the UNIX command shell processor, and C programming. Emphasis is on demonstration of UNIX tools and their application to the stepwise development of applications. Section 4.3 gives a tutorial discussion of sed, derived from the early UNIX line editor, ed. Examples using sed are compared to uses of other tools. A good description of the use of filters in general is given. Appendix 1 is a manual for ed that gives an explanation of command syntax most of which is applicable to sed.

Kernighan, Brian W., and Plauger, P. J. Software Tools. Reading, MA: Addison-Wesley, 1976. Also Software Tools in Pascal. Reading, MA: Addison-Wesley, 1981.

These two books are excellent examples of good programming style and methodology. They emphasize the development and use of tools to manipulate text files with filters and macro preprocessors. Various versions of most of the tools described are available in public domain software libraries. The earlier version has source code of interest to C programmers. The tools are available in executable form as well as source code in C and Pascal.

Kochan, Stephen G., and Wood, Patrick. UNIX Shell Programming. Indiannapolis, IN: Hayden Books, 1985.

Chapter 4, "Tools of the Trade," discusses regular expressions and UNIX tools that manipulate them: cut, paste, grep, sed, awk, tr, sort, and uniq. Several applications of sed are shown.

Marca, David. Applying Software Engineering Principles. Boston, MA: Little, Brown, 1984.

A software engineering text with examples in FORTRAN of filters, table-driven software, implementation of finite state machines, source-level debugging, tracing tools, and other applications.

McMahon, L. E. "SED - A Non-Interactive Text Editor." In UNIX Programmers' Manual, Vol. 2, 7th ed. New York: Holt, Rinehart & Winston, 1979.

The original user's manual for sed by the author who created sed by modification of ed. Read it to find more commands dealing with the hold buffer and discussion of multiple line patterns.

Sherman, Mark, and Drysdale, Robert L., III. "Producing Software Using Tools in a Workstation Environment." Proceedings of the Software Engineering Institute Conference on Software Engineering Education. Pittsburgh, May 1987.

Description of the environment provided students at Dartmouth. The standard workstation was a Macintosh on a network. An extensive list of software tools and a description of how they are incorporated in courses and student projects was provided.

Stevens, Al. C Development Tools for the IBM PC. New York: Brady, 1986.

Presents tools and techniques in C to support cache memory, data file management including B trees, screen management, and menu generation. Emphasis is on application of reusable code modules. The source code is available from its author.

Yourdon, Edward. <u>Nations at Risk: The Impact of the Computer Revolution</u>. New York: Yourdon Press, 1986.

A readable account of the impact of computers on our world for computer professionals and a general audience.

CHAPTER 12

QUALITY ASSURANCE AND SOFTWARE EVALUATION

Once upon a time there was a very proud software manager.

The manager was in charge of a software project which was looked upon in his company as a model for How To Build Software.

The project was, to be brief, Under Budget and On Schedule.

And in the halls of management, where accolades are passed out for performance on the project, there is no finer thing to be than Under Budget and On Schedule.

Once upon a time there was a very proud quality assurance manager.

The manager was in charge of quality assurance for the Software on the Under Budget and On Schedule project.

The project was, to be brief, configuration managed and standards conforming to a fair-thee-well.

And in the halls of quality, when the subject of quality itself arises, it is generally agreed that configuration and standards are What It Is All About.

Once upon a time there was a customer. The customer was very sad. The software product the customer received was a pile of excrement.

The software was produced well under budget. And on schedule. It was impeccably configuration managed. And standards-conforming.

But it did not do what the customer wanted. It did not fit in the customer's computer's memory. It did not operate as fast as the customer wanted it to. It was abysmally difficult to modify, so that the customer could not even change it to be what was wanted. And when it did operate, it failed more often than it worked.

Once upon a time there was a corporate president.

The corporate president was in charge of the manager who was Under Budget and On Schedule. The corporate president was in charge of the quality assurance manager who managed configurations and audited standards.

But the corporate president was not in charge of everyone. There was, for example, the customer.

When the customer spoke to the corporate president, he spoke of value received. He spoke of usability, and efficiency, and maintainability, and reliability. In brief, he spoke of Quality. And he was upset. The corporate president listened.

Then the corporate president spoke to his two managers. "What went wrong here?" he said.

"I was under budget and on schedule," said the software manager.

"I achieved configuration management and standards-conformance," said the quality assurance manager.

"But who is looking out for product quality?" cried the exasperated corporate president.

No one answered.

> *- Robert L. Glass, "Quality is Sometimes Only Skin Deep"*

12.A. Introduction to Quality Assurance

If you doubt that there are persistent problems with the quality of software, look at the warranty on software packages. The example shown in Figure 12.1 is not unusual.

```
Figure 12.1  A Typical Software Warranty

Crankemout Software disclaims all warranties, express or
implied, regarding the disk and related materials, their
fitness for any purpose, their merchantability, their
quality or otherwise.

In no event shall Crankemout Software be liable for any
damages suffered from the use of this product.
```

In contrast, look at the warranty on a household appliance such as a microwave oven. An appliance warranty is likely to say:

This product is warranted to perform its intended function for one year. If it should fail in that period due to any defect in materials or workmanship it will be repaired without charge. For warranty service . . .

A typical software package is not guaranteed to perform any useful functions, let alone those for which it is advertised and licensed. It should be apparent that the unwillingness of software vendors to give a reasonable warranty is because they do not have control of the quality of the product.

Software quality depends on all stages of the life cycle. Quality cannot be added on later. Quality is the result of the cumulative effort of everyone involved in the analysis, specification, design, implementation, and maintenance of a software system.

There are two basic methods of assuring a prescribed level of quality. First, we may identify factors, standards, and methods which, if competently done, will assure the creation of a good product. Second, we can demand a rigorous test of the product's quality and reject it if it does not pass the test.

Part of the problem in the quality of software has been the casual assumption that all is well, and any defects will be cleaned up at the end. This does not always work. For example, multiple interacting defects are much harder to locate and correct than single defects. The adoption of a zero defect tolerance attitude, supported by software quality assurance planning, leads to better software and more predictable development. As an additional benefit, good quality software takes less time to test since less regression testing will be required.

In one sense there is a choice. We can spend effort at the beginning on preventing the creation of defects, or we can spend more effort at the end on defect removal. The only other alternative is to continue to produce software of questionable quality. In this chapter we look at the first of these alternatives.

12.A.1. Defining Quality

In order to understand **software quality assurance (SQA)**, we need a definition of quality. For our purposes, **quality** consists of the characteristics that are wanted for a specific software product. These may vary widely from one system to another. Some aspects that may be included in the definition of quality for a particular software product may be drawn from the list in Table 12.1.

Some software will be deemed **critical applications**, which require special care in quality assurance planning. A critical application is generally one where there is high risk to human life or very high financial risk if the software should fail in service. For example, software that is to be used in a hospital in connection with patient monitoring must be thoroughly tested for all conceivable aspects of reliability and safety. An example of a high financial risk application is the management of a subscription list for a magazine publisher. While schedule compliance may be important, meeting deadlines is secondary to reliability and safety in a critical application.

Conversely, in some situations meeting the deadline is a primary factor. It is possible under some circumstances that a system that works reasonably well most of the time and meets the deadline is preferable to a perfect system turned in late. An industrial example of this might be a program that is designed to convert files from one format to another. It does not have to be completely user friendly, it just has to work well enough to get the job done.

Table 12.1 Factors That May be Defined as
          Attributes of Software Quality

Factor	Example of a Related Question
reliability	Does it compute accurately, every time?
efficiency	Does it run fast enough?
maintainability	Can it be fixed or adapted?
modifiability	Can it be enhanced or extended?
portability	Can it be moved to other hardware?
usability	Can the typical user run it?
consistency	Are the terminology and naming conventions uniform throughout the system?
understandability	Are all the documents understandable?
correctness	Does it fulfill the requirements?
testability	Can it be tested?
robustness	Does it handle insults like bad data?
structuredness	Is the code structured and modular?
compactness	Does it use a minimum of memory?
compatibility	Does it work with other systems?
integrity	Is the system secure?

In summary, quality is whatever those in charge of the project define it to be. However, it is important that quality be coordinated and defined in terms of the needs of the user. This point is illustrated in the quotation at the beginning of this chapter by Robert L. Glass. The definition of quality must be carefully considered in advance. Quality cannot be redefined at the end of the project and be expected to have any influence on prior work.

12.A.2. Planning for Quality Assurance

Quality consists of meeting a specified set of criteria for a specific project. It is important that criteria for software quality assurance be clearly specified in advance and that all team members be informed and in agreement. Otherwise, the team may find itself working at cross-purposes, with each member concentrating on what he or she believes (or has been trained to believe) is important. For example, one team member may be concerned with good documentation, another with meeting deadlines, and still another with maintainability. And, as in the opening quotation, one may only be concerned with being under budget and on schedule, while another may be concerned with configuration management and standards conformity. All of these aspects are important, but the priorities need to be rank-ordered and coordinated, along with other criteria, for a specific project.

For large projects it is essential that the elements of a **Quality Assurance Plan** be fully documented. One standard for such a document is summarized in Table 12.2. The topics in Section 6 of the table are addressed later in the chapter.

Table 12.2 is based on ANSI/IEEE Software Engineering Standard 730-1984, Software Quality Assurance Plans. The standard lists thirteen items that should be included in the plan, in the prescribed order. If any of these items is not present, the standard requires that the absence must be noted under its section heading with "This section is not applicable to this plan" followed by a justification. Additional sections may be added at the end to fill the needs of a particular project. Such a plan should be produced concurrently with the preparation of specifications during the analysis phase.

12.A.3. Quality Assurance Teams

Who stands up for quality? In one sense it must be all the project participants. However, if the project is large, there must be a designated quality assurance team that has the specific job of carrying out tasks related to quality assurance. These include negotiating standards in advance, monitoring quality throughout the project, and reviewing the results at the end. A more detailed list is given in Table 12.3.

The quality assurance team needs to be independent. For this reason it should report to management independently of the technical project manager. Those conducting a review must have the authority to tell the project manager that there is a problem to be fixed. If standards cannot be enforced there is no quality assurance. To assure quality, a development team leader cannot be allowed the option to trade schedule or other constraints against relaxation of quality standards. If there are quality problems, a higher level manager must decide any dispute between quality assurance and other team leaders. If there is a quality assurance program, then the Software Quality Assurance team must be able to enforce proper standards and practices. The time to dispute these is before the project begins.

That is not to say that every deviation from standards will be fixed. In many cases, trivial deviations will merely be noted and the product under evaluation will be approved.

Table 12.2   Outline of a Quality Assurance Plan Sections
             Prescribed by ANSI/IEEE Standard 730-1984

1. Purpose - software applied to, purpose of the software, quality goals
            and scope of the plan.
2. Reference documents - complete list of documents referred to in plan.
3. Management - describes how quality assurance is to be organized and
            managed. The organizational structure must be defined in terms
            of the hierarchy of control and responsibilities. This must
            clearly state the dependence or independence of all the indivi-
            duals/groups involved in quality assurance. The tasks to be
            carried out are to be listed with an identification of how
            responsibilities are assigned in the organizational structure.
4. Documentation required during the project - minimum documentation
            requirements listing documents and purpose of each. A minimum
            list should include:
     Software Requirements Specification
     Software Design Description
     Software Verification and Validation Report
     User Documentation
Other documents that may be required include:
     Software Development Plan
     Software Configuration Management Plan
     Procedures and Practices Manual
5. Standards, practices, and conventions - specify the standard used
            for each document. The methods of verifying each standard or
            practice must be specified.
6. Reviews and audits - list those to be done and methods to be employed
            for each. A minimum list includes:
     Software Requirements Review - adequacy, consistency, and completeness
     Preliminary Design Review - adequacy, consistency, and completeness
     Critical Design Review - acceptability, implementation standards
            compliance, compliance with requirements.
     Verification and validation review - adequacy, validity, complete-
            ness of testing
     Functional Audit - assess compliance with requirements prior to
            delivery
     Physical Audit - verify completeness of all deliverables prior to
            delivery
7. Software configuration management - by inclusion or reference to
            general plan previously documented.
8. Problem reporting and correction - procedures, standards, and assign-
            ment of duties and responsibilities.
9. Tools, techniques, and methods for quality assurance-lists the
            specific tools and methods to be employed. The purpose of
            each relating to QA is to be described.
10. Code control - plan for control and storage of software elements of
            the system covered by the plan.
11. Media control - plan for control and management of the physical backup
            media under this plan.
12. Supplier control - documents how quality assurance compliance will be
            enforced with vendor or subcontractor-produced software
            elements of the project.
13. Records collection, maintenance, and retention - describes data col-
            lection for quality assurance and how it will be managed and
            archived for future access.

12.B. Means of Achieving Quality Assurance

12.B.1. Standards

A **standard** is a mandatory guide to practices or methods employed on a project. It may be a company-developed standard or a published national or international standard. We have referred to several American National Standards Institute (ANSI) and Institute for Electrical and Electronic Engineers (IEEE) standards, which represent the consensus of many experts on particular topics.

```
Table 12.3   Tasks of a Quality Assurance Team

Collect project records and manage archives.
Manage audits and reviews.
Manage and maintain standards documentation.
Negotiate agreements on software quality standards.
Develop models for evaluating quality factors.
Develop metrics to monitor software quality.
Develop software tools to produce metrics.
Gather metric data to measure software quality factors.
Gather data on software size, complexity, productivity.
Perform trend analysis of data relating to software quality.
Analyze error reports.
Conduct verification and validation.
Evaluate cost estimation models against project cost.
```

The development of standards is a continuing process. The promotion of standards is one of the most important tasks of a quality assurance program. Software quality assurance must continually examine new development methodologies to improve software quality or productivity. If new procedures are to be adopted as a standard, the details of the standard practice must be negotiated. Once a standard is adopted there must be monitoring for compliance and data collection to determine if the goals of the standard are being achieved.

As a practical matter it is not useful to establish a standard for which there is no systematic, well-understood, objective evaluation method. To make the evaluation cost effective, there should be an automated method of evaluation that is accessible to the developer and quality assurance personnel. If a practice is not objectively measurable, a standard probably will not achieve any meaningful compliance.

12.B.2. Reviews

A **review** is a group effort at examining a software product or process. Reviews may be conducted in several forms: **walkthroughs, inspections**, or **audits**. They may be very informal, as is often the case with code walkthroughs, or very formal with extensive planning, as with an inspection. The degree of formality is flexible and can be adjusted to suit the needs of a particular project at a specific time.

Reviews are extremely important to the success of a software project, and are the primary method whereby software quality can be assured. Effective reviews can uncover errors in relatively early stages, thus keeping costs down. Adoption of standards is meaningless if they are not subject to reviews. For example, Gerald Weinberg has noted that while everyone espouses the idea of structured programming, he still finds very low compliance in impromptu code inspections.

12.B.2.a. Walkthroughs

A **walkthrough** is a group effort to review a product or documentation primarily involving those who have produced it. It involves a presentation to a group with the producers of the work available for explanations and discussion. It may be an informal or formal procedure, and is frequently used to review source code. It can consist of anything from group members getting together informally to examine each other's code to a carefully organized presentation. The purpose of code walkthroughs is frequently to find errors, but they can also be used to evaluate compliance with design standards.

At the formal end of the spectrum of walkthroughs is the **structured walkthrough**. A structured walkthrough is often used as a periodic progress review tool for management and consists of the following:

- The manager establishes a standard for the form and procedures used in carrying out the walkthroughs.
- It is scheduled periodically, such as every two weeks.
- The participant list and the role of each participant is defined.
- Each walkthrough results in a written report, with actions recorded and assigned to specific individuals.

These structured walkthroughs may or may not deal with detailed technical consideration of the current life cycle products such as source code. Nonetheless good practice dictates that within a group, peer review of technical detail should be carried out. Thus a development organization may have general progress monitoring with structured walkthroughs and also have code walkthroughs informally among the programming staff.

A code walkthrough in a classroom may consist of an informal discussion of how to approach a coding problem by presenting a source code sample. Or, more formally, it may consist of one team showing code samples to other teams and asking for a written evaluation of documentation and suggestions for testing.

Copies of the source code should be made available by advance distribution of printed copies or by providing access by electronic mail. During the presentation a video display should be provided by using overhead transparencies or by display on video monitors. The results and recommendations of a walkthrough should be documented. The walkthrough participants must take an active role. The success of the effort depends on their willingness to make and accept constructive criticisms.

An example of a form that might be used in a code walkthrough is shown in Figure 12.2.

```
Figure 12.2  Sample Form for Code Walkthroughs

Each participant is expected to complete all sections of
the questionnaire.

Code Walkthrough Evaluation     Project_____

Evaluator _____        Date   __ /___ /___

Code reviewed _____

Circle one response for each category below.
Ranks: 0 = unacceptable, 1 = poor, 2 = fair, 3 = good,
         4 = excellent,  N = Not applicable

Satisfy  requirements  0 1 2 3 4 N  Correctness   0 1 2 3 4 N
Satisfy coding std.    0 1 2 3 4 N  Error traps   0 1 2 3 4 N
Structured programming 0 1 2 3 4 N  Algorithm     0 1 2 3 4 N
Interfaces, coupling   0 1 2 3 4 N  Num. accuracy 0 1 2 3 4 N
Modularity, cohesion   0 1 2 3 4 N  Info. hiding  0 1 2 3 4 N
Quality of commentary  0 1 2 3 4 N  Efficiency    0 1 2 3 4 N

Best feature:_____
Worst feature:_____
Correction(s) required to remove reservation:
_____
Put additional comments or questions on the back of the form.

Recommend: Reject __, Accept __, Accept with reservation ___
```

Code walkthroughs are remarkably effective, finding as many as 70% of errors. They are also very cost effective, as the cost is limited to the participants' time. However, they can be incredibly boring. But for those teams who can stand to wade through each other's code in detail, the benefits are enormous. For reference, at least one study indicates that a reasonable rate of code examination is about 120 lines of code per hour. This does not work on an eight-hour continuing basis, of course. Hardly anyone can stand to go through a code walkthrough for more than about an hour at a time.

12.B.2.b. Inspections

An **inspection** is an independent review of a product and its associated documentation. An inspection may examine requirements, design, code, and/or testing of a software product. It is formal, planned well in advance, and may involve review of all existing documentation for the system. One objective is to look for defects, but the primary objective is to make sure that all required standards that affect quality are adhered to.

An inspection may involve several weeks notice and involve many people. Members of an inspection team should not be directly associated with the project and should have prior experience working on similar projects. The inspectors must have credibility with the senior software engineers and technical managers of the project under review. Many reviewers may work individually on assigned subsets of the system, each preparing a written evaluation.

The inspectors must be provided access to all relevant documents. They may also make independent tests to verify reported results. The inspectors review the materials and submit comments and suggestions in writing before an inspection review meeting. The conclusion of the inspection is generally a formal meeting in which individual review items are discussed and a final report adopted. That report may certify the compliance with standards, or if deficiencies are found, may recommend corrective measures.

At the time of an inspection meeting, any additional comments and recommendations should be written down as a matter of record. This is because it is unlikely that everything will be remembered, and something said during an inspection may turn out to be remarkably important later.

The exact details of the inspection process vary from one industry to another and from one project to another. A general outline for an inspection is shown in Table 12.4.

Table 12.4 Steps in an Inspection Process

1. Planning - define materials to be inspected, select the inspection team members, schedule meetings, distribute materials to be inspected.
2. Preparation - individual inspectors become familiar with materials, prepare evaluation.
3. Inspection meeting - establish that inspectors are prepared; read the product and record defects; review the defect list; make a decision as whether to accept the software, accept the software after defects are corrected, or schedule another inspection.
4. Rework - all items on the defect list are addressed.
5. Follow-up - inspection team verifies changes that are made.

12.B.2.c. Audits

An **audit** is an independent review to determine if the products specified have been produced according to the plan and specified standards. Such a review is primarily intended to verify that all the mandated components are in order. The primary goal of walkthroughs and inspections is to uncover defects in the system or indications of risks associated with poor quality, but audits are more narrowly focused on conforming to plan or standards. Thus audits are frequently specified as a means of verifying deliverables at a particular phase of a project.

For example, a **configuration audit** identifies that all the components specified are in fact completed and in place. It is impossible to have quality assurance without configuration management. The specific configuration to be evaluated must be absolutely fixed, not altered during the evaluation. This includes confirming that the product has been tested to show compliance with all its specified requirements and that the documentation and manuals do correspond to the specified configuration items. Configuration audits are typically a part of acceptance testing at the time of delivery of the product.

12.B.3. Evaluating Documentation

```
Table 12.5    Evaluation of Documentation

The following  evaluation criteria  are  based on those
found  in  DOD-STD-2168  Software Quality Program [DoD87].
Some  or  all of these evaluations apply to every software
product.

  Adherence to required format and documentation standards.
  Compliance with contractual requirements.
  Internal consistency.
  Understandability.
  Traceability to indicated documents.
  Consistency with indicated documents.
  Appropriate requirements analysis, design, and coding
  techniques used to prepare item.
  Appropriate allocation of sizing and timing resources.
  Adequate test coverage of requirements.
  Testability of requirements.
  Consistency between data definition and use.
  Adequacy of test cases and test procedures.
  Completeness of testing.
  Completeness of regression testing.
```

Evaluation of the software documentation may be done by any organization or a single person within the software development group. The objective of this evaluation is to make sure that all appropriate requirements for each document are fulfilled. Types of evaluations that need to be done are given in Table 12.5. These types of evaluations apply to one or more software products, and the software quality assurance plan should include a specification of which type of evaluation applies to each software document.

The specific products to be evaluated need to be determined when planning the software quality assurance program. A list of documents that might be reviewed is given in Table 12.6.

```
Table 12.6  Suggested Lists of Specific Products to
            be Evaluated under a Software Quality
            Assurance Plan

Software Requirements
      Software Development Plan
      Software Standards and Procedures Manual
      Software Configuration Management Plan
      Software Quality Program Plan
      Software Requirements Specification
Design Documentation
      Preliminary Design
          Software Top-Level Design Document
          Software Test Plan
          Programmer's Manual
          User's Manual

      Detailed Design
          Software Detailed Design Document
          Unit Test Cases
          Integration Test Cases
          Software Test Description
          Software Programmer's Manual
Test Documentation
      Coding and Unit Test Data
          Source Code
          Object Code
          Unit Test Procedures
          Unit Test Results
          Integration Test Procedures
          Software Test Procedures

      Integration and Testing Data
          Integration Test Results
          Revised Source Code
          Revised Object Code
          Software Test Procedures

      System Testing
          System Test Report
          Revised Source and Object Code
          Software Product Specification
          All Manuals
```

12.B.4. Trend Analysis

Basically, **trend analysis** means keeping track of almost anything that varies over time during the lifetime of a project. The purpose is to provide information. This is a passive process; that is, it does not directly affect the software development project. The results are sometimes surprising.

A measure that is subjected to a trend analysis is usually referred to as a **metric**. Since we do not really have a "software science" yet, quantifying aspects of software projects to try to find something measurable that correlates with quality is a continuing effort. In the meantime there will be a continuing search for useful empirical models of quantifiable measures.

Some suitable candidates for trend analysis are module complexity as measured by McCabe's complexity metric, error quantity and frequency, and compilation frequency. Although frequency of compilation may not seem to be a very serious matter, at least one study has shown that the number of errors introduced in the coding process is directly proportional to the frequency of compilation. That is, those programmers who compiled their source code most often, for any reason, also tended to produce code with the largest number of errors.

Trend analysis within a project is a requirement in many contracts, especially for the military, but the contract may be less than explicit about what it means. Trend analysis can be useful in detecting gross problems during the project and may provide the basis for identifying more subtle factors retrospectively. A competent quality assurance organization will be concerned about whether their efforts are producing long-term improvements in quality attributes. The longer term trends such as declining corrective maintenance costs are important to justify the cost of quality assurance.

12.B.5. Social Factors

The application of quality assurance involves working with the people who are producing and using a software product, as well as the product itself. Quality assurance is not so much concerned with the software product as it is with the process of creating the product. Social factors are the things that are of concern when interacting with the people who produce the software.

Quality assurance, like many other aspects of software development, involves communication. The primary means of communication are still written and spoken. An effective quality assurance person needs to have good communication skills.

One problem is that many software people lack quality assurance training. As many as half the people on a large project may have no formal training in software engineering. Of those who do, quality assurance was probably taught last, if at all. The general lack of quality assurance background in a software group can cause serious communication problems for the quality assurance staff, especially when a software quality assurance program is being started. There may be a substantial need for training before a software quality assurance program becomes effective.

Another aspect of influencing people is authority. There are two kinds of authority: real and apparent. Being able to distinguish between them is important. In the quality assurance area, the authority necessary to influence changes can rarely be enforced by management action. That is why quality assurance people must convince the developers that software quality assurance is in their best interest.

In order to maintain real authority, software quality assurance people need credibility. To achieve this, it is important to understand certain aspects of human needs. The primary requirement you need for credibility is to not only have the necessary technological expertise but also to be careful about the accuracy of your information. Be very sure of your facts if you want to be believed. One slip and you can lose your credibility and your effectiveness. Then any authority you have will quickly go from real to apparent.

On the other hand, real authority can be acquired by demonstrating competence. Keep checking your information and be prepared to keep learning. Remember, if you know all that you are ever going to know, you are not very valuable in quality assurance (or any other aspect of the software business).

Quality assurance programs should provide long-term benefits. However, this is usually accomplished through short-term hardships. It is important to keep emphasizing benefits and finding ways to be helpful to the project team whenever possible.

12.C. Verification and Validation

A key component of quality assurance is to systematically determine whether what has been done corresponds to what should have been done. Also we want to be assured that what has been done was done correctly. This is generally described by the phrase **verification and validation**, sometimes abbreviated **V & V**.

Specifically, if we are checking the results in any one stage of the life cycle against the inputs for that life cycle stage, we refer to the process as **verification**. If we are checking whether the final product satisfies the original Software Requirements Specification, we call the process **validation**. This is separate from the software testing phase, because we must consider how we are going to determine whether the software and system testing were adequate.

12.C.1. Verification and Validation Plans

To ensure that verification and validation are carried out and properly documented in large projects, standards have been developed. The outline for such a plan under the ANSI/IEEE Std. 1012-1986 Software Verification and Validation Plans is given in Figure 12.3.

As in several standards discussed earlier, the outline is a mandatory list of the sections and their order. If a section is omitted, the omission must be noted under the standard section heading, with a comment as to why it is not needed in the current plan. Additional sections that may be needed for a specific project are to be appended at the end of the standard outline.

The definition of the administrative structure for a verification and validation program is a fundamental part of the standard for a plan. The lines of authority and responsibility must be determined before the project reaches the development stage. Note that it is covered in the overview, Section 4 of the outline, as well as in the sections on reporting (Section 6) and on administrative procedures (Section 7).

Notice that a major part of such a plan is the listing of the specific activities to be carried out in each phase of the project and the overall scheduling of the reviews.

```
Figure 12.3   Outline of a Software Verification and Validation
              Plan According to ANSI/IEEE Std 1012-1986

1. Purpose
2. Referenced Documents
3. Definitions
4. Verification and Validation Overview
        4.1 Organization
        4.2 Master Schedule
        4.3 Resources Summary
        4.4 Responsibilities
        4.5 Tools, Techniques, and Methodologies
5. Life-Cycle Verification and Validation
        5.1 Management of V&V
        5.2 Concept Phase V&V
        5.3 Requirements Phase V&V
        5.4 Design Phase V&V
        5.5 Implementation Phase V&V
        5.6 Test Phase V&V
        5.7 Installation and Checkout Phase V&V
        5.8 Operation and Maintenance Phase V&V
6. Software Verification and Validation Reporting
7. Verification and Validation Administrative Procedures
        7.1 Anomaly Reporting and Resolution
        7.2 Task Iteration Policy
        7.3 Deviation Policy
        7.4 Control Procedures
        7.5 Standards, Practices, and Conventions
```

12.C.2. Compliance with Specifications

If specifications are properly written, verification may be simply a matter of auditing the properties of the items produced against the requirements documents. In the design phase this means determining that there are units whose individual specifications indicate that they carry out a specific function that will satisfy a system requirement.

There may be difficulty when a requirement is not clearly assignable to one or a few units. An example might be a performance limit. If there is a basis for evaluating a simulation we may be able to verify the consistency and assumptions made. Clearly we cannot verify that all the specifications will be met at this stage.

The uncertainties of determining whether the needs of the user are being met makes it valuable to carefully examine the use of any prototypes by users to try to verify that the specifications of the user interface are adequate. The verification goal is to prevent the introduction of defects at each stage.

When we get into the implementation stage we can be more certain of verifying the specifications of individual modules. The specifications of module interfaces and algorithmic functions may be defined precisely. Depending on the organization's standards, this may involve a representation in a program development language, algebraic notation, state diagrams, decision tables, or some other form. Precise specifications are subject to verification against the code that implements the required functions. Again, in this phase the goal is to assure by good practices that defects are not being created.

The major task of the testing phase is defect detection and removal. The major verification tasks are the determination that the testing program is properly planned and carried out according to plan. A verification and validation team may be involved in replicating some tests or conducting some independent tests.

Test results and interpretations by the test team must be inspected. Problem reports must be scrutinized to determine that when defects are identified, the test team and the developers are using consistent interpretations of the specifications. If a discrepancy in interpreting a specification is found, it must be resolved.

Especially at the end of the project it is essential to carry out a validation of the system in the intended operational environment. The ultimate test is whether the system meets all the requirements in the user's environment. The last step in a verification and validation program is to audit the delivered configuration of the system and to certify that all the software components, documentation, manuals, and so on are in the prescribed form; all the prescribed elements are present; all the specifications have been met; and the acceptance criteria have been complied with.

12.C.3. Who Does the V & V ?

A team assigned to perform verification or validation tasks will generally be chosen to cover a range of skill areas. The members of the team should not include anyone who participated in the project being examined. The team thus may be drawn from the ranks of experienced professionals from other parts of the organization. In some cases there may be a contract with an independent outside organization to supply a team and carry out verification and validation.

Independent verification and validation has a major advantage in assuring the integrity of the development. A fully independent verification and validation team effort, however, is expensive. In addition, defense contracting experience has shown that reporting and feedback from such efforts produces delays in the project.

A verification and validation team may have members from the organization who will be responsible for the maintenance of the system. If the project is being produced under contract to another organization, the contract may specify that their representatives will participate in some verification and validation activities as one of the acceptance requirements. In the case of defense contracts, the military may have a team of auditors resident at the contractor's site.

The technical skills of a verification and validation team must be highly competent and current. To ensure this, the members should not be permanently assigned to such a team. Team members should be rotated back to development, testing, and/or analysis jobs on current projects at least annually.

If your project is planning to undergo an independent verification and validation process, you want to be sure that it will pass all the examinations. Thus you will have your own quality assurance personnel working with the analysts, designers, implementors, and test personnel to establish work practices to achieve the quality goals. On the other hand, if you are not subject to independent verification and validation, the software quality assurance personnel will check quality in each phase.

12.C.4. Validation, Functional Testing, and Acceptance

The project is transferred to the users upon completion of acceptance tests carried out to verify the functionality of the system. Naturally, it is irrational to submit the system for the acceptance test until you are sure it will pass. Thus the functional system tests are important for validation of the system. These tests cover all the specified features and performance factors. Proper tests also cover aspects that are not explicitly specified but are understood to be necessary to the target application and environment. These activities involve the test team and quality assurance people.

The functional testing should involve the same (or equivalent) test data and configuration details as the acceptance test. These tests are normally extensive and should be expected to comprise about 10% of total system documentation.

The difficulty of completing the tests can depend on who designed them: the designers, an independent software quality assurance group, or the buyer. Each group has potential biases with different risks of reducing the product quality. These are summarized in Table 12.7.

Table 12.7   Potential Risks of Inadequate Functional
             Testing Based on Biases of Test Planner

Functional Test Planner	Possible Bias and Consequences
Designer	Bias toward design structural details. Validates code elements well. May be weak on operational details.
Buyer	Bias toward operational factors. Strong test of operation and performance. May have factors hard to relate to design.
Independent QA	Bias to strongly follow specification. Purely functional tests may be harder to relate to design. May not adequately cover operational concerns that are implicit, not fully specified.

The designers tend to set up tests that are biased toward structural details of the design, making it easer for them to validate code elements. This can risk producing a system of bug-free code that the user hates because it does not function well operationally.

The buyer is likely to bias tests toward operational details of most interest to them, and which they understand well from earlier systems. The risk for the designers is that it may be difficult to relate deficiencies to code elements.

An independent quality assurance team should base functional tests on the software requirements specification. The risk here depends on the adequacy of the specification. Since these biases are to be expected, it is appropriate that the functional tests required for acceptance should be arrived at by negotiation.

12.D. Statistical Quality Control

Statistical quality control rests on the assumption that we can gather suitably large samples of data to validate a statistical model of a process. Given validated models, we can get an acceptable estimate of quality for a given product based on limited measurements. Reasonable measures can be obtained from an analysis of defect removals during the testing phase of software development. Defects found can be counted and classified by severity. Presumably the defect removal process has a particular efficiency, which we might predict and hence give an estimate on the number of defects remaining.

One of the serious problems with building statistical models of defect content of software is the meager amount of published data. The vast majority of software development organizations would not dream of publishing the actual history of defects discovered through the life of a software product. If they know how to reduce defects by quantitative metrics performed on software specifications, designs, and code, they are not going to reveal their proprietary tools or publish proof that they are effective. As a result, each organization that is serious about quality must do its own data collection and build empirical models to evaluate alternative strategies.

Quality assurance cannot be legislated. Standards cannot be imposed by fiat. If quality is to improve, software professionals at all stages of the life cycle have to have an incentive to work on quality as an organizational goal. Management has to be committed to providing the resources to achieve quality.

If there is commitment to improve quality, then the necessary data will be collected. The data will be analyzed to determine what changes in procedures and combinations of tools and methods in fact improve quality. Since there is no predictive theory of how to write a correct specification or how to implement only correct programs, methods and results must be measured and compared. It costs money for training, tools, and measurement, so better quality will not be cheap.

One metric we can measure is the cumulative cost of the debugging and testing necessary to prove that defects have been eradicated. The cost per defect is highly unreliable as an indicator of quality. Bad code with lots of defects can have low cost per defect removal but high total cost, while leaving large numbers of defects to be delivered with the product. Good software may have fewer defects to be removed but they may be individually more difficult and expensive to eradicate. T. C. Jones has suggested that a metric better suited to assessing quality is defect removal cost per thousand lines of code.

The effects of alternative practices, new methodologies, and new tools must be justified on the basis of demonstration of their effectiveness. Many of the factors influencing software development will remain as stochastic variables, so inevitably our models are likely to be statistical. Thus further development of statistical quality control is likely to be a foundation of future development of software quality and reliability.

As Frederick Brooks has indicated in his provocative paper, "No Silver Bullet," there may not be any magic method to give us a breakthrough to produce better software, faster. Yet there are many reasons to expect that we can improve our methods and results. The key to achieving progress and not just change is measurement. We must continue to develop metrics and spend the resources necessary to validate the measures of software.

Summary

Software quality needs to be of concern to all software project personnel at all stages of a software project. At the present time, the state of software quality is reflected, to some extent, in the software warranties, which disclaim all responsibility for any aspect of the software.

Software quality has to be defined in context for each project undertaken. Some are concerned with efficiency, others with reliability, and still others with modifiability, to name a few parameters. Quality assurance must be planned into the entire software project from the start. Ideally, the software quality assurance team is independent from the development team.

Aspects of quality must be documented in some type of Quality Assurance Plan. One standard is ANSI/IEEE Standard 730-1984. Standards are useful in achieving software quality assurance. Standards may be set by a company or by an organization such as ANSI or IEEE.

Reviews are more important for quality assurance than anything else. They are effective and they are low cost. Reviews may consist of walkthroughs, inspections, or audits. All relevant documents for a software project need to be reviewed with quality assurance in mind. DOD-STD-2168 Software Quality Program [DoD87] mandates a specific list of documents to review.

Trend analysis, a passive activity, involves the collection of information and analyzing parameters with respect to time.

Quality assurance personnel may have many problems doing their job, partly because there is little appreciation for exactly what quality assurance is, and less appreciation for its importance when the pressure of shorter term deadlines is felt. Quality assurance people need good communication skills and a high level of credibility.

Verification and validation are used to determine quality assurance. This involves making sure that whatever was done was what was supposed to be done, and that it was done correctly. A standard for a Software Verification and Validation Plan is ANSI/IEEE Std. 1012-1986. Verification and validation may be done by a team associated with the software development company or by an outside team. The team should be independent of the development team.

Quality assurance can be assisted by keeping records on several metrics in a software project. One of these is the cost of defect removal per thousand lines of code. This and other metrics can be used to build statistical models that will help us determine the effectiveness of methodologies for software quality assurance.

Keywords

audit
apparent authority
code walkthroughs
configuration audit
critical applications
inspection
metric
quality
Quality Assurance Plan
real authority
review
social factors
software quality assurance (SQA)
Software Verification and Validation Plan
software warranty
standard
statistical quality control
structured walkthrough
trend analysis
verification and validation (V & V)
walkthrough

Review Questions

12.1.   How does a software warranty compare with other types of warranties?

12.2.   At what point in the software life cycle does quality assurance apply?

12.3.   With regard to software, what is quality?

12.4.   What factors are attributes of software quality?

12.5.   What determines the most important aspects of software quality for a specified software project?

12.6.   How does the software quality assurance team plan for quality?

12.7. What is a Quality Assurance Plan? What are the important components of such a plan?

12.8. Which team members of a software project need to be concerned with quality?

12.9. What are the responsibilities of a quality assurance team?

12.10. Whom does the quality assurance team report to?

12.11. What is a standard? Name two organizations concerned with setting standards for software.

12.12. What are software reviews? How effective are they?

12.13. What is the difference between a code walkthrough, an inspection, and an audit?

12.14. What sort of documents need to be considered before writing the Software Quality Assurance Plan?

12.15. What is trend analysis? What is it good for? What can it measure?

12.16. What is the difference between real and apparent authority?

12.17. How much training in quality assurance has the typical software engineer received? How much have you received? Do you think it is enough?

12.18. How important is credibility to software quality assurance personnel? How do you maintain your credibility?

12.19. What is meant by verification and validation?

12.20. Name a standard for verification and validation plans.

12.21. What background is needed for the verification and validation team? Whom should they report to?

12.22. What biases are likely to be introduced into tests designed for verification and validation?

12.23. What is statistical quality control? What is it used for?

12.24. What are some of the problems associated with building models to use with statistical data?

12.25. How important are metrics in software quality assurance?

12.26. Why would someone calculate the cost per defect for a software project? How useful is this parameter? Name an alternate metric for assessing quality.

Exercises

12.1. Examine the warranty provisions of the compiler you use most frequently. How does it differ from the one shown in Figure 12.1?

12.2. For a specific software project, give a list of the four most important quality factors.

12.3.   Draw an organizational hierarchy chart for a software development organization with four software project teams. Show where test teams and a quality assurance team would fit in. Assume that each project is headed by a chief programmer and that the development organization is headed by a technical manager with two ad ministrative assistants.

12.4.   Produce an outline of the steps you would take to conduct verification at the end of requirements analysis for a project to produce an interactive order processing system for a catalog sales organization.

12.5.   Describe the potential conflicts of interest involved if verification and validation are carried out solely by members of the same team that produced the system.

12.6.   List at least three different ways to count lines of code. Outline the requirements for a tool to perform the counting by each rule set.

12.7.   What is the value of reported results related to lines of code, where the counting rules and language are not reported?

12.8.   Specify a tool to generate McCabe's metric from source code text by counting keywords for conditional branches and looping. For your choice of language, what are the keywords needed?

12.9.   If the developer has no liability or responsibility beyond passing an acceptance test, what should the buyer worry about?

12.10. What is the risk to the buyer in the acceptance test if the developer has complete definition of the acceptance test and test data? What is the risk to the developer if the acceptance test and its input data are not available prior to the test?

References

Beizer, Boris. Micro-Analysis of Computer System Performance. New York: Van Nostrand-Reinhold, 1978.

> An exposition of performance modeling based on calculating module execution time requirements by analysis of the source code. The methodology is based on adding up the execution times for each operation in the algorithm, arithmetic operations, fetching an array element, testing a loop condition, making an assignment, etc. Such analyses can be done by hand or with software tools to count up every operator, with suitable factors for iteration counts, and probability of branch conditions to count on code blocks.

Beizer, Boris. Software System Testing and Quality Assurance. New York: Van Nostrand-Reinhold, 1984.

> Systematic review of system testing with extensive discussions of quality assurance activities.

Brooks, Frederick P. Jr. "No Silver Bullet." IEEE Computer 20, no. 4 (April 1987): 10-19.

> Fashioning complex conceptual constructs is the essence; accidental tasks arise in representing the constructs in language. Past progress has so reduced the accidental tasks that future progress now depends on addressing the essence.

Brown, Bradley J. "Assurance of Software Quality." SEI Curriculum Module SEI-CM-7-1.0. Carnegie-Mellon University, Software Engineering Institute, April 1987.

> Good overview of some practical aspects of quality assurance.

Cho, Chin-Kuei. Quality Programming: Developing and Testing Software with Statistical Quality Control. New York: Wiley, 1987.

> Statistical quality control is extended by analogy from manufacturing to software development. Cho sidesteps many of the methodological problems of transferring a statistical quality control method from manufacturing process control, which deals with continuous random variables, to models of computer programs, which are inherently based on many discrete variables. Much remains to be done to develop applications that really achieve statistical quality control.

Chow, T. S. ed. Software Quality Assurance, A Practical Approach. Washington, DC: IEEE Computer Society Press, 1985.

> A collection of 43 papers providing a comprehensive tutorial introduction to software quality assurance.

Christensen, K., Fitsos, G., and Smith, C. "A Perspective on Software Science," IBM Systems Journal 20, no. 4 (1985): 372-88.

> A review of a number of experiments attempting to validate various aspects of Software Science experimentally.

Conte, S. D., Dunsmore, H. E., and Shen, V. Y. Software Engineering Metrics and Models. Menlo Park, CA: Benjamin/Cummings, 1986.

> Improving software engineering practice and software quality requires experimental verification of new practices and methods of measurement. This is an introduction to essential methods for establishing quality assurance.

DeMarco, Tom. Controlling Software Projects: Management, Measurement & Estimation. Englewood Cliffs, NJ: Yourdon Press, 1982.

> An introduction to software cost estimation and project control. A variety of metrics and models of software creation factors are discussed in relation to assessing software quality.

DeMillo, Richard A., McCracken, W. Michael, Martin, R.S. and Passafiume, John F. Software Testing and Evaluation. Menlo Park, CA: Benjamin/Cummings, 1987.

> A systematic review of defense software contracting experience with quality assurance, verification, and validation.

Dunn, R., and Ullman, R. Quality Assurance for Computer Software. New York: McGraw-Hill, 1982.

> An early effort to define the emerging discipline of software quality assurance. Discusses the scope and implementation of quality assurance written for developers and managers.

Fagan, M. E. "Advances in Software Inspections," IEEE Transactions on Software Engineering 12, no. 7 (1986): 744-751.

> The paper reviews experience in performing many formal code inspections. Properly conducted inspections on code that is compiled and covers current design specifications will detect 50 to 90% of defects present.

Glass, Robert L. Software Soliloquies. Computing Trends, P.O. Box 213, State College PA 16804, 1981.

> Collection of essays on software engineering, light reading style with some profound observations. Includes "Quality is Sometimes Only Skin Deep."

Halstead, Maurice H. Elements of Software Science. New York: Elsevier North-Holland, 1977.

> A small but important book collecting the original work on Halstead's metrics.

Institute of Electrical and Electronics Engineers. Software Engineering Standards. Wiley-Interscience, October 1987.

> A collection of 13 standards documents published as one volume. Standards are revised at least once every five years and additional standards are under development. Individual standards are also published by the IEEE Computer Society Press.
>
> Includes "ANSI/IEEE Std 730-1984, Software Quality Assurance Plans," which is concerned with legal liability. It is directed toward the development and maintenance of software that concerns safety or large financial or social implications. Defines the 13-point topic outline for a quality assurance plan. "ANSI/IEEE Std 828-1983, Software Configuration Management Plans," is similar to Std 730-1984, Software Quality Assurance Plans, but limited to software configuration. Provides a means by which the steps in the software are recorded, communicated, and controlled. "ANSI/IEEE Std 983-1986, Software Quality Assurance Planning," explains the contents of a software quality assurance plan. Directed at the requirements in Std 730-1984, Software Quality Assurance Plans. An extension and clarification of ANSI/IEEE 730-1984 for application to critical applications. "ANSI/IEEE Std 1012-1986, Software Verification and Validation Plans," sets minimum requirements for verification and validation plans for critical projects and recommends minimum standards for noncritical projects.

Jones, T. Capers. Programming Productivity. New York: McGraw-Hill, 1986.

> A careful review of practical software metrics. The author carefully describes the adverse effects of many poorly chosen metrics on software productivity and quality, with a good description of the faults of various uses of lines of code counting, noting the general failure of published figures based on LOC to cite the counting rules actually used.

Lipow, M. "Number of Faults Per Line of Code." IEEE Trans. on Software Engineering 8 (1982): 437-439.

> An example of the sparse literature on error rates from the history of delivered software.

Musa, J. D., Iannino, A., and Okunoto, K. Software Reliability: Measurement, Prediction, Application. New York: McGraw-Hill, 1987.

> An introduction to statistical quality control methodology based heavily on well-developed earlier practices in industrial statistical quality control and management.

Weinberg, G. M., and Schulman, E.L., "Goals and Performance in Computer Programming," Human Factors. 16, no. 1 (February 1974): 70-77.

> A review of early experiments examining programmer performance. The importance of careful control of an experiment is outlined in view of the wide range in programmer performance which is typically observed.

Weinberg, Gerald. Rethinking Systems Analysis. New York: Dorset House, 1982.

> Discusses many realities of software development, including the low-level compliance with structured programming.

Yourdon, E. Structured Walkthroughs. 3rd ed., New York: Yourdon Press, 1986.

> This is a thorough, practical and readable description of all the details needed to conduct walkthroughs to review software projects.

CHAPTER 13

SOFTWARE PROTECTION, SECURITY, AND ETHICS

It is a very humbling experience to make a multimillion-dollar mistake, but it is also very memorable.

- Frederick P. Brooks, Jr., *The Mythical Man-Month*

Behold the mighty dinosaur,
Famous in prehistoric lore
Not only for his power and length
But for his intellectual strength.

You will observe by these remains
The creature had two sets of brains —
One in his head (the usual place)
The other at his spinal base.

Thus he could reason a priori
As well as a posteriori.
No problem bothered him a bit;
He made both head and tail of it.

So wise was he, so wise and solemn
Each thought filled just a spinal column.
If one brain found the pressure strong
It passed a few ideas along.

If something slipped his forward mind
'Twas rescued by the one behind.
And if in error he was caught
He had a saving afterthought.

As he thought twice before he spoke
He had no judgment to revoke.
Thus he could think without congestion
Upon both sides of every question.

Oh, gaze upon this model beast
Defunct ten million years at least.
- Bert Leston Taylor

13.A. Introduction

In this chapter, we examine a number of things that can happen to our software and look at ways to provide protection against damage, loss, theft, or vandalism. One aspect of protecting software involves intellectual property rights and the various means of legal protection for software. This may involve copyright, trade secrets, licenses, employee contracts, trademarks, and patents. Each has its advantages and drawbacks; the choice depends on the circumstances. The term integrity is used in connection with possible losses of data or software due to hardware or software failures, for which the primary protection is making backup copies. We will also consider software and data security against accidental or intentional damage or disclosure by users, programmers, or outside agents.

Finally, we look briefly at the subject of computer ethics, including a description of a major incident, the Internet worm, which impelled several professional organizations to issue explicit statements of ethics in regard to the use of networks. As professional computer scientists, we need to be concerned with the ethics of all aspects of computer use.

13.B. Software Protection

Software is frequently referred to as intellectual property, and the legal rights to the use of such property require protection. Software is not free; great effort is required to produce good software. The owner of the software has a reasonable expectation that economic value might be derived from it.

Software protection has two aspects: technical and legal. Technical protection schemes involve proprietary hardware and software methods of limiting the use of software products, which we will not explore here. We will survey the legal arena, because we feel that everyone professionally involved with software should be aware of the range of issues involved. Laws with regard to computer software, especially copyright laws, have changed considerably in the last decade. Furthermore, many lawsuits involving software rights and infringement are pending. A particular issue is whether user interface style and command languages can be protected by copyright. Some are claiming that the "look and feel" of an interface is protected by copyright. This issue has not yet been decided in the courts.

The general descriptions of the various legal issues in protecting software as intellectual property will help you to understand the legal battles that will continue to be waged during the next several years. To make matters more complicated, the decision arrived at in a particular case may depend, among other factors, on where the suit is brought. This is because the country is divided into several legal jurisdictions, and precedents by courts in prior cases apply in that particular jurisdiction. If two courts at the same level but in different parts of the country reached different decisions in similar cases (which has happened), then different precedents would be in effect for the lower courts in those jurisdictions. This continues until cases on the issues eventually reach the U.S. Supreme Court and are decided.

Many of these cases involve subtle points of dispute which we will not attempt to go into. Instead, in this section we will summarize briefly the major established methods of legal software protection.

13.B.1. Who Owns the Software?

One of the consequences of a software engineering practice emphasizing reusable code and group effort is that individuals who work on the code do not own it. In almost all cases, their efforts are "work for hire," in the terminology of copyright law. Hence any software produced, if subject to copyright, is owned by the employer. If the work done is a derivative of earlier copyrighted work, the copyright of the original work may determine the ownership.

Ownership rights to software also may be determined by contract. Copyrights, of course, can be transferred by written agreement of the parties involved. Thus if an individual has created a valuable piece of software and claims copyright to it, he or she should examine employment contracts carefully. The usual terms of employment contracts, unless separately negotiated, may restrict the employee from owning any software worked on while employed. That is to say, any code produced during the period of employment belongs to the employer.

Furthermore, if any of the individual's own code, previously owned, were to be used in a company project, it could be claimed by the company. The individual creator must negotiate a release from the employer in advance if he or she wants to retain rights to prior work that is likely to be used by or for the benefit of the employer.

If the rights to software are based on trade secrets, the result is the same. If you use your valuable software on the job or incorporate it into a company project, that software is not your secret anymore.

Another constraint on the rights to software is in the terms of license of the software tools required to produce it. The software tools are usually not sold, merely leased under a limited license for use. It is not unusual that a compiler for a language will be provided with a restricted license to produce programs for use on one machine. Thus any effort to propagate the software to another installation or to sell the software created requires negotiation with the owner of the compiler.

The restrictions in licenses of software to academic institutions are often very limiting since the vendor wants substantial protection and assurance against commercial use when supplying software at a discount for student use. Thus the university is usually bound not to allow its users to own software that may be created using these tools, or to require that such software be placed in the public domain.

One of the problems in dealing with managing software development is the tendency of some programmers to think that they own any piece of software that they write. Such an attitude may occur independent of any true legal claim of ownership. The tendency to adopt this sort of territorial claim on software is not supported by existing laws, which presume that work produced belongs to the employer. To claim the ownership of software, the creator must make an original creation and own, or be able to establish legitimate access to, the tools necessary to its production.

13.B.2. Copyright

Software may be copyrighted as source code or object code, or both. This was not always the case. For ninety years, the copyright law was interpreted to mean that anything that could not be read by humans could not be copyrighted. This was based on a decision involving player pianos. The Apollo Company had taken music published and copyrighted by the Smith-White Music Company and made it into a piano roll for player pianos. Smith-White sued for copyright infringement, but the Supreme

Court ruled that since the piano rolls could not be read by humans, they were not subject to copyright laws. Since object code cannot be read by humans, a direct analogy was drawn between software and piano rolls.

However, this decision was overruled by the Copyright Act of 1976 and the Computer Software Copyright Act of 1980. Both now provide copyright protection for software. To be suitable for copyright protection, the software must be an original work in any tangible medium of expression from which it can be communicated, either by itself or machine aided. This covers both source and object code variations of software.

Either published or unpublished software may be registered with the Copyright Office. In fact, the first step in establishing a copyright is to put a copyright notice in the software prior to its publication (or distribution). That can be done by inserting prominently in the software a notice of the form: "Copyright © 1990 by Crankemout Software, Inc. All rights reserved." That of course costs nothing. To complete the establishment of a copyright requires paying a filing fee and submitting a copy and a registration form to the Copyright Office.

The limitation of copyright is that it applies only to a specific expression of an idea, not the idea itself. That is, an idea cannot be copyrighted. Therefore, something that is similar in idea and appearance, but not exactly the same expression, is not an infringement of copyright. To protect an idea, the use of patent, trade secret, and license contracts are available.

13.B.3. Trade Secrets

Trade secrets protect ideas rather than the specific expression of an idea, and as such are more suitable for software protection. Trade secret law protects both source and object code. However, unlike copyright law, trade secret laws are not Federal, but a matter of state law. Each state has its own version and its own remedies for violation.

The most important consideration in protecting software by trade secret is to keep the software a secret. This means that all copies of the software, in any form, must be kept under lock and key at all times. It also means that anyone, anywhere, who sees the software in either source or object form, for any reason, must be informed that the software is considered a trade secret and should sign a nondisclosure agreement before being allowed access. It is important to keep careful records of anyone who has access to the software for any reason, and to keep copies of the signed nondisclosure forms.

13.B.4. Licenses

A license is a contractual agreement between a software producer and a distributor or user of the software. The producer retains ownership of the software. The licensed distributor agrees to market the software and pay royalties to the producer. This involves protection for both the producer and the distributor. It means that the distributor will invest time and money in inventory and advertising. It means that the producer will find out how good the marketplace thinks the software is.

If you are in the enviable position of having to choose a distributor for your software, here are some considerations to keep in mind. First, you should have confidence in the integrity of your distributor. This may be based on personal experience or the company's reputation. Second, you need to have confidence in the marketing ability of the distributor. It doesn't matter what the percentage of royalty is if the distributor can't sell many copies of your software.

As a software user you should understand the provisions of the licenses for the software you may be using. The legal penalties to you and your employer can be severe if you violate the rights of the software's owner. You should read and understand every provision of a license contract before you sign it.

13.B.5. Employee Contracts

Before you go to work for a company, you need to understand who has the rights to any software you may produce while you are employed by that company. Some companies will ask you to sign an employee contract, an explicit agreement saying that anything you create while in their employ (including software you produce on weekends working in your own home) belongs to the company.

If this sounds outrageous to you, look all the more carefully at the company you are about to work for. Under current copyright law, in the absence of any explicit agreement, any software you produce under the circumstances described above still belongs to the company. If you wish to retain the right to software you produce on your own time, you must obtain agreement from the employer before you join the company.

13.B.6. Trademark

A trademark is a word and/or symbol that distinguishes your product from the products of other companies. The trademark must not be too generic. For example, you probably could not use the term "database" as a trademark for a product, since that term is widely used in the software business. You also need to make sure that the trademark you want to use is not already in use by someone else for a similar product. This can be done by searching through trademark records in Washington, D.C.

A trademark must be registered, but this cannot be done until it is already in use. (This is partly to prevent someone from registering a trademark just to keep anyone else from using it.) This means you need to sell at least one copy of your software using the trademark you want. It is not necessary to register your trademark immediately, which is convenient. You can use it for a while to see if you like it. If you decide to change it, you won't have to go to the trouble of registering twice.

Trademark registration involves first getting the appropriate forms from the Commissioner of Patents and Trademarks, U.S. Patent and Trademark Office, Washington, D.C. 20231. You need to have made a trademark search, and you need to submit copies of your trademark design.

After submitting your application, you will be notified by the Patent and Trademark Office whether your trademark has been placed in their registers or rejected. It may be rejected because it is too similar to another trademark.

Before your trademark is registered, you may use TM next to your trademark on your products. After it is registered, you may also use the symbol ®. Then, if someone else uses your trademark, you can sue under federal trademark laws.

13.B.7. Patent

It is difficult, but not impossible, to patent software. It is relatively more expensive than other forms of protection, and the time involved in obtaining a patent is relatively long, an average of two years. For many years, there were few patent applications for software. However, recently the number of patent applications for computer software has increased dramatically.

At one time, the Patent and Trademark Office considered computer software inventions unpatentable. Computer programs were considered merely algorithms or "principles of nature." The basis for rejecting patent applications containing programs was that there are several categories of unpatentable subject matter; including mathematical formulas, arrangements of printed matter, methods of doing business, and processes involving human judgment. However, in 1981 the Supreme Court, in *Diamond v. Diehr*, held that if a process were patentable if it were not executed by a computer, it should be patentable even if it is executed by a computer.

Patents for computer software are subject to some restrictions. Computer programs are not actually patentable, but computers operated by novel and unobvious programs are patentable. Since computers are machines that implement processes, this puts them within the definition of patentable subject matter in the patent statute.

One problem with patenting software is called "prior art." This refers to publications and patents dated before the software or one year before applying for a patent. It also refers to offers for sale or public use or sale in the United States for more than a year before applying for a patent.

This means that a piece of software that is not fully developed, but is offered for sale as a new product on a test basis, can nullify qualification for patent. The trick is to be sure to apply for a patent within a year of any commercial activity.

Obtaining a patent involves filing an application with the Patent and Trademark Office and fulfilling several qualifications. The software must meet requirements of novelty and unobviousness. The patent application must include a definition of the software and a specification that completely discloses it. It is not necessary to submit the actual computer program. Flowcharts or other types of diagrams are generally preferred. The requirement is that there must be enough detail for a suitably skilled person to construct the system.

The Patent and Trademark Office reviews the application, and either issues the patent or rejects it. If the application is rejected, it may be amended so as to fulfill patent requirements, as long as nothing new is added. The Patent and Trademark Office reviews the amended application, and either issues a patent or rejects it. At this point, if the application is rejected, the applicant has the choice of appealing the decision or giving up.

During the process, the application is kept secret. If the patent is granted, the application is made public, but is now protected. If the patent is denied, the application is kept secret. Therefore, there is no risk in terms of disclosure in applying for a patent.

To maintain a patent, annual fees must be paid for up to 17 years, after which the subject of the patent enters the public domain and is no longer protected.

The protection provided by patents is enormous. A patent protects the underlying ideas in the software, and provides exclusive rights to the patent holder against anyone else using these concepts. Other software does not have to be a complete and exact copy of yours for you to claim violation of your patent rights. If another piece of software contains all the parts or steps of at least one patented claim, that software infringes the patent, even if the infringing software is an improvement over the patented software. Furthermore, if someone else has software that does substantially the same things in substantially the same way to obtain substantially the same results, patent infringement can be claimed.

Patent rights are exclusive rights. A patent may be infringed even if the infringer has no knowledge of the patent. The patent holder is entitled to a court order to the infringer to cease, and the patent holder can sue for damages. In this regard, patents provide much stronger protection than copyrights.

Patents and trade secrets are generally incompatible because the specification of the software in the patent application must give the best method of implementation. This means that the best idea for a piece of software cannot be kept a trade secret if a valid patent is desired. However, the advantage of patent over trade secret is that accidental disclosure does not nullify the claim.

13.B.8. Selection of Legal Protection Methods

Using one legal method of protection does not necessarily preclude using another. In fact, it is common to pursue more than one method simultaneously. Figure 13.1 summarizes some circumstances in which you might wish to consider specific methods of legal protection.

Before actually embarking on legal protection for your software, we recommend that you look further into one or more of these areas. Several suitable annotated references to get you started are given at the end of the chapter.

Figure 13.1 Legal Protection Methods

ACTIVITY	Copyright	Trade Secret	Contract	Trade Mark
Idea		*		
Flowchart	*	*		
Hiring programmers		*	*	
Writing code	*	*	*	
Negotiating with distributor	*	*	*	
Selling to retailer	*	*	*	*
Selling to end–user	*		*	*
Manuals	*		*	*
Program name				*
TYPE OF PROGRAM				
Source code	*	*		
Mass marketed				*
Object code	*			*
Limited distribution				
End–user programs	*	*	*	*
Operating system	*	*	*	*
Compilers	*	*	*	*

Remer, Daniel. Legal Care for Your Software, Berkley, CA: Nolo Press, 1982.

13.C. Software Security and Integrity

Threats to the security and integrity of software include accidental or intentional damage from users, programmers, outside agents, or natural disasters. **Integrity** is generally associated with assuring the correctness and preservation of machine-readable files against unintentional changes. **Security** is concerned with prevention of unauthorized access and/or intentional but unauthorized alteration of software, data, or systems.

Software needs to be protected from humans. Damage may come from accidental alteration or deletion. A user may erase files, reformat a disk, or use an executable program with an incompatible operating system. Someone entering an unauthorized part of the system may alter or erase files. Even if files are not altered, reading sensitive information from an unauthorized file constitutes a security problem. Hidden programs may be introduced into a system, such as a virus, a worm, or a Trojan horse, which can do all sorts of damage.

Unintended damage to software can result if software is moved to another system that has an incompatible machine language or operating system. Similarly, a new program that is being tested may run wild and do all sorts of things the programmer never intended. In some systems, the hardware and operating system may not prevent deleterious effects on other files.

Natural disasters may occur, such as fire, flood, lightning, earthquake, rockslide, hurricane, or tornado. Such disasters may cause physical destruction of both the hardware and software. Manmade disasters with similar effects may occur due to vehicle accidents, plumbing failures, leaky roofs, catastrophic failures in the electrical power supply system, vandalism, or terrorist attack.

The first step in a consideration of protecting software and data is a realistic assessment of the most probable threats. In addition, other threats also need to be countered not because they are highly probable, but because of the consequences if a disaster does occur.

We will first look at some ways to prevent problems, or at least minimize their consequences when they occur. These include limiting access to the system, maintaining backup copies, using error checking code, and using cryptography. Finally, we will look at some types of programs that are written for the explicit purpose of violating computer security.

13.C.1. How to Avoid Problems

Although it is true that bad programs can cause havoc, in general, they cannot harm the computer itself. Therefore, we will first concentrate on how to recover from problems associated with the software.

13.C.1.a. Thou Shalt Make Backups

Probably nothing is more important in the area of software security than to have all software backed up at all times. This does not just mean duplicate copies of files on the machine on which you are working. It means independent machine-readable files on a separate medium. Backup copies must be secure. Backups should be stored off-site, especially if the data and programs are critical. In a mainframe computer environment this is a process carried out by the computer center operations staff. In a mini-computer or microcomputer environment this is often the duty of the user who is the operator.

In addition to machine-readable backup copies, it is appropriate to have hard copy. This sometimes has been used as a last resort, since it must be retranscribed into machine-readable form. Nonetheless, it is better than no backup.

Backups, of course, do not prevent security or integrity problems. However, if a problem occurs, once the problem is identified and solved you should be able to restore the system from backups of your software and data.

13.C.1.b. Incompatibilities

Many problems in small computer systems can be caused by incompatibilities between machines and different DOS versions. If you are using, for example, an IBM-PC with the PC-DOS operating system, you need to know which version of the operating system you have. Some utilities provided with the operating system will run properly under one version but not another.

If you are working in a laboratory with several microcomputers that have different versions of the same operating system, you can cause chaos by copying utility programs from one system to another. The problem is even worse if you have several variations, such as IBM-PCs and clones, some running MS-DOS and some running PC-DOS. Good practice is, of course, to standardize the operating environments to one operating system version.

The first line of defense is to be careful in moving software between machines. You are responsible for knowing where the software came from. Commercial software licenses generally require that the software only be used on a single machine.

If a piece of software bonds itself to your machine by reading a serial number out of a ROM or from your copy of the operating system, you have little basis for complaint if it subsequently does not run properly on another machine. Don't play with pirated software. It is fine to move data files or source code files from one machine to another, but be skeptical about moving executable files.

Many people have access to microcomputers at home or at work as well as on campus. If you are using different PCs, and especially if they are using different versions of DOS, don't move copies of DOS or its utility programs between them. Use the version of DOS only on the machine it came with. If you are working with bootable floppy disks, you should label each disk for the DOS version/machine it was created for.

13.C.1.c. Public Domain and Shareware Software

If you are going to use public domain software or shareware, spend a little time testing it before mingling it with important files. Ask yourself before trying new software: Is everything that is accessible in the machine backed up elsewhere?

There is a lot of very good public domain and shareware software available (as well as a lot of software that doesn't do much, but won't cause any harm, either). However, hackers have been known to damage such software before making it available on bulletin boards. Be especially cautious when using new programs from questionable sources.

A good practice is to check the size, creation time and creation date of any new software against documentation, if any, that describes these details. In any event, protect yourself and your software with backups.

13.C.1.d. Other Problems

A natural disaster may partially damage a system. Immediate action is needed to prevent further damage. For example, a damaged building may cause a computer to be rained on. The system should have a built-in means of shutting itself off. In case of fire, the computer system should not be protected by sprinklers; rather, CO_2 or halogen fire extinguishers should be nearby. There should be surge suppressors and circuit breakers to protect against power line fluctuations. There should be standard operating procedures for orderly shutdown in the event of substantial threats to the system.

It is sometimes possible for badly written or poorly tested software to run amok and damage other files, even if the author had no malicious intent. If that program you just wrote trashes the only copy of a term paper on the same disk, who's at fault?

It is possible to protect a system to some extent from some sources of sabotage. One of the most common sources of deliberate system damage is a disgruntled employee. Therefore, one means of ensuring software security is for management to work hard to maximize job satisfaction.

13.C.2. Access Control

The first level of security for a computer system to prevent sabotage and provide confidentiality is access control of the system, including physical access to the system and its terminals. That means control of the rooms in which the equipment resides. Control of access via telecommunication lines is harder, so really secure computers don't talk on telephone lines.

When a user accesses a multiuser system, there must be access controls in the system software to authenticate the user's identity. An identification number or character string and some sort of verification code (password) are typically required. Additional means can involve constraints on what telephone lines are acceptable for remote access and what hours of operation are authorized for access, as well as limitations of accessible resources.

Surveillance of the system should be maintained to monitor its use. Access to the system must be recorded, and any access violations must be logged. Violations may take the form of a password that is entered erroneously. Any user can make a typing error, but a long list of erroneous passwords indicates that some unauthorized user is trying to break in. It is much easier to trap an unauthorized user attempting to use a system when you know that these efforts are being made. A smart system will lock up an account that is under attack by repeated attempts to guess the password.

Surveillance can be done automatically, but it won't do any good unless someone audits the resulting information regularly. This should be done at random intervals, so that knowledge of the audit procedure won't help a hacker.

Access control should be at different levels for different users. Some users may be limited to specific applications, such as running spreadsheets or databases to acquire and/or update information. These users would have access to specific files, with either read-only or read-write privileges. Application programmers would have wider access to some aspects of the system. Systems programmers often have broad access to the system, but their access must also be limited and supervised. Finally, at the highest level of access control there must be a very small number of people who have the authority to set all the levels of access. You don't want every user who has access to the system to peek into the databases or tinker with the heart of the system.

Unauthorized access is in the same category as housebreaking. It doesn't matter whether the door was unlocked; unauthorized entry is still unethical. However, sensible people will try to keep the doors locked.

13.C.2.a. Physical Security

A major problem with security of microcomputers is the portability of the software and hardware. Unfortunately it is often too easy for someone to copy sensitive data or just walk away with floppy disks. Some microcomputers have key locks that impede access by an unauthorized user. However, the possibility that someone may walk off with the entire microcomputer cannot be discounted. Physical security in this case consists of making sure that disks are locked up and that the rooms containing the systems are secure and/or the equipment is bolted down. With larger computers, the risk of someone picking them up and carrying them away is smaller. However, physical access to these computers should be limited.

Since one common method of breaking into computers is via a telephone line, security can take the form of not having telephone access to a system. This means that anyone using the system must be physically present at the system or its hard-wired terminals, and security checks can restrict these people. If the system has telecommunications access it must have reliable access controls.

13.C.2.b. Password Security

In a multiple user system, usually there are two levels of access. The first requires a user name, the second, a password. User names are often created by the system and the user has little choice of what this name is. However, passwords are almost always the brainchild of the user and are designed to be changed.

Too many users do not take the password security of their accounts seriously. Frequently users will choose passwords that are the names of popular heroes or common first names. Other commonly used passwords are trivial variations of the user name or a very short string, used by those who do not want to bother to enter a password. Several variations, as listed in Table 13.1, have been noted in software designed to break into computer networks. Often, systematically trying these variations has been sufficient to access many computer accounts. This is a common security problem.

The problem with using these passwords is that it makes it much too easy for an unauthorized user to obtain access to an account. For example, the Internet worm, described below, gained access to a large number of systems and files simply by using the variations of the user name listed in Table 13.1. Other personal data may be revealed to a hacker browsing personnel files or the company telephone book trying to guess at your password.

```
Table 13.1   How to choose an insecure password  -  The Most
             Commonly Used Passwords. Note: It is a security
             problem if any of these are used!

Passwords based on user name:        User Name:  XYZ

Password:  XYZ
           XYZXYZ
           ZYX
           X (first part of user name)
           Z (last part of user name)
also try with all lowercase letters

Other Common Passwords:
           null (i.e., no password)
           User's name
           User's birthday or anniversary
           User's spouse's name
           Part or all of user's Social Security number
```

A good password should have the attributes listed in Table 13.2. It should be easy for the user to remember, but not anyone else. That is, it should be something meaningful to the user that would not be easy for someone else to obtain from his or her personnel records; for example, your mother or mother-in-law's birth name, possibly spelled backwards. The ideal password should not be a common word, since it is possible for a saboteur to have a program try every word in the system's dictionary as a possible password.

```
Table 13.2  Attributes of a Good Password:

The password should:
           • never be written down
           • be easy for the user to remember
           • not be easy for someone else to figure out
           • not be a common word
           • be changed easily
           • be changed often
```

Password security should also be approached from the system level. It doesn't matter how careful the users are about passwords if the password file itself is not secure. It goes without saying that a file of passwords is a target for attack by an outsider. For this reason, many passwords are encrypted. However, even if an encryption system is used, the encrypted versions of the password should not be readily available.

Furthermore, since an outsider trying to get into an unauthorized account usually needs to make multiple tries at the password, such systematic trials should be detected. For example, if the password is not entered correctly on the first three tries, the user should be logged off. This discourages repeated efforts from telephone lines. Keeping records of such multiple tries can be useful in catching someone who is attempting unauthorized entry to a system.

Change your password early and change it often. Many unauthorized account users have obtained access simply by watching someone type a password at a keyboard. In more than one well-publicized incident, hackers obtained access to systems that had never bothered to alter the factory-installed password.

13.C.3. Data Integrity Checks and Procedures

Data security also means keeping track of the integrity of stored data and programs. This is especially important when sending information from one system to another.

In order to catch errors, it is important to know what restrictions there are on the transmitted information. That is, what constitutes a legal item of information? Once that is determined, not only can errors be detected, they can also be corrected.

13.C.3.a. Error Detection Codes

One standard error detection technique is the use of parity. An item of information is encoded with a specified number of bits plus a parity bit. The parity bit may be chosen so that the total number of 1 bits is even. (A finite state machine for parity checking was shown earlier in Figure 2.10.) Alternatively, odd parity may be used. Parity checks are typically used in system memory verification hardware and in verifying characters in asynchronous data communication. A parity check will detect any single bit error in a parity encoded bit string. It cannot detect an even number of bit changes.

If it is possible to repeat the transmission (or reading) of an item of information, then when a parity error is detected, the system can try again. This method has its limits, however. We don't want to try too many times or we may get a bad data item with two parity errors.

Another type of error detection code works on blocks of information with an extra character appended for checking. The check character might be the logical sum of all characters in the block. Weighted codes are often used with text strings.

As an example, let us look at a method that works well with short strings, such as Social Security numbers, credit card numbers, and employee identification information. The method gives each character a value, weighted by its position in the string, and creates a check character at the end of the string such that:

Sum of character weights modulo 37 = 0

where the sum is formed by the adding the product of each character's value multiplied by its string position as a weight. The value of 37 is the total number of letters (ignoring case), 26, plus the number of digits, 10, plus a blank. The weights of the values are based on the position of a character in the string.

For example, consider the seven-character string:

ID 1245

We need to find the check character to put on the end of the string so that the coded string is:

ID 1245?

where ? represents the check character that we are going to find. For character values, suppose we assign 0=0, 1=1, ... 9=9, A=10, ... Z=35, blank=36. Positions are counted from right to left. In this example, there are eight positions. These are shown below, along with the assigned values.

Character	Position	Assigned value
I	8	18
D	7	13
blank	6	36
1	5	1
2	4	2
4	3	4
5	2	5
?	1	x

The sum we calculate is then:

$(8 * 18) + (7 * 13) + (6 * 36) + (5 * 1) + (4 * 2) + (3 * 4) + (2 * 5) + (1 * x) = 486 + x$

To find x, we find 481 modulo 37, which gives us 5. In order to obtain

Sum modulo 37 = 0

where sum = (486 + x), x = 37 - 5 or 32. This is the value we have assigned to W. Therefore, the encoded string is:

ID 1245W

This method helps catch typical typographic errors such as transposing two numbers or letters, or confusing the letter O with the number zero. If the string to be encoded by this technique is longer than 37, modifications need to be made.

As another example, the International Standard Book Number (ISBN), which appears in this and most other books, uses a weighted code. The ISBN is a 10-digit number. The first digit indicates a group of countries (e.g., 0 is for the U.S. and some other English-speaking countries). The next two digits represent the publisher, the next six are assigned by the publisher, and the last is a check number.

13.C.3.b. Cyclic Redundancy Check (CRC) Code

An error checking code frequently used to verify the integrity of files is the Cyclic Redundancy Check (CRC) code. A CRC code is often appended to files during transfer to/from mass storage or in passage through a telecommunication channel. If you have the option of employing CRC checking in uploading or downloading files, *use it*. These codes are generated by an algorithm that combines every byte of the file. This algorithm is greatly superior to simple parity or simple checksums. It is highly effective since there is a very, very small probability that any changes can occur in a file without a failure in the CRC check. Also, if you have a stored value elsewhere of such a CRC value, it would be extremely difficult to alter a file without a detectable change in the CRC value.

13.C.3.c. Error Correction Codes

Detecting errors is important, but it is even better if errors can be corrected. Error correction codes are used in some file compression software systems, and used in some data storage systems such as CD-ROM to assure reliable data retrieval even if the media are not perfect. They are also important when critical data must be reliably transferred on an unreliable communication channel.

One very simple error correcting method is **triplicate code**, where the information is repeated three times and a majority vote determines which version will be accepted at the receiving end. Another simple technique involves arranging information in a rectangular array and creating parity bits for both rows and columns. A single bit error can be corrected by changing the bit at the intersecting row and column that localize the error by their parity errors. The weakness is that multiple errors might not be detected. But unlike single parity bit methods, a second, random error usually will not satisfy parity bits for both rows and columns.

One very good error correction method for single error correction is the use of **Hamming codes,** named for their creator, Richard W. Hamming. We will introduce this concept by example.

Let us consider the transmission of a three-bit number. For this, we will need six bits. (As the number of bits to be transferred becomes larger, the number of parity check bits becomes comparatively smaller.) Look at Table 13.3. This gives the binary representation for each position of the six bits.

```
Table 13.3  Hamming Codes: Check Positions

                    Position
          Decimal            Binary
             1                 001
             2                 010
             3                 011
             4                 100
             5                 101
             6                 110
```

Note that there is a 1 in the least significant bit for the binary values of positions 1, 3, and 5. There is a 1 in the next bit for positions 2, 3, and 6. Finally, there is a 1 in the next bit for positions 4, 5, and 6. We will use the first position in each group as the location of a parity check bit (even parity).

Suppose, for example, we wish to transmit the binary value 110. These digits will be put in positions 3, 5, and 6, like this:

```
position        1 2 3 4 5 6
binary digit    _ _ 1 _ 1 0
```

In the first position, we want the parity bit for the values in positions 1, 3, and 5. This will be a zero. Our six-bit value is now:

```
position        1 2 3 4 5 6
binary digit    0 _ 1 _ 1 0
```

In the second position, we want the parity bit for the values in positions 2, 3, and 6. This will be 1. Our six-bit value is now:

```
position        1 2 3 4 5 6
binary digit    0 1 1 _ 1 0
```

Finally, in the fourth position, we want the parity bit for positions 4, 5, and 6, which is 1. The value to be transmitted is 011110.

If the information is sent correctly, all will check. Let us look at what happens if there is an error. Suppose the information is transmitted as 011111. The error, you will note, is in position 6. Let us check the parity bits:

```
position        1 2 3 4 5 6
binary digit    0 1 1 1 1 0
received        0 1 1 1 1 1
```

The parity bit in position 1 checks bits 1, 3, and 5. These three add up to an even number, 0+1+1, so parity check 1 is correct. Parity bit 2 checks bits 2, 3, and 6. This is incorrect, since 1+1+1 is odd. Similarly parity bit 4, for positions 4, 5, and 6, is incorrect. This is summarized in Table 13.4.

Now substituting 1 for incorrect parity values and 0 for correct parity values, as shown in Table 13.4, gives us the binary value 110, or decimal 6. This tells us that the error is in bit 6. By changing bit 6 from 1 to 0, all the parity bits check.

For this method, three parity check bits are needed for up to four-bit strings, and four parity check bits are needed for five- to 11-bit strings.

```
        Table 13.4  Hamming Codes: Parity Check

            Parity bit    4  2  1
            Value         I  I  C
            Binary value  1  1  0

        Substitute I = 1, C = 0
```

13.C.4. Cryptography and the Data Encryption Standard

Cryptography is the study of secret writing. It is based on the Greek words *kryptos*, which means *hidden*, and *graphein*, meaning *to write*. The unencrypted form of a document is called **plaintext** or **cleartext**. The coded result is called **cryptotext** or **ciphertext**. The process of converting from plaintext to cryptotext is **encryption**. **Decryption** is the opposite process.

Encryption may be done by simple substitution, such as replacing each letter by the next letter in the alphabet, or it may be done by a complex algorithm.

Block encryption means that instead of character-by-character encryption, data will be encrypted block by block. With block encryption, transmission errors in any given ciphertext block do not have any affect on other blocks.

The **key space** is the set of all possible values for the key. The key is usually a sequence of letters. The algorithm determined by the encryption key is the transformation done on the plaintext to turn it into cryptotext. Similarly, cryptotext is turned back into plaintext using the algorithm determined by the decryption key.

Cryptography involves an **enciphering key** and a **deciphering key**. In a **one-key system**, these keys are the same.

There are also **two-key systems** in which the enciphering key and the deciphering key are sufficiently different that one cannot be determined from the other. This means that one of the keys can be made public without endangering the other. Such a system is called a **public key system**.

In a public key system with a public encryption algorithm, anybody can send a message, but only authorized persons, those with the decryption algorithm, can decode. Conversely, a public key system with a public decryption algorithm means anyone can decode but only an authorized source can send encrypted information.

The **Data Encryption Standard (DES)**, established in 1977 by the National Bureau of Standards as a Federal Information Processing Standard, is required to be implemented in hardware. It uses block encryption with a 64-bit block size. The DES is a one-key system with a 56-bit key. This means that the key space for the DES contains 2^{56} bits.

The Federal Privacy Act requires federal agencies to use the DES on confidential data. Any exception requires the written grant of a specific waiver.

13.C.5. Viruses and Other Maladies

Much notoriety has been generated recently by software that can attack the integrity of computer systems. Some programs, including "viruses" and "worms," are self-replicating and thus can propagate to other programs or systems. Some are designed to do more than they are advertised to do, but the additional things they do are to the detriment of the user. These are called "Trojan horses." Other problems are caused by user error or ignorance.

13.C.5.a. Viruses

A **virus** is a program that attaches itself to another, usually widely used program, for the purpose of invading a system. It is self-replicating and thus can propagate to other systems that are interconnected in a network.

Networks are created to share and communicate messages and data, including software. In some cases, a virus is made to attach itself to electronic mail packets, to an interesting data set, or to a useful piece of software. This way, it can be unknowingly transmitted to many systems along with its host, which passively carries it. In other cases directly infectious viruses have been created.

Infectious viruses not only replicate themselves but may be triggered to directly seek telecommunications paths by which they can invade other systems. How can this be achieved? One simple way is by building a table of several dozen of the most common passwords and systematically trying the list whenever entry is limited by a password.

If a virus can get into a system it may cause trouble in many ways. By replicating itself many times as a parasite it can consume storage space or execution time, depriving valid tasks of resources. Worse, a virus may misuse system utilities or commands to damage information resources. Particular atrocities include "Delete all files," or "Reformat the disk."

The creation of such viruses is clearly unacceptable and unethical behavior. Recent laws make it a felony to use telecommunication services to perpetrate such acts of unauthorized access.

13.C.5.b. Worms

Worms are similar to viruses except that, rather than being attached to another program, worms are separate, stand-alone programs. In other respects, they behave much the same way as viruses. That is, they are designed to invade a system without being noticed. They replicate themselves and work hard to invade other accounts or systems. They consume storage space and/or execution time, and generally are guilty of the same unacceptable things as viruses.

A widely publicized example of a worm that invaded a national network system, the Internet, is described below.

13.C.5.c. Trojan Horse

Another assault on computer systems is the **Trojan horse**, named after the gift horse concealing saboteurs that caused the fall of the ancient city of Troy. This form of attack is typically a gift piece of software containing an executable function other than the advertised purpose. Examples include an electronic mail system that steals passwords from anyone who uses it, a utility program that copies your data and sends it to the account of the perpetrator, and a utility that deletes all your files (including itself) the fifth time you use it.

The malcontents who have propagated these horrors in the past years have often attached their parasitic code to public domain software or shareware that is well known in legitimate versions. For example, some have propagated copies of "CHK4BOMB" and "DPROTECT," which are used to search for or protect against the ravages of a Trojan horse.

Some Trojan horses have been sold as "copy protection." The intent was to punish anyone who attempted to illegitimately copy a software package. A product called Prolock (TM Vault Inc.), used briefly by Ashton-Tate, had the effect of deleting all the files on an IBM-PC's hard disk if the software was copied onto it. The manual said that the distribution disk in a floppy drive was required for execution, but did not warn about loss of files if you executed it from a hard disk. Needless to say, it was not well liked by purchasers who tried to put their files on a hard disk for faster execution. The publicity about this problem contributed to a decline in copy-protected software.

13.C.5.d. Other Maladies

Sometimes an unexplained information system disaster is incorrectly blamed on a worm or a virus when, in fact, the users have made some kind of error. For example, in one case a word processing lab complained of a virus attack. On investigation, it turned out that they had IBM-PCs and several clones with several different versions of the operating system running in the same room. Their problems were due to incompatibilities between machines and different DOS versions. Although some utilities will produce "Wrong DOS version" messages when there are incompatibilities, in other cases errors in interpreting directory structure can lead to the loss of files or destruction of the directory data.

Another problem can arise from failure to recognize that disks do not function forever. A physical failure can cause loss of data. Such failure can be caused by fingerprints on the floppy disk, or by kicking a hard disk system while it is reading or writing. Eventually a disk may wear out or a mechanical part may fail. Sometimes there may be error messages before total failure, to warn conscientious users to take precautionary action. However, the best defense is periodic backups to other media.

13.C.6. "We Have Met the Enemy and He is Us."

Who is most likely to sabotage a computer system? An enemy agent from a foreign country? A competitor who is trying to steal your product?

Granted, this can happen, but these are not the most frequent computer security problems.

Deliberate alteration or deletion of software, data, and information is likely to be done by someone who has the easiest access to a system, that is, an insider. The student who is alleged to have created the Internet worm is someone who is knowledgeable about computers and has worked in the field of computer security. He was also an Internet user; an insider.

A common type of insider who is likely to cause computer security problems is a disgruntled employee. Someone who is being terminated should be cut off from access to any and all computer systems immediately.

13.D. Ethics

13.D.1. Case History: The Internet Worm

The **Internet** is a national computer network used by the U.S. government, industry, and the academic community. It originated in the mid-1970s as a basis for experimental network research. Since then, the Internet has become a major national facility used by a widespread, multi-disciplinary community of researchers. These users include thousands of computer scientists, electrical engineers, mathematicians, physicists, medical researchers, chemists, astronomers, and space scientists. The Internet provides a means of communication and a source of information for them. Its usefulness depends heavily on its wide availability and accessibility.

The Internet came under attack on Wednesday, November 2, 1988. Late that afternoon, a worm program was executed on one of the hosts connected to the Internet. The worm collected information from the host, network, and users, and then used the collected information to break into other machines. After successfully breaking into another machine, the worm would duplicate itself, and the duplicate program would attempt to infect other systems in the same way.

The worm was designed to be hidden from the users at the sites where it appeared. However, systems quickly became so loaded as they became repeatedly infected that they were not able to continue normal processing. Internet users who realized that they were being infected reacted in various ways. Some shut down their facilities entirely; others went after the worm.

By Thursday morning, November 3, 1988, copies of the worm had been captured by personnel at the Massachusetts Institute of Technology and at the University of California at Berkeley, and efforts had begun to head it off. Others later joined these efforts, and by working around the clock, the worm was brought under control by Saturday.

It appears that the worm was the creation of a first-year computer science graduate student at Cornell University, Ithaca NY, who worked alone. The student was immediately suspended. The Cornell Commission, which investigated the incident and published its findings, concluded that the student had "violated Computer Science Department policy on the use of departmental research computing facilities." The Cornell Computer Science Department "Policy for the Use of the Research Computing Facility" prohibits "use of its computer facilities for browsing through private computer files, decrypting encrypted material, or obtaining unauthorized user privileges."

The event, which affected at least 6000 computer sites nationally, received widespread coverage in the press. Two aspects of the incident received the most attention. First, the program did not contain any code that would explicitly damage whatever system it was running on. Second, the worm had no means of stopping itself, but was designed to continuously duplicate itself while simultaneously making efforts to avoid being identified and captured.

Reaction to the Internet worm from the computer science community was quick and virtually unanimous. The worm had interfered with the normal operation of a major national facility. It had caused the loss of many thousands of hours of research work. Several organizations issued statements of ethics. The basic content of several of these statements is summarized in the next section.

Damage done by the worm was extensive. Although it did not actually alter or destroy existing files, it did interfere with normal operation by using up system resources and causing user processes to fail. Even systems that were not overwhelmed had to be rebooted to clear the system of the ever-duplicating worms. This not only took administrative time, it forced the termination of long-running programs, as well as the interruption of normal user sessions. When it penetrated user accounts, it made it appear as if users who had nothing to do with the incident were responsible for disturbing the system.

Access to supercomputers and exchange of electronic mail were delayed because of overloads and shutdowns, sometimes for several days. Because of this, some projects were late and many others lost research time. Another major cost was the diversion of computer experts from their normal activities to track down and kill the worm.

13.D.2. Responsibility and Ethics

Open networks, like other open facilities such as highways, depend on a spirit of cooperation among all users in order to keep a system functioning smoothly. The value of a shared resource, such as the Internet, depends on the individual accountability and sense of ethics of each user. It is not possible to instigate rigid security procedures without interfering with the free use of a network, which is its hallmark and the foundation of its usefulness. Recommendations for individuals to keep in mind for network use are given in Table 13.5.

Table 13.5 Individual Actions to Provide Network Security

Access to a network is a privilege. The security of access mechanisms in a network are minimal. The idea of sharing is promoted over protection. Therefore, individuals must provide security by their actions. These actions include:

1. Confidential information, such as grades or letters of recommendation, should not be stored in the system.

2. Individuals must recognize and respect intellectual property rights. These include license, copyright, and trade secrets. Where these apply to software available on a network, the individual user has the responsibility to observe applicable restrictions. The person who puts restricted software on a network has the responsibility of making any restrictions known to users.

As a result of the Internet worm incident, several organizations, including the National Science Foundation, Computer Professionals for Social Responsibility, and the Internet Activities Board, have issued statements of ethics. These are summarized in Table 13.6.

Table 13.6 Ethics Guidelines for Network Use

It is unethical for a network user, either on purpose or through negligence, to:

1. Disrupt the intended use of a network.
2. Waste resources, including people, bandwidth, or computer.
3. Consume unplanned resources for control and eradication of an interruption.
4. Compromise the privacy of legitimate users.
5. Interfere with access by legitimate users.
6. Interfere with or alter the integrity of the system, by such means as:
   a. unauthorized use of accounts,
   b. impersonation of a legitimate user,
   c. attempting to capture or crack passwords or encryption,
   d. destruction or modification of data or programs
      belonging to a legitimate user.

All of us, as computer professionals, need to be concerned with standards of ethical behavior for all aspects of computer use.

Summary

This chapter describes software protection laws (as of 1990) with regard to copyright, trade secrets, licenses, employee contracts, trademarks, and patents. Some aspects of security that need to be considered in software systems are described, along with some typical problems and suggestions on how to avoid them. Finally, the topic of computer ethics is addressed, along with an example of security and ethical violations.

Keywords

> access control
> backup copies
> ciphertext
> cleartext
> computer ethics
> copyright
> cryptography
> cryptotext
> Cyclic Redundancy Check (CRC) Code
> Data Encryption Standard (DES)
> deciphering key
> decryption
> employee contract
> enciphering key
> encryption
> error correction code
> error detection code
> Hamming code
> incompatibilities
> integrity
> key space
> license
> parity bit
> password security
> patent
> physical security

plaintext
public key system
software protection
software security
trade secret
trademark
triplicate code
Trojan horse
virus
worm

Review Questions

13.1. What is software protection? Software security?

13.2. What are the differences between copyright, trade secrets, licenses, employee contracts, trademark, and patent? Under what conditions is it appropriate to use each of these?

13.3. If an employee of Company ABC develops an innovative piece of software, who owns the copyright?

13.4. What difference can the geographical location of hearing a software copyright case make?

13.5. What is meant by "work for hire"?

13.6. Must a copyright be filed before a copyright notice can be used? What about trademark? Patent? License?

13.7. How do you protect an idea? How do you protect an expression of an idea?

13.8. What, if anything, should be done about making backups? Where should they be kept? How often should backups be done?

13.9. What is one disadvantage of using public domain software? How can you protect yourself against this problem?

13.10. What is Cyclic Redundancy Check code? When should it be used?

13.11. What is access control? How does access control for a single-user system differ from access control for a multiuser system?

13.12. What are the characteristics of a good password? What are the most commonly used passwords? Why should you avoid them?

13.13. Once you decide on a good password, is there ever any reason to change it?

13.14. Give an example of error checking.

13.15.   What is the difference between error detection code and error correction code?

13.16.   What is parity and where and how is it used? Triplicate code? Hamming code?

13.17.   What is cryptography? Cleartext? Cryptotext?

13.18.   What is the Data Encryption Standard? Is it to be implemented in hardware or software?

13.19.   What is a virus program? A worm? A Trojan horse? How can you protect yourself against these?

13.20.   What or who is the most likely source of computer sabotage?

13.21.   What is meant by computer ethics? What standards for computer ethics, if any, are there? What do you think of them?

Exercises

13.1.   As a student, you have just created an innovative piece of software and want to try to sell it. You have used your university's computing facilities, including their compiler, for development of the software, even though you didn't get any course credit for the work. What legal entanglements may there be to unravel before you can begin marketing the software?

13.2.   Under what circumstances does an employee own the copyright to a piece of software he or she has created while employed?

13.3.   You are using a utility program that was written to be used with the operating system you are using. At some point you notice that the OS version the program was intended to be used with is not the one you have. What can go wrong? What is your legal liability? What can happen to your hardware? To your software?

13.4.   You are in charge of setting up a computer system for a small hospital. What are the security and integrity problems that might need special consideration? If the hospital is located in a politically unstable area with a potential for terrorist attack, how would you change the plans and procedures?

13.5.   Discuss the difference in backup procedures adequate for the personal computer of a computer science student and the procedures in place at a supermarket with a microcomputer networked with five point-of-sale terminals.

13.6. Suppose you have a software utility that will determine a CRC value for each file in a directory and write it as a decimal string, and write the corresponding filenames and the byte count for each to another file. Describe a procedure to determine whether any executable files have been changed if we wish to search for a virus at a later date.

13.7. Why isn't an error correcting code always used in data communications?

References

Brooks, Frederick P. The Mythical Man-Month, Essays on Software Engineering. Reading, MA: Addison-Wesley, 1975, reprinted 1982.

> Considered a classic of software engineering. Brooks presents the results of his experience as the project manager for the IBM OS 360. It is a clear exposition of the nonlinearity of manpower and project duration effects on software project management.

Denning, Dorothy Elizabeth Robling. Cryptography and Data Security. Reading, MA: Addison-Wesley, 1983.

> Introductory textbook. Includes encryption algorithms (such as DES), encryption techniques, access controls, information flow controls, and inference controls.

Enger, Norman L., and Howerton, Paul W. Computer Security, A Management Audit Approach. New York: AMACON, 1980.

> Management approach to the problems of computer security and protection of privacy.

Foster, Caxton C. Cryptanalysis for Microcomputers. Rochelle Park, NJ: Hayden Book Company, 1982.

> Examples of encryption and decryption techniques suitable for use with limited computer resources.

Gemignani, Michael C. "Who Owns What Software Produces?" IEEE Software 2, no. 5 (September 1985): 48-52.

> Addresses the question of what happens when programs rather than humans create products. This is an important issue when it comes to copyrighting student projects, as the creator of any compiler used may have a claim on the resultant software.

Glass, Robert L. "Software Theft." IEEE Software 2, no. 4 (July 1985): 82-85.

> Describes a modular decomposition technique as a way to ascertain a software theft. Glass considers the method straightforward enough for a software-illiterate judge or jury to understand.

Graham, Robert L. "The Legal Protection of Computer Software." Communications of the ACM 27, no. 5 (May 1984): 422-426.

> Excellent summary of current state of various legal protections available for commercial software.

Hagelshaw, R. Lee. The Computer User's Legal Guide. Radnor, PA: Chilton Book Company, 1986.

> Written by a lawyer associated with a computer software company, this book addresses legal aspects of acquiring computers, acquiring or marketing software, how computer professionals can limit liability, and how to start and protect your own company.

Hamming, Richard W. Coding and Information Theory. Englewood Cliffs, NJ: Prentice-Hall, 1980.

> Good description of error-detecting and error-correcting codes, especially Hamming codes.

Institute of Electrical and Electronics Engineers. Software Engineering Standards. New York: Wiley-Interscience, October 1987.

Includes "ANSI/IEEE Std 730-1984, Software Quality Assurance Plans," which is concerned with legal liability. It is directed toward the development and maintenance of software that concerns safety or large financial or social implications. Also includes "ANSI/IEEE Std 1012-1986, Software Verification and Validation Plans." Provides uniform and minimum requirements for the format and content of software verification and validation plans; defines, for critical software, minimum verification and validation tasks and their required inputs and outputs; and suggests optional tasks to be used appropriate for the particular verification and validation effort.

Jakes, J. Michael, and Yoches, Robert E. "Legally Speaking." Communications of the ACM 32, no. 8 (August 1989): 922-924.

> Description of the current state of patent law as applied to computer software.

Konheim, Alan G. Cryptography, A Primer. New York: John Wiley & Sons, 1981.

> Introductory text that emphasizes the mathematical skills needed in cryptography. Comments on DES adoption, analysis of strength, other codes.

Miles, Dana E. "Copyrighting Computer Software After Apple v. Franklin." IEEE Software 1, no. 2 (April 1984): 84-87.

> Good description of a dramatic, landmark case and analysis of its implications.

Morris, Robert, and Thompson, Ken. "Password Security: A Case History." Communications of the ACM 22, no. 11 (November 1979):, 594-7.

> This paper outlines several methods of attack on password protection that were employed by the Internet worm in 1988.

Remer, Daniel. Legal Care for Your Software, A Step-by-Step Guide for Computer Software Writers. Berkeley, CA: Nolo Press, 1982.

> Detailed description of various legal protection methods, with recommendations on circumstances for the use of each, singly or in combination.

Task Force on Legal Aspects of Computer-Based Technology. "Protection of Computer Ideawork - Today and Tomorrow." IEEE Software 1, no. 2 (April 1984): 74-82.

> Good overview of legal options and associated problems, with comments related to the size of the software company trying to protect its products.

Weinberg, Gerald M. The Psychology of Computer Programming. New York: Van Nostrand-Reinhold, 1971.

> The first attempt to systematically describe the subject; its anecdotal style makes it highly readable.

APPENDIX A

STANDARDS FOR SOFTWARE PROJECT DOCUMENTATION AND EVALUATION

The complexity of software is an essential property, not an accidental one. Hence, descriptions of a software entity that abstract away its complexity often abstract away its essence.

- Frederick P. Brooks, Jr., "No Silver Bullet"

A.A. Introduction

A.A.1. General Overview

This is a documentation standard for a project-oriented course in software engineering. This documentation standard assumes a group environment working on a project with many modules of code. These documents will be used to review and evaluate the project. The initial documents are intended to be working documents within the group, while the final documents will include individual components as well as group components.

Each group is to produce a set of initial documents indicating what they intend to do on the project and how they intend to do it. They will also produce a set of final documents indicating what they did. The final documents will be completed and turned in before the project demonstration at the end of the semester. The project evaluation will be based on the documentation and the demonstration. The demonstration is to show the functionality and performance of the software system that has been produced.

A.A.2. Format Requirements

A.A.2.a. All Documents

These documents are to be produced with a text editor. Various portions will be required for further assignments and as reference material for the group's development work, so they should be in machine-readable form for ease of change and reproduction.

Each document shall have a title page, table of contents, and numbered pages. The title page should identify the person who edited the document and the course, section, and group number, as well as listing the persons who contributed to its production. Each set of documents shall be bound with a cover. Use of a text editor means that later documents will be more efficiently produced by editing and reusing portions of earlier documents. The required format is 8.5 by 11 inch pages with adequate margins; however, it is acceptable to have the documents printed on green bar paper and cut to size with a paper cutter. Note that provision of left margin space is required for readability of source code after binding into a document. This puts a limit of about 64 columns for entering source code.

A.A.2.b. Initial Documents

There are three initial documents. They are: (1) a Software Requirement Specification that includes a Preliminary User's Manual, (2) a System Plan, and (3) a Test Specification Document. These documents are to follow the general format guidelines above as well as the specific content outlines for these documents, described in section A.B below.

A.A.2.c. Final Documents

The final documentation of the group project will consist of three sections: (1) the Test Reporting Document, (2) the User's Manual, and (3) the System Design. Each section should should be clearly identified. All three may be bound together. A page-numbered table of contents is expected for each section. Each section must start at the top of a new page.

A.A.2.d. Source Code

The primary basis of documenting the detailed design of the project is its source code. Good structured programming is expected. In the source code a wide variety of information is to be included in header (and/or trailer) comment blocks. A sample header block is given in Figure A.1.

The top of the header (the first 24 lines, or first screen) for each module shall have the most critical information to identify the module. This shall include the name of the module, a brief title, the current version and its date, author, and parameters.

The header block shall also contain a narrative, functional description of the module, inputs and outputs other than parameters, description of files used, a list of modules called and called by, and a description of side effects and global variable usage.

In order to provide for a final 8.5 by 11 inch format, lines of source code shall be limited to 64 columns.

Commentary within the code shall describe the function of each paragraph or block. This applies to all code whether in a high-level language, system procedure files, or assembly coded subroutines. The intent, function, and structure of every module must be documented within its source code. Any deviation from good programming practice must be justified in a comment where it occurs in the source code. This includes such things as tricky coding, data type mismatches, use of side effects, and subscripts out of declared range. Every GOTO used (if any) shall be commented to indicate its purpose.

A variable dictionary shall be at the end of a header block or in a trailer comment block. For readability the same convention must be used on all modules in the document, so the group must document the convention to be used before coding begins. An example is given in Figure A.1.

Modules must be limited to reasonable size and complexity (approximately 1-2 pages, or McCabe's complexity metric less than or equal to 10).

Figure A.1 Sample Header Block for Source Code Modules

```
/****************************************************************
*                                                              *
*    TRACE FLAG CHANGE                         C. D. SIGWART    *
*                                                              *
*   COURSE: CPS 410    SECTION: 1234    INSTRUCTOR: VAN MEER    *
*                                                              *
* VER. 1.0   Translated from CBASIC, MACRO 2.5,  12-11-84  CDS *
*                                                              *
*------------------------------------------------------------- *
*                                                              *
*      SAMPLE CALL: trflag()                (NO PARAMETERS)    *
*                                                              *
*   INPUTS     : TAKE FLAG VALUES FROM KEYBOARD                *
*   OUTPUTS    : PROMPT USER FOR INPUT                         *
*   SIDE-EFFECT : PUT VALUES IN GLOBAL ARRAY trace[]           *
*                                                              *
*   CALLED BY  : MAIN DRIVER          CALLS : ERROR, NUMBER    *
*   FILES USED : NONE                                          *
*                                                              *
*------------------------------------------------------------- *
*                                                              *
* FUNCTION:                                                    *
*  LETS PROGRAMMER SET ANY MEMBER, OR ALL, OF AN ARRAY OF      *
*  GLOBAL FLAGS WHICH ARE USED TO DUMP DATA FROM MODULES IN A  *
*  DEBUGGING SESSION. FLAGS ARE INITIALIZED IN MAIN DRIVER SO  *
*  ALL START IN THE OFF STATE (0). FLAGS ARE SET ONLY IN THIS  *
*  MODULE; ALL OTHER MODULES ONLY READ VALUES.                 *
*                                                              *
*------------------------------------------------------------- *
*                                                              *
* DEFINITION OF GLOBAL DATA USAGE:                             *
*  USES A GLOBAL ARRAY 'trace[#]' WHERE '#' DESIGNATES A       *
*  MODULE. ELEMENTS ARE SINGLE CHARACTERS '0' OR '1',          *
*  FOR 'OFF' AND 'ON'. USES AN ARRAY OF TRACE DESCRIPTORS,     *
*  'TRADES(#)', ONE FOR EACH ELEMENT OF TRACE.  ANY UNUSED     *
*  DESCRIPTORS ARE ALL BLANKS.                                 *
*                                                              *
****************************************************************/
```

The trace system described in this header block is given in Appendix B.

A.B. Initial Documents

A.B.1. Software Requirements Specification

This description is based in part on ANSI/IEEE Standard 830-1984, Software Requirements Specifications.

The purpose of the software requirements specification is to clearly enumerate all aspects of a proposed system in order to facilitate communication between the developer and the buyer (user). The process of creating this document should help the supplier to understand exactly what the customer wants, and help the software customers to accurately describe what they wish to obtain. The document produced should establish the basis for agreement between the customers and the suppliers on what the software product is to do. The description of the functions to be performed should assist the potential users to determine if the specified software meets their needs, or determine how it must be modified to meet their needs.

A good software requirements specification is complete, unambiguous, verifiable, consistent, modifiable, and traceable. It must include all significant requirements relating to functionality, performance, design constraints, attributes, and external interfaces. It must define the responses of the software to all realizable classes of input data in all realizable classes of situations, including both valid and invalid input values.

A software requirements specification is a specification for a particular software product, program, or set of programs that does certain things. The Software Requirements Specification must correctly define all software requirements, but no more. The software requirements specification should *not* describe any design, verification, or management details, except for required design constraints. The Software Requirements Specification limits the range of valid solutions, but does not specify design. To do so would put unnecessary constraints on the developer.

The Software Requirements Specification description we are presenting is most appropriate for new software to be developed. A sample outline is given in Figure A.2. If the project is to modify existing software, a preexisting software requirements specification should be reviewed and revised.

Methods used to express software requirements include input and output specifications; representative examples; and the specifications of models, such as mathematical, functional, or timing models.

The relative importance of each requirement should be indicated; whether it is essential, desirable, or optional. Also, the relative stability of each requirement shall be indicated; that is, whether it is likely to change over the expected life of the software.

The document shall be written in a highly structured way using structured English. Each statement shall be numbered.

```
Figure A.2  Software Requirement Specification Document
            Sample  Outline

        Title page
        Table of Contents
1.0. Introduction
        1.1. Purpose and Origin of the Need for This System
        1.2. Scope of the System Specified
        1.3. Definitions, Acronyms, and Abbreviations
        1.4. References to Related and Supporting Documents
        1.5. Overview of the System
2.0. General Description
        2.1. Product Perspective
        2.2. Product Functions
        2.3. User Characteristics
        2.4. General Constraints
        2.5. Assumptions and Dependencies
3.0. Specific Requirements
        3.1. Functional Requirements
        3.2. External Interface Requirements
        3.3. Performance Requirements
        3.4. Design Constraints
        3.5. Attributes
        3.6. Other Requirements
    Appendixes [optional]
    Glossary
    Index
```

Each statement shall be a simple declarative sentence. Care must be taken to eliminate ambiguity. Each statement shall be verifiable when the system has been implemented.

Data flow diagrams are to be used to model the system (Section 3.1). These diagrams shall separately represent high-level and detailed models of the component functions of the system in terms of required processes and data flows in the system.

The Software Requirements Specification shall address the software product, not the process of producing it. Factors that should *not* be included in the Software Requirements Specification include cost, delivery schedules, reporting procedures, development methods, quality assurance, validation criteria, and acceptance procedures. However, a good software requirements specification provides a basis for these factors.

A.B.2. Preliminary User's Manual

The Preliminary User's Manual is a specification of external interface requirements (Section 3.2) and thus is properly a part of the Software Requirements Specification. This is perhaps the most important part of the requirements specification, especially for interactive systems. It shows the formats of the system's inputs and outputs and lists all its functions from the users' viewpoint. This manual is the basis for the potential users to determine whether the proposed software will meet their needs. This is why it must describe the proposed system in a way that is meaningful to the users. It shall *not* make reference to specific modules or to the internal logic of the source code.

An online help system is not a substitute for a user's manual. A supplement to this manual may be an interface prototype. Such a prototype might be created with screen editing tools or a database management system. It is useful to capture screens from such tools to create text figures for your User's Manual.

The components of a preliminary user's manual are summarized in Figure A.3.

Figure A.3 Components of the Preliminary User Manual

1. Overview from a user's perspective of the application of the system.
2. Description of how the user initiates use of the system, including the logon procedure.
3. Description of commands available to the user and the features invoked by each.
4. Description of the prompts the user will encounter while using the system and the format of any inputs expected.
5. Description of outputs generated by the system in response to user commands.
6. Listing of error messages with description/explanation of any error recovery procedures.

A.B.3. System Plan

The System Plan represents an outline of the software development to create the required system. This plan shall be written in enough detail so that a programming team that did not participate in the preliminary design could begin writing code from it. Components of the System Plan Document are given in Figure A.4.

Figure A.4 Components of a System Plan

1. A brief narrative description of the development plan referring to figures/tables to describe major development landmarks for supporting details.
2. A hierarchy diagram of the system.
3. A list of modules by name with inputs and outputs specified by name and data type, with estimated lines of code for each.
4. Allocation of coding to team member for each module listed.
5. A schedule in chronological order showing code completion and test completion dates for each module and all integration and integration testing. Be sure to schedule at least a week for final integration and system test after the unit test of the last module.
6. Detailed description of any special resource requirements.

A hierarchy diagram (or diagrams) are to be used to represent the control structure of the software to be implemented. This represents a design choice of how to split the system into modules. Each module represented must be given a functionally descriptive name.

If event timing sequences are critical, there shall be event time sequence diagrams to specify any control sequences that are required. These are mandatory in real-time processing, distributed computation, or multi-user concurrent update file access systems.

The proposed software system is to be described in terms of a modular structure. The modules are to to be designated by valid names, and the inputs and outputs of these modules are to be listed in the form of variable declarations. A cross-reference list indicating relationships of modules to the Software Requirements Specification by specific section and paragraph numbers is highly desirable.

The overall schedule for code production and integration must be in a top-down, depth-first plan. The first item in the schedule will be a group effort to implement a high-level interactive driver.

A.B.4. Test Specification Document

This description is based in part on ANSI/IEEE Standard 829-1984, Software Test Documentation.

Standard test documentation can facilitate communication by providing a consistent frame of reference, and can serve as a checklist for completeness. The use of standardized test documents also increases the manageability of testing. These documents cover test planning, specification, and reporting; and prescribe the scope, approach, resources, and schedule for testing.

Test documentation includes test specification, described in this section, and test reporting, described in the section on final documents.

The purpose of the Test Specification Document is to (a) identify test cases, with procedures and features to be covered and pass/fail criteria, (b) document actual input values and expected outputs, and (c) identify all steps required to operate the system and exercise the specific test case. An outline of the Test Plan Document is given in Figure A.5.

```
Figure A.5  Test Specification Document - Outline

 1. Test plan identifier (name, version number)
 2. Introduction (narrative summary)
 3. Test items
 4. Features to be tested
 5. Features not to be tested
 6. Item pass/fail criteria
 7. Test deliverables
 8. Testing tasks (plus any intertask dependence)
 9. Environmental needs
10. Responsibilities
11. Schedule
12. Approvals (place for instructor's signature)
```

For each module there will be a tabular listing of the module name, the module type, and a list of all input and output parameters with the name and data types specified for each. The range of valid values for each parameter is to be specified. A set of specific values for each input parameter is to be listed which is to be used in testing that unit. The inclusion of both valid and invalid data items is required, along with the expected result. For invalid data this means the specific error message to be generated.

The environment for each test is to be specified. If a special driver or stubs are required, describe them. If a subset of the system is planned to be available as the driver, briefly describe the configuration and any necessary modifications. Note that special modifications may be required to get invalid data items to the unit under test.

Include in this document a coding/implementation schedule, the same as that in the System Plan if that schedule was accepted by the instructor; otherwise submit a revised schedule. If the data flow or hierarchy diagrams have been modified, include revised diagrams.

A.C. Final Documents

A.C.1. Test Reporting Document

The Test Reporting Document shall be, in part, an expansion and elaboration of the Test Plan Document. This is most easily done if the document is created in machine-readable form. The Test Reporting Document shall include a list of test items used, what happened during test execution (actual results as opposed to expected results), indication of the chronological order in which testing took place, a description of any event that requires further investigation, and a summary report of testing activities.

The table of contents shall indicate page references to each test. There shall be a separate subsection for each member of the software development team, containing the tests for that member's modules. Indicate the author of the code for each subsection in the table of contents. The allocation of modules to a subsection, in the case of modules with multiple authors, shall be based on the primary author. Each test shall be documented to show the environment of the test, the test items used, and the results obtained.

Compiled listings of the source code for any special drivers and/or stubs shall be provided. If the driver consists of a preexisting subset of the system, a brief note indicating what modules were present is sufficient. Do not include the entire source code in such cases, but do note any special modifications that were required.

There shall be documentation of the results of each test that has been done. The testing document is the proper place to present any code that has been compiled and unit tested but not integrated.

A.C.2. User's Manual

The User's Manual shall tell the user what the system does, how to log on to the system, what the available features are, the formats of all commands and inputs required, and the format of expected outputs. This manual must be adequate to use the software system. It is desirable to have some specific application examples of how the user would use the system. A list and explanation of error messages is required. An online help file system is not a substitute for this documentation, although such a feature of the system is a nice enhancement. If the Preliminary User's Manual was well done, this document may be a minor revision of the preliminary manual.

A.C.3. System Design and Documented Source Code

This document shall have a page-numbered table of contents, a hierarchy diagram, well-commented source code for each module, and all necessary information to implement and run the system.

A.C.3.a. System Design Overview

A complete list naming all files of source code and system procedure files to compile/assemble/link the system must be included. Also include a list of the names of all the object modules and system procedure files, and any linkage map used to generate and run the system.

This documentation should be adequate to support a maintenance programmer. Keep in mind that this document is needed as an account of the system design details for corrective or adaptive maintenance. A programmer who needs to extend and enhance the system should be able to comprehend it from this document.

The module index is an alphabetically sorted list of modules. For each module in the list the primary author must be indicated (initials are sufficient) and a page number reference to find the source code/flowcharts. This is required as a tool for anyone who has to read the code. Obviously it is the last part to be produced.

A.C.3.b. Documented Source Code

The source code for each individual group member shall be grouped together in the document. In the case of modules with multiple authors, put the code in the section of the primary author. Thus in this document there will be as many subsections of the Source Code section as there are group members. Each group member is responsible for assembling a set of source listings and any associated flowcharts for his or her subsection. Insert any flowcharts or other diagrams used in detailed code design for a module immediately after the source code for the module. Assembling this material should be no problem if individual development folders have been maintained for each module. This organization of the design material is required to facilitate individual grading of your work.

Compiled source code for every module that is integrated into the system shall be included. Each module shall begin at the top of a new page. Do not include source code for any modules that have not been integrated into the system. Source code for any modules that have not been integrated shall be included with the corresponding unit test information in the testing document.

Any system procedure files used shall be included with the source code. Source code shall also be included for any assembly coded subroutines used.

A.D. Project Demonstration

The project demonstration will be used to evaluate the performance of the software system created. The group is to present a system as it would be presented to the user, based on a set of executable files. This may include any required system procedure files or data files the system may require. In no case is system source code to be compiled at the time of demonstration.

The demonstration includes the consideration of the features available, functional integrity, ease of use, survival and recovery from user errors and bad data, and the adequacy of messages and prompts to the user. If the system has incomplete features or options, it shall issue messages to the user such as "XYZ option not yet implemented." In no case shall an error in keyboard data entry or item in a data file cause surrender of control to the operating system. Any termination of execution due to a runtime error will be considered evidence of inadequate testing.

Your instructor(s) may expect to discuss internal details of the system. This may include demonstrating execution with an internal trace feature used by the developers turned on to examine internal data flows.

The entire development group shall be present for the project demonstration. Each group member is expected to be able to answer questions about major design issues involved in the system development and specific aspects of his or her own code.

APPENDIX B

INSTRUMENTING A SYSTEM FOR AN EXECUTION TRACE

*"I can't believe **that**" said Alice.*

"Can't you?" the Queen said in a pitying tone. "Try again: draw a long breath, and shut your eyes."

*Alice laughed. "There's no use trying," she said: "one **can't** believe impossible things."*

"I daresay you haven't had much practice," said the Queen. "When I was your age, I always did it for half-an-hour a day. Why sometimes I've believed as many as six impossible things before breakfast."

- Lewis Carroll, Through the Looking Glass

B.A. Introduction

A useful testing tool is a trace system that tells you dynamically where you are in the program at any point in its execution. It is important to be sure that the source of a problem is correctly identified, especially when testing a large system. It does not help very much to work your way through the code, however systematically, if you are in the wrong module.

One programmer, who had struggled for several days with a subtle problem, finally spent an hour or two incorporating the code for a trace system into his application. When the problem appeared, along with the notice of which module was executing, his astonished comment was, "But it can't possibly be there!" But it was, and after he identified the correct location of the problem, it was quickly solved.

B.B. System Description

Briefly, the trace system consists of writing a message for each module to print when it is entered, for example, "Entering Module X," and another when it is exited, such as "Leaving Module X." Examples of this type of message are shown in Figure B.1. The system that this represents also includes a facility for indicating the number of levels of execution by an indentation system.

```
Figure B.1  Sample Trace Messages

Entering Module A
        Entering Module B
                Entering Module C
                Leaving Module C
        Leaving Module B
Leaving Module A
```

Since one does not wish to have such messages displayed for the user, there needs to be a mechanism for turning the messages on or off. Also, it is useful to be able to turn the messages on only for selected modules. Another nice feature to have is the capability of indicating the current value of any parameters. The example in Figure B.2 includes all these options.

B.B.1. Trace Flags and Descriptors

To create this system, you need a global array of trace flags (preferably Boolean or integer) with one element for each module in the program. Each array subscript value will correspond to one module. This means that there must be a method of correlating a specific module with a given array element. Many design techniques include numbering systems for modules which, if already in place, may be used. However, these numbers may have multiple decimal points and not be suitable for use.

Figure B.2 Trace System in C

```
#include <stdio.h>
#define  TRACE_SIZE  10   /* symbolic constant, max array size */
int TraceFlag[TRACE_SIZE], depth = 0;  /* global variables */

main()
/****************************************************************
*                      PROCEDURE MAIN                          *
*                                                              *
* This is a minimal program which activates the trace program *
* and calls other routines to demonstrate how the system works,*
*                                                              *
* Calls: trflg, sample1, sample2, indent     Called by: none  *
****************************************************************/
{
extern int TraceFlag[TRACE_SIZE], /* global- trace flag array  */
           depth;                 /* global- depth in hierarchy */
int   i;                /* counter                  */
char  cmd_char;         /* input command character  */
void  indent ();        /* declare function indent  */

for (i = 0; i < TRACE_SIZE; i++) {      /* initialize flags to off */
   TraceFlag [i] = 0;
   } /* end for */
cmd_char = 'R';                   /* initialize command variable */
depth = depth + 1;                /*  initial depth level        */

     /* Take command WHILE cmd_char not 'Q' */
while (cmd_char != 'Q'&& cmd_char != 'q') { /* prompt for input  */
   printf("\nRun, Trace, or Quit ? (R, T, or Q) ");
   cmd_char = getchar();          /* input character from keyboard */
   putchar('\n');                 /*   output newline = '\n'      */

   switch (cmd_char) {   /*  Handle cases of command char. values */

      case 't': case'T':         /*  On T or T  go set trace flags */
           trflag ();
           if (TraceFlag[0] == 1) {   /*   print if Flag 0 is on */
              indent (depth);
              printf("In main \n");
           }
           break;  /* go to end of switch */

      case 'R' : case 'r':
           sample1(depth);           /* calls to demonstrate trace */
           sample2(depth);
           break;
      }             /* end switch */
   }          /* end while */

if (TraceFlag[0] == 1) {          /* print message if Flag 0 is off */
   indent (depth);
   printf("Leaving main \n");
   }       /* end if */
}   /* end main */
```

```
/****************************************************************
* This initializes global array of Trace Descriptors -        *
*    note that this should normally be done in a text file    *
****************************************************************/
char TraceDesc[TRACE_SIZE][30] = {
    "Main Driver            ",
    "Trace Function         ",
    "Sample Function 1      ",
    "Sample Function 2      ",
    "Error Handler          ",
    "* ", "* ", "* ", "* ", "* "
};

trflag()
/****************************************************************
*                                                             *
*    trace flag maintenance procedure        DeSmet C 2.51    *
*       by C.D. Sigwart and G.L. Van Meer                     *
*                                                             *
****************************************************************
*    Sample Call:     trflag()              (no parameters)   *
*                                                             *
*    inputs:  take flag values from keyboard                  *
*    outputs: prompt user for input, put values in flag array *
*    side-effect: manipulates array of flags as global variables *
*                                                             *
*    called by: main                      calls: ErrorHandler *
*    files used: none                                         *
****************************************************************
* function:                                                   *
*      Lets programmer set any member, or all, of an array of *
* global flags which are used to dump data from modules in    *
* a testing session.  Flags are initialized in main so all    *
* start in the off state (0).  Flags are set only in this     *
* module; all other modules only read values.                 *
****************************************************************
*  Definition of global variable usage:                       *
*      Uses a global array TraceFlag(#)' where '#' designates  *
*      a module. Elements are single characters '0' or '1',    *
*      for 'off' and 'on' uses an array of trace descriptors,  *
*      'TraceDesc[#]', one for each element of trace.   Any    *
*      unused descriptors are all blanks.                      *
****************************************************************/
{ /* begin trflag */
extern int TraceFlag[TRACE_SIZE], depth;    /* global variables */
extern char TraceDesc[TRACE_SIZE][30];

int i, answer, response, num, tsize;        /* local variables */
void indent();                      /* declare function indent */
depth = depth + 1;                      /* increase indentation */
if (TraceFlag[1] == 1) {        /* print message if Flag 1 is on */
    indent (depth);
    printf("Entering trflag\n");
    } /* end if */

/*---------------------------------------------------------------
* get actual size of trace table : search to first blank descriptor
----------------------------------------------------------------*/
tsize = 0;
while ( strcmp( TraceDesc[tsize], "* ") != 0 ) tsize++;
```

```
/*-------------------------------------------------------------
 * prompt user and take input until 'Q' or 'q' then exit
 ------------------------------------------------------------*/
printf("This procedure allows you to set Trace Flags\n \n");
response = 'V';
while ( response != 'Q' || response != 'q') {

    switch (response) {

        case 'Q': case 'q':              /* return to calling routine */
            break;

        case 'V': case 'v':                  /* print entire table */
            printf("\n#  Module Description        Current Value\n");
            for (i = 0; i < tsize; i++) {
                printf("%d %s %d\n",i,TraceDesc[i],TraceFlag[i]);
                } /* end if */
            printf("\n");   /* add blank line for readability */
            break;

        case 'R': case 'r':                  /* set all flags to off */
            for (i = 0; i < tsize; i++) TraceFlag[i] = 0;
            printf("Flags are now all set to 'off'\n\n");
            break;

        case 'S': case 's':                  /* set all flags to on */
            for (i = 0; i < tsize; i++) TraceFlag[i] = 1;
            printf("Flags are now all set to 'on'\n\n");
            break;

        case '#':                            /* set individual flag(s) */
            while (answer != 'q' && answer != 'Q'){
                printf("\n Which flag number do you want to change?\n");
                scanf("%d",&num);          /* get integer from keyboard */
                    if (num>=0 && num<tsize) {
                        printf("\nCurrent value: %d ", TraceFlag[num]);
                        printf("%s\n",TraceDesc[num]);
                        printf("Enter:  0 -> off   1 -> on");
                        printf("    Q -> quit\n");
                        answer=getchar();   /* get input from keyboard */
                        putchar('\n');
                        switch (answer) {
                            case 'q': case 'Q': break;
                            case '1': TraceFlag[num] = 1;
                                    break;
                            case '0': TraceFlag[num] = 0;
                                    break;
                            default: /* bad value,  print message */
                                    ErrorHandler (1);
                                    break;
                            } /* end switch (answer) */
                        } /* end if, flag range check */
                    else {                   /* flag number error */
                        ErrorHandler (2);    /* print message     */
                        } /* end else flag range check */
            } /* end while loop in case '#' */
            answer = ' '; /* reset for next time # is asked for */
            break;
        default:                   /* case of incorrect 'response' */
            ErrorHandler(3);       /* print error message          */
            break;

    } /* end switch (response) */
```

```
        if (response != 'Q' && response != 'q') {
            printf("  Do you wish to: view the entire table  ? (V)\n");
            printf("                   reset -> all flags off ? (R)\n");
            printf("                   set   -> all flags on  ? (S)\n");
            printf("                   set individual flag(s) ? (#)\n");
            printf("                   quit -> to main menu    ? (Q)\n\n");

            response = getchar();           /* get input from keyboard */
            putchar('\n');
        }
        else break;        /* on 'q' OR 'Q' end while */
    } /* end WHILE menu 'response' NOT 'Q'  */

    if (TraceFlag[1] == 1) {        /* print message if Flag 1 is on */
        indent (depth);
        printf("Leaving trflag\n");
        } /* end if */
    depth = depth - 1;  /* decrease indentation  */
    return;
/****************************************************************
 * variable dictionary                                         *
 *    type           variable            definition            *
 *    integer        i                   local counter         *
 *    integer        MenuRepeat          flag for while loop    *
 *    integer        tsize               max size of trace table *
 *    integer        TRACE_SIZE          current size of trace table *
 *    integer        TraceFlag[]         array of trace flags   *
 *    integer        answer              input from user, flag change *
 *    char           response            command from user, menu select*
 *    char           TraceDesc[]         descriptors of trace item  *
 ****************************************************************/


/****************************************************************
 * sample usage of conditional trace:                          *
 *                                                             *
 *        xxx (y,z)                                            *
 *        integer y, z;                                        *
 *        {                                                    *
 *        if (TraceFlag[11] == '1') {                          *
 *            printf("Entered  xxx(y,z)\n");                   *
 *            printf("x = %d, y = %d\n",y,z);                  *
 *            }                                                *
 *                                                             *
 *            .                                                *
 *            .          body of routine                      *
 *            .                                                *
 *        if (trace(11) == '1')                                *
 *            printf("Leaving xxx with y = %d, z = %d\n",y,z); *
 *        }                                                    *
 ****************************************************************/
} /* end trflag */
sample1(x)
    int x;
/****************************************************************
 *                      procedure sample1                      *
 *                                                             *
 * This function is a stub, used only to demonstrate the       *
 *    trace system.                                            *
 *                                                             *
 * Calls: indent           Called by: main, sample2            *
 ****************************************************************/
```

```
{
extern int TraceFlag[TRACE_SIZE], depth; /* global variables */
void indent();     /* declare function indent */
depth=depth + 1;   /* increase indentation */
if (TraceFlag[2] == 1) { /* print message if Flag 2 is on */
    indent(depth);
    printf("Entering sample1(x), x= %d\n", x);}
        /* Print message and value of parameter, where   */
        /*   '%d' us format specifier for numeric value  */

if (TraceFlag[2] == 1) { /* print message if Flag 2 is off */
    indent(depth);
    printf("Leaving  sample1\n");}
depth=depth - 1;  /* decrease indentation  */
} /* end sample1 */

sample2(x)
    int x;
/********************************************************************
*                         procedure sample2                       *
*                                                                 *
* This function is a stub, used only to demonstrate the trace     *
* system. It calls another stub to further demonstrate.           *
*                                                                 *
* Calls: sample1, indent              Called by: main            *
********************************************************************/
{
extern int TraceFlag[TRACE_SIZE], depth; /* global variables */
void indent();     /* declare function indent */

depth = depth + 1;   /* increase indentation  */
if (TraceFlag[3] == 1) { /* print message if Flag 3 is on */
    indent(depth);
    printf("Entering sample2(x), x = %d\n", x);}

sample1(depth); /* additional call to stub to demonstrate trace */

if (TraceFlag[3] == 1) { /* print message if Flag 3 is off */
    indent(depth);
    printf("Leaving  sample2\n");}
depth = depth - 1;  /* decrease indentation  */
} /* end sample2 */

ErrorHandler(n)
/********************************************************************
*                        procedure ErrorHandler                   *
*                                                                 *
* This is a minimal functional error handler -                    *
*    note that this should normally be done in a text file        *
*                                                                 *
* Calls: indent      Called by: any function with error traps     *
********************************************************************/
int n;
{
extern int TraceFlag[TRACE_SIZE], depth;  /* global variables */
void indent();     /* declare function indent */
depth = depth + 1;  /* increase indentation  */

if (TraceFlag[4] == 1) { /* print message if Flag 4 is on */
    indent(depth);
    printf("Entering ErrorHandler\n");
    } /* end if */
```

```
switch (n) {
   case 1: printf ("Valid choices are 0, 1, and Q\n");
           break;
   case 2: printf ("That is outside the range of valid flags\n");
           break;
   case 3: printf ("That is not a valid response; ");
           printf ("Enter V, R, S, #, or Q \n");
           break;
   default: printf ("There is no error message with that number\n");
           break;
   } /* end switch */

if (TraceFlag[4] == 1) {  /* print message if Flag 4 is off */
   indent(depth);
   printf("Leaving ErrorHandler\n");
   } /* end if */
depth = depth - 1;  /* decrease indentation */
} /* end Error Handler procedure */


void indent( d ) /* returns no value */
    int d;       /* parameter declaration */

/*****************************************************************
*                       procedure indent                       *
*                                                               *
* This function sends a string of blanks to the screen          *
* 4 times the depth count. Warning and depth printed if >=      *
* depthlim.  Used for structured trace output. No trace         *
* messages are printed since it is used with every trace        *
* message in other modules.                                     *
*                                                               *
* Calls: none      Called by: main, any function with trace     *
*****************************************************************/


{
int depthlim = 10;
static char line[70] = /* blank string to generate indentation */
"                                                                ",
    *p;         /* variable pointer to blank string       */

/*****************************************************************
*  Warn on excessive depth, and stop indenting                  *
*****************************************************************/
if( depth >= depthlim ) {
   printf("WARNING : depth = %d \n",d);
   d = depthlim ;
   } /* end if */

/*****************************************************************
*  Output 4 blanks per level of depth                           *
*****************************************************************/
p = line + strlen(line) - d * 4 ;   /* get pointer value */
printf( p );
} /* end indent */
```

An alternative is to create a numbering system that, for example, corresponds to the order of integration. For a program already in existence, any convenient order, such as the order the modules are listed in the source code, can be used. However, it is important to keep track of which module corresponds to which array element.

This correspondence can be incorporated into an array of character string descriptors. This array can be local to the trace procedure and should read the descriptions from a text file. Use of a text file, as described in Chapter 6, has the advantage that additions and modifications can easily be made without recompilation.

B.B.2. Additional Code in Program Modules

Each module in the program will need a conditional statement at the entry point and another at the exit point. For example, for a Boolean array TraceFlag, the entry message might be:

if (TraceFlag[1]) then print ("Entering Sample1")

For the exit, the message might be:

if (TraceFlag[1]) then print ("Leaving Sample1")

The message needs to be meaningful, though brief. In a program with reasonable module names, those names can easily be used in the trace statements. Take care to use the correct index value and make sure it is the same value in both the entry and exit statements.

A trace system may add about 10% to the source code, depending on the language and the system used. Most people who have used it in system testing feel that the benefits are worth the additional effort and overhead.

B.B.3. Options for Turning Flags On and Off

The trace flag maintenance module itself is designed to give the developer the option to turn specific flags on and off. Options in the menu include looking at a list of all modules (with flag values and module descriptors), turning all flags on or off, turning individual flags on or off, and returning to the calling program.

Because it is unlikely that anyone will remember the numbers assigned to modules, especially in a large program, it is appropriate to have access to a list. Since this list should be in a text file, the list may be available in hard copy and/or online. The program in Figure B.2 is designed to allow the programmer to reexamine the table of modules and other options repeatedly.

The arrays of flags and descriptors are initialized using as a limit a symbolic constant (TRACE_SIZE in the example in Figure B.2) which is intended to be greater than or equal to the number of modules. The array of descriptors is initialized to blanks or nulls. Then, after the descriptions are added, the array can be examined for the number of nonempty strings. This number, "tsize" in the example, can be used for printing the table. For very large programs, an additional feature could be to print the list one screenful at a time.

B.B.4. Structured Trace Output

It is convenient to know not only which module you are in, but also which module most recently made the call. The code in Figure B.2 includes an indentation procedure that enhances readability and indicates how many levels deep you are in a program, even if not all the trace flags are turned on. In this way the trace output will graphically portray the hierarchical structure of pattern of execution.

This is done by writing a function that does not return a value ("void" in C), but which prints a specified number of blanks. This will effectively indent the output of the print statements, which indicates that a module is being entered or exited. The number of blanks we have chosen is a multiple of four. The function is called using an integer parameter, and that parameter is multiplied by four. This is the number of blanks printed.

The parameter is a global integer variable, which we call "depth." This integer is initialized to 0. Then when each module is entered, the value of depth is increased by 1, and when each module is exited, depth is decreased by 1. Thus if Module A calls Module B, which in turn calls Module C, the trace messages would be as shown in Figure B.1.

B.B.5. Dynamic Display of Data

The next extension of this methodology is to use the conditional print statements to show variable names and current values referenced to the source code. Thus the trace mechanism can be used to test the current state of parameters at the interface and on selected internal paths. In that way the trace system becomes an important tool for integration testing. The best time to consider where to put conditional print statements in a module is when the code is being implemented.

It is in integration and regression testing that the utility of being able to turn selected trace flags on and off becomes apparent. In any system with several dozen or more modules it is not reasonable to examine the trace output when *all* modules are dumping notices of entry, exit, and internal data. In that circumstance the trace output is voluminous and unwieldy. But is is very easy to examine the execution of a module when the trace is turned on only for a module under test and the modules it calls or is called by. Any errors in presumed paths may be detected by the indentation system.

B.C. Example of a Trace System

The example in Figure B.2 is a trace system implemented in C. There is a stub for a main function at the beginning and additional stubs at the end for the error handler and two additional sample functions, sample1 and sample2.

Because of the brevity of the program, and for reading convenience, the strings for the descriptor table and the error messages in the error handler are included in the code. However, we strongly recommend the use of text files in both cases for actual implementations, as described in Chapter 6.

The array TraceFlag is declared as a global array of integers, which is initialized to 0 (off) immediately in the main program. No entry message is included at the beginning, as it would not be printed. Instead, a message is inserted immediately after the call to the trace function, trflag. An exit message is included at the end.

The comment block at the beginning of trflag gives credit to the authors, provides a sample call, and describes inputs, outputs, and side effects. It lists modules called and called by, and gives a brief description of the function. The data dictionary is included in a trailer block, along with an example of how to use the program.

After the declarations, the TraceDesc array is initialized to blanks. (Recall that in C the declaration is an array of character arrays and requires two subscripts; in usage, only the first subscript is needed). Then the desired description strings are assigned, and the response character initialized to a blank.

In order to avoid using any part of either the TraceFlag or TraceDesc arrays that do not refer to existing modules, tsize is set to the size of the trace table.

A while loop gives the programmer the choice of viewing the table, setting individual flags, setting all flags to 1 or 0, or leaving the procedure. These choices are presented repeatedly until the last one (quit) is selected.

If the programmer selects the option of setting individual flags, a prompt for flag number is written. If the flag is outside the range in use, an error message results and the prompt reappears. If a valid flag number is selected, the various choices are listed. This procedure is repeated until a choice to quit is entered; then control is returned to the main menu of the function.

Two sample functions, sample1 and sample2, are included for demonstration. They consist only of stubs with the trace messages and a call by sample1 to sample2. The results of running the program with various options are shown in Figure B.3.

```
Figure B.3  Sample Output from Running Trace Program

Run, Trace, or Quit ? (R, T, or Q) r
Run, Trace, or Quit ? (R, T, or Q) t
This procedure allows you to set Trace Flags
#   Module Description          Current Value
0 Main Driver                       0
1 Trace Function                    0
2 Sample Function 1                 0
3 Sample Function 2                 0
4 Error Handler                     0
   Do you wish to: view the entire table  ? (V)
                   reset -> all flags off ? (R)
                   set   -> all flags on  ? (S)
                   set individual flag(s) ? (#)
                   quit -> to main menu   ? (Q)

s
Flags are now all set to 'on'
   Do you wish to: view the entire table  ? (V)
                   reset -> all flags off ? (R)
                   set   -> all flags on  ? (S)
                   set individual flag(s) ? (#)
                   quit -> to main menu   ? (Q)

x
                Entering ErrorHandler
That is not a valid response; Enter R, S, #, or Q
                 Leaving ErrorHandler
   Do you wish to: view the entire table  ? (V)
                   reset -> all flags off ? (R)
                   set   -> all flags on  ? (S)
                   set individual flag(s) ? (#)
                   quit -> to main menu   ? (Q)

v
#   Module Description          Current Value
0 Main Driver                       1
1 Trace Function                    1
2 Sample Function 1                 1
3 Sample Function 2                 1
4 Error Handler                     1
   Do you wish to: view the entire table  ? (V)
                   reset -> all flags off ? (R)
                   set   -> all flags on  ? (S)
                   set individual flag(s) ? (#)
                   quit -> to main menu   ? (Q)

r
Flags are now all set to 'off'
   Do you wish to: view the entire table  ? (V)
                   reset -> all flags off ? (R)
                   set   -> all flags on  ? (S)
                   set individual flag(s) ? (#)
                   quit -> to main menu   ? (Q)

3
```

```
That is not a valid response; Enter R, S, #, or Q
Do you wish to: view the entire table  ? (V)
                reset -> all flags off ? (R)
                set   -> all flags on  ? (S)
                set individual flag(s) ? (#)
                quit -> to main menu   ? (Q)
#
Which flag number do you want to change?
3
Current value: 0  Sample Function 2
Enter:  0 -> off  1 -> on    Q -> quit
1
Which flag number do you want to change?
That is outside the range of valid flags
7
Which flag number do you want to change?
2
Current value: 0  Sample Function 1
Enter:  0 -> off    1 -> on    Q -> quit
q
Do you wish to: view the entire table  ? (V)
                reset -> all flags off ? (R)
                set   -> all flags on  ? (S)
                set individual flag(s) ? (#)
                quit -> to main menu   ? (Q)

s
Flags are now all set to 'on'
Do you wish to: view the entire table  ? (V)
                reset -> all flags off ? (R)
                set   -> all flags on  ? (S)
                set individual flag(s) ? (#)
                quit -> to main menu   ? (Q)

q
        Leaving trflag
    In main
Run, Trace, or Quit ? (R, T, or Q) r
        Entering sample1(x), x= 1
        Leaving  sample1
        Entering sample2(x), x = 1
            Entering sample1(x), x= 2
            Leaving  sample1
        Leaving  sample2
Run, Trace, or Quit ? (R, T, or Q) z

Run, Trace, or Quit ? (R, T, or Q) q
    Leaving main
```

B.D. Hiding the Trace System from the User

The example in Figure B.2 shows how to implement a trace system, but does not explain how to hide the system from a user. The experienced programmer has probably already figured out at least one way to do it. We will describe two methods. Either way, all flags must be initialized to off.

B.D.1. Using Recompilation

The first method completely suppresses the system, making it impossible for the user to invoke the trace module. This involves deleting the call to the trace module, possibly by putting the call into a comment block. In C this can also be done using #define and #undefine. The drawback is that recompilation is required to use it, but the advantage is that the trace module does not need to be included with the executable part of the program. However, it must be kept available for use by the maintenance programmer, along with adequate documentation, including instructions on how to use it.

B.D.2. Hidden Menu Option

The second method leaves the trace system available as a hidden option. For example, some unusual character, when used in the main menu, could activate the system. We have found * to be satisfactory. It is unlikely to be used otherwise in a menu, even by accident.

However, when using this option, care must be taken to guard against the possibility that it will be accessed by the user. One might, for example, respond to the prompt with a message such as:

> You are in a trace procedure intended for program maintenance.
> Are you sure you want to be here? (Y/N)

If the curious user decides to try it out, it probably won't hurt anything.

When using this second option, instructions to the programmer should be included in the source code and in the programmer's manual, though not, of course, in the User's Manual.

B.E. Conclusions

Implementing a trace system requires adding additional code, and a considerable amount of organization and planning. While the time commitment in design and coding is relatively small, it can save a large amount of time in system testing. Frequently a lot of special code must be written to conduct tests. This system reduces that need and provides a systematic way to retain the required test environment for later use by maintenance programmers. It is also possible for such a system to be incorporated in an existing system by maintenance programmers.

Because of the required overhead and effort, people who have never used the system, if given a choice, will often opt to ignore it. However, those who have once tried the method are usually permanent converts and strong advocates of the system. Our recommendation, therefore, is to try it once. You may find that you can't live without it.

GLOSSARY OF SOFTWARE ENGINEERING TERMS

Software is an isolated, esoteric field, fraught with semantic casualness and a paucity of terms.

The computer is still in its infancy ... and the technological world is still struggling to evolve a vocabulary that is comprehensive, consistent, and clear....

Anyone discussing computers and software must be aware of the accidental confusion caused by different understandings of even common terms.

...many glossaries do not distinguish between close, neighboring concepts. Such glossaries are harmful; they perpetuate confusion.

- Joseph M. Fox, <u>Software and its Development</u>

Acknowledgment

This glossary is based, in part, on IEEE Standard 729-1983, IEEE Standard Glossary of Software Engineering Terminology, copyright (c) by The Institute of Electrical and Electronics Engineers, Inc., 345 East 47th Street, New York NY 10017.

acceptance criteria: the standard a software product must meet to successfully complete a test phase or meet delivery requirements (IEEE Std 729-1983).

acceptance testing: testing conducted to determine whether or not a system satisfies its acceptance criteria and to enable the customer to determine whether or not to accept the system (IEEE Std 729-1983).

accessibility: the extent to which software facilitates selective use or maintenance of its components (IEEE Std 729-1983).

adaptability: the ease with which software allows differing system constraints and user needs to be satisfied (IEEE Std 729- 1983).

adaptive maintenance: maintenance performed to make software usable in a changed environment (IEEE Std 729-1983).

analysis phase: see requirements phase

analytical model: a representation of a process or phenomenon by a set of solvable equations (IEEE Std 729-1983).

ANSI: American National Standards Institute

application prototype: a preliminary version of an application program which demonstrates the user interface or some other properties of a software system, but is not completely functional. It may simulate or even use faked data instead of carrying out many internal functions that will eventually be implemented (see rapid prototyping).

application software: software specifically produced for the functional use of a computer system (IEEE Std 729-1983).

ASQC: American Society for Quality Control

audit: (a) an independent review for the purpose of assessing compliance with software requirements, specifications, standards, procedures, instructions, codes, and contractual and licensing requirements (see code audit).

(b) an activity to determine through investigation the adequacy of, and adherence to, established procedures, instructions, specifications, codes, and standards or other applicable contractual and licensing requirements, and the effectiveness of implementation (IEEE Std 729-1983).

automated design tool: a software tool that aids in the synthesis, analysis, modeling, or documentation of a software design (IEEE Std 729-1983).

automated test generator: a software tool that accepts as input a computer program and a representation of its specification, and produces, possibly with human help, a correctness proof or disproof of the program (IEEE Std 729-1983). (see automated verification tools)

automated verification tools: a class of software tools used to evaluate products of the software development process. These tools aid in the verification of such characteristics as correctness, completeness, consistency, traceability, testability, and adherence to standards (IEEE Std 729-1983).

backup: provisions made for the recovery of data files or software, for restart of processing, or for use of alternative computer equipment after a system failure or a disaster (IEEE Std 729-1983).

bottom-up: pertaining to an approach that starts with the lowest level software components of a hierarchy and proceeds through progressively higher levels to the top level component (IEEE Std 729-1983).

bottom-up design: the design of a system starting with the most basic or primitive components and proceeding to higher level components that use the lower level ones (IEEE Std 729-1983).

boundary test: a test designed to operate at the edge, or boundary of the class of values. For example, if an input condition specifies a range from x to y, then values near x and y should be tested, both above and below.

change control: the process by which a change is proposed, evaluated, approved or rejected, scheduled, and tracked (IEEE Std 729-1983).

code audit: an independent review of source code by a person, team, or tool to verify compliance with software design documentation and programming standards. Correctness and efficiency may also be evaluated (IEEE Std 729-1983). Related term: code inspection (see inspection)

cohesion: the degree to which the tasks performed by a single program module are functionally related (IEEE Std 729-1983).

comparator: a software tool used to compare two computer programs, files, or sets of data to identify commonalities or differences (IEEE Std 729-1983).

complexity: the degree of complication of a system or system component, determined by such factors as the number and intricacy of interfaces, the number and intricacy of conditional branches, the degree of nesting, the types of data structures, and other system characteristics (IEEE Std 729-1983). Related terms: McCabe's metric, Halstead length metric

component: a basic part of a system or program (IEEE Std 729-1983).

configuration: (a) the arrangement of a computer system or network as defined by the nature, number, and the chief characteristics of its functional units. May refer to a hardware configuration, or a software configuration.

(b) the requirements, design, and implementation that define a particular version of a system or system component.

(c) the functional and/or physical characteristics of hardware/software as set forth in technical documentation and achieved in a product (IEEE Std 729-1983).

configuration audit: the process of verifying that all required configuration items have been produced, that the current version agrees with specified requirement, that the technical documentation completely and accurately describes the configuration items, and that all change requests have been resolved (IEEE Std 729-1983).

configuration control: (a) the process of evaluating, approving or disapproving, and coordinating changes to configuration items after formal establishment of their configuration identification.

(b) the systematic evaluation, coordination, approval or disapproval, and implementation of all approved changes in the configuration of a configuration item after formal establishment of its configuration identification (IEEE Std 729-1983).

configuration identification: (a) the process of designating the configuration items in a system and recording their characteristics.

(b) approved documentation that defines a configuration item.

(c) the current approved or conditionally approved technical documentation for a configuration item as set forth in specifications, drawings and associated lists, and documents referenced therein (IEEE Std 729-1983).

configuration management: (a) the process of identifying and defining the configuration items in a system, controlling the release and change of these items throughout the system life cycle, recording and reporting the status of configuration items and change requests, and verifying the completeness and correctness of configuration items. (see also change control, configuration identification, configuration control, configuration audit.)

(b) a discipline applying technical and administrative direction and surveillance to (i) identify and document the functional and physical characteristics of a configuration item, (ii) control changes to those characteristics, and (iii) record and report change processing and implementation status (IEEE Std 729-1983).

confinement: (a) prevention of unauthorized alteration, use, destruction, or release of data during authorized access.

(b) restriction on programs and processes so that they do not access or have influence on data, programs, or processes other than that allowed by specific authorization (IEEE Std 729-1983).

contract: A legally binding agreement between parties wherein one or more parties agree to perform particular services or deliver specifically a agreed product in exchange for specified compensation.

conversational: pertaining to an interactive system that provides for interaction between a user and a system similar to a human dialogue (IEEE Std 729-1983).

copyright: A right to control reproduction, distribution, and publication of a work of authorship. Such a right protects the expression of authorship in literal form, but does not protect the ideas or concepts that are contained when expressed in another form. Such a right belongs to the author(s), unless the work was done at the direction of, and for the benefit of, an employer in which case the right is vested in the employer. Such rights may be transferred, bought or sold by those possessing such rights.

corrective maintenance: maintenance performed specifically to overcome existing faults (IEEE Std 729-1983).

correctness: (a) the extent to which software is free from design defects and from coding defects.

(b) the extent to which software meets is specified requirements.

(c) the extent to which software meets user expectations (IEEE Std 729-1983).

coupling: a measure of the interdependence among modules in a computer program (IEEE Std 729-1983).

cryptography: The art of devising and implementing procedures to transform information into coded form to make it unreadable, This is known as encryption. Cryptography also includes the inverse, the devising and implementing of procedures to the related art of devising and implementing the inverse procedures to decode and make coded information readable. This latter is known as decryption.

data abstraction: the result of extracting and retaining only the essential characteristic properties of data by defining specific data types and their associated functional characteristics, thus separating and hiding the representation details (IEEE Std 729- 1983). (see information hiding)

data dictionary: (a) a collection of the names of all data items used in a software system, together with relevant properties of those items.

(b) a set of definitions of data flows, data elements, files, data bases, and processes referred to in a leveled data flow diagram set (IEEE Std 729-1983).

data directory: see data dictionary

data flow diagram: a graphic representation of a system, showing data sources, data sinks, storage, and processes performed on data as nodes, and logical flow of data as links between the nodes (IEEE Std 729-1983).

data flow graph: see data flow diagram

defensive programming: adherence to a programming practice which assures reliable or testable execution even in the presence of bad data.

definition phase: see requirements phase

delivery: (a) the point in the software development cycle at which a product is released to its intended user for operational use.

(b) the point in the software development cycle at which a product is accepted by its intended user (IEEE Std 729-1983).

design: (a) the process of defining the software architecture, components, modules, interfaces, test approach, and data for a software system to satisfy specified requirements.

(b) the result of the design process (IEEE Std 729-1983).

design analysis: (a) the evaluation of a design to determine correctness with respect to stated requirements, conformance to design standards, system efficiency, and other criteria.

(b) the evaluation of alternative design approaches (IEEE Std 729-1983). (see preliminary design).

design analyzer: an automated design tool that accepts information about a program's design and produces such outputs as module hierarchy diagrams, graphical representations of control and data structure, and lists of accessed data blocks (IEEE Std 729-1983).

design methodology: a systematic approach to creating a design, consisting of the ordered application of a specific collection of tools, techniques, and guidelines (IEEE Std 729-1983).

design phase: the period of time in the software life cycle during which the designs for architecture, software components, interfaces, and data are created, documented, and verified to satisfy requirements (IEEE Std 729-1983).

design requirement: any requirement that impacts or constrains the design of a software system or software system component (IEEE Std 729-1983). (see requirements specification)

design review: (a) a formal meeting at which the preliminary or detailed design of a system is presented to the user, customer, or other interested parties for comment and approval.

(b) the formal review of an existing or proposed design for the purpose of detection and remedy of design deficiencies that could affect fitness-for-use and environmental aspects of the product, process or service, and/or for identification of potential improvements of performance, safety and economic aspects (IEEE Std 729-1983).

design specification: a specification that documents the design of a system or system component (IEEE Std 729-1983). (see requirements specification)

detailed design: (a) the process of refining and expanding the preliminary design to contain more detailed descriptions of the processing logic, data structures, and data definitions, to the extent that the design is sufficiently complete to be implemented.

(b) the result of the detailed design process (IEEE Std 729- 1983).

development life cycle: see software development cycle

development methodology: a systematic approach to the creation of software that defines development phases and specifies the activities, products, verification procedures, and completion criteria for each phase (IEEE Std 729-1983).

development specification: synonymous with requirements specification (DOD usage) (IEEE Std 729-1983).

DFD: Data Flow Diagram

document: (a) a data medium and the data recorded on it, that generally has permanence and that can be read by person or machine. Often used to describe human readable items only.

(b) to create a document (IEEE Std 729-1983).

documentation: a collection of documents on a given subject (IEEE Std 729-1983). (see user documentation, software documentation, system documentation)

DoD (or DOD): Department of Defense

driver: a program that exercises a system or system component, possibly by simulating the activity of a higher level component (IEEE Std 729-1983).

editor: (a) a computer program that permits selective revision of computer-stored data (IEEE Std 729-1983).

(b) a person who examines a document and modifies it, where necessary, for completeness, consistency, readability, and neatness.

efficiency: the extent to which software performs its intended function with a minimum consumption of computing resources (IEEE Std 729-1983). Not to be confused with lines of code (e.g. fewer lines of code does not necessarily imply greater efficiency, and in many cases may be counterproductive.)

encapsulation: the technique of isolating a system function within a module and providing a precise specification for the module (IEEE Std 729-1983). (see information hiding)

error: (a) a discrepancy between a computed, observed, or measured value or condition and the true, specified, or theoretically correct value or condition.
(b) human action that results in software containing a fault (IEEE Std 729-1983).

error analysis: (a) the process of investigating an observed software fault with the purpose of tracing the fault to its source.

(b) the process of investigating an observed software fault to identify such information as the cause of the fault, the phase of the development process during which the fault was introduced, methods by which the fault could have been prevented or detected earlier, and the method by which the fault was detected.

(c) the process of investigating software errors, failures, and faults to determine quantitative rates and trends (IEEE Std 729-1983).

exception: an event that causes suspension of normal program execution (IEEE Std 729-1983).

failure: (a) the termination of the ability of a functional unit to perform its required function.

(b) the inability of a system or system component to perform a required function within specified limits. A failure may be produced when a fault is encountered.
(c) a departure of program operation from program requirements (IEEE Std 729-1983).

failure recovery: the return of a system to a reliable operating state after failure (IEEE Std 729-1983).

fault: (a) an accidental condition that causes a functional unit to fail to perform its required function.

(b) a manifestation of an error in software; a fault, if encountered, may cause a failure. Synonymous with "bug" (IEEE Std 729-1983).

fault tolerance: the built-in capability of a system to provide continued correct execution in the presence of a limited number of hardware or software faults (IEEE Std 729-1983).

feasibility: the capability of being done under the set of constraints that have been assumed. This means that an informed judgment has been made that a proposal is internally consistent and that no factors have been identified which would necessarily lead to the failure of the proposal if carried out in a competent manner.

feasibility study: a systematic effort to gather information to make a judgment of feasibility regarding a proposed system or set of procedures. This may include costs, benefits, constraints, resource requirements, and technical methods needed to realize a proposed system, and a plan in order to make a judgment on its feasibility.

flowchart: a graphical representation of the definition, analysis, or solution of a problem in which symbols are used to represent operations, data, flow, and equipment (IEEE Std 729- 1983).

formal specification: (a) specification written and approved in accordance with established standards.

(b) in proof of correctness, a description in a formal language of the externally visible behavior of a system or system component (IEEE Std 729-1983).

formal testing: the process of conducting testing activities and reporting results in accordance with an approved test plan (IEEE Std 729-1983).

functional decomposition: a method of designing a system by breaking it down into its components in such a way that the components correspond directly to system functions and subfunctions (IEEE Std 729-1983). (see hierarchical decomposition)

functional design: the specification of the working relationships among the parts of a data processing system (IEEE Std 729-1983). (see preliminary design)

functional requirement: a requirement that specifies a function that a system or system component must be capable of performing (IEEE Std 729-1983).

functional specification: a specification that defines the functions that a system or system component must perform (IEEE Std 729-1983). (see performance specification)

Halstead's length metric: formula derived by M. Halstead for calculating program length, based on the total usage of all operators and operands in the representation of a program.

hierarchical decomposition: a method of designing a system by breaking it down into its components through a series of top-down refinements (IEEE Std 729-1983). (see functional decomposition, modular decomposition, stepwise refinement)

hierarchy: a structure whose components are ranked into levels of subordination according to a specific set of rules (IEEE Std 729- 1983).

host machine: (a) the computer on which a program or file is installed.

(b) a computer used to develop software intended for another computer (as opposed to target machine).

(c) a computer used to emulate another computer (IEEE Std 729- 1983).

IEEE: Institute of Electrical and Electronics Engineers

implementation: (a) a realization of an abstraction in more concrete terms; in particular, in terms of hardware, software, or both.

(b) a machine executable form of a program, or a form of a program that can be translated automatically to machine executable form.

(c) the process of translating a design into code and debugging the code (IEEE Std 729-1983).

implementation phase: the period of time in the software life cycle during which a software product is created from design documentation and debugged (IEEE Std 729-1983). (see installation, checkout phase, test phase)

implementation requirement: any requirement that impacts or constrains the implementation of a software design; for example, design descriptions, software development standards, programming language requirements, software quality assurance standards (IEEE Std 729-1983).

information hiding: the technique of encapsulating software design decisions in modules in such a way that the module's interfaces reveal as little as possible about the module's inner working; thus, each module is a "black box" to the other modules in the system. The discipline of information hiding forbids the use of information about a module that is not in the module's interface specification (IEEE Std 729-1983). (see encapsulation) inspection: (a) a formal evaluation technique in which software requirements, design, or code are examined in detail by a person or group other than the author to detect faults, violations of development standards, and other problems (see code audit).

(b) a phase of quality control that by means of examination, observation or measurement determines the conformance of materials, supplies, components, parts, appurtenances, systems, processes or structures to predetermined quality requirement (IEEE Std 729-1983).

installation and checkout phase: the period of time in the software life cycle during which a software product is integrated into its operational environment and tested in this environment to ensure that it performs as required (IEEE Std 729-1983).

instrumentation tool: a software tool that generates and inserts counters or other probes at strategic points in another program to provide statistics about program execution, such as how thoroughly the program's code is exercised (IEEE Std 729-1983).

integration: the process of combining software elements, hardware elements, or both into an overall system (IEEE Std 729-1983).

integration testing: an orderly progression of testing in which software elements, hardware elements, or both are combined and tested until the entire system has been integrated (IEEE Std 729- 1983). (see system testing)

integrity: the extent to which unauthorized access to or modification of software or data can be controlled in a computer system (IEEE Std 729-1983). (see security)

interactive: pertaining to a system in which each user entry causes a response from the system (IEEE Std 729-1983). (see conversational)

interface: (a) a shared boundary. An interface might be a hardware component to link two devices or it might be a portion of storage or registers accessed by two or more computer programs.

(b) to interact or communicate with another system component (IEEE Std 729-1983).

interface requirement: a requirement that specifies a hardware, software, or data base element with which a system or system component must interface, or that sets forth constraints on formats, timing, or other factors caused by such an interface (IEEE Std 729-1983).

interface specification: a specification that sets forth the interface requirements for a system or system component (IEEE Std 729-1983).

interface testing: testing conducted to ensure that program or system components pass information or control correctly to one another (IEEE Std 729-1983).

ISO: International Standards Organization

KISS principle: "Keep It Short and Simple"

level: (a) the degree of subordination of an item in a hierarchical arrangement.

(b) a rank within a hierarchy. An item is of the lowest level if it has no subordinates and of the highest level if it has no superiors (IEEE Std 729-1983).

level of documentation: a description of required documentation indicating its scope, content, format, and quality. Selection of the level may be based on project cost, intended usage, extent of effort, or other factors (IEEE Std 729-1983).

licensing: a contract to use a system under a set of specified constraints and limitations in exchange for payment of the license fee. Software is most commonly distributed under licenses which do not transfer ownership and which specifically limit copying, distribution and disclosure of the software and its documentation

life cycle: see software life cycle

LOC: lines of code

macro: (a) a predefined sequence of instructions that is inserted into a program during assembly or compilation at each place that its corresponding macroinstruction appears in the program.

(b) synonymous with macroinstruction (IEEE Std 729-1983).

maintainability: (a) the ease with which software can be maintained.

(b) the ease with which the maintenance of a functional unit can be performed in accordance with prescribed requirements (IEEE Std 729-1983).

maintenance: see software maintenance

maintenance phase: see operational and maintenance phase

McCabe's metric: a measure of program complexity defined in graph theoretical terms, i.e. based on a control flow representation of a program. This measure is often used to determine whether a module exceeds a reasonable level of complexity for adequate testing.

menu: a list of selections available to a software user.

model: a representation of a real world process, device or concept (IEEE Std 729-1983). (see analytical model)

modification: (a) a change made to software.
(b) the process of changing software (IEEE Std 729-1983).

modular decomposition: a method of designing a system by breaking it down into modules (IEEE Std 729-1983). (see hierarchical decomposition)

modular programming: a technique for developing a system or program as a collection of modules (IEEE Std 729-1983).

modularity: the extent to which software is composed of discrete components such that a change to one component has minimal impact on other components (IEEE Std 729-1983).

module: (a) a program unit that is discrete and identifiable with respect to compiling, combining with other units, and loading; for example, the input to, or output from, an assembler, compiler, linkage editor, or executive routine.
(b) a logically separate part of a program (IEEE Std 729- 1983).

module strength: see cohesion

object: an entity that has a state, or value. Analogous to "noun" in English. A program usually creates an object by a declaration. A class of objects is a group of the same general kind of entity.

object oriented development: a method which maps abstractions of the real world directly to the architecture of solutions, wherein each module in the system denotes an object or class of objects from the problem space.

Occam's razor: the principle that if two alternate choices are otherwise equal, the simpler should be selected.

operation and maintenance phase: the period of time in the software life cycle during which a software product is employed in its operational environment, monitored for satisfactory performance, and modified as necessary to correct problems or to respond to changing requirements (IEEE Std 729-1983).

operational reliability: the reliability of a system or software subsystem in its actual use environment. Operational reliability may differ considerably from reliability in the specified or test environment (IEEE Std 729-1983).

optimization: the design or redesign of a system or part of a system to achieve the best possible state of some attribute(s). This might be to maximize speed of execution for some function or in another case might be to minimize the use of storage space.

partial correctness: in proof of correctness, a designation indicating that a program's output assertions follow logically from its input assertions and processing steps (IEEE Std 729- 1983).

patent: a right to control the manufacture and sale of merchandise which uses or is based on the invention which is covered by the patent. A patent holder may collect a royalty payment for the use of the invention covered by the patent. Such a right is granted by, and registered with, the U.S. Patent Office when it has been determined that the applicant has demonstrated the earliest claim to the invention. A mathematical algorithm, or computer program is not patentable, although a device with an embedded computer and software may be patentable.

perfective maintenance: maintenance performed to improve performance, maintainability, or other software attributes (IEEE Std 729-1983).

performance: (a) the ability of a computer system or subsystem to perform its functions.

(b) a measure of the ability of a computer system or subsystem to perform its functions (IEEE Std 729-1983). (see performance requirements)

performance evaluation: the technical assessment of a system or system component to determine how effectively operating objectives have been achieved (IEEE Std 729-1983).

performance requirement: a requirement that specifies a performance characteristic that a system or system component must possess (IEEE Std 729-1983).

performance specification: (a) a specification that sets forth the performance requirements for a system or system component.

(b) synonymous with requirements specification (U.S. Navy usage) (IEEE Std 729-1983).

(c) (see functional specification)

preliminary design: (a) the process of analyzing design alternatives and defining the software architecture. Preliminary design typically includes definition and structuring of computer program components and data, definition of the interfaces, and preparation of timing and sizing estimates.

(b) the result of the preliminary design process (IEEE Std 729-1983).

(c) (see design analysis, functional design)

preprocessor: a computer program that effects some preliminary computation or organization (IEEE Std 729-1983).

product specification: synonymous with design specification (DoD usage) (IEEE Std 729-1983).

profiler: a tool used to analyze program execution by counting instructions, statements, procedures, or clock time used.

project plan: a management document describing the approach that will be taken for a project. The plan typically describes the work to be done, the resources required, the methods to be used, the configuration management and quality assurance procedures to be followed, the schedules to be met, the project organization, etc. (IEEE Std 729-1983).

prompt: (a) a message informing a user that a system is ready for the next command, message, or other user action.

(b) to inform a user that a system is ready for the next command, element, or other input (IEEE Std 729-1983).

proof of correctness: (a) a formal technique used to prove mathematically that a program satisfies its specification.

(b) a program proof that results from applying this technique (IEEE Std 729-1983).

protection: an arrangement for restricting access to or use of all, or part, of a computer system (IEEE Std 729-1983).

protocol: (a) a set of conventions or rules that govern the interactions of processes or applications within a computer system or network.

(b) a set of rules that governs the operation of functional units to achieve communication (IEEE Std 729-1983).

prototype: an initial or trial version of a system under development. It generally will not be completely functional within the system specifications, and may be used to test system concepts and be used as a basis for developing the eventual system by stepwise refinement.

qualification testing: formal testing, usually conducted by the developer for the customer, to demonstrate that the software meets its specified requirements (IEEE Std 729-1983). (see acceptance testing, system testing)

quality: (a) the totality of features and characteristics of a product or service that bears on its ability to satisfy a given need (IEEE Std 729-1983).

(b) (see software quality)

quality assurance: a planned and systematic pattern of all actions necessary to provide adequate confidence that the item or product conforms to established technical requirements (IEEE Std 729-1983).

rapid prototyping: a prototype of an application program emphasizing the user interface and generated during requirements analysis to evaluate user needs. (see application prototyping)

redundancy: the inclusion of duplicate or alternate system elements to improve operation reliability by ensuring continued operation in the event that a primary element fails (IEEE Std 729-1983).

regression testing: selective retesting to detect faults introduced during modification of a system or system component, to verify that modifications have not caused unintended adverse effects, or to verify that a modified system or system component still meets its specified requirements (IEEE Std 729-1983).

reliability: (a) the ability of an item to perform a required function under stated conditions for a stated period of time (IEEE Std 729-1983).

b) (see software reliability)

reliability assessment: the process of determining the achieved level of reliability of an existing system or system component (IEEE Std 729-1983).

reliability evaluation: see reliability assessment

requirement: (a) a condition or capability needed by a user to solve a problem or achieve an objective.

(b) a condition or capability that must be met or possessed by a system or system component to satisfy a contract, standard, specification, or other formally imposed document. The set of all requirements forms the basis for subsequent development of the system or system component (IEEE Std 729-1983). (see requirements analysis, requirements phase, requirements specification)

requirements analysis: (a) the process of studying user needs to arrive at a definition of system or software requirements.

(b) the verification of system or software requirements (IEEE Std 729-1983).

requirements phase: the period of time in the software life cycle during which the requirements for a software product, such as the functional and performance capabilities, are defined and documented (IEEE Std 729-1983).

requirements specification: a specification that sets forth the requirements for a system or system component. Typically included are functional requirements, performance requirements, interface requirements, design requirements, and development standards (IEEE Std 729-1983).

retirement phase: the period of time in the software life cycle during which support for a software product is terminated (IEEE Std 729-1983).

reusability: the extent to which a module can be used in multiple applications (IEEE Std 729-1983).

review: see design review

robustness: the extent to which software can continue to operate correctly despite the introduction of invalid inputs (IEEE Std 729-1983).

security: the protection of computer hardware and software from accidental or malicious access, use, modification, destruction, or disclosure. Security also pertains to personnel, data, communications, and the physical protection of computer installations (IEEE Std 729-1983).

semaphore: a shared variable used to synchronize concurrent processes by indicating whether an action has been completed or an event has occurred (IEEE Std 729-1983).

side-effect: processing or activities performed, or results obtained, secondary to the primary function of a program, subprogram, or operation (IEEE Std 729-1983).

software: (a) computer programs, procedure, rules, and possibly associated documentation and data pertaining to the operation of a computer system.

(b) programs, procedures, rules, and any associated documentation pertaining to the operation of a computer system (IEEE Std 729-1983).

software development cycle: (a) the period of time that begins with the decision to develop a software product and ends when the product is delivered. This cycle typically includes a requirements phase, design phase, implementation phase, test phase, and sometimes, installation and checkout phase.

(b) the period of time that begins with the decision to develop a software product and ends when the product is no longer being enhanced by the developer.

(c) sometimes used as a synonym for software life cycle (IEEE Std 729-1983).

software development plan: a project plan for the development of a software product. Synonymous with computer program development plan (IEEE Std 729-1983).

software development process: the process by which user needs are translated into software requirements, software requirements are transformed into design, the design is implemented in code, and the code is tested, documented, and certified for operational use (IEEE Std 729-1983).

software documentation: technical data or information, including computer listings and printouts, in human-readable form, that describe or specify the design or details, explain the capabilities, or provide operating instructions for using the software to obtain desired results from a software system (IEEE Std 729-1983). (see documentation, system documentation, user documentation)

software engineering: the systematic approach to the development, operation, maintenance, and retirement of software (IEEE Std 729- 1983).

software life cycle: the period of time that starts when a software product is conceived and ends when the product is no longer available for use. The software life cycle typically includes a requirements phase, design phase, implementation phase, test phase, installation and checkout phase, operation and maintenance phase, and sometimes, retirement phase (IEEE Std 729- 1983).

software maintenance: (a) modification of a software product after delivery to correct faults.

(b) modification of a software product after delivery to correct faults, to improve performance or other attributes, or to adapt the product to a changed environment (IEEE Std 729-1983). (see adaptive maintenance, corrective maintenance, perfective maintenance)

software quality: (a) the totality of features and characteristics of a software product that bear on its ability to satisfy given needs.

(b) the degree to which software possesses a desired combination of attributes.

(c) the degree to which a customer or user perceives that software meets his or her composite expectations.

(d) the composite characteristics of software that determine the degree to which the software in use will meet the expectations of the customer (IEEE Std 729-1983).

software quality assurance: see quality assurance

software reliability: (a) the probability that software will not cause the failure of a system for a specified time under specified conditions. The probability is a function of the inputs to and use of the system as well as a function of the existence of faults in the software. The inputs to the system determine whether existing faults, if any, are encountered.

(b) the ability of a program to perform a required function under stated conditions for a stated period of time (IEEE Std 729-1983).

software tool: a computer program used to help develop, test, analyze, or maintain another computer program or its documentation (IEEE Std 729-1983).

specification: (a) a document that prescribes, in a complete, precise, verifiable manner, the requirements, design, behavior, or other characteristics of a system or system component. (see design specification, formal specification, functional specification, interface specification, performance specification, requirements specification)

(b) the process of developing a specification.

(c) a concise statement of a set of requirements to be satisfied by a product, a material or process indicating, whenever appropriate, the procedure by means of which it may be determined whether the requirements given are satisfied (IEEE Std 729-1983).

SRS: software requirements specification

stability: (a) the ability to continue unchanged despite disturbing or disruptive events.

(b) the ability to return to an original state after disturbing or disruptive events (IEEE Std 729-1983).

stepwise refinement: a system development methodology in which data definitions and processing steps are defined broadly at first and then with increasing detail (IEEE Std 729-1983). (see hierarchical decomposition, top-down, bottom-up)

structured design: a disciplined approach to software design that adheres to a specified set of rules based on principles such as top-down design, stepwise refinement, and data flow analysis (IEEE Std 729-1983).

structured program: a program constructed of a basic set of control structures, each one having one entry point and one exit. The set of control structures typically includes: sequence of two or more instructions, conditional selection of one of two or more instructions or sequences of instructions, and repetition of an instruction or a sequence of instructions (IEEE Std 729-1983).

structured programming language: a programming language that provides the structured program constructs and that facilitates the development of structured programs (IEEE Std 729-1983).

stub: (a) a dummy program module used during the development and testing of a higher-level module.

(b) a program statement substituting for the body of a program unit and indicating that the unit is or will be defined elsewhere (IEEE Std 729-1983).

sub-menu: a list of menu selections accessible from another menu.

syntax-directed editor: an editor designed to help enforce the syntax of a specific language.

system design: (a) the process of defining the hardware and software architectures, components, modules, interfaces, and data for a system to satisfy specified system requirements.

(b) the result of the system design process (IEEE Std 729- 1983).

system documentation: documentation conveying the requirements, design philosophy, design details, capabilities, limitations, and other characteristics of a system (IEEE Std 729-1983).

system reliability: the probability that a system, including all hardware and software subsystems, will perform a required task or mission for a specified time in a specified environment (IEEE Std 729-1983). (see operational reliability, software reliability)

system testing: the process of testing an integrated hardware and software system to verify that the system meets its specified requirements (IEEE Std 729-1983). (see acceptance testing, qualification testing)

systems analysis: The art of investigating the need for a system, determining the requirements, costs, benefits and feasibility of proposed systems and the preliminary design and planning of system development.

target machine: (a) the computer on which a program is intended to operate (as opposed to host machine).

(b) the computer being emulated by another computer (IEEE Std 729-1983).

termination proof: in proof of correctness, the demonstration that a program will terminate under all specified input conditions (IEEE Std 729-1983).

test log: a chronological record of all relevant details of a testing activity (IEEE Std 729-1983).

test phase: the period of time in the software life cycle during which the components of a software product are evaluated and integrated, and the software product is evaluated to determine whether or not requirements have been satisfied (IEEE Std 729- 1983).

test plan: a document prescribing the approach to be taken for intended testing activities. The plan typically identifies the items to be tested, the testing to be performed, test schedules, personnel requirements, reporting requirements, evaluation criteria, and any risks requiring contingency planning (IEEE Std 729-1983).

test procedure: detailed instructions for the setup, operation, and evaluation of results for a given test. A set of associated procedures is often combined to form a test procedures document (IEEE Std 729-1983).

test repeatability: an attribute of a test indicating whether the same results are produced each time the test is conducted (IEEE Std 729-1983).

test report: a document describing the conduct and results of the testing carried out for a system or system component (IEEE Std 729-1983).

testability: (a) the extent to which software facilitates both the establishment of test criteria and the evaluation of the software with respect to those criteria.

(b) the extent to which the definition of requirements facilitates analysis of the requirements to establish test criteria (IEEE Std 729-1983).

testing: the process of exercising or evaluating a system or system component by manual or automated means to verify that it satisfies specified requirements or to identify differences between expected and actual results (IEEE Std 729-1983).

tool: (a) see software tool;

(b) a hardware device used to analyze software or its performance (IEEE Std 729-1983).

top-down: pertaining to an approach that starts with the highest level component of a hierarchy and proceeds through progressively lower levels (IEEE Std 729-1983).

top-down design: the process of designing a system by identifying its major components, decomposing them into their lower level components, and iterating until the desired level of detail is achieved (IEEE Std 729-1983).